T0349035

PODCAST STUDIES

PODCAST STUDIES
Practice into Theory

LORI BECKSTEAD and **DARIO LLINARES**, editors

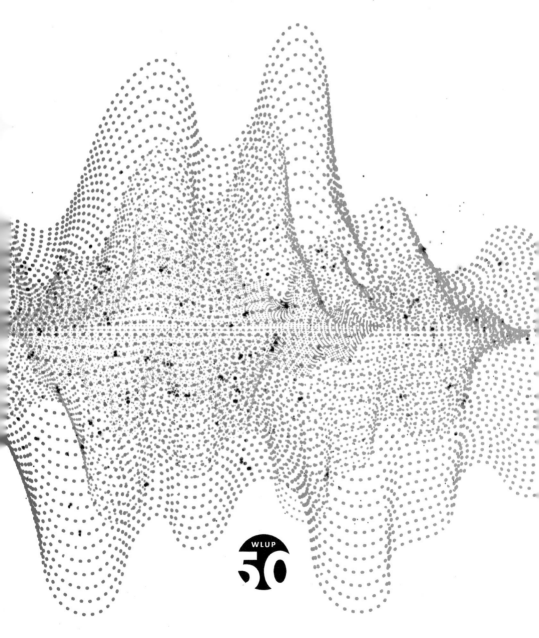

WLUP 50

Wilfrid Laurier University Press acknowledges the support of the Canada Council for the Arts for our publishing program. We acknowledge the financial support of the Government of Canada through the Canada Book Fund for our publishing activities. Funding provided by the Government of Ontario and the Ontario Arts Council. This work was supported by the Research Support Fund.

Library and Archives Canada Cataloguing in Publication

Title: Podcast studies : practice into theory / Lori Beckstead and Dario Llinares, editors.

Names: Beckstead, Lori, editor. | Llinares, Dario, editor.

Description: Includes bibliographical references and index.

Identifiers: Canadiana (print) 20240338375 | Canadiana (ebook) 20240338391 | ISBN 9781771126434 (hardcover) | ISBN 9781771126458 (EPUB) | ISBN 9781771126465 (PDF)

Subjects: LCSH: Podcasting. | LCSH: Communication in education—Technological innovations. | LCSH: Education, Higher—Technological innovations.

Classification: LCC LB1033.5 .P63 2025 | DDC 371.102/2—dc23

Cover and interior design by John van der Woude, JVDW Designs.
Front cover image: "Sound waves," Sandipkumar Patel, iStock.com.

This book is printed on FSC® certified paper. It contains recycled materials and other controlled sources, is processed chlorine-free, and is manufactured using biogas energy.

Printed in Canada

Wilfrid Laurier University Press is located on the Haldimand Tract, part of the traditional territories of the Haudenosaunee, Anishnaabe, and Neutral Peoples. This land is part of the Dish with One Spoon Treaty between the Haudenosaunee and Anishnaabe Peoples and symbolizes the agreement to share, to protect our resources, and not to engage in conflict. We are grateful to the Indigenous Peoples who continue to care for and remain interconnected with this land. Through the work we publish in partnership with our authors, we seek to honour our local and larger community relationships, and to engage with the diversity of collective knowledge integral to responsible scholarly and cultural exchange.

Contents

Acknowledgements

We set sail on this academic odyssey four years ago, charting a course with a meticulously crafted timeline. However, the journey has perhaps been longer and more windswept than anticipated. With the book finally ready to greet its readers, it is clear that the intricate web of collaboration, laced with a generous measure of patience, has been the cornerstone of our endeavour.

Our primary and most profuse thanks goes, of course, to our authors, whose insightful, curious, authentic, and inspiring contributions are nothing short of foundational in the ever-evolving edifice of podcast studies. Their collective wisdom not only elevates the stature of our field, but also embodies the very spirit and purpose of this anthology. Collaborating with each one has been both an honour and an inspiration, and our gratitude for their participation is immeasurable.

It's noteworthy that the intellectual generosity which underpins much of podcasting, especially the analytical discourse that forms the backbone of our academic journeys, is often a labour of love—a testament to the benevolent spirit that fuels academia. But this is consistently taken for granted. In this context, we want to thank all the guests on the podcasts we have produced. In a real sense their minds and voices are the intellectual and aesthetic material that allows us to podcast. But not only that, their willingness to speak and share expertise and emotion underpins podcasting as a space of connection.

We have had incredible support from our publishers, who have believed in our vision for the project from the very start, and helped us navigate when we ran into difficulties. The process of oversight has helped us make the book the best version of itself. Siobhan McMenemy, our contact at Wilfrid Laurier University Press, has been an extremely supportive guide and we are so grateful that she saw the value in the project from the start.

We'd like to thank our peer reviewers, who, as is customary, shall remain nameless, but you know who you are and we are grateful for your diligent work, which made this volume so much better.

Dario wishes to extend a special acknowledgment to Neil Fox, whose cama-
raderie and shared passion for podcasting have been a source of cultural guidance. Our dialogues, particularly through *The Cinematologists* podcast, have
been a wellspring for my engagement with the medium. Stacey Copeland's
insightful critiques of our introduction and my chapter were invaluable, while
Anne Korfmacher, through our intellectual exchanges during PhD supervi-
sions, consistently provided fresh perspectives that broadened my horizons.
Richard Berry stands as a pillar of the podcast studies community, offering
unwavering support and guidance. To my partner, Bea, I owe a profound debt
of gratitude. Her perspicacity and incisive feedback pierced through my rhetorical fog, bringing much-needed clarity to my work. Her presence—stead-
fast in support, graceful in understanding—has been a sanctuary, allowing
me the solitude for reflection and the companionship for encouragement.
Bea, you are the unsung hero of my every day. Finally, but most significantly,
my sincerest thanks to Lori, without whom this project might have faltered.
While I was in the tumultuous seas of job transitions, it was she who stead-
fastly took the helm. Her diligence, perspicuity, and meticulous attention to
detail not only compensated for my occasional absences but also elevated the
quality of our collective work. Lori, your partnership is treasured, your friendship cherished, and I am hopeful that the whirlwind of this experience only
serves to fortify our collaborative spirit for future ventures.

Lori wishes to acknowledge the financial support of the Creative School
at Toronto Metropolitan University. Dario, I wish to thank you for inviting me
to co-edit this volume with you, which helped give me the confidence to see
myself as a worthy expert in this field. From the get-go you have been a wellspring of exciting ideas and deeply perceptive thought, as well as an inspiring
model of someone who Gets Shit Done. I admire your intellect and your motivation, and frankly, I don't know how you do it all, but I am grateful to have
had this opportunity to learn from you. Finally, I'd like to thank my life partner Dave Rose, who is my rock as well as my soft place to land, and without
whom, I think, nothing would be possible.

This book, a tapestry of voices and ideas, stands as a testament to the collective endeavour of many. To all involved, we are eternally grateful.

The PRACTICE of PODCAST STUDIES

LORI BECKSTEAD and DARIO LLINARES

As a scholar, to identify with the discipline of podcast studies is to attempt to orient oneself to a sound medium that is not yet two decades old, with a heterogeneous set of technological, structural, and practical requirements, and with a uniquely complex, even ambiguous set of impacts and engagements. Since the mid-2000s coining of the term podcasting to define a burgeoning field of "internet radio" facilitated by RSS (Really Simple Syndication) subscription technology, the study of podcasting has mirrored the uneven evolution of the medium. It is perhaps indicative of the scholarly mindset that much formative research work on podcasting was largely concerned with pedagogic utility. Many teachers were early adopters and saw practical applications for podcasting as an enhancement or a disruption to the limitations to analogue teaching through a digital revolution.

Research into podcasting began to diversify quickly with the affinities and divergences from radio, often provoking challenging questions around medium specificity and even, at times, an antagonistic sense of scholarly propriety. The question of whether podcasting is something distinct from radio rather depends on the ontological criteria one sets out. Artefactual, experiential, technological, and even attitudinal criteria indicators are used to make arguments for and against the specificity of podcasting. Commenting on the rationale for their 2022 *Routledge Companion to Radio and Podcast Studies*, editors Mia Lindgren and Jason Loviglio suggest that the mingling of radio studies and podcast studies in their book "reminds us that neither 'radio' nor 'podcasting' should be approached as static objects of analysis; instead both are constantly changing, shaping each other and other media" (2022, 1).

Many podcast scholars use the starting point of technology as a foundational demarcation. The underlying digital infrastructure (i.e., RSS, which acts as a standardized method of content distribution; iTunes as a default directory for podcast organization; the initial popularity of the iPod and the subsequent ubiquity of Wi-Fi–enabled smartphone;, and the expansion of podcast-hosting and -listening apps) facilitated the production and distribution of the sound artefacts that we call podcasts.

·ı|ı·ı|ı·ı|ı·

As podcasting has expanded from being a small, largely independent labour of love for a committed cadre of audio enthusiasts to a mainstream industry with huge infrastructural and artistic investment, expanding listening numbers and significant socio-cultural impact, the academic focus on what podcasting is and does further expanded and diversified. Pointedly, in the first ten years of the medium's development, and before anyone thought to designate a field of study, there was always a significant overlap between those who practise and those who study podcasting. Because of the relatively low barrier to access production tools and the culture of autodidactic learning via YouTube, sound recording and editing was not subject to gatekeeping.

As podcasting reached a point of mainstream crossover in the mid-2010s, the disciplinary framework of podcast studies began to take shape. Although there were antecedents that have come to be retrospectively recognized as foundational podcast studies research (see Berry 2006, Bonini 2015, and Markman 2012, for example), it was the publication of two books—Llinares, Fox, and Berry's edited collection *Podcasting: New Aural Culture and Digital Media* (2018) and Spinelli and Dann's monograph *Podcasting: The Audio Media Revolution* (2019)—that symbolized a concerted move towards the designation of a field of inquiry. The expansion of critical analyses of podcasting in the wake of these texts has shaped a cross- and interdisciplinary examination of processes of production, distribution, and engagement. Nele Heise's open-source list of podcasting research attests to the ever-expanding number of outputs and approaches to researching the medium.[1] From within this scholarly critical work, recognizable discourses have emerged, such as podcasting's DIY independence, its intimacy and parasociality, its disruption of broadcast orthodoxies, its (re)invention of audio genres and forms, its liminal position in digital media, and its adoption by non-mainstream voices and communities. Furthermore, researchers from adjacent fields in

---

1   Heise's list can be found here: https://rb.gy/iz22i. Access must be requested.

the arts and humanities naturally draw upon theoretical and methodological cal paradigms established in media studies, cultural studies, sound studies, sociology, literary studies, and radio studies, among others. Along with this is a sense that academic podcasting offers the chance to challenge orthodoxies of the academy, largely deriving from the use of sound, and more specifically the voice, as the prism through which knowledge is created and articulated. The challenging of text as the primary source of academic knowledge is still something of an insurgent one; here we are writing a book after all.

As editors of this book, we come to the field from different entry points. For Lori, as a professor of media production with a radio and journalism background, podcasting has been something of an adaptation. Applying existing audio production and narrative skills in a new medium naturally led to investigations into the nature of the new medium. Dario, on the other hand, comes to podcasting from film studies. Podcasting was an avenue through which his academic role as a film lecturer and researcher found a new outlet. As our respective podcasting practices developed, our interest was piqued not only by the possibilities of practice-led research and the creative possibilities of podcasting, but also the epistemological affordances of sound mediation relative to text and image.

There is an ever-expanding culture of academics utilizing podcasting as a tool for articulating and disseminating research. Such practice raises self-reflexive questions in terms of podcasting's actual and potential role in academia, and wider questions about the nature of communication and knowledge in the contemporary media, technological, social, and political landscape. Our discussions and collaborations across the burgeoning network of "podacademics" have revealed the medium's value and significance in a wide range of academic contexts: the creative and intellectual potential of sound, the capacity to distribute knowledge beyond academic audiences, as a means of collaboration, as a methodological research tool, as a method of peer review, and the potential for diversification of voices and perspectives to speak and be heard.

A key question of podcast studies, indeed the driving motivation of this book, is how and why academics use podcasting as a practice. The production of podcasts by lecturers, researchers, administrators, and students offers a wealth of creative and intellectual work, as well as potential for access and engagement in ways that academic books and journal articles do not afford. However, the examination of this ever-expanding range of work in the context of practice-led, practice-informed, or practice-based research, along with further study of the outcomes and uses of scholar-produced podcasts, is in need of a greater analysis and schematization. As Jorgensen and Lindgren point out, "Practice-based approaches provide radio and podcast researchers opportunities to reveal the practice of producing audio content, thereby revealing implied knowledges and decision-making processes" (2022, 52). In putting together this book, we wanted to provide space for key thinkers aligned with podcast studies to reflect on how podcasting practice, in the broadest understanding of that notion, feeds into conceptual thinking about knowledge production and communication. In other words, how do academics theorize podcasting in light of the praxis—enaction, realization, or application of ideas through practice—that the medium affords? We're flipping the oft-used subtitle of academic textbooks, "Theory into Practice," to explore how the doing of podcasting can contribute to theorizing the medium. We are not proposing an edict—that legitimacy as a podcast studies scholar hinges on producing one's own podcast. However, the intention of this book is an engagement with academic podcasters in their exploration of the motivation, production process, and context, and, crucially, their critical reflections on how the practice of podcasting influences their thought.

IF AN ACADEMIC PODCASTS, IS IT AN ACADEMIC PODCAST?

While the academy maintains its reliance on text-based publication as the primary, "legitimate" form of academic knowledge production, scholars are increasingly turning to podcasting as a venue for exploring ideas, collaborating, and creating and disseminating knowledge. In tandem, the question of what constitutes an academic podcast—or the specifics of academic podcasting as a process (as potentially distinct from commercial, hobbyist, or any other type of podcasting)—is an explicit issue for podcast studies to grapple with. But it's a multi-layered issue: Does an academic podcast have to be produced or hosted by an academic? (And who exactly is an "academic" in this context?) Does it need to have some fundamental association with an academic institution? Is there a difference between an academic podcast and, say, a journalistic podcast that utilizes the expertise of academics? (Many popular podcasts rely on scholars, via interviews, to produce the research underpinnings or to provide expert information and analysis.) What does an academic podcast even sound like? Such questions are woven implicitly through many of the chapters in this book.

The idea that an academic podcast is, or could be, engaged with peer review is a key consideration in podcast studies today. Indeed, Beckstead, Cook, and McGregor suggest that scholarly podcasts are distinct from other forms of podcasts in that they have the potential to be subjected to peer review; they are "podcasts that create new knowledge; whose content is accountable to a community of peers, whether they be scholars or others; where it is possible for knowledge to be interrogated, cited, and in some disciplines reproduced; and, crucially, where podcast series are able to respond to comments, critiques or suggestions either before publication or afterwards as part of a series or through additional material" (2024, 3). Such a definition makes clear the academic- and public-service usefulness of scholarly podcasting. Nonetheless, in many academic disciplinary fields, the podcast is still seen as, at best, a quaint side project and, at worst, a derided affront to "proper" academic work. As Woods and Wood state in relation to the use of podcasting in writing studies,

> [A] case could be made that podcasts *as scholarship* is still an unpopular opinion, particularly in English departments that prioritize traditional forms of publication (e.g., alphabetic texts), and thus, assign greater value to a singular mode of composing. We believe many teacher-scholar-podcasters find themselves in a peculiar position where they need to take into account how their podcasts are perceived and valued in their local context, and how podcasting is situated in the politics of that ecology. (2023, 2)

Podcaster-academics in many disciplines regularly face such issues. But if the field of podcast studies has a singular political aim, it is to fight against a kind of academic segregation. Academics who podcast often do so, with little to no resources, because they recognize the benefit to their research and to the wider community of engaging in public conversations. But the enthusiasm for performing unpaid labour of this type diminishes when many university administrators, policy-makers, and evaluation committees do not yet value podcasting in the same way as traditionally peer-reviewed publications.

Mack Hagood's chapter "The Scholarly Podcast: Form and Function in Audio Academia" is a useful reference point which unpacks how podcasting sits within a range of "nascent genres, formats, and practices, only some of which fall neatly into the popular conception of 'podcasting'" (2021, 181). Audio journals, audiobooks, audio lectures, campus and community radio, audio documentaries, and podcasts sit on a continuum which he describes as "audio academia." Hagood argues that quality is one of two differentiating factors amongst types of scholarly podcasts, distinguishing between "hi-fi, mid-register" podcasts (highly produced, presenting academic knowledge to a general audience) and "lo-fi, high register" podcasts (of low production value, with the use of specialized academic knowledge). With academic podcasters often producing independently, usually with no specialized training and without any recognized guidance or criteria of evaluation from universities themselves, there is arguably no frame of reference for what makes a successful, good, or excellent academic podcast. Nonetheless, as Newman and Schwarz (2018) have shown, audio quality can impact the perception of the quality of the research; listeners perceive the research and the researcher less favourably when their talk or interview is presented in poor audio quality. While good audio quality may be imperative, elements that determine both the independent and commercial understanding of podcasting quality, such as subjective critical praise or empirical metrics (download numbers, for example), are potentially less relevant from an academic viewpoint. And insofar as the corporatization of higher education is perceived as a growing problem (see, for example, Price-Williams, Nasser, and Sasso 2020; Spinrad, Relles, and Watson 2022), such blunt metrics are potentially dangerous to academic freedom and the very notion of what types of knowledge and research are "worth" pursuing.

THE AIMS OF PODCAST STUDIES

To taxonomize a list of aims, requirements, or goals for a disciplinary field always comes with the potential of being rather reductive, if not exclusionary. Furthermore, the criteria can quickly become obsolete as disciplinary boundaries and areas of inquiry evolve. Spinelli and Dann put forward a list of "podcasting features and concepts" (2019, 7) which served as a useful, tentative blueprint for podcast studies at the time. However, even just these few years later, this list reads more like a set of definitional parameters for podcasts as a form of mediation, rather than a set of disciplinary concerns. Rime, Pike, and Collins (2022), in an article that goes back to the fundamental question of what a podcast is, set out six pairs of tensions or "immutable attributes that the medium has entailed since its inception" (1262) through which to consider podcasting: personalization and automation, independent and mainstream production, unique and universal content, current audience and possible demographic, immersion and interactivity, art and technology. Richard Berry (2022) considers the medium through technical, cultural, and sonic lenses, while Tzlil Sharon (2023), in questioning whether there is in fact, or should be, such a thing as podcast studies, lays out three central approaches through which podcast researchers have conceptualized podcasting to date: technological, socio-cultural, and formalistic. (To the relief of many a podcast scholar, Sharon concludes that yes, there is and there should be.)

Thus, standing on the shoulders of podcast researchers of the last two decades, and despite our reservations about being reductive, we march boldly into the taxonomization minefield to offer this (by no means exhaustive) snapshot of what we consider the core intersecting concerns of podcast studies. To this end, areas of inquiry in this discipline include:[2]

---

2   These categories are of course not isolated and are more often than not interrelated in the methodologies and foci of podcast studies research.

- **Definitions:** How podcasting and the podcast is understood on a fundamental level, what the correlations with and differences are between both "old" and "new" media, as well as how podcasters define themselves and their craft. (e.g., Berry 2006 and 2018; Bonini 2022; Llinares et al. 2018a)

- **Form and Content:** The study of the artefact of the podcast itself, which may encompass elements such as genre, form, structure, style (e.g., Lindgren 2016; O'Meara 2015; Spinelli and Dann 2019; Rae 2023), as well as analyses of the fact of the podcast being primarily a sonic artefact (e.g., Fariello 2019).

- **Production Practices:** How the podcast is crafted (e.g., McHugh 2022), who is crafting them and why (e.g., Markman 2012; Markman and Sawyer 2014; Millette 2012), and under what conditions they are being crafted (e.g., Sullivan 2018 and 2021a).

- **Audiences:** How and why listeners relate to, engage with, or are affected by podcasts (e.g., Chan-Olmsted and Wang 2022; McClung and Johnson 2010). Within this category are both quantitative approaches to audience behaviour using empirical data (e.g., Edison Research 2022; McLung and Johnson 2010) and qualitative approaches, which may look into aspects of podcasting such as intimacy (e.g., Euritt 2023; Sienkiewicz and Jaramillo 2019), parasociality (e.g., Schlütz and Hedder 2022), fan culture (e.g., Wrather 2016), participatory ecosystems (e.g., García-Marín 2020), and listening (e.g., Tobin and Guadagno 2022).

- **Technologies:** Explorations of the technical mechanisms through which podcasting emerged, developed and continue to change; the study of interrelations between technologies that position podcasting in the wider media ecosystem; and analysis of the impact of technological developments that have changed distribution, reception, and listening practices (e.g., Bottomley 2020; Llinares 2022; Morris and Patterson 2015; Swiatek 2018).

- **Political Economies:** Analyses of podcasts and podcasting in the context of democratic media structures, and the question of public and private spheres in the digital age; the interrelationship between podcasting and local, national, and global economic systems; analyses of podcasting as a commercial industry (e.g., Crider 2023; Cwynar 2019; Sellas and Bonet 2023; Sullivan 2018).

- **Cultural Practices:** How, why, and by whom podcasting has been adopted or utilized as part of collective or individual cultural expression, and how podcasting has been deployed to challenge systemic hierarchies and affirm marginalized voices and viewpoints (e.g., Florini 2020; Fox, Dowling, and Miller 2020; MacDougall 2011; Royston 2023; Vrikki and Malik 2019).

- **Pedagogy and Scholarship:** Analyses of podcasting as a pedagogic practice at all levels of education (e.g., McGarr 2009; Verma 2021); how podcast studies articulates itself through podcasting (e.g., Hoydis 2020; Llinares 2022; McGregor 2022; Sharon 2023); and how scholarship is created, evaluated, and disseminated via podcasting (e.g., Beckstead, Cook, and McGregor 2024; Cook 2023; Hagood 2021).

Due to the porous boundaries between these groupings, they should not be considered discrete categories. If the study of podcasting offers anything, it is the opportunity to amalgamate scholarly interests, approaches, and methodologies. As you will see, the chapters that follow encapsulate an interdisciplinarity of both focus and form of research. However, it is the relationship between podcasting and scholarship that drives the central motivation for this book as a whole. Podcast studies is inherently a practice as well as an object of study.

In contemplating the relationship of podcasting, practice, and scholarship, we posit that, perhaps more than for any other medium, the study of podcasts and podcasting actively necessitates the doing of podcasting. This is something of a bold claim. Podcasting arguably places an onus on podcast studies scholars not only to be analysts and critics of podcasting, but also to be creators themselves—to actually use the medium itself to engage with the conceptualization of that medium. Scholars of other media have not previously found themselves in a similar position; a film or TV scholar, for example, has not necessarily been expected also to be a practitioner of said medium. Yet we encounter this often among podcast scholars. In a basic sense, the accessibility of the medium in terms of cost and know-how makes this possible far more than with established media. But more importantly, the ability to participate in podcasting through multiple approaches (as producer, listener, hobbyist, educator, researcher, etc.) points to podcasting as what Swiatek (2018) calls a "bridging medium," and speaks to what Llinares (2018) might call the liminality praxis—occupying the intermediary space between the doing and the thinking, the what and the why. The praxis of podcasting is that, in the doing of it, there is the potential to re-engage with ideas and possibilities on a theoretical, conceptual level. The relationship between voice, self, and knowledge is a case in point here. The practice of thinking, speaking, and reacting to others' thinking and speaking in the recording space, then engaging with that audio in the editing and distribution process, effects a perpetual cycle: practice into theory and theory into practice. Even the word podcast itself is used interchangeably as both a noun and a verb—an object as well as an action or process. If podcast scholars study both the objects and the processes, should not the output of those studies (that is, the published scholarship) be likewise both object and process? We feel this approach strengthens the foundations of podcast studies, allowing the discipline to be especially reflexive about not only podcast creation and distribution, but also about listening, audiences, form and content, socio-cultural impact, and so on.

We are aware of the counter-arguments. We recognize that valuable insights come from podcast scholars who are not practitioners, just as scholars of English literature, for example, do not have to be published literary authors in order to be taken seriously as scholars. Our intention here is not to be exclusionary about whose perspectives and contributions carry weight in podcast studies; in fact, as we stated earlier, one of the key motivations of podcast studies is to fight against academic segregation. The discipline welcomes, of course, research from a variety of perspectives. Nonetheless, scholar-practitioners bring a particular set of perspectives that are a valuable part of the wide-ranging scope of the discipline, which is why we have chosen to focus this book on the relationship between podcasting practice and scholarship.

Underpinning our central concern with how practice provides a context for theory, we also posit a series of themes that shape this assertion through the book. In the following sections, we schematize the interdisciplinary nature of podcast studies, academic podcasting's self-reflexive tendency, challenges to the traditional gatekeeping boundaries of academia, and the potential for access and inclusion. The themes we highlight are by no means exhaustive; you will undoubtedly find your own tributaries of connection through the chapters. But these themes will, we hope, provide the reader with a layer of context for engagement with this book.

INTERDISCIPLINARITY

There is a case to be made that podcast studies is a field made up of bandwagon jumpers. The shared attraction to the medium is arguably grounded in the affordances it gives to scholars to expand the scope of their "original" field. But in the practice of podcasting, many scholars feel a sense of reinvention or rearticulation of their field of interest, creating exciting possibilities. Interdisciplinarity in the field of podcast studies, then, immediately draws from conceptual interests and methodological approaches in obvious cousins such as media studies, sound studies, and, of course, radio studies. Then there are more conceptual and thematic connections shared with areas such as cultural studies, sociology, literary criticism, and film studies, among others. But disciplinary affinities in podcast studies research are often attributed not just to the content but also the form of sound production (again an allusion to the possibilities of practice into theory). For example, Julia Hoydis, writing on feminism, gender, and podcast studies, and drawing from Stacey Copeland, states:

> podcast and gender and queer studies appear to be a natural fit—not least because podcasts, as oral [media], draw our attention to a constitutive part of personhood: If one considers its etymological roots, stemming from the Latin personare (to sound through), it captures, Stacey Copeland reminds us, "the human understanding of the sound of voice as an indisputable part of both an embodied self and performative identity." (Hoydis 2020, 222)

Many of our contributing authors take on the parameters of interdisciplinarity in their chapters. Simon Barber alludes to the notion that new academic fields are inherently interdisciplinary as he elides songwriting studies with podcast studies in chapter six. Parinita Shetty's Ph.D. project, which she and Dario discuss in chapter twelve, is situated in a natural affinity between fan studies and podcast studies. Martin Feld's chapter (chapter two) is not just interdisciplinary, but multidisciplinary, bringing together fan studies, technology, and podcasting using an autoethnographic method to explore the form, content, and context of his practice.

But whether the authors articulate the parameters of interdisciplinarity with explicit intent or not, their research and critical work is inculcated with the theoretical methodological hallmarks of more established fields of knowledge—the relative youthfulness of podcast studies requires such epistemological appropriation. The question of methodological affinity across disciplines is just as important as aesthetic, conceptual, or political intersections. Methodologies such as interviews, focus groups, and audio-diary recordings are central pillars of ethnographic and autoethnographic research approaches, as well as foundational methods in podcasting. With this in mind, we next think through the use of autoethnography and the "self-reflexive tendency" (Llinares 2019) as what have emerged as two of the guiding methodological approaches of this book.

ACADEMIC PODCASTING AND THE SELF-REFLEXIVE TENDENCY

Inherent within the praxis of podcasting, and made explicit in many of the chapters of this book, is the sense that the medium fundamentally lends itself to self-reflexivity and even autoethnographic analysis. The very process of voicing ideas, concepts, or outcomes of research projects gives a sense of the subjective connection to the researcher. This is in fairly stark contradiction to the disembodied and mostly impersonal expectations of "normal" scholarship, in which the author generally removes themselves from the narrative, using the third person and passive constructions to depersonalize the work. The presence of an interlocutor is a humanizing influence, and conversation, particularly when interrogating motivations and contexts for academic assertions, can engender self-reflection. In academic podcasting, reflections on why the researcher did the research, on the political context in which it was done, or even the personal psychology of the researcher is foregrounded.

The element of a self-reflexive or autoethnographic underpinning to academic podcasting emerges partly from one of the inherent aspects of podcasting structure: serialization. The nature of podcasting's distribution mechanism lends itself to structures of series made up of episodes. While it's fairly obvious what these structures can do for a popular podcast genre such as, say, true crime, perhaps under-theorized is the potential that this serialized structure has for academic podcasts. Audio recordings can certainly be scholarly and even reflexive by nature, but true reflexivity is an affordance of the ongoing nature of podcasts. Podcasting is a reminder that scholarship is about reinterrogating one's position constantly, and opening oneself up to challenges that force one to engage with a productive evolution.

Another aspect of the self-reflexive tendency often explicitly points to podcasting's emergence in the era of digital publication, and the associated breakdown of the producer/consumer binary. For Llinares and Fox (2022, 95) the self-reflexive tendency is a "feature of many non-fiction podcasts, [and] is indicative of amateur and professional practitioners reckoning with the possibilities of a burgeoning medium in an uncertain communications ecosystem." Podcaster-academics very often explore the processes, motivations, and outcomes of the practice of their podcasting, echoing a history of self-reflexive writing and methodological approaches that acknowledge and even centre the researcher in relation to the research. The tendency is also prevalent in podcasting more broadly; Mia Lindgren (2016) has examined this phenomenon specifically in relation to the popularity of journalistic podcasts which use personal and subjective approaches to storytelling.

Reflexivity, as described by Barbara Probst, is "the embodiment of an epistemology in which the knower is always present" and offers "a means for using self-knowledge to inform and enhance the research endeavor" (2015, 46). With the voice as a primary attribute, the tone of self-reflexivity is highly imbued into the content of podcasting. Some of our authors define their work explicitly as autoethnography. While not a prerequisite, we have encouraged the authors in this book to translate the tone of reflection into their writing.

The self-reflexive tendency, ideally, leads podcaster-academics to an interrogation of their own positionality, which in turn engenders analyses of social and political identity. The work of Sarah Florini, for example, theorizes how podcasting can capture everyday interactions as a Black sociality, providing an implied audience of Black "listeners with a downloadable, mobile, sonic recreation of these Black social spaces" (2015, 215). This is taken up by Fox, Dowling, and Miller (2020) who posit Black podcasting as a "discursive cultural guide" in the twenty-first-century digital ecosphere.

Probst does, however, note a limitation of the role of reflexivity in research: that "we can only reflect on what strikes us as requiring reflection, what we become aware of with our conscious minds...the very things one most needs to examine may be those that are most deeply hidden" (2015, 46).

CHALLENGING TRADITIONS OF KNOWLEDGE PRODUCTION AND DISSEMINATION

For many academics, podcasting provides a voice, both literal and ideological, which is much less restricted than in more traditional areas of academia (Cook 2023). Podcasting facilitates a freedom of expression in the use of the voice to articulate knowledge, but also freedom to break out of the formalized tone of voice disciplined by the academic text or formal lecture. Podcasts sound more like the post-conference chat with colleagues at the bar, where we feel free to ask questions and offer feedback and insight in the form of everyday discourse, rather than the kind of tightly edited, perfected, and finished piece of written feedback that might be expected in more traditional publication fora. Podcasting, fully rooted as it is in conversation, can be free-flowing, vulnerable, and even messy and imprecise (Beckstead, Cook, and McGregor 2024)—characteristics not normally ascribed to the usual outputs of academia, but nonetheless crucial aspects of knowledge creation. Academic podcasting offers something of an escape from the ivory tower.

Having thus broken out, the natural next question is one of rigour. Once we leave the confines of the tower with its gatekeeping and formalized structures of peer review, can academic podcasting measure up to the perceived rigour of traditional academic publication? One attitude towards podcasting is that it does not possess the value or rigour that is inherently accepted for the journal article or book. However, podcasts can certainly be peer-reviewed in the traditional sense, with disciplinary experts weighing in on the benefits and outcomes of a podcast; see, for example, *Secret Feminist Agenda* (McGregor 2017–22). Podcasts can also be the vehicle through which peer review is conducted—see, for example, the *Open Peer Review Podcast* (Beckstead 2020). But podcasting, because it is built on a foundation of conversation, cannot be anonymized in quite the way that written scholarship can be. Assumptions that anonymous review is imperative to ensure academic rigour have been contested (see Bastian 2015), and podcasting's swift take-up among scholars and researchers will necessitate a re-evaluation of such assumptions. Beyond simply adapting academic podcasts to existing norms of rigour and peer review, which could surely suck the joy out of podcasting and replace it with rubrics and administrative box-ticking, podcast studies is interested in how academic podcasting might engender new ways of thinking about not only how scholarship can be deemed valid (and by whom), but also how scholarship is created in the first place.

While the producers of scholarly podcasts might assume they're addressing an audience of other scholars in their field, they are no doubt aware that a wider public also has access. For audiences beyond academia, it's incumbent upon the podcaster to provide the context for a layperson or a non-academic public listener. If done successfully, this facilitates an accessibility to the research, to the scholarship, and to academia in general that is not necessarily available in journal articles or via the other typical structures through which academic work is distributed, and helps to (re)position academia as a site for publicly engaged scholarship. This public accessibility further enables discourse with a broader range of communities than are normally available to scholars. Thus academic podcasting potentially engenders new communities in which a wide range of perspectives are drawn together to create new insights, either with regard to podcasting itself or with wider disciplinary fields, or both.

Another connecting theme of this book is the role that podcasting plays in the broader structures and traditions of the university. In many facets of podcast use, whether we are talking about production or distribution of knowledge and information, there is often an allusion to its disruptive potential. Llinares describes it as a "positive destabilisation: an exciting and potentially revelatory disruption of the boundaries that tie disciplines and fields of inquiry to specific forms of expression and institutional practice" (2018, 135); Ian M. Cook characterizes scholarly podcasting as "insurgent" (2023). Certainly throughout this book, podcast scholars reflect on the opportunities for scholarly practices that challenge the status quo. On the flip side, however, there are also concerns about labour exploitation. Academic podcasters will have individual motivations for podcasting, but for now this usually comes from a place of personal interest. Is academic podcasting just another strand of the individualized expectations of contemporary academia, in which various forms of unpaid scholarly activity are assumed or expected to take place? Paradoxically, then, the insurgent, positive disruption that the podcast form and structure may facilitate is dependent on an academic having or making the time to produce a show. Academic podcasting is thus subject to many hierarchies of opportunity that can restrict the progression of equity-deserving persons through traditional structures of scholarly development.

Indeed, assumptions about accessibility need to be interrogated in podcast studies. An active advocacy for the diversification of voices, as well as a globalized, pluralistic approach to the development and understanding of the medium, does underpin many examples of podcast studies research. Vrikki and Malik (2019, 273), for example, have analyzed podcasting's role in facilitating new forms of social affiliation and anti-racism in the context of an "intensifyingly hostile environment for black and minority ethnic groups and a digital and creative sector marked by social and cultural inequalities." Sibanda and Ndlovu (2023) have studied the role of podcasting in forming "communities of resistance" amongst Zimbabwean youth, while Park (2017, 245) has shown that citizen news podcasts in Korea motivate "ordinary individuals who are left largely disillusioned from mainstream journalism to engage in elite-challenging political action." Nevertheless, the notion that podcasting is utilized to address niche interests and ignored histories, and to give voice to what might be considered by some as "controversial" political identities cannot be assumed, and needs to continue to be at the forefront of concern for podcast studies.

As we set out to create this book, we were keen for the makeup of the content to be as diverse as possible and to include viewpoints not solely Western-centric. The fact that we have only partially succeeded attests to the fact that podcast studies is not outside of the hierarchical structures of academia, and that the study of the medium is beholden to barriers of language, culture, geography, and indeed, bias. Podcast studies risks being articulated primarily through the lenses of whiteness and Eurocentrism if this is not attended to carefully by researchers in the discipline, academic mentors and supervisors, and those who inadvertently contribute to a ready-made "canon" of podcast scholarship by failing to consider the politics of citation. Accessibility and inclusion is of course a problem in academia as a whole, but we hope that given podcasting's subversive potential and insurgent qualities (Cook 2023), podcast studies can contribute to breaking down these barriers rather than upholding them. With this in mind, it was our original aim to produce a much more radically non-Eurocentric list of authors. The struggle of writing and editing on the back of the COVID-19 pandemic is by no means an excuse, but it took its toll on academics generally, and most notably on those from underprivileged backgrounds and contexts. Having noted those caveats, we are proud to have a chapter by Indigenous scholars Tanya Ball, Sheila Laroque, and Kayla Lar-Son, writing what we think is amongst the first academic chapters on Indigenous podcasting. In addition, chapters such as those from Yemisi Akinbobola, Stacey Copeland, Hannah McGregor and Katherine McLeod, Jasmine Harris, and Tzlil Sharon and Nicholas John provide vital access points for thinking through inclusive possibilities and critiques of podcasting.

THE FRAMEWORK AND FORMAT OF THIS BOOK

Podcasting has the potential to circumvent and maybe even break through academic barriers. However, we are fully aware that in writing this book there is something of an inherent contradiction: Why write a book at all if we are such ardent evangelists of the podcast form? There are several responses to that. First, it reflects the fact that even with the adoption of podcasting in many academic areas, the written text is still the definitive benchmark of academic production (a condition we hope will change over time). Second, we have attempted to reflect in this book something of the conversational process and tone of podcasting: in an early meeting with prospective authors we asked them to keep in mind that this is a book that wants to be a podcast. Indeed, several of the chapters are recorded conversations that have been adapted for print publication. This approach reminds us that, as Copeland, McGregor, and McLeod point out in chapter seven, "knowledge is always situated in relation to the contexts through which it is generated."

In developing this book and working with the authors, we did not want to impose a certain academic style on the writing. This is something of a critical/political stance. We have produced this book because it's still taken for granted that the written word is more important, but did not want to insist on formal modes of address, especially because our underpinning approach was to encourage authors to reflect on their own experiences. Furthermore, in discussions with the authors, we found there was a clear desire for the language to be as accessible as possible. Just as podcasting opens up academic knowledge to a broader audience, so too can the written word be made more accessible, beyond the boundaries of traditional academic norms. We want to show it's possible to be academically rigorous without necessarily being bound by the perceived requirements of academic structure or language.

And finally, this will come full circle when this book is released and we speak to each author about their chapters for a series of *The Podcast Studies Podcast*. Thus the book will break out of its textual status and become sonically "alive" through the embodied voices of authors who can expand on, qualify, and contextualize the written text.

INTRODUCING THE CHAPTERS

Part 1: Podcasting as Academic Practice

The chapters in part one look directly at the definition, practices, motivations, and implications of academic podcasting: how academic podcasting reframes disciplinary boundaries and methodological approaches, along with notions of academic selfhood through podcasting as research practice.

Dario Llinares reflects on the use of the term "space" within podcast studies literature as a rhetorical mechanism to amalgamate physical, technological, experiential, and conceptual allusions to the practice of podcasting. He grounds this common but often imprecise or contradictory definitional approach in Henri Lefebvre's media critique *The Production of Space* (1991), as well as in Donna Haraway's notion of "situated knowledge" (1998). Using a self-reflexive analysis of his own academic practice on *The Cinematologists* podcast, he maps out the overlapping parameters of spatial interpretation in an attempt to define a clearer sense of "podcast space."

In "'It's in the Show Notes': Autoethnography of an Amateur Tech Podcaster," **Martin Feld** conceptualizes the relationship between his interest in both technology and podcasting as a listener turned producer, and how this underpinned his podcast Ph.D. by practice. Using an autoethnographic approach of positing researcher as subject, Feld deconstructs his form of academic fandom (aca-fandom) and how his podcast *Hemispheric Views* became the central podcast case study. Thinking through the dynamics of collaboration and the act of practising production in public, Feld advocates for the academic podcast to embrace the identity of amateur. He argues, through the work of Rachel Fendler (2013), among others, that podcasting affords a nomadic pedagogy whereby experiential learning takes place in non-traditional spaces and forms.

Samuel M. Clevenger explores how podcasting might respond to the maladaptive demands of contemporary life through an analysis of the "idle podcast." He argues that podcasting has the capacity to promote "restful and pleasurable idleness"—in opposition to pervasive neoliberal demands of compulsive productivity and constant self-improvement—and contemplates the mindfulness and self-care podcast genres in the context of his own *Field Recordings* podcast.

In his chapter, **Robert E. Gutsche Jr.** begins with the premise that the existing power dynamics in both journalism and journalism studies are in need of a reckoning, and explores whether podcasting has the potential to engender such change. Using his own experience as producer of *The J Word: A Podcast by Journalism Practice*, Gutsche reflects on the ideological underpinnings of the process of developing and producing podcasts aimed at journalism theorists and practitioners.

Liz Giuffre analyzes her podcast *Music Mothers and Others* as a model to explore the interrelationship between podcast research, industry, and audience engagement for academics who are parents and/or carers. Produced during phases of intense work and family disruption during the state-imposed COVID-19 lockdown in Australia, the creation and release of the podcast allowed Guiffre and her podcast partner Shelley Brunt to theorize their creative industries work through the multi-layered parameters of podcast production.

Simon Barber reflects on his own practice drawing upon analysis of song-writing podcasts which inform wider academic projects related to the craft of songwriting. As a co-creator of the *Sodajerker* podcast, Barber's self-reflection examines the challenges and limitations of making a popular podcast for a general audience while engaging with the "liminal space" between practice and theory. Barber then offers critical interpretations of podcasting in the wider scholarly context of songwriting studies.

Part 2: Podcasting as Social and Cultural Practice

In this section authors explore contexts and practices of podcasting that directly create and reflect socio-cultural concerns, including spaces of feminist and racial articulation and activism, storytelling, selfhood, language, and fan practice to shape identity.

Based on a "kitchen-table conversation" (or as close to one as Zoom can approximate), **Stacey Copeland**, **Hannah McGregor**, and **Katherine McLeod** explore the possibilities of podcasting as a feminist practice. The sense of place, as both a physical and conceptual context for feminist conversation, is the basis for a self-reflexive yet dialogic exploration of both their podcast practice and engagement with podcast studies. The conversational form of the chapter and the sense of rigorous scrutiny for which they advocate is an acknowledgement of a feminist practice of continual learning, building, listening, and rebuilding within the sonic space.

Erin Cory's chapter outlines her *Picturing Home* research project and podcast, an examination of the experience of migrants forging a home in Sweden. Migrants share a wealth of stories, memories, and traditions with each other; the resulting podcast is a collaborative amalgamation of research and activism, and thus challenges both the problematic discourses around migrants to Sweden and the academic boundaries of knowledge production. Cory problematizes the research in podcast studies around marginalized communities as too focused on the end product rather than the foundation of community-building labour, and suggests a highlighting of liminoid spaces of "play and experimentation *around but outside the podcasting moment.*"

From their point of view as hosts and producers of *masinahikan iskwêwak: Book Women* podcast, **Tanya Ball**, **Sheila Laroque**, and **Kayla Lar-Son** explore the connection between podcasting, Indigenous ways of Knowing and Being, and what they call "vibrations of resurgence." They describe how key aspects of Métis ontologies such as Relationality, Land, and Ceremony are expressed and taught via Storytelling,[3] and unpack the ways in which podcasting facilitates the telling of Stories and resistance of the colonial narratives of mainstream media.

Tzlil Sharon and **Nicholas John** reflect on differing narrative contexts of one singular narrative, a gay Jewish couple's struggle to become parents using a Ukrainian woman's eggs and two Indian surrogates. Sharon and John document how this story is covered in three different podcasts by two different production teams based in two different countries and in two different languages. They examine in detail the differences of approach and emphasis between long-form podcasts *Radiolab* and *Sipur Yisraeli*. In this adapted-for-print conversation, Sharon and John reflect on the importance of language and identity in the intentions of podcasters across differing cultural contexts and, in turn, how comparative analysis is a viable tool for podcast studies in analyzing narrative non-fiction.

Yemisi Akinbobola created the *HerMediaDiary* podcast as a platform for African women to share their experiences as they navigate careers or pathways to careers in media. Here, in contemplating her podcast through an academic lens, Akinbobola provides insight into podcasting's potential as a non-traditional site for academic publishing, and—critically—one that offers the potential to bridge the gap between academia, sites of African feminist activism, and media practice.

Fan podcasts are a huge segment of the medium's output. Many fan studies academics have deployed podcasting as a bridge between their scholarship and the enactment of their fandom itself. **Parinita Shetty** talks to **Dario Llinares** about her Ph.D. in which she posits that fan podcasts act as sites of public pedagogy and intersectional literacy. As part of the methodology, she created the podcast *Marginally Fannish*, allowing her to bring a diversity of fans into an academic space of analysis and create a collaborative relationship between researcher and participant. This is another example of how a podcast conversation can provide the basis for a written publication, where the framework and tone add to the self-reflexive aspect of the theorization.

---

3   Some words are intentionally capitalized here in accordance with how Ball, Laroque, and Lar-Son have written them, who in turn have taken cues from Greg Younging's *Elements of Indigenous Style* (2018).

Part 3: Podcasting as Production and Pedagogic Practices

Part 3 brings together reflections on broader aspects of podcast production, including but also beyond the practice of making podcasts, with reflections on visual contexts of podcast creation and on the labour of podcasting, and analyses of various modes of pedagogic function and outcome.

Challenging the idea that podcasts are an audio-only medium, and based on her experience creating the necessary visual imagery and digital texts to make a podcast publicly available, **Lori Beckstead** argues that podcasts are "made present" (Genette 1997) in the world via their text-based and graphic paratexts, such as cover art, show descriptions, show notes, and so on. Using the lens of literary theory, she analyzes two important podcast paratexts in particular, cover art and transcripts, and makes the case that any ontology of podcasting must consider the means, usually visual, by which audiences arrive at or alternatively experience podcasts.

Leslie Grace McMurtry uses her own podcasting practice to critique structural inequalities of labour that often go unseen and undiscussed across both commercial and academic contexts of production. Furthermore, using an autoenthnographic reflection on her own podcast, *Shattered*, she interrogates her own motivations for engaging in "hope labour" (Kuehn and Corrigan 2013), and argues that multiple parameters of creative and logistical labour associated with drama production have the propensity to push producers towards burnout.

For **Neil Fox**, podcasting is a form of curation that shapes our cultural landscape. In his chapter, Fox situates podcasting as "collection-making," which can be reductively defined as a form of commercial and nostalgic consumer need. However, he suggests the democratic potential and accessibility (which remains somewhat intact, for the time being at least), can engender a form of archiving that brings to the fore historical and cultural erasure. In this context he interviews podcasters Mary Wild and Sarah Cleaver about their *Projections Podcast*, a show that uses psychoanalytic film theory, which they discuss as having potential for curatorial activism.

When COVID-19 suspended in-person learning, **Kelli S. Boling** made a pedagogical pivot to become a producer of educational podcast content. Instead of a one-way transmission of information from professor/producer to student/listener, Boling describes how podcasting enabled interactive engagement amongst learners, professor, and special guests for students studying social justice and the media.

Jasmine L. Harris reflects on her experiences using podcasts and the production of podcasts as pedagogic tools that have the potential to subvert colonial expectations of learning and assessment. In her constructivist approach to pedagogy, Harris includes podcasts to help legitimize "non-traditional" language (i.e., language and ways of speaking often used amongst racialized groups) in an academic context, as well as to break down colonial assumptions of who creates knowledge and in what format. In her chapter she provides useful details about assignments she successfully implements in her classroom.

How should educators balance the theoretical and practical aspects of podcasting for their students? Where and how do podcast studies fit into undergraduate classrooms? **Lori Beckstead, Richard Berry**, and **Kim Fox** are educators who each have one foot firmly planted in the practice of podcast production and the other in podcast research and scholarship. In this conversation, they discuss how they approach "teaching podcasting"—teaching with podcasts, about podcasts, and how to podcast.

With this eclectic range of voices and perspectives, we hope that this book offers valuable explorations into podcast studies from practitioners thinking through the implications of their work. From an editorial standpoint, we have learned so much from descriptions of academic podcasting in terms of form and theme, but also from the interpretations and analyses that have emerged. As the scope and form of academic podcasting continues to expand, the work in this collection, we believe, offers both a snapshot of a discipline still defining itself, and inspiration for academics and students to take up the practice.

PART ONE

PODCASTING AS ACADEMIC PRACTICE

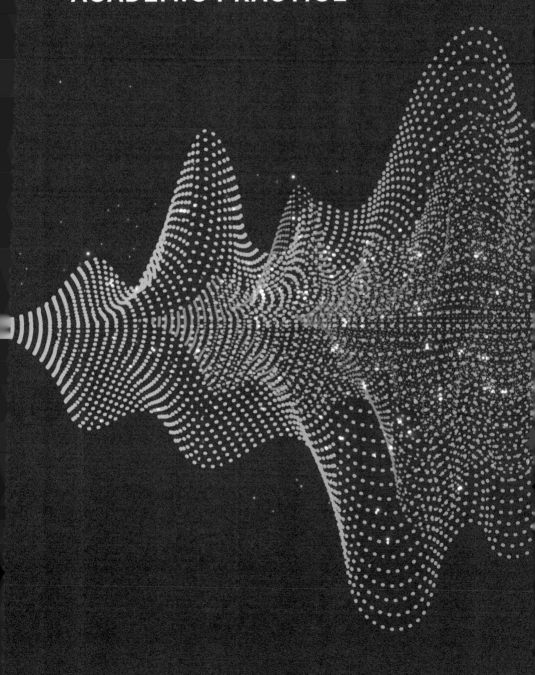

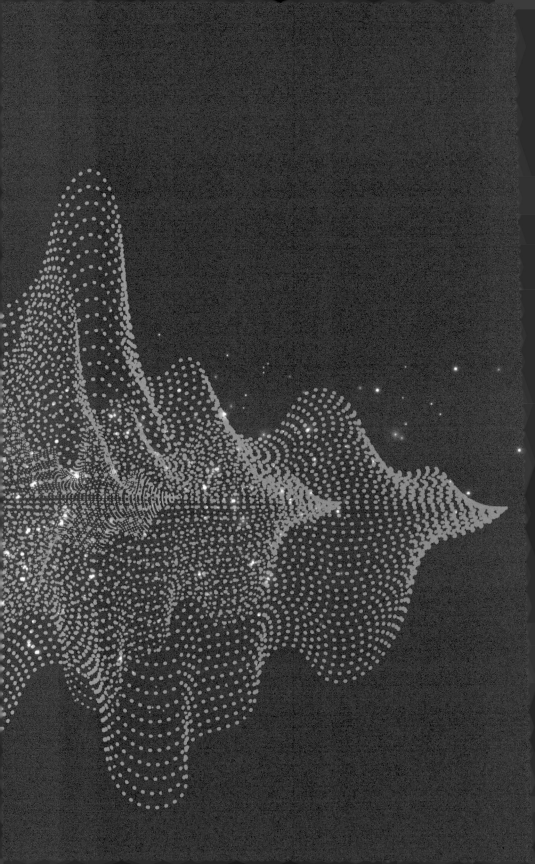

CHAPTER 1

ACADEMIC PODCASTING
Media Practice in the "Podcast Space"

DARIO LLINARES

W hat a useful word "space"[1] is when grappling with the ambiguities of our mediated lives. It allows us to think across the physical grounding of experience, yet simultaneously implies a state of being and thinking. We might walk into a friend's apartment for the first time and remark, "What a wonderful space"; yet in that space we might later have a conversation about our life using the lament, "I'm not in the right headspace." Paradoxically, these two applications of the word space often fold into each other in enigmatic ways. Think of the use of "safe space," which operates at the nexus of literal and ideological function. This elasticity of application is especially useful when thinking about the contemporary digital world, and our use of, immersion in, and engagement with media. Within media studies, many theoretical frameworks employ the conceptual utility of space to amalgamate a sense of objective reality, of material being in the world, with subjective allusions to human thought, emotion, and conscious experience. As we operate across the "real" and "virtual," "space" as a concept has become central to the way we think about mediation. For Brajković and Dokić (2014, 393), "When digital media appeared, they quickly established domination, not only over the term, but also over the category of space itself."

---

1 I have used the quotation marks—"space"—in my first instance of the term only. However, through the essay space should always be understood as a contested concept.

Within podcast studies, the application of the term space also reflects this pliability, often asserted as a rhetorical bridge between podcast production, distribution, and consumption. Furthermore, through the expansion of research that can be defined within podcast studies, the phrase podcast space is used to draw a range of connections and causalities between podcasting's technological affordances and its socio-cultural implications. In my own research, I have deployed the term space in such multi-conditional ways. Referring to its unique techno-historical development, I claimed podcasting to be a "space for academic discourse" and an "idiosyncratic audio space" (Llinares 2018). Indeed, within this very book, the word space has been used by *every* contributor, with diversity of intent and application.

Analyses of space in the context of mediation are not new. Much direct scrutiny of the philosophical history of space as a grounding concept for epistemology and ontology leads back to Henri Lefebvre's *The Production of Space* (1991). Lefebvre's critical inquiry begins from this position of questioning the specificity and intention of various philosophical lines of thought, and indeed the rhetorical abstractions of specific philosophers in their application of space. He traces this back to Descartes as a moment of rupture, where space as a concept is split between an abstract notion of cognitive perception to a more absolutist, totalizing idea of objective material experience. Through critiques of the likes of Kant, Chomsky, and Foucault, Lefebvre argues that conceptual use of space is a negotiation between a logic of objective space and a more modern, epistemologically abstract notion of mental or conscious space.

In this chapter, in attempting to think through a specific framework as to how one might consider the manifestation of a "podcast space," I begin by outlining various applications of the term space influenced by Lefebvre's insights on space as a conceptual paradigm. I begin by analyzing many instances of space being deployed by media and podcast studies scholars to navigate different modes of practice and experience. I then reflect on my podcasting as an academic practice on *The Cinematologists*,[2] synthesizing how the production process and sonic form emerges from the contested "spaces" (both physical and ideological) of the university, and exploring how the technical, experiential, and cultural parameters of the podcast space forges the possibility of a specific type of conversational practice. I conclude with an attempt to "map out" the complex dynamics that manifest the podcast space from the standpoint of an academic podcaster. This is a template of sorts to be sure, but has the intention to provoke further reflection in podcast studies regarding the application of space as a definitional term.

---

2   Dario Llinares and Neil Fox. *The Cinematologists*. https://www.cinematologists.com.

SPACE, MEDIA STUDIES AND CONTESTING SITUATEDNESS

The expanding literature on podcasting invokes space as a way of considering complex, intersecting dynamics. In Richard Berry's reflection on ten years of podcasting, he states, "Podcasting has become a distribution route, as well as a space for innovation and remediation—where content can be shared with listeners in a way that linear transmission systems cannot facilitate" (2016b, 665). In this short sentence, space is applied to allude simultaneously to both a place as well as a cultural or artistic movement. Yet, this is also rhetorically anchored to technological distribution and reception affordances. It is further implied that the space is a product of remediating audio content (usually broadcast radio), and associated with online sharing culture that facilitates digital networking. To be clear, none of this I disagree with. Having said that, the designation of space is doing a lot of conceptual work here. Later in the same piece Berry also states that episodes "are frequently recorded in a podcaster's own personal or domestic space" (666). Again, a statement that I wouldn't contest, yet this spatial rhetoric demarcates podcasting (amateur, hobbyist, DIY) from radio (professional, vocational, polished)—a tension that underpins much of podcast studies scholarship.

It's clear that the use of the word space in podcast studies draws from the wider media studies lexicon, where the intersection of physical or material applications provides a grounding for both explicit and implicit allusions towards practice, experience, socio-cultural impact, and even notions of "cognitive space," or "mental space," as Lefebvre would call it. In an editorial introduction of *Continuum* focused on media spaces in 2014, Stephen Monteiro highlights how a spatial turn in media theorization, influenced by Lefebvre, posits how physical, mental, and social space intersect in the production of dynamics of power and resistance. This focus on power, perhaps the most acute concern of late twentieth- and early twenty-first-century media and cultural studies scholars, has arguably begun to be supplanted by a new direction of inquiry: one that reckons with the mobile, fractured, voracious, unbounded cartographies of digital experience. Monteiro cites Haraway's (1998) notion of "situated knowledge," which, from a feminist perspective provokes a challenge to "objective knowledge." Haraway points to and critiques the use of space as a context for anchoring the body and thus the perspective of viewing from the body, through which we project a reality of the world and ourselves within it. Haraway, like Lefebvre, challenges the term space, its multivariate yet contradictory application, to reckon with the conditionality of our own "situatedness."

Haraway's notion of situated knowledge clearly had a directly political feminist intention, but in hindsight it reads like something of a blueprint, pointing to the impact of the digital media experiences to come. Theoretical media analyses of the internet era are arguably forced to conceptualize space not just theoretically but practically. Our everyday use of media technology disperses our sense of grounded physical location and facilitates a symbolic construction of our lives and identities, forcing us to constantly "situate" ourselves. This adds a further layer of complexity to the idea, explored by Lefebvre, of knowledge as an assumed property of an ideologically neutral mental space: "The quasi-logical presupposition of an identity between mental space (the space of the philosophers and epistemologists) and real space creates an abyss between the mental sphere on one side and the physical and social spheres on the other" (6).

We are constantly confronted with, reflecting on, and thinking through how digital life simultaneously creates, yet alienates or even atomizes, our situatedness. The well-expressed media discourses regarding shifting dimensions of time and space, the possibilities of alternative, augmented, and virtual realities, and new disciplines of media architecture and media geography all operate in the nexus of mediation, space, and contested situatedness. In the next section, I look specifically at how podcast studies scholars have deployed the rhetoric of space to conceptualize the podcasting media complex.

PODCAST STUDIES AND THE "PODCAST SPACE"

The application of space within podcast studies encompasses a cross-section of theoretical assertions applied to the affordances of the medium. Whether they use the term deliberately or abstractly, scholars grapple with a sense of material and conceptual situatedness. This can relate to the (dis)embodiment of producer or listener, the complexities of the physical, online, and sonic environments of podcast creation, institutional spaces (e.g., Spotify, the BBC, or universities as spaces where podcasts are defined and created for different purposes), the role of technological apparatuses as the grounding of more conceptual attributions of space, and the listener herself, who simultaneously occupies various forms of spatial situatedness. Assertions regarding the designation of podcast space within podcast studies are made up of a constellation of technological, spatial, aesthetic, social, and political elements (with differing configurations).

Richard Berry states: "Unlike broadcasting, the distribution systems and technologies for podcasting are in the public domain and so producers and consumers have been able to bend and define the "podcast space" to fit their own needs without the need for regulatory change or expensive engineering solutions" (2016b, 668). This exemplifies an often used application of space: the technological specifics related to the mechanics of production and distribution. The associated outcome, for Berry, implies that the podcast space is outside, or circumvents, the boundaries of traditional broadcasting. In this sense, space is co-opted into the discourse of "new" media and aligns with utopian ideas associated with the internet as a "space for visibility and participation, critically interrogating the relations between the new and the old" (Geiger and Lampinen 2014, 339). Certainly, in the reckoning that brings together, navigates, or synthesizes between "old" and "new" mediation, space offers a conceptual designation that usefully fuses technological affordances, social outcomes and assumptions around online spaces as separate spheres of influence (see Markman 2015).

Podcasting has also been posited as a form of public sphere, where the interrelation of subjectivity and activism emerges from the technological infrastructure of the medium and the emotional resonance of the storytelling voice. Podcasting as a space of democratic participation (Jarrett 2009) thus aligns with discourses of political liberation and utopianism potentialized by the open-access culture of the internet. Chang Sup Park, writing on citizen journalism in Korean podcasting, analyzes examples through the lens of Bakhtin's carnivalesque, suggesting, "carnivalistic citizen podcasts are the 'space' for the public to express dissent to the established order, creating an 'anti-structural' sphere, where dominant social relations are inverted or levelled" (2017, 258).

A specific invocation of podcasting as a potential space of political or ideological disruption links to its deployment as feminist praxis. Tiffe and Hoffmann combine a reading of sound scholar Yvon Bonenfant's work on how sound resonates between the body in space, and how feminized bodies and voices have been traditionally marginalized in a variety of spaces. While being careful not to imbue podcasting with a utopian aura, they state: "we are hopeful about the potentiality of podcast space for traditionally-oppressed voices, given our own experience being embraced as loud and occasionally vulgar women podcast hosts, and observing the success of other minority podcast hosts" (2017, 118).

In Freja Sørine Adler Berg's (2022) analysis of independent women podcasters in Denmark and their use of the medium to challenge conceptions about their own identities and lives, the "podcast space" is defined as an alternative to the gatekept spaces of traditional broadcasting, yet deemed potentially innovative in offering a non-visual space of personal expression. In Tiffe and Hoffmann (2017), the podcast space is deployed in both a material and ideological sense, where the voice has freedom and safety to designate selfhood through the complexities of experience and emotion. Hannah McGregor, Stacey Copeland, and Katherine McLeod, who have all written previously about the potential of podcasting as a feminist space, think and talk through the methodological, political, and conceptual in chapter seven in this book, stating: "through a self-reflexive form of feminist collaboration, we position feminist practices within podcasting as being in a state of continual learning, building, listening, and rebuilding sonic spaces that embody feminist politics." The emphasis here is on the development, use, and shaping of a space of praxis, through remaking, rethinking the politics of physical environment and embodiment, and as a result, a specific form of active feminist listening. Such an approach undoubtedly echoes Haraway's call to a reflection on "situatedness" in reckoning with selfhood, social experience, and knowledge itself.

In a similar vein, but focused specifically on race and UK politics of the last decade, Vrikki and Malik (2019) suggest that the technological possibilities of the medium facilitate a "civic urge" to tell stories about lived experience or marginalization:

> In an international climate that bolsters populist rhetoric around minority cultural groups, podcasts occupy a rare marginal space for articulating the lived experiences of these groups, whilst challenging broader patterns of racialised disenfranchisement, including in the digital creative industries. (275)

Drawing on hooks (1989), they suggest podcasting as a space which enacts and articulates "subaltern counterpublics," thus challenging established media narratives around race through a "curation of experiences, a contemporary way to build a space, assemble, engage one another in discourse, as well as to create a resilient platform for creative work" (285). From a similar ideological perspective, Fox, Dowling, and Miller (2020) invoke a range of applications of space, linking the technological "digital audio space" with socio-cultural claims of a "Black discursive space" which is part of a wider online space of resistance and Black social justice (drawn from Florini 2015; Cole and Guy-Sheftall 2003). Cory and Boothby (2021b) deploy podcasting as a "boundary object"—a technology that is a site for communication between groups. Their ethnographic study in a community arts project defined a collaborative practice of podcasting in spatial terms, with the dynamics of production, recording, and editing forging a kind of collaborative storytelling.

Within podcast studies, an often repeated claim relates to notions of intimacy. Alyn Euritt's (2023) research is the most-developed schematization of podcasting intimacy, and is very much coupled with questions of space (and time). Fundamental to this are multivarious reflections of physical and symbolic "closeness." Medial affordances of podcasting technology and practice, in the making and the listening, have the effect of navigating complex dynamics of space, public and private, embodied and disembodied, along with sound as a shaping, materializing force on experience. In the context of shifting journalism practices in the podcast era, Mia Lindgren points to aural intimacy as a space listeners both enter into and experience through aural technological mechanics: "The personalized listening space created by head-phones further accommodates the bond created between voices in the story and the listener" (2016, 23).

There are few studies that actively posit a critique of manifestations of a podcast space. Sharon and John's analysis of the first season of *Invisibilia* and its interpellation of an ideal listener through the use of adult colouring books and a listening-party kit published alongside it, suggest a space of "childlike listening": "The notion of 'getting lost in the sounds' suggests that the pod-cast offers an enchanting tale with the magical ability to transport us from one space to another, not unlike a bedtime story" (2019, 337). Though it is not directly stated by Sharon and John, the analysis chimed with the underly-ing sense that the podcast space can be a safe space. Here again we see a use of space that crosses the physical or psychological application: the listening practice of using earbuds or headphones is suggested as a means to designate an immersive auditory bubble (linking back to Euritt and intimacy).

The possibility of open dynamics of thought, untethered from and therefore potentially disruptive of traditional, institutionalized practices of knowledge production and communication, is arguably why a certain strand of scholars are attracted to podcasting. With this in mind, I now reflect on the spatial dynamics practice with more direct contextualization in terms of scholars who have explored the specifics of "academic podcasting."

PODCASTING AS, AND IN, ACADEMIC SPACE

As is summarized in the introduction and discussed throughout this book, the emergence of podcasting as a technology, a medium, and a practice, and its subsequent adoption within academia or by academics, has complex dynam-ics reflecting multitudinous possibilities and difficulties (see also Llinares 2022). This of course provides the driving impetus for podcast studies. The analyses, reflections, and motivations of academic podcasters have, when discussing their own audio work, that of other academics, or the structural relationship between podcasting and academia, drawn copiously upon the rhetoric of space. Again, this often provides a way of transitioning between quite different elements in the framework of a holistic view of podcasting, amalgamating physical, conceptual, practical, and creative components. But what is implied by the podcast space becomes more specific (or complicated) by further spatial parameters, often woven through analyses, when associ-ated with academia.

Mack Hagood's (2021) exploration of scholarly podcasting and the useful umbrella term *audio-academia,* as distinct from podcasting, is a case in point. Interestingly, he follows the pattern of using space—i.e., the "heterogeneous space of RSS feeds" (183)—to demarcate podcasting from radio, while also pointing to the possibility of sonic aesthetics manifesting space of thought and reflection for the academic listener. Hagood's taxonomy of specific "scholarly podcasts" provides a blueprint for thinking about the relationship between form and content. He counterposes "high-fi, mid-register" shows, which combine "high production values and accessible, often narrative-driven exploration of academic ideas" with "lo-fi, high-register" examples (189). The latter are usually produced by academics for an academic audience, with a lexicon that implies specialist knowledge in the listener. The lo-fi aspect is something of an implicit criticism, suggesting less emphasis on recording and production values or the general aesthetic considerations of the information being communicated.

Hagood then puts forth a third way, which draws upon the strengths of two aforementioned types of academic podcast, reflecting on the production of his own excellent *Phantom Power* podcast. Hagood's thesis regarding this third way is defined through the concept of space:

> I am in favor of opening up a space between the two aforementioned genres of scholarly podcasts—"a third way" that draws upon the strengths of both. The premise of this work is that scholarship—and particularly sound studies—can and should be done *in sound.* (190)

This third way reminded me somewhat of the "third space" in its application by the post-colonial theorist Homi Bhabha. In this context, the idea that subjective uniqueness, regarding a person or context, is always a formation that manifests through hybridity. In linking this notion to podcasting we can understand the podcast space as liminal (Llinares 2018)—the result of overlapping structural requirements of a medium that draws from many different technical, social, and creative elements.

There are examples in podcast studies research that directly highlight academic podcasting as a space for an open form of public intellectualism and collaborative dialogue across disciplinary and nationally specific boundaries (see Barker, Chod, and Muck 2020; Lundström and Lundström 2020). Writing in the area of social work education with a detailed qualitative and quantitative focus on his own *Social Work Podcast,* Jonathan Bentley Singer (2019) highlights potential advantages of the medium in terms of dissemination, access, and participation, and methodology, particularly for social care interaction. His discussion also points to a range of familiar "barriers":

financial, conceptual, attitudinal. On the last point he states, "Podcasts live in the space between entertainment and education" (Bentley Singer 2019). This is another definition of podcast as occupying an in-between or "liminal space," which Singer goes on to suggest can "bring research findings to life in a way that peer-reviewed journal articles cannot" (585).

There is expanding work by academics from beyond the humanities, arts, and media drawing upon podcasting both as a methodology and as a tool of distribution. For the Rogers et al. (2020) project "The City Under COVID-19: Podcasting as Digital Methodology," urban scholars provided voice-recorded reports of their experiences building stories around more-than-human cities, social solidarity, quarantine, social control, and the urban environment. The element of space is used rhetorically in the article: the space of the city, the sonic space as aural representation, and podcasting as a space of scholarly communication. These reflections on the affordances of podcasting in scholarly contexts demonstrate how space is a useful concept for thinking through complexities between media production, academic research, collaboration, distribution, knowledge production, and the site of the university itself, in a physical and ideological sense. In the next section, I explore these complexities through my own experiences producing *The Cinematologists*.

THE CINEMATOLOGISTS AS PODCAST SPACE

Considering the dynamics of space in my own podcasting practice provokes a bewildering array of possibilities. The nomenclature of academic podcast is one I have attached almost in retrospect to *The Cinematologists*, a podcast I started with my colleague Dr. Neil Fox in 2015. Yet, what this has come to mean requires a multi-layered reflection—not merely on academic practice, in terms of scholarship, research and pedagogy, but also on one's academic identity and mediated selfhood. I have written previously on the liminal structures of podcasting praxis, a concept I intended to encapsulate through a holistic interaction between doing and thinking (2018). Drawing upon Paulo Freire (2017), I argued that the doing of podcasting (the many technical skills, thought process, even physical and emotional requirements) opened up a space in which cultural and intellectual possibilities of scholarship found new forms of articulation and relevance. Concomitant to this was a sense that being a podcaster meant joining a community of practice, facilitated through the affordances of first listening as a podcast fan, and then eventually production.

Seeing the podcast as a forum or space where an academically informed conversation intersects with as many perspectives, voices, and forms of articulation on the subject of film culture is the organic outcome of reflection, rather than a specific research intent. Without predesignated research methods or a question driving the motivation for making the show, or for that matter a specific scholarly outcome, my podcast work was imbued from the start with a vocational motivation. Since we had neither a defined methodological approach nor a defined scholarly publication intention in the early development of the podcast, there was no requirement to structure the podcast in a similar vein to a journal article—for example, with a research context or review of literature. Indeed, it was only after more than a year, when we had gained an audience and some recognition, that the question of schematizing, retroactively, how the podcast could fit recognizable academic criteria arose.

Where podcasting fits with regard to academia is a complex, even ambivalent question that is at the heart of podcast studies. There are, of course, podcasts and podcasters that attempt from the outset to define the academic criteria of their work; some of these receive funding which allows for more, dare I say, professionalized production values (Kinkaid, Brain, and Senanayake 2020). There are also an increasing number of M.A. and Ph.D. students who create podcasts as part of their theses (see Olivia Trono's *My Master's Thesis, But It's a Podcast (About Podcasts)*). My version of academic podcasting has remained adjacent to my university work, yet it's never been a part of my contract. It has received occasional financial support, but only when I stipulated I would produce a journal article to "academicize" the work. In some ways, this has been frustrating. Yet, for me, it is precisely the idea of podcasting as a "liminal space," in between but not fully anchored to the physical, ideological, structural practices of the university, that provides flexibility of scholarly practice and value outside of prescribed academic criteria.

In hindsight, this sense of having an anointed academic position, with a pedagogic practice informed by the lexicon of film, media, and cultural studies, was the foundation of the content and tone of *The Cinematologists*. As academics teaching the same film course, our central motivation—to screen and discuss films we wanted to talk about for a live podcast—had two corollary advantages: a space to watch, and a potential ready-made audience of students. Because of this, in its production, *The Cinematologists* reflects interrelation between the physical spaces of recording, which define the sonic aesthetics of the podcast, and the influence of the university as a historical and ideological space (i.e., its associations with learning and freedom of thought). But also, in a vital sense, the podcast became an independent, creative, and intellectual space, in which we could interrogate and critique institutional norms ingrained by the university or by cinema. So in this sense, the space of the podcast was at once physical, conceptual, and creative, thus enabling a kind of scholarly freedom.

The early format of the show combined discussion between co-hosts with interviews and Q & As with audiences, recorded live after film screenings.

Discussion portions of the show were recorded in one of our university offices, homes, or occasionally a local café. We don't purposefully not record in a studio. But the podcast was produced, logistically and economically, around liminal times and spaces of our university work. Reflecting on this now, though, I realize that recording the podcast is somewhat symbolic of a medium that exists at the periphery of acceptance in academia. Indeed, as podcasting began to take a more central role in my research and conceptual thought, it did so as an alternative or parallel to my formalized teaching and participation in recognized academic engagements, such as conferences.

The centre of most early episodes was a recorded introduction and Q & A that took place around the live screening of a film. This was often within the Falmouth University's lecture theatre/screening room and the audience was mostly students. Screenings and recordings were always organized as extra-curricular activities for students, rather than being embedded within modules or other pedagogic structures. The main reason we started the podcast was to screen and discuss films we liked. So, the invitation to attend would be self-selecting rather than mandated. Upon reflection, I believe this live format was adopted because of the desire we had to connect the podcast to the screening experience. Even pre-pandemic, the sense that auditorium viewing was becoming a mere viewing option, rather than the grounding principle it had once been, was something that interested us. The sonic atmosphere of liveness and the shared experience of cinema viewing, when listened to on a podcast, evoked an element of what I subsequently came to write about as an "audio-cinematic" aura (Llinares 2020a).

As I gained more experience in the technical aspects of sound recording, production, and editing, this furnished a desire to explore the creative, artistic possibilities in which the space of sonic experience is just as important as the information being articulated. Underpinning this was the development of both the technical skills and craft required to create a podcast. Sound record-ing and editing was primary, but alongside this I gained an understanding of RSS hosting, web design and social media marketing. It's difficult to under-estimate just how important this learning process was in shaping my subsequent sense of the medium's broader conceptual applications. This autodidacticism was multi-faceted, fostering a range of specific skills related to the technical elements of podcast production, as well as the gradual appreciation of more abstract skills, such as the beats of interviewing or the subtle resonances one can produce through audio mixing. Recorded sound I began to understand as the raw material, the manipulation of which can shape the spatial dimensions of the listening experience. Furthermore, I found that the affordances of pod-casting as a space for creative praxis began to reframe how I perceived the rela-tionship between practice and theory, through the very doing of podcasting.

The notion of a podcast space then, is a conceptual centre; a holistic affordance emerging from a combination of physical, technical, social, and cultural praxis. The material of sound, formed and shaped by the podcaster(s) through these "spatial" interactions, is then available for immersion by a listener.

Episodes entitled "Knowing Sounds" and "The Cinematic Voice" think through *The Cinematologists* as a space of experience that the listener enters into. How could the voices and discussion of what were interviews or points made by audience members of a live Q & A become the materials for sonic shaping of sound? And how can sound effects and music add to an experience that is cinematic? In my approach to these episodes, Hagood's third way once again resonated with me in terms of how academic podcasting can utilize the "sonification of pre-existing scholarship or as an original work produced in the audio medium," which allows the use of "affordances, aesthetics, and evidentiary power of sound" and therein effects a scholarly communication "with expert, interdisciplinary, and public audiences alike while bypassing editorial and aesthetic filters of intermediaries such as public radio broadcasters" (190).

I now want to focus more directly on the specifics of what might seem quite an abstract notion: scholarly communication. The academic attraction to podcasting, on a fundamental level, is the communication of academic ideas and research within a formal context, but imbued with the freedom and sense of personal investment and passion that are deliberately exorcized from a journal article.

THEORIZING A SPACE OF
COLLABORATIVE PRODUCTIVE DIALOGUE

An essential factor in thinking about podcasting within an academic context is how the complex apparatus of production and distribution manifests a space for what I will call collaborative, productive dialogue. As my sense of podcasting as a space forged through technological affordances, my practical skill development, and a variety of knowledge applications intersected, the importance of the specific type of conversational interaction became more evident. From the outset, the anchor of *The Cinematologists* was a specific form of dialogue that draws upon academic collegiality, cinephilic knowledge and passion, and friendship imbuing intimacy and respect. Despite the variety in the shows we have produced, it is the discussions "in the moment" that define the thematic content and sonic identity of the podcast. Perhaps one might criticize the idea that this is somehow a unique process. Is this just a recorded chat, no matter how you dress it up? The genre of the "chatcast" imbues the sense of an informal authenticity that can either be extolled as one of podcasting's fundamental virtues or derided as aimless gossipy navel-gazing.

Conversation-based podcasting is fundamentally reliant on how the interplay of voices articulates content, as much as it is on the content itself. To be clear, I have created podcasts of differing formats, structures, and sound aesthetics, but the conversation is the underlying principle and material. Whereas obviously there were many spaces, academic and informal, where I and my co-host engaged in conversation, the organizing structure of recorded conversation is inflected by factors such as the apparatus and situation of recording, the awareness (developed over time) of how dialogue is the raw material of a podcast's overall sonic materiality, and the fact that the dialogue is intended for an audience.

In order to understand the specificity of "collaborative, productive dialogue," we can draw on what Schegloff calls "interactional episodes," in which "different speech exchange systems are the products of different practices, and accordingly have different features" (1999, 409). The academic podcast, then, (as with other conversation-based podcasts) provides a unique context for intersecting characteristics that shape a dialogue in intrinsic (voices, patterns of exchange, relationship between speakers) and extrinsic (focus or theme, requirements of the podcast structure) ways. There are forms of academic podcast in which the correlation to recognized academic methodologies and structures of articulation are forwarded explicitly. However, academic podcasting as exemplified in my practice started and continues to be defined by how the medium facilitates a space for productive thought and a working through of ideas that is based on progressive, dialectical, and multilectical exchange.

Conversational exchanges are not solely reduced to the dialogue of myself and my co-host. *The Cinematologists* from the outset aimed to bring a multitude of voices into the podcast space, effecting what Paulo Freire calls "polyvocality" (2017). This notion of polyvocality echoes the way I and, indeed, other academic podcasters think about the value of conversation within the structure of the podcast. For Kinkaid, Brain, and Senanayake, the use of the voice recording as a trigger for affective engagement with a subject area provides a form of connection to knowledge that is inaccessible with the written form:

> we suggest that hearing the emotion and tone in a speaker's voice may evoke different affective engagements between the audience and the research content. In our case, this modality generated insights into the embodied and emotional spaces inhabited by graduate students that could not have been produced through written text. We are excited by the potential of podcasts to communicate similar affective data about the embodied spaces occupied by the various populations with whom geographers work. (2020, 79)

There is clearly further research to be done on whether this kind of positive dialogue is influential on the parasocial relations that audiences form with podcasts, or how much the labour of listening reiterates a mirroring of ideas that is often lamented as an enclosed ecosystem. In this sense, I'm not suggesting that "collaborative, productive dialogue" defines podcast conversation as a whole, or even academic podcasting specifically. Yet, academics who deploy discussion-based formats are often attempting not only to shape and distribute knowledge as though it's some objective material, but to utilize the form to expand, interrogate, and analyze what it means to know. This may be a grand claim, but through my experience, if the podcast space has an essential value in academia it's to manifest the conditions for thinking, speaking, and listening as concerted, intentional practices.

MAPPING AN ACADEMIC PODCASTING SPACE

It would be reductive to suggest that the use of sound, in some purely ontological sense, triggered an epiphany in my understanding and practice of mediation. Sound is the essence, but it is the complex, integrated processes of podcasting, its multi-faceted phases of planning, recording, reflecting, and disseminating, that brought me to the point of thinking about mapping the interrelated elements of a specific podcast space. In Figure 1.1, I have attempted to schematize these spatial dynamics to show how the material production, and creative and intellectual aspects intersect to manifest the podcast space. The outer rings represent the developmental, logistical, technical, and environmental elements that all feed into the specific manifestation of a podcast as an audio artefact. I would suggest these four overarching spatial fields need to be in place: (1) conceptual, (2) physical, (3) technological, and (4) organizational. The constitution of these fields will differ not at all, slightly, or considerably, depending on the context of the podcast.

The conceptual field dictates the fundamental theme and focus of the podcast: what it is about, what genre it might belong to, how the producer or host conceives of the work in a holistic sense. This is essentially the space of thought and ideas, but is not confined to the planning and development. It permeates the entire production and distribution process. As an academic podcaster, I would also ground this in relation to the disciplinary field with which the podcast is concerned. This might be in a formalized way; for example, the podcast itself might be structured as part of a research project that has specific parameters. Or it might be more informal; i.e., the podcast speaks to or from an academic subject area.

The physical space of the podcast may seem obvious. The venue and physical space of recording is defined by logistical and economic factors, but also

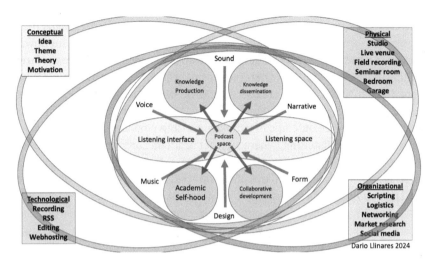

FIG. 1.1. Spatial map of academic podcasting. *Source: Dario Llinares*

ultimately defines the aesthetics of sound and therefore listening as a spatial experience. Academic podcasts might have a specific relationship to spaces within the university for recording, as I have outlined with regard to *The Cinematologists*. But many academic podcasts may also record in a studio. Obviously, the rise of remote recording software means that multiple physical spaces of recording are connected through the conduit of a digital space.

In terms of technology, we might consider more uniformity here. All podcasts will use editing software and a hosting platform, and (until quite recently) were distributed through RSS. The specific technologies of this may vary, but the fundamental technological architecture of the internet has to be a given when we consider a spatial connection between the production and reception of podcasts.

The organizational parameters of the podcast make up the fourth field. This is arguably the most undervalued and understudied element of podcasting's entire mediation complex. Producers in commercial podcasting constantly think through marketing and distribution, as these are key to audience growth and monetization. There is often an entirely different mindset underpinning the motivation for a podcast relating to research dissemination, creating new methodological and theoretical approaches to producing knowledge, challenging institutional traditions, and finding a space for a greater diversity of voices.

The inner circle of the map defines the production and creative processes that manifest a podcast into a specific kind of audio aesthetics artefact. Sound, form, narrative, design, music, and voice are the tools a podcaster deploys in the creative labour of podcasting, contextualized with the outer fields (particularly, at this stage, uploading to a hosting site and distributing for downloading or streaming). Any resultant audio episode—and I recognize the "tree falling in the forest" analogy here—does not become a podcast unless it is listened to. Thus, the central area of the matrix—the podcast space—is not specific to a certain physical (or digital) space in which a recording happens. Nor is it solely a unique outcome of a dialogue within a podcast recording. Nor is it in the space of listening, where another academic or student, for example, reflects on ideas or gains specific knowledge. It is the complex apparatus of production and thought that manifests through all of the elements of creation and consumption of a podcast. The "podcast space" is also a material space of listening, which is layered in a similar vein. One may be listening in a physical space, but then the listening act creates an immersion into a space of aural engagement. This in itself will have different facets depending on the form of listening one has adopted—i.e., whether using headphones, listening while in the car, or via your home smart speaker. At the moment of entering the listening *space* through a specific listening interface, all the previous spatial dynamics are activated and a singular, holistic "podcast space" can be said to have manifested.

I have also acknowledged a series of outcomes that have the potential to occur as a result of the podcast space being "entered." In this matrix, the outcomes reflect the intentions that might be aligned with a specifically academic podcast such as *The Cinematologists*. Outcomes for other podcasts may differ, and indeed may be more numerous. Such outcomes may, for commercial podcasts specifically, be more concerned with empirical scrutiny—e.g., listen or download statistics—which in turn can be used as a measure of success. The outcomes I have stipulated are more abstract and less open to objective measurement (although this is not beyond the realm of possibility).

CONCLUSION

In this by no means exhaustive attempt to theorize "space" through analysis of podcast scholarship and my own reflections on practice, I have begun to unpack the complex dynamics of application and implication. Thinking in spatial terms undoubtedly reflects the complexity of processes that producers and scholars think and act through when podcasting. But that is the advantage and weakness of using space as a conceptual framework. Often implied as mutually material and conceptual, creative and ideological, space is useful because it allows for a shorthand for the multi-faceted elements of podcast production and consumption. However, its application can be ambivalent and even contradictory.

One of the obvious critiques of the foray into defining a podcast "space" more thoroughly, particularly, perhaps, through the map, is its two-dimensionality. The problem is not so much the lack of the three-dimensional spatial graphics that would add more depth to the interrelationship of fields, tools, and outcomes that manifest the podcast space. It is a lack of acknowledgement of time as a key factor in what is undoubtedly a spatiotemporal process. Also, this kind of mapping has the potential to generalize academic podcasting practice in a way that actually creates boundaries. My intention is for this framework to be the starting point for thinking through the podcast as a media space that is open and adaptable to non-white, non-male, non-Western experiences and reflections. Mapping, after all, can be understood as a colonial tool.

Furthermore, the academic podcast space might be critiqued as the preserve and privilege of a certain type of scholar who can integrate the labour required into their circumstances. Yet, academic podcasting that challenges the traditional structures of academia does run up against issues, both those specific to podcasting and those indicative of the transforming economic and technological milieu of higher education, which also have to be acknowledged. What I have characterized as a largely positive "space" of practice outside the often staid forms and functions of academic life could be to someone else just another unwanted, unpaid, unused example of digital labour in the neoliberal university.

In thinking through Lefebvre's theoretical reconciliations between material, cognitive, and social rhetoric, "space" provides a way of reckoning podcasting's complex practices and outcomes—particularly with regard to how abstract, esoteric ideas around thought and knowledge need to be understood alongside the material conditions of their emergence. As Lefebvrian scholar Rob Shields highlights,

> Because Lefebvre is referring to not only the empirical disposition of things in the landscape as "space" (the physical aspect) but also attitudes and habitual practices, his metaphoric l'espace might be better understood as the spatialisation of social order. In this movement to space, abstract structures such as "culture" become concrete practices and arrangements in space. (1999, 154–55)

For me, the experience of the podcast space is one of positive engagement with media ontology. Academic podcasting has been a revelatory avenue affording a unique space of praxis, where practical creativity and social function have led to new ways of thinking about the relationship between knowledge and subjectivity. Even with a healthy set of caveats and critical reflections, particularly the shifting academic and media landscape where technological transformations and attendant socio-cultural implications have led to a fracturing of epistemological certainties, podcasting facilitates the potential of a culturally progressive, positively disruptive space for scholarship.

CHAPTER 2

"IT'S IN THE SHOW NOTES"

Autoethnography of an Amateur Tech Podcaster

MARTIN FELD

When I began my part-time Ph.D. project in 2019, I was driven by my fandom to explore tech-podcast case studies and how they foster a collaborative production environment based on RSS, interviewing producers and listeners within the genre. RSS stands for "Really Simple Syndication" and is an open technology that delivers updates on web content (NotePage, Inc. 2019), enabling podcasting and its connected directories and apps. What I did not anticipate was my supervisors' suggestion to start producing podcasts myself. Their point was clear: beyond listening, producing podcasts could enhance my understanding of the medium and feed back into my own theory.

I accepted this suggestion and created two different RSS-based podcasts on separate platforms, experimenting with different apps, services, and formats: *Lounge Ruminator* on WordPress, connected to my pre-existing blog as a site for academic journalling and media discussion; and *Feld Notes*, a microcast about family history on the open-web social-networking platform Micro.blog. Murray (2019a) defines microcasts as "mini-podcasts" of around seven to ten minutes in length, which are ideal for frequent communication with listeners. Alongside my research, exposure to different services and audiences has facilitated a greater appreciation of the effort required to create chumcasts (or chatcasts), which, as termed by Julie Shapiro, are podcasts "in which two or more hosts riff off each other, chatting in a casual or rambunctious manner around a theme, making the listener feel included in a private no-holds-barred conversation" (McHugh 2016, 70–71).

My Ph.D. project, titled *Really Specific Stories*,[1] seeks to expand the discussion of independent, RSS-based tech podcasts as a participatory culture within podcast studies (Jenkins 2013). I approach this from the position of Jenkins's "aca-fan" (or academic fan), which he asserts is "in a constant movement between these two levels of understanding [academic and fan] which are not necessarily in conflict but are also not necessarily in perfect alignment" (2013, 5). As an aca-fan, I am interested in the ongoing commitment to RSS as the original vehicle for open podcasting, along with community discussion of the value of *podcasting about podcasts*. Marco Arment (2016), creator of podcast app Overcast and co-host of tech show *Accidental Tech Podcast*, explains the benefits of podcasts' RSS basis, stating that they still work like "old-school blogs," and that "It's completely decentralized, free, fair, open, and uncontrollable by any single entity, as long as the ecosystem of podcast-player apps remains diverse enough that no app can dictate arbitrary terms to publishers (the way Facebook now effectively controls the web publishing industry)."

My two podcasts, *Lounge Ruminator* and *Feld Notes*, also align closely with Brabazon's (2019, 27–35) list of ten suggested methods or "genres" for undertaking podcasting in doctoral studies: (1) when delivering a seminar, public lecture, or presentation, produce a high-quality recording before the event and upload it after the live presentation; (2) create microcontent through microinterviews; (3) podcast the Ph.D. candidature; (4) promote research publications; (5) podcast from the field; (6) capture and disseminate high theory and abstract ideas; (7) talk through an argument before it is written; (8) interview interesting people and leaders in a field; (9) record a seminar on a key new article or book with your friends, colleagues, and fellow Ph.D. students; and (10) configure your content for new audiences. In her article, Brabazon uses the term *genre* to denote the very different types of Ph.D. podcasts that result from the decision to embrace one (or a combination) of the suggested methods.

I propose an eleventh genre for Brabazon's list, which is the focus for this chapter: become your own research subject.

With two fellow microbloggers and tech enthusiasts, Andrew Canion and Jason Burk, I began a fun side project in 2020: a tech podcast named *Hemispheric Views*, which has now become one of the key podcast case studies for my Ph.D. Andrew and Jason had tried podcasting before; however, they were motivated to try something new and collaborative after discovering my aforementioned solo projects. Through my work with them, as well as my own podcasting about podcasting and practising my production skills *in public*, I have come to embrace my identity as an amateur. Based on this stance as

---

1   Martin Feld. *Really Specific Stories*. https://www.rsspod.net.

an amateur, I advocate for the use of what Fendler (2013) terms nomadic pedagogy, whereby "experiential learning" takes place in "unfamiliar territory" across eventful spaces away from the fixed location of a school—mine are digital (Crang and Thrift 2000, in Fendler 2013).

In the following sections, I demonstrate the value of becoming your own research subject and embracing and critiquing your amateur status, thereby fuelling Ph.D. podcasting theory and practice. This is based on what I present as the complementary methods of performative autoethnography (Ellis and Bochner 2000; Spry 2011) and social c/a/r/tography (Fendler 2013), a visual map of rhizomatic relationships that result in collaborative, nomadic learning. With these methods, I offer podcast scholars an example of how to analyze their own development reflexively: I map the creation of my tech podcast and the nomadic personas and identities that develop across eventful spaces of learning with different technologies, audiences, and collaborators.

EMBRACING THE AMATEUR AND COMBINING TWO METHODOLOGIES

Evans and Stasi found that, in fan studies, there has been a lack of explicit reference to research methods and why they were chosen. They argue that this is a result of the field's interdisciplinarity and its roots in media and cultural studies, and "by its very nature willingly showing disdain for definitions and categories, emphasizing flexibility and fluidity with the aim of proceeding as a bricolage collective of methods, theories, ideas and concepts" (2014, 8). Furthermore, Evans and Stasi assert that reflexivity, more explicit methodological discussion, and a focus on mapping the mobility of fans' online activity can uncover the ontology of the aca-fan and lead to radically different ways of researching.

Although I aim to contribute to the discrete field of podcast studies here, as an aca-fan, my study is also situated within the field of fan studies—demonstrating its interdisciplinarity. In developing my eleventh suggested genre of *becoming your own research subject*, I include an explicit discussion of two combined methodologies, which represent my growth as a scholar in podcast studies theory and amateur status as a tech podcaster: autoethnography and social c/a/r/tography. First, however, I define amateurism and why embracing this status has been so important to achieving reflexivity and creating in public.

Embracing

My use of the term amateur is based on the more positive, open definitions of the word by media ecologist Lewis Mumford and media arts researcher Olga Gurionova. Mumford, known for his concepts of art and technics, argues that the work of the amateur "is a necessary corrective to the impersonality,

the standardization, the wholesale methods and products of automatic production" (1967, 415), and that creativity is a social product that is transmitted
between people through traditions and techniques. Goriunova (2011) explains
how amateurs generate "technopublics" and creative production, and while
they are conflicted, they are not antonymous with professionals:

> An amateur has wonder and enthusiasm, and it is through her chaotic and
> processual movements amplified by the technopublic dimension brought
> about by art platforms that such play reconfigures the schemes, circuits,
> and boards constituting the plane of the possible into reciprocal making,
> perceiving, taking part…It is worth noting that the amateur is not opposed
> to the professional here. The amateur can be professional (the professional
> should maintain the ardent love of the amateur) and a professional can
> be nonprofessional. An amateur feeds on raw autocreativity, whereas the
> nonprofessional professional works with cooked creativity, servicing the
> apparatuses…an amateur is a rather overextended and conflictual figure…
> to cover the proactive consumer as well as to address the economy of con-
> tribution in the new brands management. (107–8)

Throughout my project, I have defined myself as an amateur, not in reference to my skill or any remuneration, but as a descriptor for participation in
and the focus on making. Whether my work is "professional" or not is of little
concern; it is the enthusiasm in producing that is significant. Through this
practice, I echo Thumlert's call to address negative connotations of amateurism, based on Prior's (2010) work on "new amateurs": traditionally, amateurs
are seen as lacking competence, when in fact "new amateurs might challenge
our most enduring pedagogical fictions" through their multimodal production
(Thumlert 2015, 124). In the "chaotic" process of my multimodal creativity, I
have reflected on my simultaneous presentation of both amateur and professional identities: undertaking podcast work for personal interests, my studies,
and even as requested by my employer. I explore this complex development
later in the chapter through a series of identified events (or "epiphanies").

Fuelling the art platform that Goriunova describes is participation within
what Kelty (2005) calls a recursive public, which "comes into being through a
shared concern for taking care of the technical means that bring them together
as a public" (Goriunova 2011, 92). I am an amateur within a recursive public,
the genre and fan community of tech podcasts, whose "raw autocreativity"
is underpinned by RSS. Such a social imaginary engages in what Kelty terms
"arguments-by-technology," which seek not only to discuss the features, uses,
and effects of devices, but in this case also the underlying benefits of openness in technologies such as RSS. Kelty asserts that openness "is a practice

and a concept on which recursiveness depends," and that "this commitment to openness bears similarity to J.S. Mill's version of a liberal polity in which all ideas are allowed to circulate because it strengthens and highlights the best ones" (186–87). This idea of a recursive public connects to Sarah Murray's (2019b) work in the field of podcast studies on podcast collectives—representative of networks such as Relay FM (Heeremans 2018). Murray states that working with others creates a "self-in-process," where participants "demonstrate intimate soundwork and collective individualism as integral to this era of audio storytelling, but more broadly as flexible frameworks applicable across all digital cultures of social storytelling" (314). As an aca-fan, I have accepted and now advocate my amateur status in both approaching theory in podcast studies and practising the art of podcasting. It has made me more comfortable with experimentation and *learning from my mistakes in public*. Channelling this into my reflexive study, my newfound openness led to the following question: Why not try to combine two seemingly incompatible methodologies, then see what happens?

Combining

I now shift to an explicit discussion of methodology. In my Ph.D. project, as I engage with the content and networks of RSS-based tech podcasters, I undertake a narrative-inquiry approach (Clandinin and Connelly 2000), revealing the stories and personal experiences of those from my chosen case studies. To demonstrate here the value of reflexivity and becoming your own research subject, I combine the qualitative methodologies of performative autoethnography and social c/a/r/tography to trace my personal development as a nomadic researcher or learner-traveller (Fendler 2013). From here, I map (visually) the various personas and roles that are established across the resulting eventful spaces, in and through which I practise podcast production and complementary content creation. These spaces include human and non-human agents across digital networks (Crang and Thrift 2000, in Fendler 2013; Taffel 2019).

Fan studies researchers Jenkins (2013) and Hills (2002) advocate the use of alternative qualitative methods to capture the fan experience, with the latter arguing that autoethnography can address the issue of relying on a discursive mantra in fan studies, whereby the researcher is encouraged to question their self-account repeatedly. Three pioneering autoethnographers who guide my approach are Ellis and Bochner (2000) and Spry (2011)—informing the written theory and method and the act of oral autoethnography in my own podcasting practice. Ellis and Bochner demonstrate in their own first-person accounts the power of autoethnography to reveal multiple layers of consciousness and connect the personal to the cultural. Through my podcasting and by reflexively writing *and* podcasting about podcasting, I become what

Ellis and Bochner call a "complete-member researcher," as I am absorbed into my recursive public (Kelty 2005).

Performance as an autoethnographer is advocated by Spry (2011), linking mainly to discussion of the stage but also applicable to intimate voice work. While producing my podcast *Lounge Ruminator*, for example, I engage in performative autoethnography. As Spry explains: "knowledge is constructed through performance as fully as through composition" (29). Through public performance, my analysis of podcasting theory fuels my creative podcasting practice; subsequent lessons learned as an amateur producer then loop back to enhance my understanding of the field and my writing.

The act of performing and practising in public begins with making podcasts, then extends to the writing of an autoethnography in this chapter. At every stage, I present a *performative-I disposition*, which helps to construct a story with others in the culture (or public) that I have chosen (Spry 2011), while critically reflecting on my own performance in public. Elements of my performance are captured here in nested vignettes (Humphreys 2005), featuring highlighted excerpts of my own authenticity, exposure, reflexivity, and application.

To analyze pivotal moments in my own narrative, I identify *epiphanies*, as proposed by Denzin (cited in Savin-Baden and van Niekerk 2007), which have influenced my own creative practice and realization of different roles and personas across a transmedia environment. There are four different types of epiphany (Savin-Baden and Niekerk 2007, 465), which I will use to examine and critique my experiences in a later autoethnographic section:

- **Cumulative epiphany:** an event that is symbolic of profound changes that may have been going on for a number of years or be a turning point in one's life caused by the accumulation of numerous related experiences.

- **Illuminative epiphany:** a point in time or particular experience that reveals insights; or an event that raises issues that are problematic.

- **Major epiphany:** an event or experience that is so traumatic or challenging that its meanings or consequences are immediate.

- **Relived epiphany:** an event or issue that has to be relived in order to be understood.

My intended categorization of selves—including roles and personas—links to close-listening research by Yee (2019) in the field of persona studies, exploring the connection between podcasts and personal brands. Altogether,

I propose the use of autoethnography to show the development of skills in research and creative practice over *time*.

The identified eventful spaces that emerge from my epiphanies are visualized through social c/a/r/tography (Fendler 2013). Fendler builds upon the work of Irwin et al. (2006), who advocate the use of a/r/tography: a practice-based research methodology in education and the arts (Sullivan 2004, in Irwin et al. 2006). They explain further: "The name itself exemplifies these features by setting art and graphy, and the identities of artist, researcher, and teacher (a/r/t), in contiguous relations. None of these features is privileged over another as they occur simultaneously in and through time and space" (Irwin et al. 2006, 70). With the addition of the letter C, this method emphasizes mapping and space. Moreover, by demonstrating equal identities, the social c/a/r/tographic method connects to persona studies, based on graph theory and network theory, "mapping the social and spatial dynamics of networks and cultures" and facilitating the "rendering of computational and network as visible and legible to the human" (Marshall, Moore, and Barbour 2015, 294). Mapping has been encouraged as a technique in storytelling by other writers, such as Turchi (2004, chap. 1), who states they help us "to see our knowledge in a new way."

While autoethnography shows developments over time, for podcast scholars I propose that this form of mapping displays one's developments (and their relationships) without chronology in *space*.

My transmedia environment is revealed through the complementary processes of autoethnography and social c/a/r/tography, amounting to what Kuhn and Callahan (2012) term a scholarly remix, combining interdisciplinarity and "media electracy"—a new, "writable," and curated public sphere (Ulmer, in Kuhn and Callahan 2012) to appreciate the nomadic nature of Ph.D. podcasting as a participatory archive. In the next section, I share an autoethnographic account of my work in podcasting theory and practice over time, as I contribute to a participatory archive. Ultimately, I present a model for other podcast scholars—using epiphanies and vignettes from oral and written work—to appreciate and critique their own development, interaction with human and non-human agents (Taffel 2019) and choices in theory and practice.

AN EPIPHANY-DRIVEN AUTOETHNOGRAPHIC ACCOUNT OF PH.D. PODCASTING

A Return to Study

Several years ago, when I commuted to Sydney for work, I learned to pass the hours and delve into my Apple brand fandom through tech podcasts such as *The Talk Show with John Gruber*, *Accidental Tech Podcast* and Relay FM shows like *Connected* and *Upgrade*. Podcasts became my go-to medium whether in the car, on the train, or walking, as they felt much more involving than music—a truly fun and engaging way to escape and learn something new while exploring my Apple fandom at length. After starting a new role in my hometown of Wollongong, I was no longer commuting and my listening habits changed, but I was afforded extra time to contemplate my consumption. This led me to enroll in a Ph.D. to study tech podcasts, as I had considered returning to university studies for some time and had finally devised an appropriate research idea. This discovery came in the form of a *cumulative epiphany*: after growing up with a propensity for enjoying visual media such as television, films, and books, my consumption habits had changed significantly to favour audio. Podcasts were my new focus and I wanted to learn more about them. This epiphany also led me to critique my own privilege, as I not only had the time to listen to tech podcasts and could afford the devices they discussed, but now I also had the luxury of being able to study my fandom.

Working with supervisors Dr. Kate Bowles and Dr. Christopher Moore, our early meetings led them to ask, "Beyond listening, have you considered making podcasts yourself?" This was my first *illuminative epiphany*: I enjoyed podcasting so much as a listener that I had never even thought of this possibility. The result of this epiphany has been to use my podcasting to reflect on what I learn about the medium in my research and the development of my creative practice, including the willingness to feature in my own and others' podcasts. In March 2019, I participated in my first-ever podcast as a guest. I was invited by Jean MacDonald, community manager at Micro.blog, to join episode fifty-three of the *Micro Monday* podcast, a show in which new users on the blogging platform are highlighted (MacDonald 2019). This was my first exposure to using tools like Skype, QuickTime Player, and Audio Hijack for running and recording shows. Around this time, my supervisor, Kate, also suggested that I also keep a handwritten journal of my experience, creating a multimodal mix of microphone and pen—an eventful space to record my own epiphanies during my travels as a learner. Excerpts of these entries feature in this very autoethnography.

Baby Steps

When it came to making my own podcast, I realized that I knew very little. I decided to take a dual approach, making two distinct podcasts on separate services, in order to practise and gain exposure to different interfaces and ideas.

The first show that I devised was *Feld Notes*,[2] a somewhat sporadic family-history podcast in which I interviewed my maternal grandmother about her

---

2   Martin Feld. *Feld Notes*. https://feldnotes.com/podcast/.

life and migration to Australia from former Yugoslavia. I decided to publish this show on the site Micro.blog: an eventful space that came in the form of an ad-free alternative to Twitter and Instagram. One of the paid plans allows the publishing of "microcasts" up to twenty minutes in length, using a separate app by the developer, called Wavelength. Micro.blog seemed the right way to start, as I met friendly, supportive people on the network, and the imposed limit of twenty minutes meant that I could start small. I wasted no time and kicked things off in September 2019, using the app Ferrite Recording Studio for editing and exporting: a suggested technology from my Apple-centric recursive public (Kelty 2005).

The second podcast that I created was *Lounge Ruminator*,[3] based on my WordPress site of the same name, which was the initial blog that I used during my undergraduate studies—albeit renamed and redesigned in the years since. This was perhaps the greater learning curve, as I had to learn how to adjust settings on WordPress, interact with its RSS feed and upload audio files with a specified blog post category. In this eventful space, my episodes would explore media topics, ideas connected to my tech fandom, and an audio journal of my studies. The first episode, in a monologic format, was published on 24 September 2019, and saw my first foray into actively participating in my tech podcast fandom. This was expressed in the description of my first episode show notes:

> In this first episode of the *Lounge Ruminator* podcast, Martin is inspired by a recent blog post by John Siracusa to discuss the lost art of super-short, printed film reviews and how they can help us to improve our digital communication today. (Feld 2019)

Linking my own creative practice to existing podcast studies literature, I experienced the same positive feelings that were described by Markman and Sawyer (2014), who surveyed independent podcasters to understand their motivation and reasons for doing so: "As with the public creativity factor, podcasters in the produsage cluster remain engaged with podcasting because they have found a community where they can receive feedback to help them improve their skills, while at the same time having fun and enjoying the process involved in podcast production" (32).

Although my effort with *Feld Notes* continued occasionally, my podcasting on *Lounge Ruminator* picked up steam as I committed to a weekly schedule. Various topics linked back to my Ph.D. literature review as I explored the field of media ecology—the basis for my ideas about podcasting as an environment.

---

3   Martin Feld. *Lounge Ruminator*. https://loungeruminator.net/podcast/.

Soon enough, friends and even colleagues discovered my show and I became more willing to promote myself, but remained sensible about my place in the long tail, as I noted on 4 November 2019 in my handwritten journal:

> I felt really encouraged by this and decided to push it even further, sharing the episode (altogether) on Twitter, Micro.blog, Mastodon, LinkedIn and even through specific messages...I sent a link to the Media Ecology Association, which later retweeted it...I don't expect a mass following—I'm realistic—but I need to get used to promoting myself more and putting my work in front of those who are experts.

I experienced an *illuminative epiphany* about the value of participating after publishing my third *Lounge Ruminator* episode, "It's the Principle of Thing." In this instalment, I discussed media ecologist Carlos Alberto Scolari (2012) and his work on design and interfaces (in a media-ecological context). A link to the show I published was subsequently retweeted. While I had received feedback from listeners before, at this moment I felt that I was contributing to scholarly discussion online and actively reproducing some of the methods (or genres) suggested by Brabazon (2019). Despite my status as an early researcher, I started to see the value of my ongoing communication of high theory and abstract ideas—talking through my research and ideas before writing them and configuring content for new audiences. However, I did discover the dependence on social media (and others' interaction or reposting) to have my content discovered.

Discussing academic concepts led to another *cumulative epiphany* in my twenty-sixth episode, titled "Bibliophilia": with more regular explicit discussion of my research and literature review in every episode, I felt that I was more actively podcasting my Ph.D. candidature. As suggested by Brabazon (2019), I decided to include a new recurring segment called "Research Rumination" to act as the more official time to share lessons from my research. This segment has addressed technology education, niche communities, the history of radio, persona studies, and the primacy of visual media in Western culture in episodes such as "27. Stillness," "29. Mass versus Niche," "30. The Martin Feld Retail Photo Collection," "35. Personas and Pets," and "38. Typos and Consoles." *Lounge Ruminator*, which had started as my attempt to better understand the production methods of podcasters, had therefore become a more pronounced fusion of my creative practice and the theory underpinning my project. Meanwhile, I extended my interviewing and editing skills by talking to a friend who conducted Ph.D. research in public health and a fellow Ph.D. student at my university in the respective episodes "32. Tackling Sports Betting" and "36. Mapping Entrepreneurial Narratives."

When I reached episode forty-five, titled "A Ticking Clock," I had completed one full year of podcasting on *Lounge Ruminator*. Planning and recording this episode led to a relived epiphany: as I reflected on my path, I found myself podcasting about podcasting, fixating on meta discussions about the underlying medium and technology, which is typical of the niche discussion that occurs in the technopublic of Apple-centric podcasting. To warp the words of McLuhan, my medium had become my message, as I asked people to ruminate on a skill that they had developed in the course of their own work or creative pursuits. In that episode, I described my podcasting experience (Feld 2020, 06:58):

> When I look back, I didn't start off with theme music, I wasn't using chapter markers in the same way—or at all! I wasn't necessarily using MP3 chapter artwork or following the sort of conventions that I wanted to establish for show notes or lists....You know what? The learning happens during this procedure. (Feld 2020, 06:58)

With this relived epiphany on the first anniversary of both of my podcasts, not only was my podcasting feeding my theory and my literature review, but my scholarly ideas and handwritten journalling were enhancing my creative production. My practice went back into my theory, which then continued to inform my practice. This was the moment that I began to actualize my persona as an *academic podcaster*, stemming from my role as Ph.D. student researcher, but also that of a *tech podcaster*, using the medium to discuss the medium. I was not just a writer anymore; in fact, the majority of the creative work on my main blog had become academic audio. Revisiting the work of Goriunova (2011) and Thumlert (2015), I was engaging with scholarly research in a technopublic dimension and challenging my own pedagogical fictions: learning through audio production instead of remaining fixed to the page.

Later, in 2021, I also realized point five in Brabazon's (2019) list, "Podcasts from the Field," in which I interviewed two generous participants who fulfill the general roles desired for my intended Ph.D. research: producer and listener. These interviews took place in episodes "65. Becoming an Independent Developer" and "66. An Aca-fan Moment" and acted as examples of fieldwork and my narrative methodology in action, as they fit the chumcast format with a focus on unstructured interviewing. Brabazon explains that this is one strategy

> ...to maintain a connection with both the home base and the field, alongside a reflexivity about the research method...Actual impressions can be captured in real-time and then they are available to cycles of interpretation and analysis. These podcasts can also be referenced in the doctoral thesis as a sonic diary of the process. (2019, 32)

Through undertaking, transcribing, and analyzing the practice interviews with my narrative approach, I realized that while my unstructured method gathered rich qualitative information, I was drawing too much from each participant and would need to adapt my decision-making and writing for interviews with the tech podcasting community in my eventual thesis discussion.

I practised all of this in public as an *amateur* and I encourage other podcast scholars to make these (perhaps difficult) discoveries about themselves. Be willing to adapt your work out in the open.

It Was Accidental

Rewinding from episodes sixty-five and sixty-six, however, it was the production of episode twenty-eight that led to two epiphanies—one *cumulative* and one *major*—which spawned an entirely new direction in my research and is discussed later in this subsection.

Episode twenty-eight was the *cumulative epiphany*, as I reached a milestone in my recording skills and produced something for the first time in my own fan genre. On 31 May 2020, I wrote the following in my Ph.D. journal:

> I asked Microblogger and all-round nice guy from Perth, Andrew Canion, to join me on the podcast. This twenty-eighth episode was titled "A Potted Computer History" and we explored our respective introductions to technology...along with our computing habits, preferences and where we see technology going in the future.

Andrew and I had spoken before on Micro.blog and he was a very supportive listener who generously spent his time providing feedback about my show. Following this cumulative experience, the episode was the opportunity to engage with his narrative and get to know him. For some time, I had also been communicating with an American Micro.blog user named Jason Burk, who, like Andrew, was supportive and reviewed my podcast. Jointly excited by the result of Andrew featuring on *Lounge Ruminator*, we began to plan our own shared podcast. To test our idea for a chumcast, we used *Lounge Ruminator* to launch a pilot episode, which we called "39. International Mac Nerds." We received enthusiastic feedback from other Microbloggers; this commentary was the final push that we need to launch a fortnightly podcast, which became *Hemispheric Views*.[4] This was the first sign that I had begun to engage in what Hansal and Gunderson (2020) describe as "fannish methodology": accepting my own dual position as fan and researcher, while breaking

---

4   Jason Burk, Andrew Canion, and Martin Feld. *Hemispheric Views*. https:// hemisphericviews.com.

down "academic walls" (Ahmed 2017 in Hansal and Gunderson 2020) to build connections and share knowledge with fellow fans.

On 16 September 2020, I reflected on how we worked as a team to launch our podcast on the service Fireside, and how Andrew and Jason brought their skills as fellow amateur fans of tech podcasts to share our first official episode, "001: Tim Tam Slams," while feeling "pleased with the results, as Jean MacDonald from Micro.blog shared it...In the first 48 hours, we had 66 listeners, which was a pleasant surprise."

Hemispheric Views constitutes a major epiphany in my Ph.D. journey so far, and perhaps the greatest eventful space for my podcasting practice—linking to many other spaces online (see section on social c/a/r/tography). It is the accidental transition into being a tech podcaster that has garnered the greatest insights into the podcast genre that I love. *Hemispheric Views* now functions as a Ph.D. case study alongside the shows that first inspired my research. This was not my intention when I began my research in 2019. I had accidentally become my own research subject, thereby fulfilling my suggested eleventh genre for Brabazon's (2019) list. Our continued production has also led to the creation of supplementary media—or paratext (Genette 1997)—and the fostering of our own community that is growing beyond the pre-existing friendships on Micro.blog. We three fulfill the personas of tech podcasters; however, it is fair to say that we play different roles for our listening audience and friends online. Andrew is the business guy, Jason is the creative tech guy and I am the artsy research guy. Reflecting on role and persona, I believe I have shifted from a purely academic-podcasting role to that of a performer in the genre, realizing a new tech podcaster persona that has been channelled into the launch of my Ph.D. podcasting project, *Really Specific Stories*.

As a fan of tech podcasting, I was proud of *Hemispheric Views* and positive about contributing to the community; as a practising academic, I was becoming critical of my own participation. Adopting Spry's (2011) performative-I disposition, I came to recognize my own performance as a stereotypical white male podcaster with other white men—having met in an online space that is perhaps more likely to attract such an audience. This is not necessarily a problem, but something of which I need to be aware.

As an additional point in the story, my creative activity was recognized online by my employer, BlueScope (a global steel manufacturer based in Australia). Managers subsequently asked me to develop *Voices of BlueScope*, a podcast to share stories from people across the company, spanning from grassroots to leadership. This may call into question the definitions of amateurism and its supposed antonym: *professionalism*. Recounting Goriunova's statement on the issue: "The amateur can be professional...and a professional can be nonprofessional" (2011, 107–8). I am paid for the work that I perform for the *Voices of BlueScope* podcast[5] as a part of my professional full-time employ-ment; however, it is fuelled by an amateur enthusiasm. It may, however, raise questions for some about my authenticity, as I am representing a company rather than undertaking a personal project.

With this autoethnographic account, I have come to appreciate the rela-tionship between my work in podcasting theory and practice over time. I now turn to a discussion of my journey in space.

SOCIAL C/A/R/TOGRAPHY

Building on my autoethnography, the following diagram shows how one's Ph.D. podcasting journey—through theory and practice—may be presented visually as social c/a/r/tography. It displays human and non-human agents (Taffel 2019) across my digital network and tertiary experience as a series of rhizomes, which include people, profiles, apps, courses, and services. The process of mapping reveals other agents, which did not spring to mind during the act of writing chronologically, as eventful spaces in my theoretical and practical work as a learner-traveller. The resulting hand-drawn social c/a/r/tographic map was produced without any final image in mind. Connections and movement are more important here than chronology.

As I trace each movement, it becomes clear that the personas and roles that I have adopted along the way start to bleed into each other. My persona as an academic researcher might have led to the persona of tech podcaster on a podcast like *Hemispheric Views*, where I play the role of the artsy research guy; however, those performances have then fed into my persona as a paid "professional" podcaster on *Voices of BlueScope*, which in turn loops back to alter my perception of what constitutes amateur creative practice. Among all of these connections is communication with other producers, listening fans, and fellow podcast studies researchers, across networks such as Micro. blog, Twitter, Discord, and Slack, and of course, the technology that makes open audio distribution possible: RSS. My decision to map this interaction with the aforementioned non-human agents, as well as the podcasts that I have published and spread across the web, prompts the following reflection: What has been the material effect of my creative work? How much energy has been used to publish it and how much has been used every time someone has downloaded it? Taffel (2019) asserts the need to think about the material infra-structures that underpin what appear to be immaterial, virtual environments. I propose that other podcast scholars also consider the ecological effects of

---

5   BlueScope. *Voices of BlueScope*. Produced by Martin Feld. https://www.bluescope .com/life-at-bluescope/voices-of-bluescope-podcast.

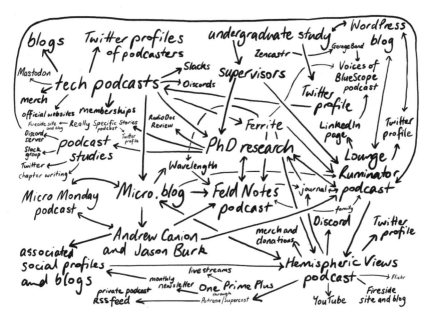

FIG. 2.1. Social c/a/r/tographic map of podcasting and research experience.
Source: Martin Feld

their research and creative projects, and how they occupy physical space in reality. One solution is to "sing the praises of small-file aesthetics," which, as Marks (2020, 51) cites from Goriunova (2012), operates "In contrast to corporate ideologies of high resolution, lossless compression, and 'immersion,'" and "emphasizes the physical affordances of digital media and the ingenuity of their makers and receivers."

My mapped journey reveals a different view of myself as a research subject, along with the relationships between my podcast research and creative practice, and how my supposedly immaterial work occupies real physical space. I have used this map to understand my shifting identity as a podcast researcher, and how I may be perceived when approaching potential participants for my research interview show, *Really Specific Stories*. This method can be adopted by any podcast scholars seeking to understand the eventful spaces in which they learn and the agents they encounter along the way.

EPILOGUE: A GLITCH BEHIND THE SCENES

Now, it's time for a little autoethnographic twist.

In 2023, well after I first drafted this chapter and as my work on the *Really Specific Stories* podcast began, my ability to publish regularly on *Lounge*

Ruminator and *Feld Notes* diminished significantly. When the time came to renew my WordPress plan for *Lounge Ruminator*, I decided to downgrade it, keeping all of my blog posts and updates, but removing unnecessary plug-ins. After following the process correctly, somehow the downgrade severed my RSS feed's connection to podcast directories and changed all of my content URLs; this led me to confront a lengthy repair process and to request help from different podcast app providers.

The podcast is working again, but this experience has led me to reflect on my most recent *major epiphany*, which challenges my notions of openness and ownership in the recursive (techno)public of tech podcasting: If I stop paying a host to distribute my creative work through RSS, or indeed something simply goes wrong, then who is really in control? Who "owns" the content in the community? I may claim to be "authentic," but if people cannot hear what I have promoted, how does that break my image or persona as a "professional" podcaster? Would it reinforce the negative connotations of amateurism?

When I began my Ph.D. travels, eager to understand RSS-based tech podcasting, I did not appreciate the breadth of podcast studies, nor foresee that I would become an active member of both communities or understand the material effects of my work and how it really lives on the web. Through podcasting, my creative practice led me to the suggested eleventh genre of *becoming my research subject*, which has since helped me to rethink my Ph.D. writing and theory as an amateur learner-traveller.

I propose that a combination of performative autoethnography and social c/a/r/tography offers other learner-travellers in podcast studies two different perspectives of the creative podcasting process. Autoethnography encourages more chronological reflexivity and first-person intimacy—like podcasting itself has achieved as a bridging medium (Swiatek 2018). Vignettes reveal moments of recorded experience and epiphanies, and when classified appropriately, act as signposts for moments of profound growth and development. Autoethnography can help us to appreciate our experience over *time*. Social c/a/r/tography highlights visually the movement through and accumulation of eventful spaces of learning as rhizomes, displaying how lessons in theory and practice lead to and feed back into each other. Mapping in this way can help us to appreciate our experience through *space*.

As I reflect on becoming my own research subject, I pose the following five questions to other scholars who may wish to do the same:

1. How has your own persona or relationship with your topic shifted over the course of your investigation?
2. What are the material, ecological effects of your research and digital work?

3. Who or what controls the availability or distribution of your ideas?

4. In writing and recording about yourself, how can you show your work behind the scenes, critiquing your dual identity as an amateur and professional, and challenging notions of academic performativity and perfectionism?

5. How do you reinforce or challenge social norms in your performance as a complete-member researcher or podcaster?

I continue to ask myself these questions, and as is the case with any personal account, my story will continue well after this printed (or digital) page makes its way into your hands. *Seismic personal and technological shifts happened in the course of writing of this very chapter.*

As I continue to practise in public, I hope to see you somewhere along my travels; make sure to say hello.

CHAPTER 3

ON IDLENESS AND PODCASTING

SAMUEL M. CLEVENGER

O n 16 March 2020, a producer for BBC Radio 4 named Eleanor McDowall tweeted that she was starting a new podcast "inspired by heartbreak and burnout" (McDowall 2020). Titled *Field Recordings*, the new podcast would consist simply of field recordings either created by McDowall or submitted by other audio-makers. When you listen to an episode of the podcast, you do not hear topics of discussion or interviews, not even a formal introduction or theme song. You just hear the field recordings themselves—birds chirping in a garden, or rain falling in a forest, or commotion on a city street—along with the occasional audible rustlings and movements of the field recordist. There is a relative aimlessness to each episode's content—a lack of an intended purpose or objective beyond the act of listening to the sounds—that results, at least in the mind of the present author, in a calming sonic ambience and a restful, pleasurable listening experience. The creation of a calming podcast seems to have been one of McDowall's goals in the project: in a review in *The New Yorker*, McDowall noted that she "just wanted to stand still and listen to the birds" after feeling burned out and exhausted (Larson 2020). She hoped the podcast would provide her with "a bit of space and respite" (Wilding 2020).

My fascination with *Field Recordings* lies in how it suggests that podcasts can be creatively designed to promote, intentionally or otherwise, restful and pleasurable idleness. In his recent book on the subject, the Irish philosopher Brian O'Connor argues that idleness can be understood as a form of human freedom if it is defined as "experienced activities" that are bereft of some guiding purpose and disconnected from any kind of task-oriented productivity, or what he calls "disciplined self-monitoring" (2018, 6). For O'Connor, the absence of purpose and the disconnection from some coercive urge to be productive fosters a "feeling of noncompulsion and drift" that possesses "restful and pleasurable qualities" (5), for the idle experience offers an escape, if only temporary, from the stresses of work and daily performance. With life under a particularly capitalist mode of production, idleness is often experienced serendipitously: following O'Connor, we "slip" into idleness for brief or sometimes extended periods when we are not compelled to work or complete the tasks necessary for the production and maintenance of life (5). Idleness is not a monolith, and is as conceptually complex and dynamic as any other human activity, manifesting in a variety of forms and taking different meanings throughout history. What is compelling about the case of *Field Recordings* is that, while the podcast is not explicitly designed to advance a form of idleness along the lines described by O'Connor, the apparent purposelessness of its ambient soundscape expands the possibility of an affective listening experience akin to the experience of restful, pleasurable, aimless forms of idleness.

Yet, does this mean that *Field Recordings* is an example of what we might call an "idle podcast," meaning a podcast that fosters purpose-free listening and provides a restful and pleasurable listening experience through that deliberate lack of purpose? The podcast would not be idle from the perspective of the producer, for they are purposefully attempting to produce a restful and pleasurable soundscape, and deliberately choosing to create a podcast that seems to have little purpose other than listening to the produced sounds. Rather, the idleness of the idle podcast lies in its reception and the possibility that the listener is affectively moved by purposeless sonic vibrations, and experiences a pleasurable and contemplative form of rest. Is this an idle podcast? What is an idle podcast? Why is it important to contemplate the possibility of idle podcasts, if the creation of such a podcast is even possible?

This chapter considers the questions posed above and explores the relation between podcasting and idleness in twenty-first-century life, with a specific focus on podcasts produced and consumed in the United States (US) and the United Kingdom (UK).[1] Asking what constitutes an idle podcast can be a key part of a broader discussion of the place and value of podcasting in the advancement of healthier and more humane ways of being and interacting in the world. By exploring podcasting in terms of its capacity to promote restful and pleasurable forms of idleness, I hopefully shed light on at least one way that podcasting can be used to respond to the deleterious effects of contemporary capitalist life on human well-being, notably the prioritizing

---

1   I delineate the limits of my study here to avoid overgeneralizing the analysis to podcasting cultures in other parts of the listening world.

of compulsive productivity, performance, and self-improvement over restful inactivity as the necessary and morally superior activities in a meaningful life. In the first section, I briefly sketch the importance of considering idle podcasting, specifically as it relates to the conditions of life under capitalism in the twenty-first century and what scholars have referred to as the neoliberalization of podcasting (Cwynar 2019). Next, I discuss the cultural meaning of two particularly prominent kinds of podcasts that relate in important ways to the question of idleness: "mindfulness" podcasts, and self-care podcasts designed to help listeners fall asleep. Finally, I return to the case study of *Field Recordings* and reflect on the ways in which podcasting can be used to promote an idle listening experience.

ON THE NEED FOR IDLE PODCASTS

If we associate idleness with activities that lack instrumentality and are pleasurably disconnected from any sense of purpose or productivity, it is difficult to envision a truly "idle" podcast, at least from the standpoint of production. After all, is not the idea of a podcast necessarily predicated on a conscious purpose, artistic, economic, or otherwise, guiding its creation? If the creation of an idle podcast is possible, what would that entail for the producer? What kind of audio production would it require? Since podcasting at its most basic level depends on the productive task of developing content for episodes, would that then render the notion of an idle podcast impossible? This does not even consider the ways in which the podcasting ecosystem today exemplifies the production and consumption processes of the "culture industries" of late capitalism (Adorno 2001, 98). Even if the producer sees the podcast creation process as pleasurable and a hobby that they freely enjoy in their non-work time, it still requires purchasing consumer goods (i.e., audio production equipment) and utilizing commercial streaming services and distribution platforms on the internet.

From the standpoint of podcasting as a growing industry, a podcast is never idle, since it serves the purpose of generating capital for an entrepreneur or organization attempting to profit from its production and/or distribution. As scholar John L. Sullivan notes, there has been an ongoing development in the world of podcasting in the past several years: "the slow transformation of an amateur medium into a new vehicle for commercial media content" (2018, 34). Entrepreneurs and media corporations, Sullivan argues, "have rapidly expanded their interests in podcasting as a business, bringing professional standards and the logics of capital with them" (34). According to a recent study, podcasting is now a multi-billion-dollar industry in its own right, with the global podcast market in 2020 estimated to have a value of $11.46 billion and an expected growth rate of over 30 percent through the decade (Grand View Research 2021). In this context, the production and distribution of a podcast serves the particularly economic and productive purpose of generating capital for the commercial media platforms and streaming services facilitating their distribution.

Moreover, an increasing number of podcast listeners access programs through corporate streaming services, meaning even niche, small-audience, and DIY podcast productions are not autonomous from the ongoing commercialization and corporatization of the podcasting ecosystem. Over 60 percent of podcast consumers in the US rely on the streaming service of either the multinational technology giant Apple's streaming service or Spotify, the world's largest streaming provider, with a market capitalization estimated in the tens of billions of dollars (Buzzsprout 2022; Ingham 2021). Corporations are signing lucrative distribution deals for the exclusive rights to broadcast celebrity podcasts with large listening audiences (Berr 2021). Spotify paid over $230 million to purchase Anchor.fm, a service that hosts and distributes podcasts free of charge (Morris 2021b). Spotify's acquisition of Anchor.fm underscores the ongoing corporatization of online podcast distribution, such that even niche, personal, small-audience, and DIY podcasts can be seen as contributing to the market value of the corporate streaming platform distributing them. According to scholar Jeremy Wade Morris, podcasts, regardless of their popularity or the size of their audience, are being "spotified" (2021b, 221): they are becoming increasingly dependent on commercial streaming platforms for their distribution. The ongoing spotification and "platformization" of podcasting means that they serve the particular purpose of helping to generate revenue and expand the market value of the commercial distribution platform (Sullivan 2019).

The corporatization and commercialization of podcasting, however, does not negate the social significance of the medium, particularly as a means of amplifying the perspectives and lived experiences of marginalized and disadvantaged communities. In the UK context, scholars Photini Vrikki and Sarita Malik contend that podcasts are "an emergent space for a diverse and typically marginalized range of U.K. citizens to mobilize as a counterpublic against the grain of dominant racialised representations and narratives produced by mainstream media" (2019, 274). Amidst the enduring racial, gender, and class inequalities in creative and cultural industries in terms of access, resources, and representation (O'Brien et al. 2017), social groups can use podcasts to articulate the complexities of their experiences, augment and extend feminist and other social activist discourses (Tiffe and Hoffmann 2016), build and maintain community relationships, unsettle the normative social codes and expectations that proliferate in the corporate media landscape

(Copeland 2018a), and help different groups and listening publics connect and communicate information through a medium that is arguably more intimate, personal, and emotionally powerful (Swiatek 2018). Though podcasts are tethered and impacted by the impulses of a commercial industry and the broader corporate media ecosystem, that does not necessarily determine or limit the complex social meaning of podcasts for the listeners.

Can a podcast, however, encourage listeners to "do nothing," in the sense of disconnecting, albeit briefly, from the overstimulation of contemporary lived experience, and immersing themselves aimlessly in a sonic ambience? The American artist Jenny Odell (2019) argues that people are being overstimulated and exhausted by what she calls the "attention economy" of contemporary capitalism, leading them to perceive their value based on their ability to stay productive and stimulated by social and digital media. Relegating large portions of their free time to the consumption of digital and social media forms, people are left in a "state of anxiety, envy, and distraction" that is financially lucrative for the commercial media corporations (xii). In her book, Odell calls on people to do nothing, so that a seemingly nonproductive practice, like sitting in a park, enjoying a meandering conversation with other people, or watching and listening to birds without an objective, becomes an end in itself. The doing of nothing is only nothing from the standpoint of the capitalist logic of productivity: as an experienced activity in a certain time and place, doing nothing is pleasurable and restful because it is counterproductive in the sense that it ignores the "inwardly generated methods of self-scrutiny and enhancement that typify discourses of work and productivity under capitalism" (Gregg 2018, 10). With that said, is the podcast, as an intimate aural medium, capable of advancing Odell's cause of doing nothing and pursuing more pleasurably idle experiences?

In my own research, I started contemplating the possibility of podcasting as a purveyor of idle listening while reading philosophical works on the deterioration of free time under twenty-first-century "neoliberal" capitalism.[2] Philosopher Byung-Chul Han argues that the technologies of power and domination of the neoliberal capitalist mode of production increasingly target the human psyche, turning people into self-interested consumers who self-impose the neoliberal dictates of maximization and productivity, and exploiting

---

2 Following the political scientist Wendy Brown (2015), "neoliberalism" refers to the "normative order of reason" dominating Western social, political, and economic thought today. In her historical perspective, neoliberalism "developed over three decades" in the late twentieth century and is now "a widely and deeply disseminated governing rationality" (9), viewing "every human domain and endeavor, along with humans themselves" in terms of their economic value and productivity (10).

their desires and motivations (2017a, 21). This has resulted in a powerful "psychopolitics" in which the neoliberal logics of economization, productivity, and hyperactivity have effectively colonized conscious and unconscious human desires, transforming human subjects into "projects" who compulsively seek their own optimization in the pursuit of a healthy, productive life. In Han's depiction of neoliberal psychopolitics, as human projects strive to perpetually improve themselves, consume self-help products, cultivate self-management skills, and compulsively engage in physical and mental training, they come to desire the very things that are integral to the domination of the self under neoliberalism (29). In this endless pursuit of therapeutic improvement and of the maximization of all human activity, humans enter a state of what Han calls "perpetual self-optimization," becoming self-exploiting entrepreneurs as they strive to constantly reinvent their skill sets and adapt to the precariousness and competitiveness of job markets (Han 2017a 28; Cwynar 2019).

The psychopolitics of neoliberalism fuels rampant psychological exhaustion, burnout, and widespread mental health maladies, because it glorifies and normalizes the neoliberal ideal of the productive "self-as-a-work-of-art" (Han 2015). The neoliberal human project, desiring to embody a self-as-a-work-of-art, lives in a state of endlessly, compulsively working to improve themselves and accumulate achievements (Han 2017a). This ideal, however, is a dehumanizing illusion because it fetishizes work and economic productivity, denigrating in the process the virtuous qualities of restful inactivity and aimless contemplation. Here Han bases his understanding of virtuous contemplative rest on his reading of the Greek philosopher Aristotle, who "situated the beautiful and noble outside of what is useful and necessary, that is, outside of work" (Han 2017b, 86). In Han's reading of Aristotle, the highest form of happiness for human beings lies in the "contemplative lingering on beauty" and the "turn towards those things that are imperishable and unchanging, the things that rest entirely in themselves" (87). This exemplifies what he calls the "*vita contemplativa*," a form of human experience centred on the capacity for one to step outside, if only temporarily, of the stresses and overactive stimuli of everyday existence, and contemplate one's relation to the immensities and forces of nature and life (Han 2015, 14). The *vita contemplativa* is not equivalent to inactivity; in fact, a life of contemplation is an active life, as it entails learning, the sharing of knowledge, the appreciation of art, and the expression of human creativity (Han 2017b, 102). Yet, the *vita contemplativa* represents a restful state of being because it does not co-opt rest as a tool for self-improvement (for example, as a means of becoming more refreshed for work or some other task). It is a rest that exists in itself and for itself.

Under twenty-first-century capitalism, however, digital technologies have become key sites for the valorization of productivity and optimization through self-regulation. According to Han, the *vita contemplativa* has been driven out of twenty-first-century life, and what philosopher Hannah Arendt (1998) called the *vita activa*, a life of human action, is privileged and reinforced through the neoliberal "self-as-a-work-of-art" ideal. By severing the dialectic between action and contemplation, and turning the *vita activa* into an "absolute value," everything "that is not an act or activity" is denied value and meaning (Han 2017b, 109). The neoliberal regime, pushing humans to constantly improve themselves and maximize the worth of their activities, both in terms of work and leisure, leads to mental exhaustion and disorders such as depression and anxiety. Human projects "optimize ourselves to death...Relentless self-exploitation leads to mental collapse" (Han 2021, 14). In this era of digital self-tracking, we can see evidence of the influence of the exhausted neoliberal "self-as-a-work-of-art" through apps and wearable technologies that offer to help consumers be more disciplined and productive by optimizing their "mundane" and "dormant" bodily functions such as sleep (Lyall 2021, 144). Rest itself has become a site for capital accumulation and an activity to fine-tune for the purposes of remaining productive in life.

Thus, the ability for a podcast to promote a restful, idle listening experience, akin to Han's *vita contemplativa*, depends in part on the extent to which the podcast gravitates towards the pursuit of self-optimization and the valorization of economic productivity. Research already shows the often close links between podcast production and the promotion of entrepreneurial activity. Scholar Christopher Cwynar, in a study of the reality podcasts *StartUp* by Gimlet Media and Stable Genius Productions' *ZigZag*, argues that such productions try to appeal to listeners by presenting compelling stores of "entrepreneurial individuals struggling to establish themselves in a society entirely structured by the values and ideologies of the marketplace" (2019, 318). Both podcasts are anchored by personalities who previously worked in public radio and are using their podcasts to convert the social capital they accumulated from their public radio experience into a new entrepreneurial project. Their podcasts venerate the stories of individuals who have adopted an entrepreneurial subjectivity and have embraced the hardships of reinventing themselves in a competitive marketplace in order to attain individual and economic success (330). The podcasts, in other words, offer stories that celebrate, rather than question, defining self-worth through entrepreneurial activity and economic productivity. If podcasts can promote the virtues of entrepreneurialism and economic productivity, presumably they can also promote psychopolitical discourses by approaching ordinary bodily functions, such as sleep, as functions in need of optimization, and the issues of rest and self-care as issues to address in order to stay productive in life.

"RESTFUL" PODCASTS?

Online and on streaming platforms, there is already an array of podcasts that attempt to address the mental health and burnout maladies of contemporary life by offering listeners an opportunity to experience rest and cultivate skills in self-care. One prominent manifestation of this can be termed the "mindfulness" podcast. A quick search reveals plentiful, freely available mindfulness podcasts offering listeners a guided session of mindful meditation, a discussion of the importance of mindfulness and its role in improving one's health and happiness, or a combination of both (Nortje 2020). Typically, the podcasts are framed as resources for self-help and self-management: listeners learn how to "manage stress, reduce anxiety, and feel more energized" (Lindberg 2020). For example, *Daily Meditation Podcast* teaches listeners "different styles and techniques to...manage stress, sleep better, gain focus, and find clarity" (para. 16). *Meditation Minis*, a podcast that has reportedly been downloaded by tens of millions of listeners, offers short guided meditations so that listeners can obtain some quick relief from their stress and practise how to "better be that best version of you" (Hamilton 2022, 00:30). If the various "best of" lists available on the internet are any indication (de Wolfe 2020; Reardon 2020), listeners have access to a healthy array of short, easy-to-follow podcasts designed to help them learn the basics of mindfulness meditation and establish a meditation routine within their already busy schedules. Though each podcast is distinctive in terms of its approach and conception of mindfulness, what tends to link the podcasts is their general focus on self-help and self-optimization: audio resources with "techniques that will carry you to your most calm self" (Reardon 2020, para. 9); and free guided meditations to "calm your anxiety, help overcome negative thinking, increase your confidence and sharpen your mental focus" (para. 8).

A particularly neoliberal conception of mindfulness often permeates such podcasts, in that they promote the practice of mindfulness as an individualized coping strategy for dealing with the stress and anxiety of twenty-first-century life at the personal level. The Buddhist psychotherapist Miles Neale (Fisher 2010) and scholar Ronald Purser call it "McMindfulness": the practice of mindfulness is secularized, commodified, and "reduced to a technique for just about any instrumental purpose" for the consumer (Purser 2019, 17). The discussion and practice of mindfulness is disconnected from Buddhist teachings on ethics and interdependence, as well as a consciousness of the ways in which social structures and historical forces impinge on our everyday lives. Instead, consumer products like mindfulness books, seminars and classes, meditation apps such as Calm and Headspace, and podcasts offer "basic concentration training" that is essentially a "tool of self-discipline, disguised as self-help" (8). As Neale says, it is meditation "for the masses, drive-through style, stripped of its essential ingredients, prepackaged and neatly stocked on the shelves of the commercial self-help supermarkets" (Fisher 2010, para. 15). In the case of mindfulness podcasts, listeners are persuaded that "the causes of suffering are disproportionately inside us, not in the political and economic frameworks that shape how we live" (Purser 2019, 8). Listeners are reminded that

> It is not the nature of the capitalist system that is inherently problematic; rather, it is the failure of individuals to be mindful and resilient in a precarious and uncertain economy. Then they sell us solutions that make us contented mindful capitalists. (10)

Such podcasts and apps market a privatized form of mindfulness "as a vehicle for personal gain and gratification. Self-optimization is the name of the game" (11). Though mindfulness can be a vehicle for critical thinking and for a critical awareness of one's relation to everything and everyone else (Forbes 2019), it is a particularly secular, privatized, and individualized form of mindfulness that is advanced by the podcasts, presenting mindful meditation as a means of managing one's productivity and optimizing one's level of happiness (Illing 2019).

Such McMindfulness podcasts illustrate the ways in which the neoliberal regime absorbs and commodifies "idle time" and time for leisure pursuits into the processes of production and capital accumulation. As Han (2017a) writes, "idleness that might otherwise be devoted to activities free of purpose and constraint are integrated into the operations of Capital" (51). With life processes being shaped by capitalism's mechanistic logics of efficiency and productivity, non-work time becomes "only breaks, work-free interim periods in which the regeneration from work takes place in order to be fully available again for the process of work" (Han 2017b, 92). All time, including one's available free time, is transformed into either an instrument for production, a commodity for consumption, or an opportunity to engage in self-optimization through the consumption of self-care products (Lutz 2021, 65). "Free time," the German philosopher Theodor Adorno writes, is "tending toward its own opposite" and is "becoming a parody of itself" (2001, 188). Thus, even potentially restful and contemplative activities (i.e., meditation exercises) are commodified and marketed as mindfulness-based consumer products, designed to help individuals manage their daily stress and optimize their mental and physical health (Purser 2019). The consumption of self-care and self-help commodities becomes an integral part of the individual's pursuit of what yoga scholar Andrea R. Jain terms the "transformative and salvific process of personal growth" (2020, 2). Neoliberalism exploits human freedom by turning it into "manifold forms of compulsion": the "freedom" to compulsively consume, compete, work, produce, and optimize one's life (Han 2017a, 2).

This is just one particular way some podcasts present mindfulness as a self-management tool. There are other podcasts, for example, that focus on the historical, particularly Buddhist, origins of mindfulness meditation, and the promotion of ethical compassion, notions of human interdependence with nature and other beings, and the relation between mindful concentration and the enactment of social change. The Rubin Museum of Art in New York City, which showcases the art and ideas of Tibetan societies, has produced a weekly podcast on mindfulness meditation since the beginning of the COVID-19 pandemic. Each episode includes a short talk by a respected meditation teacher or scholar and a guided meditation session. The Rubin Museum of Art's series of podcasts often situates the importance of meditation within Tibetan Buddhist traditions, while speakers stress the importance of understanding one's interdependence with other humans, nonhumans, and environments, freeing oneself from self-centred attachments, and the importance of compassion in one's engagement with the world. The podcast also presents the practice of mindfulness as a tool for self-betterment, but also as an opportunity for listeners to practise how to "quiet the mind, open the heart, and engage with the world more consciously" (Mindfulness Meditation Podcast, n.d., para. 2).

Similar to mindfulness podcasts, in terms of their focus on encouraging a state of rest and relaxation for the listener, there are other podcasts with affective soundscapes deliberately designed to help listeners fall asleep. In 2013, podcaster Drew Ackerman created the now-popular *Sleep With Me* podcast, with each episode consisting of Ackerman telling a meandering bedtime story with his "gravelly voice" and "mazelike" sentences "that turn on countless 'if's, 'or's, and 'so's" (Caplan-Bricker 2016). The idea is to be so boring that listeners fall asleep to Ackerman's slow, low voice and circuitous stories designed to be almost, but not quite captivating (Ackerman 2022). *Sleep With Me* has been hugely successful, at one point reaching over two million downloads per month (Carpenter 2017). Ackerman's *Sleep With Me* is one of the more successful examples of podcasts created to help listeners fall asleep or alleviate their struggles with insomnia and other sleep-related ailments. Another more recent iteration is podcaster Kathryn Nicolai's *Nothing Much Happens*, which parallels the approach of *Sleep With Me* by telling slow, uneventful stories to "soothe your mind and help you sleep" (Nicolai 2022). In each episode, Nicolai speaks closely to her microphone and employs a soft, almost whisper intonation, creating sounds that bring to mind podcasts dedicated to autonomous sensory meridian response (ASMR; Hanna 2019). Like *Sleep With Me*, *Nothing*

Much Happens has also become a "hit" podcast, with an accompanying book published by Nicolai (Harper and Mackenzie 2020). Both Ackerman and Nicolai earn money from their podcasts through sponsorships and listeners purchasing premium subscriptions or paying for ad-free versions of the episodes. The two podcasts are also just two of the more popular sleep podcasts available online and through commercial streaming platforms. The relative popularity of sleep podcasts, which has increased in recent years and during the COVID-19 pandemic (Nicholson 2021), suggests that there is widespread desire among podcast consumers for programs that can help them improve their sleep patterns.

There is an important affective dimension to both the sleep and mindfulness podcasts,[3] in that their purpose typically revolves around the goal of creating a soundscape capable of producing the felt sensations of either restful contemplation or falling asleep. What this suggests is that the podcasts can also potentially create the aural conditions for a kind of idle experience, regardless of the podcast producer's intentions. Sound, if we follow the thought of scholar Michael Gallagher, is affective: its vibrations and waves move "through and between bodies" and material entities; it is "sensed, felt and responded to by sentient beings" (2016, 43). The experience of listening to sounds, whether via podcasts, music, or everyday noise, is an embodied, felt experience as the listener is pre-cognitively moved by the vibrations of the sounds (Clevenger and Rick 2021). The podcast in particular, as an "intimate aural medium" that one listens to with headphones, can create "a deep affective experience" for the listener (Copeland 2018a, 209). In the case of sleep-inducing podcasts like *Sleep With Me* and *Nothing Much Happens*, listeners can *feel* restful, less anxious, and sleepy, and the producers of the podcasts employ strategies—speaking in a low voice, whispering close to the microphone, crafting and reading purposely boring and nonsensical stories—to further facilitate the embodied experience of rest. These techniques do not guarantee a particular affective response, however. The produced sounds create a vibrational "aura" with the capacity for both predictable and unpredictable affective transmission (Thompson and Biddle 2013). Listeners may be moved by the sound waves in ways conducive to sleep, but the sensations will be particular to the somatic context of the listener and can possibly deviate from the intentions of the

---

3   My understanding of affect draws from the work of philosopher Brian Massumi (2002), who argues that affects entail "belief in the world—a non-cognitive, embodied belief in the world's potential, directly felt, and no sooner felt than acted upon" (Massumi et al. 2019, para. 6). This understanding of affects is more abstract than emotions, in that affects are seen as pre- and extra-conscious, as well as intensely felt by the body. This approach to affect helps me engage with the idea that sounds in the world not only have affective capacities, but can move the body in particular, sometimes unpredictable and unconscious, ways.

podcast. Indeed, all podcasts that entail voice, music, or other sonic waves can produce an affective experience, which helps explain why some podcasts can "accidentally" help create listener drowsiness due to the voice of the narrator or the calming qualities of the soundscape (Foussianes 2020).

Like mindfulness podcasts, podcasts designed to induce sleep do not exist in a historical and social vacuum. On the one hand, podcasts like *Sleep With Me* and *Nothing Much Happens* can aid individuals suffering from insomnia, anxiety, and other stressors by providing a kind of sonic palliative that helps the listener fall asleep. Their popularity and their promotion as aural palliatives for the complex trauma and anxieties associated with the COVID-19 pandemic indicate that the podcasts are providing some form of relief to listeners (Dibdin 2021). Yet, as Han argues, the deeply personal problem of mental well-being is also always a historical and societal problem, with "contemporary psychic maladies" such as depression and anxiety being the result of the neoliberal regime's emphasis on compulsive achievement and valorization of overworking. There is no discussion of the deleterious aspects of contemporary capitalism on podcasts like *Sleep With Me* because such a discussion would presumably inflame the anxieties of those listeners who want to calm their nerves. The podcasts necessarily approach the personal trouble of sleeplessness as an individualized problem that can be mollified through the choice of self-help, which serves to implicitly promote a privatized understanding of sleeplessness and keeps the podcasts aligned with the neoliberal dictate of personal responsibility. This is not necessarily meant to critique the content or intentionality of these podcasts, but rather to consider their limitations and situate such programming within the historical conditions of neoliberalism. By trying to help people sleep and rest, the podcasts accept and reinforce, unintentionally or not, the psychopolitical logics of the neoliberal order that is arguably contributing to sleeplessness.

There is a seeming creativity, playfulness, and open-endedness to sleep-inducing podcasts like *Sleep With Me* and *Nothing Much Happens*. The stories often have a whimsical essence that is bolstered by the host's frequent digressions and asides, all purposely included to enhance the boringness of the episode. This is perhaps best exemplified in *Sleep With Me*, with Ackerman telling listeners at the beginning of each episode that he will purposefully veer from the supposed topic of the episode and engage in "pointless meanders" (2022, 05:56) and "superfluous tangents" (05:58), always communicated through Ackerman's "lulling, soothing, creeky dulcet tones" (05:50), to help create a sonic ambience in which listeners will feel safe and able to forget racing thoughts and feelings. In fact, Ackerman often veers off on tangents even as he explains the purpose of the podcast. The point of *Sleep With Me* is not to provide information about the issue of sleeplessness or discuss the problem of sleeplessness with guests, nor are listeners supposed to listen intently to the stories. Moreover, there is little overt emphasis on the importance of cultivating self-help and self-optimization skills. Rather, the meandering, pointless bedtime story is supposed to do the work of creating a safe place to sleep for the listeners. All the listeners need to do is lie in bed and listen to the episodes. The creativity, playfulness, and relative aimlessness of the content of sleep-inducing podcasts like *Sleep With Me* suggest a kind of semi-autonomy from any task of helping listeners cultivate their self-management skills through mindfulness practice.

However, it also seems like the playful content camouflages important parallels between sleep-inducing podcasts and the mindfulness podcasts discussed previously. They both are founded on the guiding purpose of providing an individualized aural remedy for anxiety, stress, and sleeplessness through podcast production. The sleep-inducing podcasts do not exhibit the "individualistic spirituality" of the mindfulness podcasts, which often present a secularized form of mindfulness that is packaged and proffered as a convenient product that does not require the consumer to substantially change their lifestyle or question dominant cultural values (Purser 2019, 18). Yet, both frame stress, anxiety, and sleeplessness as personal troubles that can be ameliorated through the cultivation of more effective habits, whether that is maintaining a consistent meditation routine or listening to a particular podcast before attempting to sleep. As a result, sleep-inducing podcasts rest, so to speak, on a difficult contradiction between their intended purpose and the framing of their content. On the one hand, the objective of creating a sonic ambience in which the individual listener feels safe to forget their racing thoughts and fall asleep means that the podcasts purposefully avoid discussing difficult, potentially anxiety-inducing topics. The narrators speak directly to the listeners in soothing tones to help create a soundscape attuned to the individual listener and their suffering of sleeplessness. On the other hand, the framing of insomnia as a personal trouble obscures any contextual links between mental health and the conditions of life under neoliberal capitalism. This decontextualizing of sleeplessness risks the reinforcement of neoliberal conceptions of sleep as something that can be fully understood and improved through consumer products that seek to optimize one's life performance, and not as symptomatic of the organizing logic of the neoliberal regime.

TOWARD THE "IDLE PODCAST"

What if the possibility of an idle podcast depends in part on the spontaneous affects registered by listeners as they feel the reverberations of the produced soundscape? It is important to remember that the cultural meaning of podcasting is not reducible to its status as a commodity, nor does the commodification of podcasting determine its meaning for the listeners and the consumers. In the mid-twentieth century, Adorno wrote that it would be a mistake to assume that the production process and ideology of the cultural industries totally dominate "consumer-consciousness," the mental life of the consumer (2001, 195). "What the culture industry presents people within their free time," Adorno wrote, "is indeed consumed and accepted," but there is still often "a kind of reservation" in the mind of consumers, "in the same way that even the most naive theatre or filmgoers do not simply take what they behold there for real" (196). The meaning of a cultural product for a consumer does not always reflect the ideological message encoded in the production.

Can we apply Adorno's notion of the consumer's "split consciousness" to the practice of listening to podcasts, and say that it is also possible for a listener to consume an audio production for reasons alternative to the supposed purposes of the production? A 2018 episode of the podcast *99% Invisible* explored the history and cultural meaning of the British Broadcasting Corporation's (BBC) *Shipping Forecast* radio broadcast. Host Roman Mars notes in the episode that many British citizens would listen to the *Shipping Forecast* "for something entirely different from its intended purpose": to help them fall asleep (Mars 2018, 08:05), or to help them "cure their insomnia" (09:08). *99% Invisible* itself is also known for the calming and sleep-inducing qualities of Mars's voice. On a Reddit message board concerning podcasts one can "fall asleep to," one anonymous post read, "*99% Invisible* is so calming I can no longer listen to it while driving. Roman Mars has the most soooooothing [*sic*] voice" (spacejamorjelly 2020). Perhaps Roman Mars is pleased to know that his podcast has a calming influence on listeners, but it is doubtful he would say the point of his podcast is to induce listeners to fall asleep.

What I am suggesting is that perhaps there is something about the process of producing a podcast and the affective conditions of podcasting that suggests that podcasts can engender listening experiences related in some meaningful way to idleness. In terms of production, there is still a creative semi-autonomy that stems from the fact that podcasting, despite its growth and popularity, still sits "on the periphery of mainstream media" (Llinares, Fox, and Berry 2018b, 7). There is still (digital) space "for niche and cult content that caters for the more idiosyncratic cultures of interest" (3), as one can create a podcast that is creatively bereft of purpose or topic, and still make it available online through multiple distribution platforms. Further, there is the "relatively inexpensive production costs" of podcasting (Morris and Patterson 2015, 222), as well as the absence of editorial gatekeeping which prevents creators from posting their content online (Clevenger and Rick 2021). In terms of consumption, there is an affective quality to a podcast that is not reducible to its intentionality as a digital commodity. Because a podcast has no necessary visual referent, the listener is intimately immersed in the sounds, sharing time and space with what they are hearing (Voegelin 2010). Without a visual object to provide a sense of certainty, there is an "immediate sensibility" to sound, "unordered and purposeless, always now" (169). Further, the immediate sensibility of the sound is affectively charged, as the sonic waves and vibrations move the listeners in ways that can be unconscious or unexpected. As intentional sleep-inducing podcasts like *Sleep With Me* and *Nothing Much Happens* demonstrate, the vibrational energy of sound can be harnessed through creative and playful techniques (i.e., slow, digressive, circuitous storytelling) to produce an immediate sonic sensibility with possibly restful and pleasurable attributes.

The meaning of idleness in podcasting, however, is not limited to issues of sleep or the unpredictable and unintentional affections of podcast productions. *Guardian* journalist Mark Wilding (2020) noted the rise of what he terms "slow audio" podcasts, which often consist primarily of ambient recordings with no narration or dictated purpose. Take, for example, American writer Jon Mooallem's *Walking* podcast, which consists of recordings of Mooallem walking through woodlands near his Pacific Northwest home. There is a minimal amount of narration, sometimes in the beginning or midway through an episode, leaving the listener to primarily focus on the sounds of the woods, sometimes rain, the rustling of leaves and earth as Mooallem walks, the wind as it comes into contact with his recording device, and the sounds of Mooallem's moving body (Mooallem 2020). In terms of creative intention, *Walking* exhibits an important similarity with Eleanor McDowall's *Field Recordings* podcast: both provide a sonic ambience that is without an explicit narrative or intentionality, and neither is framed as a self-help tool. This frees the listener to experience the sounds without a guiding purpose and without an impulse to use the podcast for productive purposes (i.e., to optimize one's mental health). The "lack of narrative," Wilding (2020) writes, "leaves listeners free to choose their own meaning." It also means the potential restful, contemplative, pleasurable, or otherwise idle qualities of the podcasts lie in the ambient recordings themselves. As *Vulture* magazine writer Nicholas Quah notes, with Walking, it is the "sheer banality of the recordings" that "both clears and focuses the mind, and willful surrender to the pure sensory experience can send sparks of warmth across your shoulders" (Quah 2019, para. 5).

Are *Field Recordings* and *Walking* the closest examples of an "idle podcast"? There are other similar productions of "slow audio" available on the internet (Wilding, 2020). One prominent example is BBC Radio 3's *Slow Radio* show, which offers listeners the sounds of nature, calming music, and other sonic landscapes designed as "an antidote to today's frenzied world. Step back, let go, immerse yourself: it's time to go slow" (*Slow Radio*, n.d., para. 1).

There may also be other imaginative podcasts out in the ecosystem that seek to create an ambience of restful idleness and contemplation and have not yet received much attention from podcast reviews and websites. The availability of free online streaming platforms, less expensive audio-editing software, and free recording apps on phones presumably means that there are more than a few people out there who are recording ambient sounds and posting them online as a means of sharing their calming sonic creations. I hope that is the case, at least, and look forward to listening to other, new manifestations of idle podcasting.

If the existence of podcasting is inseparable from technological, production, and consumption processes integral to the capitalist mode of production, then the notion of an "idle podcast" is a contradiction: from the standpoint of production, there can probably be no truly idle podcast, as its form is tied to the accumulation of capital through the consumption of cultural commodities. However, by simply asking this question, we compel ourselves to explore the ways in which podcasts can usurp the productive ethos of neoliberal capitalism, even if in brief, miniscule, or unintentional ways, through their affectively charged soundscapes. The examples of *Field Recordings* and *Walking*, and in certain ways the sleep-inducing podcasts *Sleep With Me* and *Nothing Much Happens*, demonstrate that by approaching podcasting as an intimate aural stage for playful sound art, with a meaning and purpose that is largely left to the listener, it is possible to craft an affective soundscape that, at the very least, temporarily gestures towards the ideals of the *vita contemplativa*. A podcast can be, and, as noted earlier, often is marketed as a self-help tool that a listener can purchase and consume from the podcasting marketplace, but there are always other, creative ways to approach podcasting. A podcast can also consist of uninterpreted field recordings, leaving the listener free to listen for reasons unrelated to social pressures or expectations. In this sense, perhaps there is something about podcasting that can be used not only for the valorization of quiet contemplation, inactivity, and idleness, but also to question the productive and growth-oriented ethos of neoliberalism.

CHAPTER 4

PODCASTING TOWARDS RECKONING
A Journalistic Tool for Academic Subversion

ROBERT E. GUTSCHE JR.

Note to the reader: This chapter is based on a talk, "Podcasting Toward Reckoning: Developing a Tool for Journalistic Reflexivity," presented at the Department of Mass Communication and Journalism of Pazhassiraja College in India, in 2021. The talk has been reproduced as a bonus episode to season three of The J Word, *which can be heard at https://www.buzzsprout .com/1208318/9637132.*

Theoretically, journalism (including podcasts, such as *The Daily, The Tip Off, The Brief,* and *S-Town*) is a space where conflict is examined, human agency is evoked, and the powers that be can be held to account. But what happens when journalism (and the academic field that studies it) requires a reckoning of its own issues of power dynamics (Callison and Young 2019)? Can podcasting provide a place for a range of voices, in terms of their ideas, geographies, and sounds, to represent a field of practice and study? And from another vantage point, can podcasting provide a digital place for solutions and change by connecting theory and practice through conversation?

In this chapter, I explore theoretical and practical underpinnings of subversion inherent in the academic-but-public-facing podcast *The J Word: A Podcast by Journalism Practice*.[1] This podcast, which I have produced and

---

1   Gutsche Jr., Robert E. *The J Word: A Podcast by Journalism Practice.* https:// thejword.buzzsprout.com/.

hosted since the summer of 2020, is connected to the academic journal *Journalism Practice*. My intentions for the podcast—having emerged through a period of reflection on my own decades in journalism, journalism education, and now journalism research—are for it to be a journalistic-academic tool, a site for production targeted at public consumption using the genre's audio forms and distribution apparatus.

First, I provide a brief scene-setting of the problems of the journalism world and the need for a reckoning. Second, I discuss a bit of the "pre-podcasting" (Besser, Blackwell, and Saenz 2021) that I underwent in the development of a podcast with its ambitious aim of garnering an audience of practitioners and theorists. Third, I unpack the theory-to-practice (and maybe back again) process of producing the podcast to identify its ideological underpinnings related to sense-making, social capital, performative power, access to scholarship, and ranting as a "podcastual approach."

AN AGE OF RECKONING?

Journalism(s)[2] has been under fire, and rightfully so, for its lack of inclusivity in its ranks and reporting (*The J Word* episode 3.1). With some promise, a recent term, *reckoning*, has been applied to discussions of journalisms' problems—namely its rootedness in power structures and interpretations of and for white men in the "Global North."[3] Candis Callison and Mary Lynn Young (2019, 3) define *reckoning* as a "coming to terms with unfinished business, a settling of scores and/or past mistakes." They identify two main points of the field—and how we imagine it. First, they identify that Western journalism has long (since its beginning) had a problem in its diversification of newsrooms, and that the dominant coverage is of things that matter to the rich. Second, they argue that over generations the same solutions have been posed, and promises to do better have been broken by news organizations, university journalism programs, and individual journalists. These solutions have included diversifying hiring practices and creating reflective journalism that identifies power structures, even in the most banal of situations (see Harp, Callison, and Young 2020).

Other changes in US journalism in recent years include the following areas of improvement and discussion:

---

2   I write *journalism(s)* to refer to the extensive range of what can be considered journalism outside of the dominant, elite, and mainstream standards.

3   While I appreciate the political concerns surrounding the need for terms such as *Global North* and *Global South* to represent inequalities, we should also recognize that the terms construct a lumping together of the diversity and varying inequalities and identities within geographic classifications of the globe.

- By 2020, more non-white women than before were in leading positions in newsrooms (Beer 2021).
- More newsrooms have publicly acknowledged dangerous and racist aspects of their histories, including *The Kansas City Star* (Fannin 2020), the *Los Angeles Times* (LA Times 2020), and *National Geographic* (Goldberg 2018).

Work remains. Still, similar discussion within scholarly fields (in the Western/US context) has also emerged in recent years by

- rightfully pushing and propagating the campaign #CommunicationSoWhite (Chakravartty et al. 2018; Crittenden and Haywood 2020) to unveil racial (and gendered) disparities in research and academic hiring within communication fields; and
- debating approaches to geographic, gendered, and racial aspects of scholarly reciprocity and reflexivity within journalism studies (Borges-Rey 2020; Gutsche et al. 2017; Kligler-Vilenchik and Tenenboim 2020).

Still, work remains.

There are limitations to the progress that's being made, including in Western-centric areas of journalism. As an editor at the journal *Journalism Practice*, I am afforded a unique, albeit small, viewpoint into the challenges of entering into the pillars of scholarship for early-career researchers. I see, thankfully not frequently, how academics operate to maintain their own positions of power in their reviews of what they deem publishable. I have seen—without divulging anything top secret—the rise of select voices in my field, many that revolve around digitization, metrics, tweets, and notions that journalism is vital to "democracy." As a result, and as I have written elsewhere, scholars continue to maintain a divide between social science and critical or cultural studies approaches to journalism that reproduces normative assumptions of how media work, while marginalizing voices, tones, and critiques on journalism as a source of power and social control (Gutsche 2015; 2021). Simultaneously, there is a furthering of "academic professionalism" in our field that is undoubtedly and unforgivingly practice-led, where, in addition to conducting top-notch, theoretical, and impactful research, scholars train media workers, including in journalism and strategic communication (Franklin and Mensing 2010; Roush 2017), to work in neoliberal media worlds.

While reflecting upon the state(s) of my field, the immense growth of the podcasting genre, and the opportunity to circumvent, disrupt, and challenge systems of oppression embedded in academic publishing and institutions, oft-incestuous scholarly collaboration and citations that advance some and leave others behind, and the theory-to-practice divide, *The J Word* emerged, to me, as a means for reckoning.

MAKING *THE J WORD*

The J Word came about in the middle of the COVID-19 pandemic when academics were working from home and the podcast form was seeing (yet another) revitalization (Quah and Crampton 2020). I, like so many others, found myself "sheltered" in my home in England through a mixture of doctor's orders and governmental stay-at-home rules. In my escape from the pandemic, I did what any sane person would do: I thought more about life. One of those areas of my life that remained consistent—and that could be done easily online and away from the world—was my role as an associate and engagement editor at *Journalism Practice*, the first journal I ever published in, and one that has an aim to encourage connections between theory and practice. In this reflection, I asked: How did we as a journal and editorial team position ourselves in the debates and discussions mentioned above? To what degree did our scholarship adequately reflect the diversity of ideas and identities in the field? What voices were heard, both in terms of their ideas but also their accents, dialects, and other ways in which voice serves as a marker of and for identity?

By 2020, I had become familiar with podcasts on journalism, from *On the Media*, *It's All Journalism*, *The Data Journalism Podcast*, and *New Books in Journalism*. These were grounded in a normative approach to how journalism is made, and less so in the ideological and cultural aspects of journalism (see Berkowitz 2011). Other podcasts offered a different tone, one that unpacked a bit more in terms of cultural explanations of what journalism covered—and how. *Journalism History*, *El Café Latinx*, *BuzzMachine*, and the video blog and related podcast *Deuzevlog* provided a baseline for tone and topics that I thought would be helpful to expand upon (Gutsche 2020). I was also struck by the quality of their sound production and by their focus on problem-solving through diversity and innovative thought.

I was, however, still unsure if the problems I see with journalism and its related scholarship that have led to calls for a "reckoning" were being adequately addressed or simply viewed as fixable rather than endemic (Gutsche et al. 2022). I wondered whether there was room or interest in treating journalism as much as a "democratic tool" as one that is rooted in social oppression and indoctrination (Tischauser and Benn 2019). No, I concluded; there remains a thorny knot yet to be adequately untangled, and without unpacking all of my ideological intentions to the journal for which I work,[4] I pitched the podcast as a product that could elevate the journal's prominence, expand its reach, and have it stand out in a crowded field of journalism studies publishing.

Today, here is how *The J Word* works: I scour through the articles that come across our desks and are ultimately published, often first online, and almost always behind a paywall. Authors from at least three articles are invited to an episode to outline their work and to engage in accessible, applicable, and (I hope) theoretically challenging discussion. This forms ten hour-long episodes per season twice a year that I produce and host. Articles that are discussed on the podcast are made "free access" for about a month after the episode drops to allow greater access to what otherwise would remain behind a paywall. I promote the episode and the authors through our social media channels, where I include the researchers' headshots, tag them, and highlight an audio snippet of the interview as a hook.

Thus far, I have found working on *The J Word* a rich experience, one that tries to help an academic journal do more for society and communities of practice and theory, while helping make the information in the journal articles that are featured on the podcast more accessible, in terms of their applicability and their financial cost. To some degree I am limited in my own critiques of the podcast's production quality and its measurements of success, as *The J Word* has become a bit synonymous with my version of "the podcast self." However, in the discussion below I hope to unpack theoretical and practical underpinnings of subversion and reckoning at the core of *The J Word*, and comment on the ability of podcasting to bring truth to power by "hearing" ideas and identities.

PODCASTING AS SENSE-MAKING PRODUCTION: PROBLEMATIZING BY APPEARING

Sense-making is a process by which individuals reflect upon and through processes of organizational chains and activities, and their media experiences and interactivities (Reinhard and Dervin 2012). It asks what participants believe is happening (or what has happened) in a moment, or in a process over time, with the aim to address gaps or disruptions that can lead to greater understanding of the process and its related social or cultural implications and forces. Recent work in sense-making and journalism has

---

4   As a point of transparency, I am paid a marginal stipend as an associate editor and have the costs of the hosting and recording software paid for by the journal's publisher.

examined how audiences make sense of media messages (Edgerly 2022). I also apply a type of sense-making to *The J Word* by initially engaging with my guests in two main ways. First, I like to recognize with guests that they are content creators, both by having produced their research articles, and by contributing to the construction of the podcast discussion. Second, I advocate for the idea that they are also an audience to the discussion they are having, asking them to reflect upon not just their own works but on the ideological meanings within which their works are embedded and that are expressed throughout our talk.

To be sure, I turn much of our conversations into reflections on the powers that be in terms of ideologies, personalities, and power performances shaping dominant characterizations of and explanations for journalism in today's media spheres. This is particularly the case when our discussions revolve around the popular focus on "new," "trendy," and "techy" contributions to journalism research that emerges from the "Global North" (Perloff 2019; Raetzsch et al. 2021). My aim in discussions on journalism and trust, mis- and disinformation, climate change, Instagram, AI, design, and news sources is similarly focused on complicating the contributors' work, when applicable, through critical evaluation of such aspects of their work as method, theory, and meanings for the practitioner, student, or "average citizen." This real-time reflection on their own work that is captured in sound hopefully unveils the potential power forces that shaped their decisions in making a study and influenced their conclusions. Such an approach is less about an interrogation of their academic selves as it is an anthropological one embedded in "destabiliz[ing] the typified voices of authority...by proposing another way of creating such authority" (Cook 2020, 15). In other words, while guests retain a sense of authority through their identities, and their speech and voices on the podcast, they are also removed from the typical (and typified) scholarly settings of a conference, classroom, or article read in a library carrel. The sense-making that emerges, then, is of a scholar reflecting upon herself, her work, and the input of her colleagues to amass new conclusions—or to affirm prior ones—through live discourse.

This sense-making is also a route to a larger means of involving emerging or established voices that become elevated to contribute, if not lead, field-wide discussions of our "reckoning" (for more on what guides my approach, see McHugh 2022; Mutsvairo, Bebawi, and Borges-Rey 2020). Indeed, from how journalism covers #MeToo in Europe, China, and Australia, to the role of AI in journalism in the UAE, Pakistan, the US, and Nigeria, I try to be global in curating the voices that appear on the podcast (*The J Word* episodes 1.4, 2.10, 3.6, and 4.2). Yet, the sense-making approach helps make these discussions less descriptive and less based on geography, as my questions never (and

I mean never) sound like, "How are journalists using AI in Qatar?" Rather, because of the people who are participating, they themselves engage with the ideas of interactions of the local and the global in journalism research, challenge each other to complicate domestic interpretations and global overreach in explanations for how journalism works.

Guests frequently follow a pattern I set to challenge the Western-based, dominant rhetoric that states that all things are the same, articulating, for instance, that climate change and disinformation in Argentina is quite different, unsurprisingly, than how journalists may fact-check climate change data in the UK. Articulating those differences in the context of interrogating journalism's function are the purpose of the podcast. The sense-making further emerges when our conversations move into how and why scholars and popular discourses support false equivalencies. From that discussion alone we are able to meet one of my sense-making aims that's influenced largely by my podcast support system—namely my wife. Speaking from both her scholarly and Colombian positions, she reminds me in our frequent post-recording kitchen meet-ups that white Westerners (of which I am one) love to learn *about* "others" but never *from* "them."

SOCIAL CAPITAL: CASTING PODCAST PARTICIPANTS

One listening to a podcast on journalism scholarship would expect (if not hope) to hear the "big voices" of the field. What if, though, *those voices* were put on the margin? Would that be a way to address a reckoning? For *The J Word*, I appreciate the storied, tenured/permanent, and popular academic voices who have published in the journal and contributed to an episode or two. But a reckoning must note that those voices already get a lot of traction as invited keynotes, publication collaborators, leaders of organizations, and as beneficiaries of journal articles, books, and teaching. I have wanted *The J Word* to be different, with a focus on women, non-Western voices, and critical scholars. In turn, guests are encouraged to promote themselves and their ideas, to share the temporary free access to their articles once their episodes drop, and to add their podcast-as-public engagement to their CVs and profiles. I also want them to feel a sense of affirmation from the conversation.

In some ways, this is easier said than done; I am dealt as guests those who publish in the journal. So, taking this into consideration, at the 2019 Future of Journalism conference held at Cardiff University in the UK, scholar Nikki Usher presented initial data on just who is leading scholarship on journalism from the field's leading journal editorial boards (including *Journalism Practice*'s). Might this be a way to also address who gets published in our journals? Usher found that roughly 78 percent of the scholars on boards across journalism studies identified as white. Nearly 60 percent identified as male, with the majority of the board members' affiliations located in Europe, the US, and Australia. And while there might be some concerns about how these data were compiled (Usher and a research assistant surmised some of the data based on names and interpretations of identities, though in some cases they reached out to individual board members to capture how they themselves identified), the quantification of centralized power in this case articulates rising vocalized concerns of how journalism scholarship is structured, at least from the vantage of the ivory tower.

With that in mind for the purpose of *The J Word*, I intentionally spread some of the known or recognizable voices across each season so that they do not bulk up in one discussion or another. Such a programming choice might be good marketing—spreading out the voices we think people are more likely to listen to could ensure more listens. Still, such programming (and inclusivity) decisions spread these known voices' social capital across episodes and seasons to increase the chances that lesser-known scholars are "heard." Here is what the approach is not intended to do. First, early-career researchers and emerging voices do not need a popular name as a buttress to their legitimacy; their ideas stand on their own, though they may be marginalized based on social and cultural influences of the academy. Second, the episode does not need a "star voice" to guide or influence conversation.

What I have found through this approach, however, is that the podcast experience demystifies the "star voice" even when they do appear. No longer are these voices coming from behind a podium at a conference that only the privileged can afford to attend in person. Nor are these voices coming from the pages of a prestigious book or journal article. During the podcast, some of these known voices crackle under poor broadband connections. They overspeak, correct themselves, and put their feet in their mouths like the rest of us. I am not suggesting the podcast can create a fully level playing field. Still, when a deferred-to voice is featured with three other voices in an episode where ideas that conventionally appear under separate individual article titles merge with others', or when a voice that usually comes uninterrupted from a pulpit during a twenty-minute keynote competes with other voices throughout a longer discussion, maybe the podcast does level things a bit. Most interesting in this mingling of known and emerging voices is when you hear the well-cited (and by no means do I mean to suggest they are so undeservingly) showcasing their own "sense-making" of research and practice in a way that surprises even the most cynical of us, as guests emerge quite equally in their critique and support of each other.

PERFORMATIVE POWER: THE ACT OF PODCAST PARTICIPATION

Perhaps more than anything, I have found guests using *The J Word* to practise their public speaking—or their speaking in public—and in so doing, performing their power. Performative power emerges in the agency enacted by one who reveals overtly their positionalities, practising representation in which "every performance, every identity [is] a new representation of meaning and experience" (Denzin 2003, 328). Such is the case of vocality (Magnat 2019). Indeed, there is a sense of performative power that emerges from the very act of participating in the podcast. I have found three very interesting themes emerging from guests' sense of audio presentation related to their voices, articulations of self, and academic contexts. First, based upon the Global North–ness of our field, scholars with non-Anglo names provide me with pronunciations of their names as they are spoken in their home countries *and* as they are spoken in the "North." I find that providing an alternative pronunciation is thoughtful and a form of self-preservation, which I wish was not necessary in their minds. I understand that not everyone will know how to pronounce my last name, which comes from a German background. In fact, I do tell people to say it as they would the Italian brand Gucci and then make some bad joke about how I don't have that level of brand awareness or financial abundance. But there still seems to be something different when a guest recognizes that their institution or their name is not spoken enough for others to just recognize it on first reference.

In response to their clarification—and often thinking of my own sons who may have to do the same with their Latin names and spellings throughout their life—I try to acknowledge the guests' thoughtfulness. To help reduce any concerns they may have about my own pronunciation of their names, I ask the guests to say their names as I am recording so that I can hear it (and try to repeat it) correctly when I start post-production. This back-and-forth may be considered its own kind of performative power in the sense that it is agency one uses to reinforce the accurate presentation of self and a sense of ownership, not just of self-identity, but of the branding and reproduction of the content they are co-creating through their participation in the podcast. My performance is to recognize my power position as host and producer, to try to acknowledge my limitations and my responsibility in how they will be represented.

The genre of academic podcasting, as *The J Word* might be, removes the individual from the computer screen and keyboard, turning them into a different sort of actor who can be "heard" through their breath, their accent, their diction, and their silences. Sometimes, my guests for whom English is an additional language express great hesitation about their participation based on how they may be perceived given their academic rank or longevity, their geographic location, and their voice and use of language. Bravely, they still have come on the podcast to perform their power. While I do not provide in advance of the recording questions or comments about the podcast—only the articles being discussed by the two or three scholars to be featured—I have agreed with some guests (at their request, or if I sense it would be helpful) to record their conversations separately from the other guests. I also offer to have the guests write out their answers in English and read them back to us, all during the recording. Any silences from that process are edited out, a behind-the-scenes performance of my power to edit and represent.

There is yet another aspect that leads me to believe participating in this podcast is an act representative of performative power. Some guests—early career and otherwise—have told me that they haven't spoken to other scholars formally outside of a classroom or conference space about their research. This can be for any number of reasons. Perhaps they were not invited, or they feel their research wouldn't be accepted, or they are concerned about the platform and their abilities, as I discussed above. I understand in that I myself have often felt slighted for the things I say about journalism, education, institutions, and ideologies, which sometimes make conferences feel a bit hellish. Some of this comes from the social and institutional pressures about what makes someone, some place, or something popular. Having once taught at a Hispanic-serving research institution in the US, even as a straight white man from the Midwest, I felt the marginalization of my ideas (and of my students) at conferences where people seemed to be less-than-impressed with not just the institution (a fine one, I should say), but also with the types of people they imagined I served. I cannot fully appreciate how I would feel if my marginalization was based upon more than the status of my institution.

In addition to the performative power that I hope *The J Word* assists in, my hope is that it also provides fodder and experience through which a guest's performative power can be extended into the halls of academia. At the same time, I recognize that podcasts at large still seem to fall short of the traditional means by which an academic measures reach, success, and acknowledgement against institutional benchmarks (Fox et al. 2021). That said, beyond maybe serving as an initial, though brief "training ground" for one's public engagement, perhaps the podcast can become a line in a CV, a social media engagement, a form of evidence of value and worth. Maybe even a metric that can be added to a list for promotion or advancement, and "evidence" through one's discussions of one's power to speak and be heard in and around important issues of today.

CIRCUMVENTING NEOLIBERAL CORPORATIZATION
OF SCHOLARSHIP: PODCASTING AS AUTONOMY

While writing this chapter, I tweeted, "How many academic podcast episodes should equal one peer-reviewed article?" The answer might make it possible for me to spend more time on *The J Word* (beyond the ten hours I do spend on each episode, from research and scheduling to post-production and distribution). However, I did not get many responses to my question, and I really do not have an answer for this myself. At my own institution, I am not even able to adequately present an episode, or the podcast as a whole, as a recognized research output, and I am open to the fact that not everyone who creates a podcast—or participates in one—would want it classified as one type of output over another.

Instead, I remain more fascinated about the question itself, recognizing it is wrapped up in a neoliberal, corporate reporting of outputs as some kind of justification and creation of authority for scholars. As podcasters continue to search for meaningful measurements of their work at the risk of understanding cultural meanings of labour and industrialization (Morris 2021a), I also struggle with the constraints of sharing the podcast as "scholarship" and the disappointment that such work is not conventional enough to earn scholarly citation. Some of this may be the difficulty related to searching individual parts of a podcast. A solution to this could be to add podcast chapter markers or create transcripts of each episode, but that again seems as though it might be diminishing sound in favour of the printed word.

In attempting to answer my question about how academic podcasting fits into conventional academic measurement, I find that for institutions to answer this they would have to undermine the conventional research project in a sort of reckoning of its own limitations and inequalities. Without outlining all of what might be on that list, let us take up the ideas of time and ownership. The first, time, is an easy one. Though it does take time, the podcast can be done with much less time than an essay, chapter, or other publication. Certainly, these avenues of discourse offer very different things, but put simply there is freedom in discussing research (and like in *The J Word*, I think, coming to new scholarly ideas) in a podcast via its absence of the inordinate length of time it takes to receive "constructive" reviewer feedback, revise, and publish an article.

I also think we have created some new ideas via "out loud" research (Hagood 2021), during the podcast. Amid a set of episodes focused on journalistic coverage of climate change (*The J Word* episodes 4.4 and 4.5), for instance, we attempted to build new ideas of "synergistic effects" of climate change—in this case, that in covering climate change, practices of journalism had been impacted and changed in a synergistic relationship to the social, cultural, and environmental influences of global warming (Gutsche and Pinto 2022). We were able to test out the idea through conversation. Perhaps more importantly, we were able to get the idea out there, including amongst each other, faster than through conventional publication. How we might have been cited for that idea from the podcast and not the related publication is either a failure of the genre or at the very least a failure of academia to acknowledge a podcast in the same way as an article.

Still, podcasting has been found to provide various forms of autonomy for scholars and content producers, particularly in terms of freedom from the mandates of conventional language, argumentation, and labour (Sullivan 2018). Some of that labour that exists within conventional scholarship is controlled by the peer-review process, for better or for worse. With the podcast, we are free to say some things about research and practice, even if we are spitballing, that might not make it past the conservative and curmudgeonly Reviewer 2, known throughout scholarship for demanding scholars write their work as Reviewer 2 would (Peterson, 2020). In fact, the scholarly reviewing that doesn't go into the making of the academic work of *The J Word*'s participants' conversation has also been recognized for its racisms, sexisms, and hyper-Westernizations (Steinberg, Skae, and Sampson 2018). To be sure, the articles featured on the podcast have already appeared in the academic journal, having traversed that conventional track and possibly Reviewer 2.

The podcaster's freedom may not be perfect, though. I haven't yet had to deal with a guest who "goes rogue" enough to warrant editing out (as I have with some journal reviewers), so maybe on *The J Word* we still comply with forms of conventional speech and ideas. I would like to think, however, that podcasters have a bit more freedom for thinking through ideas, making comments without citations, and putting ourselves out there in a sense of "talking back" to the system and of doing scholarship "out loud" without the worry of Reviewer 2's disposition.

One of the most tangible forms of autonomy from neoliberal corporate structures of academia that *The J Word* provides revolves also around related conventions of academic publishing. To spread research and good ideas—that often are a byproduct of taxpayer and philanthropic funding to our academic institutions that employ scholars—by making articles discussed on *The J Word* free access, the podcast becomes a space to critique systems of power in terms of corporate control over intellectual property. (Of course, it is the journal publisher, not I, who ultimately breaks through the paywall, but I will take credit for the idea.) I am not arguing that the publisher makes articles free access for altruistic reasons and that by doing so they are releasing their power over what is arguably the product of, in many cases, public investment in education and knowledge-building.

Free access, even if established because of the aims of the podcast, means more eyes on the document, and more activity and engagement points for the journal's website; this becomes "indicative" of the audiences' desire, upon which the publisher can base its subscription rates for libraries and individuals. Free access might also make the notion of scholar-paid open access more attractive, bringing in more money for publishers (for critical discussions on open access, see Gutsche 2021; Haelewaters, Hofmann, and Romero-Olivares 2021; Liverpool 2021; Reidpath and Allotey 2019). Yet, I have seen the power in providing free access from the perspective of my guests. Several have told me that the free-access status was the only way they were able to download their own articles without paying.[5] By circumventing the corporate paywall in the roughly thirty instances per season when articles are provided to the public at no (further) cost, *The J Word* meets another of its aims of subversion and reckoning.

MOVING TO A CONCLUSION: RECKONING THROUGH RANTING

I want to conclude this essay on using the podcasting genre as a unique digital place for subversion and reckoning by highlighting the potential of podcasting to move beyond academic convention through the rant. Certainly, "the rant" can be associated with more oppressive forms of speech and discourse in popular podcasts, particularly those from some polarized political perspectives. Here, the rant is associated with conspiracy theory and a lack or manipulation of "fact" to disregard and repress counterthought (see, for example, Van den Bulck and Hyzen 2020). Podcasts like *The Joe Rogan Experience* rise to the top of the list in such a category, where the podcast becomes a space for seemingly endless moments of speech, convoluted and incoherent wide statements of fact and assumption, with an assumed aim of alienation and silencing (Hyzen and Van den Bulck 2021). Yet, the rant also appears in early episodes of interviews with a US Southerner speaking about inequalities, global oppression and collusion of the powerful, culture, language, and agency in the seminal Serial Productions podcast *S-Town* (Waldmann 2020). Here, the subject of the podcast speaks about interconnectedness among societies, cultures, behaviours, and ideologies that cause the listener to (hopefully) pause and consider complexities embedded within the discourse and

---

5   Note that the publisher does offer authors fifty free downloads of the published work, though the authors I spoke with said they were not aware of this offer and relied on the free access resulting from their involvement in the podcast.

form of speech. The rant, in this case, is on the surface an amalgamation of life's spheres of influence that can easily be written off as a crazy speech. But for the careful listener, a welcome pause could bring meaningful reflection. Within that is the subversive power of the rant.

Such subversion operates when structures and expectations associated with those structures are reversed. As I have addressed in this essay but only now directly articulate, a reckoning is more than just a smart observation. It is even more than an articulation of that observation. Subversion requires action or intentional inaction. Here, I argue that the podcast—and its participants—are taking action. *The J Word* does not operate with the expressed intention of action, nor do I expect or ask participants to share or define their action as I do my own. Yet, the reckoning of journalisms' challenges and the restrictions and parameters of journalism scholarship would be clear to the avid listener, I hope.

The rant is one of the characteristics of (my) podcasting—and, to me, of reckoning-engaged subversion. But what is ranting, and how and why may it appear in podcasting? Popular definitions of rant are aligned with "blowing off steam" in an aggressive and dishevelled manner, with "rambling" and "going off track," and, unfortunately, with much of what Western cable talking heads and polarizing media pundits and politicians do (Davis 2018). That said, ranting or rambling, when one extends one's ideas into a larger landscape of meaning and discussion that revolves around an initial topic or idea, can uncover deeper meanings of one's discursive evidence, argument, and positionality, even if the means do not conform to conventional, logical flow (Bjørnholt and Farstad 2014). As an academic, I have often been accused of ranting in my classes, partially because it is harder to follow along with someone who is "on a rant" than the static monotony of a PowerPoint or the dullness of the Oxford Union.

On *The J Word*, I am cognizant that anytime I am speaking for over three minutes it might be considered a rant, while I am making transitions or segues or trying to drive a conversation one way or another. In the classroom and on the podcast, the rant becomes more obvious, I am told, when I am saying something that may make the listener uncomfortable. As the rant emerges, they are able to drift away from the narrative, back to the original discussion and argument, without complicating it further. In turn, they are using the rant and this distance from it to release themselves from the responsibility of truly understanding the argument's meaning, which is also included in the evidence of the rant. While not really articulated, the notion of the rant appears in podcasting—even if most overtly in the titles, such as *The Recap Rant, The Nightly Rant, Xennial Rants. The Guardian* (2020) inadvertently defined ranting in a review of *The Ranting Atheist* when the reviewer wrote,

The anonymous host of this podcast is unafraid to ask tough questions, even though he knows that what he is saying is grossly unpopular in a country where churches are full every weekend and street preachers are on every street corner. His courageous and unapologetic approach is what attracts me to listen.

I'd like to think on *The J Word*, some of my rants on the troubles of persistent technological determinism in the fields of journalism and journalism research, the dangers of lacking inclusivity in the "cool kids club" of scholarship that "matters," and the uncovering of embedded inequalities in practice and scholarship come through. Indeed, ranting is an impassioned voice that elevates oppositional narratives and can be at the centre of an inclusive and international dialogue (Kennedy 1999; Neale 2008; Scott 2018). And what better place than the podcast, which we already recognize as a place for intimate and emotional exchange and immersion (Swiatek 2018)?

There certainly is a lack of evidence that ranting is a unique podcasting character trait or a journalistic one, but if I am to do anything in this chapter, it is to justify and represent the diverse modes of communication—from diction and dialect to ideological vantage point and delivery style—that emerge and can exist on podcasts. And in so doing, my hope is to justify the moments when a speaker goes off track—whether that be over the course of a recorded five minutes or an eighty-word sentence. We might not be able to adequately reckon without a rant. I invite further research on this issue.

CONCLUSION: RETURNING TO THE START

I started this chapter with three questions: 1) What happens when a field of practice and study requires a reckoning? 2) Can podcasting be a place for diverse voices in that reckoning? 3) Can that place provide solutions and change by connecting theory and practice? To the first, I argue here that what I hope is my own pathway through this podcast, from its planning to its production and reflection, is further evidence of the power of the individual to assess and take action against inequalities within the neoliberal academy. Such action need not involve podcasting, but I do believe, in answer to the second question, that I (with my guests) have been able to find a place where the unique qualities of sound and vocality can speak (back?) to Western-centric approaches to a field of practice that breed inequality. And as I have tried to emphasize, this speaking must be acknowledged not just by the ideas that are presented but in the accent, diction, and performative power of the speakers' voices. Lastly, in respect to the third question, I am not sure it can be answered fully. The best I can say as to "change," thus far is in the celebration of one's agency, the affirmation expressed to me by my guests, and the collaborations and interactions among guests that have emerged from their recordings and their listens. Perhaps, in the end, those measurements mean more than any other metric.

CHAPTER 5

POD-A-BYE BABY

Podcasting as a Pathway to Continued Participation for Academic Parents

LIZ GIUFFRE

P articipation in academic outreach and engagement activities can be particularly challenging for academics who are parents/carers. Using as a case study the podcast *Music Mothers and Others*,[1] made by Australian academics and parents Liz Giuffre and Shelley Brunt, this chapter positions podcasting as an accessible way for academics who are parents/carers to continue to conduct research while also engaging with their peers and a general audience. Further, the content and context of *Music Mothers and Others* is offered as a model to demonstrate how research, industry, and audience engagement can be achieved through podcasting.

This chapter considers a specific example of podcasting and parenting practice with the cross-city podcast collaboration *Music Mothers and Others*. Produced, written, recorded, and edited by me, Liz Giuffre, and my colleague Shelley Brunt, *Music Mothers and Others* was conceived as a way to research how parenting/caregiving and creative industries work can best coexist. Shelley and I chose podcasting as a medium to explore and expand our existing research into parenting and creative industries. We also created the podcast during intense periods of our own working and family lives—at a

---

1   Giuffre, Liz and Shelly Brunt. *Music Mothers and Others*. https://musicmothersandothers.com/.

time when we each have children under school age, and during state-imposed COVID lockdowns. We are both based in Australia, albeit in cities that are separated by a distance of about eight hours by car—Shelley in Melbourne, myself in Sydney. Although Shelley and I have extensive experience in the creative industries as practitioners and theorists (as traditional academic researchers and in industry as arts workers), the process of creating and releasing the podcast allowed us to bring into action the "theory" of creative industries work by serving as the podcast's audio producers, talent bookers, editors, scriptwriters, social media monitors and creators, and website publishers.

The practice of podcasting has been an important way in which we have been able to engage with our research subjects. Without *Music Mothers and Others*, Shelley and I would have become academically (and socially) isolated during the Australian COVID lockdowns of 2020 and 2021. As creative industries academics who often engage in qualitative analysis, ethnographic audience engagement and close textual analysis at live performances, the closure of arts venues and cancelling of tours meant that many of our usual sites for research were just not available to undertake "business as usual." Similarly, access to resources like state and federal archives, libraries, and other physical research spaces were closed during these times, and universities restricted access to campus buildings, and by extension, any books or items we had in our own offices. My institution, the University of Technology Sydney, offered suggestions for "adapting research methodologies in the COVID-19 pandemic" (Garcia and Barclay 2020); there are now well-established digital methodologies available for use in media, audio, and cultural studies (see, for example, Sayers 2018). However, in practice, to fully convert to online takes years of expertise to master, and further requires necessary practicalities like ensuring access to appropriate technology and support at home. Significantly, the tightest restrictions during lockdown meant that there was no recourse to child care, formal or casual.

Podcasting provided a way for Shelley and me to continue our work from home during lockdown. This proved practical for us as producers because recording and editing audio was more achievable than trying to engage in deep written analysis without normal child care support. The podcast also provided an accessible invitation for our research subjects, as our guest artists or creative workers tended to be more familiar with podcasting as a format than with academic writing. As I'll discuss later in this chapter, increasingly podcasting is being recognized by researchers and audiences as a way to engage with each other and supplement, or even circumvent, the often-paywalled and much-delayed paths of the traditional academic publishing environment (Levy 2020; Rogers et al. 2020). While making *Music Mothers and Others* Shelley and I have had a shared understanding of the value of what Berry calls "podcastness" (2016a, 11), a distinct type of connection between produ-cers, guests, and audiences in podcast practice. For us this includes the way research is done, as well as the type of data received. Prior to starting the pod-cast, Shelley and I gained ethics clearance from our respective universities to interview creative industries professionals about caregiving and professional practice. However podcasting allowed us to use tone and nuance of emotion to go deeper. That is, we may ask the same questions in an academic exchange as in the podcast, but we can present those findings in sound form with a dif-ferent affect than in academic writing. This is similar to the detail McHugh describes with her work on oral histories and sound texts, as "[l]istening to the recording, as opposed to reading a transcript, gives a sense not just of who is speaking but of subtle dynamics and narrative rhythms" (2012, 188–89). The style of the final podcast became closer to what might be considered an older broadcast-style approach, or "chat-based" audio (Ames 2016), as Shelley and I presented our podcast as a conversation between researchers and guests. This enabled an active exchange of ideas about our research with guests (who are also research subjects) and in the process provided a fruitful way to expand, and sometimes challenge, our original frames of reference. Our experience as independent podcasters, as well as academics, has also allowed us to reflect on "podcasting and participatory practice" as Markman considered it (2012). Markman found many podcasters to be driven by a combination of interests in "technology/media, content, or personal motives" (2012, 557). In devising and executing *Music Mothers and Others*, Shelley and I were also drawn to these three factors, and further, considerations of how best to combine them.

The practice-led research—or practice-led academic engagement—that *Music Mothers and Others* employed is comparable to other forms of work/life media forms, such as the (in)famous "mommy/mummy blog" phenom-enon of the 2000s (Hunter 2016; Lopez 2009; Morrison 2011; Van Cleaf 2015). Podcasting provides an added intimacy that written blogs cannot—with the sounds of the artists' work, as well as interruptions, such as those from children and other environmental factors—delivering a heightened ability to "provide and receive emotional validation" which Van Cleaf considered fundamental to mommy/mummy blogs (2015, 247). For example, when I am heard interacting with my children as part of the podcast (or in some cases explaining their crying in the background and assuring the listener that they are fine), this is a demonstration of parenting in real time. In the case of one episode in particular (Brunt and Giuffre 2020a, 00:04), I needed to add an extra introduction to assure the listener that the crying baby in the back-ground of the recording was not actually in prolonged distress. This addition to the podcast episode provided emotional validation as well as emotional clarification—letting an understandably distracted or concerned listener know about the welfare of the child and my response as a parent. This emotional connection can also provide a sense of vulnerability and evoke empathy—as later discussed with relation to the episode with Nardi Simpson in particular (Brunt and Giuffre 2020a).

Importantly, the work of active parenthood is one that has been explored via podcasting in various ways. From an affect point of view, work like Hyland Wang's account of "motherwhelm" in the sound of NPR's *ZigZag* stands out (2023, 7–8). However, unlike Wang's account of the sound of active parenthood as producing "audio [that] is cluttered—[as] cars whiz by, mouthfuls of salad crunch and wind blows incessantly into microphones—by the ambient sounds of [mother/parent's] rushed lives" (2023, 8), in *Music Mothers and Others* the sounds of domestic parenting and the general domestic circumstances of recording are not necessarily that of "clutter," but an authentic soundscape rather than that of a sterile recording studio. These sounds of babies crying, family members co-inhabiting and other media playing in the background may not be desirable from a purist (and pre-pandemic) podcasting perspective, but provide a vivid audio context for the listener. Ultimately, Hyland Wang concludes that "the affect produced by the [*ZigZag* podcast] is despair—the feeling of looking at walls too big to scale" (2023, 22) when considering how one might persist in creative industries while actively being a working mother (or parent). Perhaps because Shelley and I were in the eye of the storm while creating the first seasons of *Music Mothers and Others*, and with the benefit of having continuing work as creative industries academics, the affect of our work was somewhat less bleak. Since these first seasons were created we have also released an academic monograph, *Popular Music and Parenting* (Brunt and Giuffre 2023), in which we explored parenting and its influence across various aspects of creative industries, including as creative inspiration for artists; as a way to engage intergenerational audiences; and as a concept more generally within the creative industries. Our podcast served as an important research gathering tool for that work, as well as a way to broaden conversations beyond traditional "academic circles."

Podcasting as an academic method has been explored by a variety of social scientists. Notable examples include geographers Kinkaid, Brain, and Senanayake (2020), ethnographer anthropologist Cook (2020), historians Kerrigan, Criticos, Kerrigan, and Ritchie (2021), and journalist and broadcaster McHugh (2014). It has also been explored within arts and cultural critique (McHugh, McLean, and Neale 2020; Fox and Llinares 2018) and broader autoethnographies for broad education practices (Lowe, Turner, and Schaefer 2021). There is also a growing number of podcasts exploring parenting experiences, such as the audio (auto)biography documentary podcast series *Not By Accident* chronicled by Zehelein (2019). As Rogers and a collective of twenty-four other academics proclaimed in the critical commentary "The City under COVID-19: Podcasting as Digital Methodology," podcasting has "allowed researchers [and subjects] to collaborate in new ways, and this podcast project pushed at the boundaries of what a research method and research community might be" (2020, 438). Personally and professionally I have also found the experience of podcasting akin to the theory and practice Llinares describes, specifically the "foster[ing of a] spirit of community, respectful and reasoned debate, and even a space and time for academic discourse that is arguably becoming more marginalized in the university itself" (2018, 124). In the case of our podcast, which explores how creative industries workers and academics navigate professional and personal lives as parents/carers, we have found Llinares's point to be particularly true when discussing precarious work and insecure employment. Although both full-time, permanent employees now, my colleague and I both spent long periods as casual and contract workers, and these conditions remain the reality for many working in the creative and academic industries. As was brought into sharp focus during the COVID-19 lockdowns, these types of workers are often marginalized or completely left out of discussions of value and worth by institutions and governments (Harris, Smithers, and Spina 2020; Adams 2021).

THE ANATOMY OF *MUSIC MOTHERS AND OTHERS* (A.K.A. "LITERATURE REVIEW")

The tagline for *Music Mothers and Others* is "an audio parenting group." I originally proposed the podcast as a way to supplement the academic research Shelley and I were both undertaking in relation to popular music and parenting—having written independently about children's music and media cultures (Giuffre 2013; Brunt 2021), and with a co-authored book project, *Popular Music and Parenting* (Brunt and Giuffre 2023). The idea was that the podcast would serve as a way to gather additional data, connections, and insight for the research rather than be its main data source. As the pandemic has continued, the findings and connections to industry we have made via the podcast have guided the research in ways that have allowed our original vision for the book to evolve (and we have gained ethics clearance from our respective universities to ensure we can use it for this purpose if we choose). However, more important than this has been the shared sense of solidarity and community we have been able to build locally, nationally, and internationally.

The podcast was launched on 30 August 2020, broadcast weekly on Monday evenings via 2SER, a Sydney-based community radio station, and then released as a podcast either that night or the morning after. We write, produce, and edit the audio for the podcast; write copy for, produce, and maintain the podcast website (www.musicmothersandothers.com); make content for the podcast social media outlets (Instagram, Facebook, and Twitter), and make a Spotify-based song playlist for each episode relating to each guests' professional practice. The final "product" is independently produced by me and Shelley Brunt, with a "radio edit" made for 2SER FM, as well as a specialist edit for Australia-wide distribution via the Community Radio Network (CRN), which is part of the Community Broadcasting Association of Australia (CBAA). We created fifteen original episodes in 2020, thirteen original episodes in 2021, as well five "best of" compilation episodes including an episode celebrating International Women's Day, and two combining guests' responses to key questions relating to innovation in industry and co-listening.

Music Mothers and Others is interview-based, with episodes structured roughly around the same four questions or topics for discussion. These are provided to the guests in advance and are modified if required.

1. How do you describe your place/role in the music/creative industries?
2. What is your earliest childhood memory/influence that has informed your current practice?
3. How do you negotiate between family life and your work life now, and do you have any advice for the industry to make this negotiation easier/more accessible?
4. Can you finish the sentence "The kids and I are listening to..."?

In practice we did have some variation in the way we asked or approached these questions, but the main aims remain. Of the utmost importance is using the podcast as a place to host a conversation, so that the guest can describe, in their own terms, the relationship between creative industry work and parent/family life; as well as how formative (childhood) experiences have come to bear on their contemporary practice. The question of "advice for the industry" is deliberately practical in nature and has yielded quite specific responses relating to the guests' particular needs and experiences. The final piece, "The kids and I are listening to...," invites the guest to engage with our research relating to co-listening and relationship-building through music.

In our pilot (which later became our first episode), Shelley and I interviewed each other about the podcast's aims and answered these core questions from our own perspectives. This served as an introduction to our audience as well as a model for future guests—and, importantly, it allowed us to reflect on our own past and current experiences. As I will discuss later, the relationship between our own lived experiences as creative arts workers, creative arts academics and parents/carers continues to be an active part of the content and context of the podcast. We use the medium as a place to discuss, explore, and share these in discussion. We also use the medium as a way to explore the relationships between children and parents/carers using the specifics of sound. This includes recordings of children (ours or our those of our guests) used as station IDs or intros, as well as illustrations of content where permission has been granted. At times this provides simple sonic diversity, but at other points this is a sonic demonstration of the content and context of the discussion. For example, in the first episode Shelley and I feature recordings of our children singing, or making early verbalizations in response to the music we've talked about using as a way to calm them down—illustrating the way the music is being used, and received, as part of our parenting practice and the children's development. This process of demonstrating practice and context in the *Music Mothers and Others* podcast can be compared to the way Rae, Russell and Nethery (2019, 1038–39) have adapted Schafer's earlier work on "earwitnessing" (1977) to apply to more recent podcasting practice. Although our approach, genre, and topic is very different to the example Rae, Russell, and Nethery provide with *The Messenger* podcast and its exposition of Australian offshore detention centres and their occupants, by including the voices of the children we are parenting alongside our discussion of this process, we invite our audience to be drawn into the affective experiences being explored sonically through the podcast. That is, our immediate need to negotiate between the roles of being an academic and being a parent can be heard in real time as we record in houses, spaces that also clearly have other family members making noise in close proximity, and where audio levels cannot be smoothed adequately because of different recording locations for ourselves and our guests.

During lockdowns especially, we were, like working parents in many places around the world, expected to perform both tasks simultaneously. As I have written elsewhere, the expectation to successfully work and parent at home simultaneously has been hugely unbalanced with regard to gender and associated class politics (Giuffre 2020). As hosts and producers Shelley and I are always very open about our experiences with family life, and the podcast has allowed us to talk freely about our experiences as academics, too. The conversations with working creative industry professionals allows us to compare the "theory" of our craft with the practice of everyday industry workers—at times discovering, in those recorded conversations, the continued divides between these two worlds. Pleasingly though, we are also able to find continued connections between these worlds, and a shared purpose, particularly during these times of financial and industrial pressure for both arts practice and arts academia.

THE PRODUCTION CONTEXT FOR
SERIES ONE (OR "METHODOLOGY")

The first podcast season—consisting of fifteen episodes lasting twenty to thirty minutes each—was recorded in different cities across Australia and Europe, all in isolated conditions due to government-imposed COVID-19 lockdowns. I was recording in Sydney, which was locked down for three months and did not allow visitors or the use of external premises without exceptional circumstances. Shelley was recording in Melbourne, a city that was locked down for five months with even stricter restrictions placed on citizens' movements, including on how far and for how long people could leave their homes, even for exercise or to buy essential items. The lockdown restrictions presented obvious logistical challenges—compounded by our dual roles as working academics and parents of young children. Shelley and I were both due to be on research-intensive work allocations during the second half of 2020, and we had planned to travel to work in person together where we could, with the anticipated support of formal and family daycare systems. Australian COVID-related restrictions changed much of this, and the ability to freely leave our houses, let alone our cities, was swiftly removed by respective state and federal governments for months at a time in both 2020 and 2021. Our academic institutions undergoing significant financial constraint following the loss of international student numbers in our sector, and the threat of looming job losses provided extra pressure for those of us left to perform above and beyond.

Lockdown conditions meant the podcast could only be recorded remotely using whatever technology was at hand. We used what we called a "good technique with basic technology" approach, recording at each end local tracks that were relatively interference free and with clear focus on our individual vocals so that we could mix them together later. Where possible we mirrored the effect of studio conditions to allow ourselves to hear one another and ourselves separately, using "two different earbuds" at once—one to allow us to listen via Zoom to respond, and another linked to an external recording device to serve as a makeshift cardioid microphone to capture a clean version of our own voices locally. We then synced these separate tracks manually in post-production, using a single-tracked Zoom recording as a guide or backup track if needed. Finally, we used the free open source program Audacity serving as the DAW for the project and Google Drive or Dropbox to share and save rough audio, draft edits, and final media.

Beyond the technology itself, the recording environment was also manipulated to allow for the best possible sound. This included recording in the best "dead" sound contexts we could find (bedrooms, cupboards, inside cars, or even in beds), but also at times of day that would be least likely to have noise bleed from other household members or neighbours. In lockdown conditions, this was especially difficult, given that whole families were present at home for much of the day and night, and also that neighbours were also nearby, if not only at home, also—as in my case—on both sides of my apartment building, using lockdown as an excuse to undergo building works. In short, this meant that recording had to ideally be scheduled according to guest availability, during baby or toddler nap times and in line with construction workers' lunch breaks. Where there were exceptions that needed to be made to meet guest availability (or when children or workers would not stick to schedule), Shelley and I did our best to improvise, and finally, compromise. Given the podcast's focus on the relationship between family life and creative industries, we felt the audience would excuse the odd "noise bleed" associated with family members working and living together closely. We had to be careful to keep this to a minimum and to ensure it did not distract from the actual guest and conversations. At worst, there were some cases where parts of interviews had to be abandoned because the sound of kids in the background was simply too overwhelming. For much of the first series I recorded my end of the podcast with my then-six-month-old son either strapped to me to get him to sleep, or attached to me as he breastfed.

Although other media forms provided scope for the sharing of ideas and experience, podcasting allowed for emotional and contextual exchanges, with children literally, as well as metaphorically, often interrupting the work. As audio, these interruptions had to be dealt directly as part of the content of the show—and when our own children or those of our guests could be heard during the interviews, we made comments about it rather than ignoring it. Of course, there were times when these sounds were too distracting and we needed to edit them out or re-record small sections, but this negotiation, in practice, reminded the listener, the guests, and ourselves of the point of the podcast—to explore (and even celebrate, if but for a moment) the necessary negotiations made as work and family life coexist. I had previously experienced this as a print journalist when my daughter was only a few months old, while interviewing Virginia Hanlon Grohl to promote her book *From Cradle to Stage: Stories from the Mothers Who Rocked and Raised Rock Stars* (Hanlon Grohl 2017). Given the content, the guests' experience, and a lack of other babysitting help, I conducted the phone interview with my daughter strapped to me, and I began by telling Virginia about this and apologizing in advance in case the little girl interrupted or needed my attention. Virginia was not only empathetic, but spoke directly to my daughter when the infant started to babble during the interview, joking that she had perfect pitch. We later included this interview as an "archive special" for the *Music Mothers and Others* podcast as additional content during a production break in 2020, recording an introduction to explain the earlier context and acknowledge Virginia's book as source material and ongoing inspiration for our research work into parenting and creative industries (Brunt and Giuffre 2020d).

As of July 2021 we were again recording in lockdown in Sydney and with travel restrictions in Melbourne. This time, restrictions on movements outside the home were not quite as strict, so we were able to record outside or in our academic offices (if these were open). For series two I was also able to use a small pool of research-allocated funding to pay an emerging producer, a former audio student of mine, to assist with the consolidation and technical production. Although Shelley and I still did all the pre-production and recording of podcasts (including sourcing guests; writing scripts, social media and website content; and uploading), the student producer, Nina Longfellow, was able to be a fresh "pair of ears" as much as a technical support. The process of training her for the role was also an important learning experience for both her and me, as we moved from a teacher-student relationship to a collegial industry-based relationship. Her background is in music and sound design and communications, but her interest is in the broadness of community media—whatever that will come to mean in the future. By the end of the second season in October 2021, Nina had been paid as producer for the series, and we will apply again for funding for her into the future. She has also gained other paid work subsequent to this, being able to use *Music Mothers and Others* as a launching pad.

THE PODCAST'S CONTENT (OR "FINDINGS")

At a time when we were physically restricted by COVID-19 lockdowns and travel restrictions, the podcast also provided a platform to directly ask creative industry practitioners about their own relationship to industry and its relationship to family life. Lockdown meant creative industry workers and academics needed to rethink how they were able to work, if at all. Conventional support like child care, schooling and going "on tour" (or to an office or other workspace) were not available. In conversation, the changing workplace was being discussed in real time. For example, in our episode with Australian musicians Stephanie Ashworth and Paul Dempsey from the band Something for Kate (Brunt and Giuffre 2020b), the husband-and-wife musical team reflected on their need to continue to make music while unable to tour a new album. As twenty-year veterans of the mainstream Australian music industry, the award-winning artists had returned to making music and touring together after a period away to raise their then small children. They were just about to return to work when the pandemic commenced and lockdown conditions were enforced. However, in the absence of being able to tour, they were able to connect with as broad an audience as they could, remotely, via independent media like our podcast. The domestic conditions also allowed for a candid discussion and invited reflection on the relationship between family and working life. As we sat in our respective domestic spaces with children's toys, instruments, and other work/life apparatus all combined together, it became easier for the artists and the academics to talk, via Zoom, about the shared experience of needing to "cope with the new reality." Shelley and I shared stories of connecting with students remotely, while Stephanie and Paul discussed ways to connect with their fans while not being able to tour live. We also talked in turn about the negotiations we had all made around screen time with our families (that is, where old rules had been broken when deadlines were looming), allowing Stephanie and Paul to reflect on their relationship with their children through musical practice and preferences. In particular, Paul recalled how he had noticed their children listening to his and his partner's work, the children having "taken the iPad into their room or something and gotten on Spotify and they're listening to us [Something For Kate]; they just want to listen to it without us knowing that they're listening to it, so that's kind of cute" (Brunt and Giuffre 2020b, 24:30–24:41). Stephanie explained that "in the lockdown we've been having to listen to our own album a bit, which we don't normally do, but just to approve mixes and all those sorts of technical things…you know [the kids] really get into it, they really go through the journey with us. And in fact, my son was listening to one of our singles yesterday and he said 'Mum, I think I can hear the bass now!'" (Brunt and Giuffre 2020b, 23:52–24:21). This last point Stephanie recalled while laughing, explaining not just that her son could hear her at work (which was relatively unusual), but also his own expectation of being part of the process of musical decision-making—as if his acknowledgment of the bass was also an acknowledgment of the success of the song's final mix.

The ability to pre-record and post-edit podcasts has allowed for a flexibility that other outlets like live broadcasting or performing simply do not. As many of our guests told us, working in those less flexible media spaces has significantly restricted their ability to have work-life balance, with some completely opting out of creative industries during periods of intense parenting/caring responsibilities. Multi-platform artist Alexandra Plim described how her work with her husband, touring DJ Hot Dub Time Machine, had necessarily been put on hold when they had their small children, with the pair deciding he would tour while she stayed home (Brunt and Giuffre 2020e). When lockdown hit and that avenue for work (and also revenue) was paused, a new intensity was placed on her time and their work/life routine. As a visual artist she discussed her need to have an outlet that was her own, and the way this was negotiated—literally around nap times and other processes of "tag-teaming" childcare. Similar periods of change were also described by many of the guests, including journalist Andrew P. Street, and administrators Dale Packard and Heidi Braithwaite. Often these periods of change provide catalysts for career adaptation and change: Packard moved from independent freelance work to formalized arts administration while Braithwaite pivoted in her work life when she had her child to form her own company. As Braithwaite explained, "when he [my son] was about six months old, a friend of mine contacted me and she was managing a band. She said, 'I need a publicist to do this tour, the label won't do it'...that was literally the start of my company. After that I, you know, got a business name and set myself up properly and worked from the kitchen table in my house. And the jobs just kept rolling in. And I just didn't look back...he was actually the motivation it was that I want to—I want him to grow up and see I was able to do this, I wanted to kind of make him proud" (Brunt and Giuffre 2020c, 03:28–04:28).

In some cases, guests talked about dropping out of creative work altogether for a time to accommodate the needs of their families. In addition to negotiations discussed already, then-radio broadcaster and producer Shevonne Hunt described a point when she realized that she would no longer be able to continue her career as a radio broadcaster within the freelance environment she had been in, noting in particular how the demands of either breakfast or drive shifts were simply not compatible with breastfeeding and interrupted nights. Shortly after this realization, however, she appealed to friends on social media for advice, and was able to gain work with a start-up digital radio outlet focused on parenting, for which she helped establish its own (now strong) podcasting arm: "a friend of mine at [ABC] Radio National saw the post, and she'd been offered the job that I was to end up having...it was the absolute best thing for me at that point in my life. I didn't want to have to stay on top of current affairs because I'd been up with a baby all night, I didn't want to wake up and read about death and destruction." (Brunt and Giuffre 2021b, 20:01–20:53). One of our most recognizable guests, Murray Cook—from the original lineup of iconic Australian children's entertainers the Wiggles—explained how it was the needs of his teenage children that helped him decide to retire from that part of his working life. In his episode, Cook, now as part of a new "grown-up" group, the Soul Movers, discussed how he had taken his family on international tour with him at one of the heights of the Wiggles' fame to balance family and creative life: "We were spending, you know, six weeks at a time in America, you know, three times a year. And you know, I really did miss a lot. One tour, we just hired our own bus so that the family could come with us...But yeah, that was a struggle." (Brunt and Giuffre 2021a, 19:46–20:08).

The conversations in the podcast were also opportunities to learn from our guests beyond a conventional researcher-subject relationship. Award-winning Australian Indigenous artist Nardi Simpson provided an important insight into the intersectional demands of the creative arts industry, scholarship (she is herself a Ph.D. candidate) and cultural nuance and heritage (Brunt and Giuffre 2020a). As a Yuwaalaraay writer, composer, musician, and culture keeper, Nardi described in her episode the relationship between being a teacher as a parent and a teacher as an artist, but also being a cultural teacher for her own community and broader Australia. As part of this episode, her frank discussion about the pressures as a woman in these multiple roles particularly resonated, as she (and we as hosts) questioned where and how performing creative work may be thought of as "selfish" in light of the other demands from personal and professional obligations. The nuance of this conversation is extremely difficult to convey in words and text alone, with tone of voice in particular providing important detail, as the calm tone and relatively slow pace of Nardi's delivery drew Shelley and me in as listeners and participants in the podcast. Even while listening again now I am aware of what can be heard in the podcast—the relative pace and urgency in my own voice, as I try to ignore the sound of my son crying in the background and continue the interview, trusting that my husband will attend to him. In contrast, Nardi's advice is provided with an even and direct tone, as she explains how she has learned to "not be hard on herself" and realize how to "not feel guilty about being creative" (Brunt and Giuffre 2020a, 19:19–21:16). With a podcast, the way the words are spoken is just as important as the words themselves, and in conversation Nardi, as a creative artist, academic, parent, and scholar, provides an important counterpoint to my own multiple positions of academic, worker, and parent.

Music Mothers and Others has been careful to consider music in relation to the "village" of child-rearing and family life, too. For example, musician and performer Koko and industry innovator Chris Carey are both guests featured on the podcast who are not parents themselves, but actively incorporate inclusive practices to allow for families to engage with their work. In her episode (Brunt and Giuffre 2020g), Koko explained how as a musician she has a particular passion for creating work that is "child friendly" or "child oriented," as evidenced by her work with the independent Australian group the Pogogo Show and her associated "live with Koko" sessions on social media. Similarly, as an arts administrator and manager, Chris Carey discussed his ambition to make industry events "parent friendly" by ensuring nursing parents and those who need to bring children with them to events were able to be accommodated (Brunt and Giuffre 2020h). Carey's commitment is one I had experienced first-hand, having first met him when I attended his Fast Forward industry conference in Sydney while still on parental leave with my daughter, who was then so small she was strapped to me during the duration of the talks. We discussed this first meeting in the episode and used it as a launching pad to unpack Carey's stance, as he was acutely aware of the potential loss of talented women especially in the music and creative industries when they have children. In this episode Carey also explained his commitment to family life and industry, informed in part by his experiences growing up helping to raise his much younger brother.

THE MUSIC COPYRIGHT "PROBLEM," AND A NICE QUIRK (A.K.A. "HAPPY ACCIDENT" AND EXTRA FINDINGS)

Podcasting has provided a way to reflect and re-engage with parenting and creative practice. One common language to create connections between hosts, guests and audiences for *Music Mothers and Others* has always been music—in its discussion, creation, use as a parenting or family-bonding tool, and for sheer enjoyment. However, gaining copyright clearance to use music in podcasts is complex—owing to the international nature of the publishing form, with music publishers, record companies, and artists often unclear themselves about how to licence works. Even when they are clear, the terms for licensing are themselves confusing—how can an independent podcast say, in clear terms, how long it expects to be "live" or how many listeners in how many territories it will have? And when releasing and creating a podcast for free, where would a budget for such clearances come from, anyway?

In Australia podcasters can purchase a "mini-licence" from the combined industry bodies the Australasian Performing Right Association Limited (APRA) and Australasian Mechanical Copyright Owners Society (AMCOS). Depending on the anticipated revenue to be raised from the podcast, as well as the anticipated listenership and the amount of music to be used, this licence is only a few hundred dollars for a year and covers publishing rights ("Online Mini Music Licence," n.d.). However, this does not cover mechanical copyright—meaning that we can feature music that is written by other people as long as we re-record (or "cover") the work; we have access to the song, but not an existing recording of it.

Many podcast producers faced with this practical restriction around music use simply make their own completely, give up, or—to put it bluntly—"chance it" by using music illegally in the hope that various "fair use" clauses in copyright law will cover them. While we did take this approach in some ways—Shelley wrote and recorded the *Music Mothers and Others* theme tune herself, for example, and we have avoided including pre-existing recorded music in our podcast at all if possible. The one exception is a small snippet of a recording by Nat Bartsch used in the episode featuring her as guest, after a lengthy but ultimately fruitful appeal to her record company, ABC Music. Of course, when we have interviewed artists whose work (and therefore copyright) is completely independently owned, then we have also been able to feature their recordings—as with T. Wilds and Ben Green, for example. We were also free to include music we had recorded and written ourselves, or music that we had recorded ourselves that was otherwise out of copyright (such as common nursery rhymes like "Mary Had a Little Lamb").

As music and media academics, we were determined to work beyond this practical restriction if possible, and have settled on a solution that satisfies the content and context of the podcast. Where possible, Shelley and I now include original recordings of children or families that our guests have made or that we have made ourselves—sounds that illustrate the episodes as well as provide show IDs and edit breaks. In particular, this works well as part of the regular question "The kids and I are listening to...," where we invite guests to talk about co-listening with their families. Following this question (when guests have often spontaneously broken into song as they describe and illustrate this co-listening practice), we have often asked if they were willing to record those sessions and share snippets of them with us for inclusion in the podcast. We began leading by example, with simple voice memo recordings of ourselves talking to/with our children or singing with/to our children. These included songs that we had built relationships with but may not be considered "traditional" children's songs—for example "Rocket Man" by Elton John, which my daughter favoured as a lullaby, or "It's Oh So Quiet" by Björk, which Shelley's daughter enjoyed as a play song.

Our guests also provided examples, and recordings of these. Following Andrew P. Street's discussion about his young son's love of The Cure's "Boys Don't Cry," the young boy's voice singing the song is featured—serving to illustrate the intimacy he talks about in the conversation (as well as being just a lovely moment!). Similarly in his episode Ben Green talks about his son's love of a particular football song, and while the discussion itself is engaging, being able to follow this with an example of the young boy singing the song really brings the episode to life. During the COVID-19 lockdowns in 2021 we invited audience members to contribute their own recordings for this segment, and we anticipate some interesting results.

CONCLUSIONS: WHY PODCAST AS *"MUSIC MOTHERS AND OTHERS"*?

Music Mothers and Others is a hybrid a research-informed podcast that can provide research outputs (or at least preliminary data for future academic inquiry), but it is also an industry-based creative work that meaningfully engages with artists in a diverse range of roles and with a variety of life and work experience. We have deliberately tried to feature a range of genres, generations, genders, and types of "others" as our guests. The podcast has allowed for the communication of academic research interests and experience with a broader audience. Podcasting has also provided a rare way to continue to engage with creative industries as well as continue to meet our obligations as parents of young children. Although the logistics of what it means as an "academic research output" are still in flux, organized at the individual university level, and sometimes even at the individual faculty and school level, if nothing else the practice of making the podcast has provided us with the momentum to stay interested and motivated to complete our other "traditional" academic work, like engaged teaching and peer-reviewed publishing.

Music Mothers and Others is by no means the only podcast to explore the relationships between personal and professional obligations. However, being founded and created under the conditions of pandemic lockdown does make the podcast distinct. Our intention is to continue to create new episodes and engage our audience for as long as is practical, and as long as the feedback we receive continues to be positive. As an additional note, we are especially concerned with ensuring that diversity of experience relating to gender and precarious work is also discussed and openly explored through this project—as women and those in freelance or casual positions, tend to overwhelmingly be those who are engaged with the show's content. As former long-term casuals and contractors in creative industries and then in academia ourselves, we are particularly sensitive to the relative precarity that means participation (or not) in industry is for many not a mere choice, but rather something that circumstances dictate. In many cases, parents, and particularly mothers, may withdraw from creative life altogether. We are careful to acknowledge that continued work in creative industries is difficult for many, particularly women and minoritized people, and we continue to learn from guests who explain to us their periods of rest, change, and complete absence from creative work if necessary, too. The dual demands of family and professional life are complex and individual, and while podcasting as a practice and research tool has provided us with many benefits, we also are aware of the added pressure this can place on already-stretched resources. In response to this, we have continued to make *Music Mothers and Others* into 2022 and 2023, but with fewer episodes per season and adjusted time frames where necessary.

CHAPTER 6

FROM THE IVORS TO THE IVORY TOWER
Using Podcasting to Study Songwriting

SIMON BARBER

S ince its inception after the turn of the millennium, podcasting has achieved increasing acceptance as a method of content distribution (Spinelli and Dann 2019). One of the affordances of podcasting that can be readily observed is the opportunity to gather insights from world-leading professionals and to develop a body of knowledge about their practices. For instance, music podcasts such as *Song Exploder, Switched on Pop*, and my own *Sodajerker on Songwriting*[1] adopt a variety of approaches to document the reflections of notable musicians concerning the processes behind their work. In recent years, these podcasts have become the subject of academic research interrogating their contributions to knowledge about popular music creation (Giuffre 2022; Henderson and Spracklen 2017; Skjerseth 2022). While these podcasts have different ways of presenting and conveying insights into creativity, it is primarily the long-form interview that has been central to my podcasting practice and has fed into academic projects I've initiated around songwriting. I'll return to the importance of this format later in the chapter.

The art and craft of songwriting itself has been explored in mainstream media (Rachel 2013; Seabrook 2015; Zollo 2003), and from a number of perspectives within academia, such as how it has been organized historically

---

1 Simon Barber and Brian O'Connor. *Sodajerker on Songwriting.* https://www
.sodajerker.com.

(Inglis 2003), the importance of creativity (McIntyre 2008), and the dynamics of collaboration (Bennett 2011). Attention to songwriting as a field of study has increased since 2019, following the creation of the Songwriting Studies Research Network (songwritingstudies.com), which unites scholars, industry workers, and practitioners in a forum for the exchange of ideas about songwriting. Drawing on what Stahlke Wall (2016) has called "moderate autoethnography," and with reference to wider critical frameworks from popular music, media, and cultural studies, I use this chapter to explore the role that podcasting has played in the emerging interdisciplinary field of songwriting studies. Focusing on my experiences as a co-creator of the *Sodajerker* podcast, I reflect on the challenges and limitations of making a popular podcast for a general audience while experimenting with podcasting's potential as a research methodology. I am interested in whether podcasting is capable of spanning what Llinares (2018) calls the "liminal space" between practice and theory, mainstream production and academia, and I begin by providing some context about my work as a podcast producer and how this activity connects to my scholarly research. I offer this overview not to bolster my own credentials, but simply to provide some background detail about the podcast that I have been working on for the past twelve years. I then explore some of the key decisions made during my own podcast making and offer critical interpretations of how these factors either contribute to or detract from the podcast's potential to inform wider scholarly initiatives.

REFLECTIONS ON PODCAST MAKING

I first entered the world of podcasting in 2011. At the time, podcasting was less a world than a burgeoning community, with practitioners like me discovering the parameters of the medium through a largely autodidactic process of making and uploading audio content. Though I had been in academia for a couple of years by that point and had questions about the nature of songwriters' creative work, my motivation for starting a podcast was just as much to do with my work as a musician. In 2010, I had formed a songwriting team under the name *Sodajerker* with my long-time creative collaborator, Brian O'Connor. We reasoned that a podcast based around long-form interviews with songwriters might engage a listenership who would come to know us as hosts and then be motivated to care about the songs that we ourselves were writing.

The first episode of *Sodajerker on Songwriting* was published on 9 November 2011 and featured the American songwriter Billy Steinberg in conversation about his writing process and hit songs from his career. The idea was novel at the time and we quickly found an audience. There are now more than 250 episodes available, featuring a variety of well-known songwriters, from Sir Paul McCartney, Burt Bacharach, Alicia Keys, Paul Simon, and Sting to St. Vincent, Beck, Elvis Costello, Nile Rodgers, Jon Bon Jovi, Lindsey Buckingham, and Diane Warren. As the years passed, the podcast became more embedded in UK music culture. In 2016, we were commissioned by the BBC World Service to produce a radio documentary entitled *The Secrets of Songwriting*. In 2019, we were asked to attend and record a special episode about the Ivor Novello Awards, a prestigious ceremony, held annually in London, which has honoured excellence in songwriting since 1956. In 2020, we reached a further milestone when our ongoing audio archive was added to the British Library's Sound and Moving Image Catalogue. Today, the podcast has achieved almost ten million downloads and has charted in more than eighty countries (Chartable).

During the course of creating the *Sodajerker* podcast, I obtained a large volume of information about songwriting and creativity, which I explored through academic articles and book chapters. These publications examined key themes identified by our subjects, such as the ways professional songwriters rationalize their emotional investment in their work (Long and Barber 2015); the history of organized approaches to song production (Barber 2016); how songwriters conceptualize creativity while working within the wider infrastructure of the music industries (Long and Barber 2017); strategies and techniques for song generation (Barber 2017); and the role of the recording studio in songwriting (Barber 2020). However, it was not until 2018 that my colleague Dr. Mike Jones and I were able to draw on the body of knowledge produced via the *Sodajerker* podcast to help frame the study of songwriting as an interdisciplinary academic field. Funded by the Arts and Humanities Research Council (AHRC), the Songwriting Studies Research Network launched in March 2019, bringing together academics, practitioners, and industry workers for conversations about the value of songwriting to a variety of stakeholders. Events held during the first few years of the network focused on themes such as practice and production, streaming and sustainability, and motivations for songwriting. As indicated previously, these themes emerged directly from the voices of professional songwriters speaking on the *Sodajerker* podcast, and were then consolidated through academic scholarship.

Alongside the literature on songwriting, there is a growing body of work dealing with the study of podcasting in a range of contexts: for example, its historical development and the growth of the field of podcast studies (Berry 2015; Llinares, Fox, and Berry 2018a; Spinelli and Dann 2019); listener motivation, participation, preference, and use (Chan-Olmsted and Wang 2020; McClung and Johnson 2010; Perks, Turner, and Tollison 2019; Wrather 2016); podcasting's relationship to radio and listening (Markman 2015; McHugh

2016; Nyre 2015); the motivations of podcast producers (Markman 2012; Markman and Sawyer 2014; Hamilton and Barber 2022); and podcasting as a research methodology (Kinkaid, Brain, and Senanayake 2020; Lundström and Lundström 2020; Mollett et al. 2017). In this chapter, I focus on the process of podcast making and the complexities involved in creating content that is intended to be useful in more than one context. The *Sodajerker* podcast is intended for an audience of songwriters and music fans, and acts as a resource for scholars interested in studying songwriting from a variety of interdisciplinary perspectives.

While podcasting has long been used in academia as a tool to augment learning (Heilesen 2010) and more recently to disseminate the findings of research projects (Mollett et al. 2017), using insights from podcast interviews as the foundation for a new area of research is a relatively under-explored area of the literature. It is in this space that I locate my reflections on practice. As I document and reflect on my own experiences in podcasting, I draw on autoethnography, a method of qualitative inquiry incorporating reflexivity and personal narrative. This approach has been subject to some criticism for its tendency towards self-indulgence, fuzzy use of terms like *autobiography* and *narrative*, and a lack of evidence of sociological contribution (Stahlke Wall 2016, 6). However, Stahlke Wall also argues that by taking a systematic approach, linking personal experience to social, cultural, and political issues, while maintaining a critical view of dominant discourses and an awareness of ethical issues, one can better justify the use of this label and also provide enough analytical rigour (in this case from engagement with wider conceptual thinking) that the focus on the researcher's experiences is not understood as self-absorption.

Although podcast interviews are ostensibly no different than any other kind of interview, the premise of *Sodajerker on Songwriting* is that it obtains access to leading practitioners and subjects them to a rigorous line of questioning about creative process. The podcast is then made available to an active audience of professional songwriters, amateur enthusiasts, and music fans who consume the information and make use of key insights or lessons in their own practice. The production and consumption of the podcast by its primary audience and the impact it has for listeners is therefore relatively straightforward. However, relying on podcast interviews as an evidence base for research necessitates a greater level of awareness and understanding of the layers of mediation involved in their creation. I explore this problem in the remaining sections of the chapter by reflecting on my experiences of making the *Sodajerker* podcast. I consider how the concept of independence informs editorial decisions and the economic status of the show; how narratives constructed by podcast guests evolve through interventions like editing—but also through the need for creative workers to reassert their status as creative workers; and how live podcast events can be used to further bridge the gap between industry and academia.

INDEPENDENCE IN PODCAST PRODUCTION

In popular music studies, independence is a concept that continues to wield power, particularly in relation to DIY music cultures such as punk (O'Connor 2008) or forms of alternative rock described as "indie," which are closely tied to the philosophies and practices of independent record labels (Kennedy and McNutt 1999; Strachan 2007). Typically, the use of the term *independent* suggests that an artist, band, or organization has rejected the economic and cultural machinations of major labels in order to retain control of its work. However, in reality, the complex nature of acquisition, ownership, and distribution within the music industries means that this is not always the case (den Drijver and Hitters 2017).

Podcasting has also been understood as a space where utopian ideas of democratization, authenticity, and self-expression have flourished (Sullivan 2018). One of podcasting's key attributes is how it facilitates the discursive practice of meaning making. As songwriters ourselves, my partner, Brian, and I came to podcasting with a natural curiosity about why people write songs, how the work is done, and what it means to spend a lifetime pursuing a creative act. To answer these questions, we independently embarked upon creating a series of conversations with professional songwriters. By publishing these conversations in the form of podcast episodes, we regularly share new insights with a community who has become engaged both conceptually and practically through the answers our guests provide. Members of the podcast's audience frequently engage with us via social media or email to discuss how they have absorbed new approaches, strategies, and techniques in their own work, and evolved their thinking about creativity. This feedback is important as it helps us as podcast makers to understand how the information is taken up, and the impact it has in the lives and work of our listeners.

In keeping with this philosophy of independence, the structure, editing style, and marketing of the *Sodajerker* podcast emerges from a two-person DIY operation. We rely primarily on regular communication with each other and our own intuition to decide how we should describe and present the material contained within the episodes and the tone we adopt on social media. All of the work of creating the podcast's episodes, including research, recording, editing, and promotion, is therefore carried out by the co-presenters. Following the model of commercial radio, where the viability of a media enterprise typically depends on acquiring listeners to sell to advertisers (Barnard

2000), podcasting has, since its inception, sought to develop relationships between advertisers and consumers (Vilceanu, Johnson, and Burns 2021). However, in the case of the *Sodajerker* podcast, an awareness of the ethical principles of academic research, and a desire for independence and control have meant that we have not accepted sponsorship for any of its more than 250 episodes to date and don't incorporate advertising messages. Instead, the podcast operates on the basis of a voluntary donation system, which has a dedicated space on the *Sodajerker* website. This approach has consistently provided enough capital to cover the costs of production, without requiring us to interrupt the listening experience. By way of contrast, the requirements of commercial advertising on podcasts can often involve the insertion of external audio segments at pre-roll, mid-roll, and post-roll locations in a program. This can mean less time spent talking about the topic at hand, and an emphasis on decision-making that prioritizes the agendas of sponsors. For example, commercial podcast producers frequently spend time monitoring the CPM (cost per thousand) of user exposure to advertising messages and the conversion rates of listeners on sponsor sign-up pages, and are under pressure to tailor their content to appeal to the largest possible audience. While we are not against relationships with sponsors that require less intrusive methods of advertising, such a situation is generally undesirable for us if it has the potential to compromise decision-making about the content.

To combat this issue, expenses are kept to a minimum. Unlike some commercial podcasts, which require a staff and therefore must generate a significant income to fund the enterprise, costs incurred making the *Sodajerker* podcast are minimal, and primarily for audio hosting via the Libsyn podcast platform and membership for premium video-chat services like Zoom. Since the COVID-19 pandemic, travel for interviews has been seldom. This allows the podcast to remain sustainable and assert its independence from economic control. This does mean, though, that the podcast is not a profitable enterprise and will always require a personal subsidy of unpaid time and effort. This situation is also indicative of the position of privilege that we occupy as people who make their living from other forms of work. My co-presenter, Brian, is a professional musician and I am a salaried academic working within a UK university. As a result, we are able to devote time and resources to the podcast without worrying too much about its economic status. This might not be the case for full-time podcasters, or those of lesser means, who might only be able to sustain their podcasts by accepting outside support. And of course, there are independent podcasts for whom sponsorship generates a substantial income, and those that obtain prestige through being popular enough to sustain the interest and support of advertisers. Independent status, then, can be complicated and shouldn't be equated with an absence of commercial support.

To add further nuance, it is important not to overlook the fact that despite my attempts at transparency, *Sodajerker on Songwriting* is made primarily for a general audience of music fans and it exists and functions as part of the promotional infrastructure of the music industries. As such, there are a range of responsibilities involved with meeting the needs of guests and their representatives, and these considerations inevitably inform the delivery of the product. For example, the vast majority of our interviews are agreed to as the result of pitches received from publicists working on promotional campaigns for forthcoming record releases. Such agents often request that the publication of press activity should take place on or around the release date of the record, or at least within the time-limited scope of the campaign. In order to maximize exposure for the episodes and maintain our reputation with these partners, we typically plan the production schedule to meet these requests. Usually there is no editorial control demanded by third parties, though it is expected that we will mention forthcoming releases or tours in a promotional context. As a result of these relationships, there is always the potential for the agendas of publicists, managers, and artists to narrow the scope of our insights into the creative work. Moreover, changes made in response to any demands could impact the podcast's potential to contribute to scholarly initiatives.

As independent podcast producers, Brian and I are fortunate to be able to take a broad view of songwriting craft, regardless of genre, resulting in an archive that includes episodes focused on songs from Disney films, musical theatre, rock, pop, country, rap, and jazz. Despite this inclusive stance, we still require a steady flow of high-profile guests with new work to promote who are willing to talk at length about creativity. As such, we are subject to their availability and their receptiveness to engage with the topics we propose to them. Despite attempts to stimulate diversity by pursuing and booking guests directly, the majority of high-profile guests offered to us through publicists in the UK and the US take the form of established white male artists working in prominent genres like those listed above.[2] This situation highlights long-standing inequalities within the music industries, and raises questions about the extent to which gender, race, and genre might affect an artist's chances of being understood as a songwriter. From a scholarly perspective, it reveals the limitations and potential harm of building a body of knowledge around the ideas and concepts of those whose voices are most prominent, and the danger of unconscious bias resulting from our own musical tastes and preferences. It is therefore incumbent upon us to use our independence

---

2   During our run of 258 shows to date, just sixty guests have identified as women and thirty as people of colour.

to make better decisions in the production process in order to increase not only the diversity of voices made available to listeners, but also the richness of the data available for study. As the podcast continues to grow, the concept of independence remains a productive lens for critical reflection about the usefulness of podcast interviews as research.

SHAPING SONG STORIES

As Llinares, Fox, and Berry (2018a) demonstrate, over the past fifteen years, podcasting has come into its own as a new aural culture, and one in which narrative is absolutely central. Storytelling abounds in fiction and non-fiction podcasts like *Welcome to Night Vale* and *Blockbuster*, but stories are also an important part of podcasts, like *Sodajerker on Songwriting*, that utilize an interview-based format. Indeed, we often seek to draw out the stories contained within song lyrics, but perhaps more importantly, the stories about how a song was written. By studying what songwriters say about the process, and by thinking critically about narratives of song creation, we can get closer to understanding songwriting practice. The songwriter interview provides a window into that process. And yet, through the telling (and retelling) of stories and the process of podcast editing, there is the potential for these narratives to be shaped and their meanings transformed, which can compromise the integrity of the data.

As a podcast producer, I am regularly faced with questions about my own agency in the process. While I endeavour to record conversations in which guests feel that they can express themselves authentically and at length, the editing process presents me with an opportunity to "optimize" these performances. This can involve not only improving the clarity and legibility of the sound via post-production processing, but also the removal of non sequiturs, repeated words, crosstalk, coughing, and other aspects of speech that might restrict effective communication.[3] This situation leaves me with a number of questions. For instance: To what extent do my interventions transform the narrative or its meaning? Would we reach different conclusions about the intended meaning if the raw audio was transcribed verbatim? Should we therefore consider the edited media product inauthentic in a research context? With a research agenda in mind, it is essential that every effort is made

---

3   Some might rightly argue that natural components of speech (such as repetition for emphasis, or a passionate intake of breath) can enhance communication, but I am referring primarily here to those elements that tend to divert attention from the point being made, such as unnecessary repetition, sentences without conclusions, interruptions, coughing, irrelevant background noises, or audio distortions like mouth clicks and plosives.

to ensure that editing is limited to enhancing listenability and is not focused on placing emphasis on minor themes, or dramatically transforming the tone or meaning of the artist's discourse. One notable example in the *Sodajerker* catalogue is episode eighty-three featuring rapper Scroobius Pip, who speaks with a stammer (Barber and O'Connor 2018). Although one could argue that listenability might be enhanced through the smoother flow provided by editing, I chose instead to preserve the authentic expression of his natural speech. As a result, I did not edit any of the instances in which Pip stuttered during our conversation. From this experience, I concluded that each case must be considered on an individual basis in order to find the best way to represent the guest and their intentions.

As I've argued elsewhere (Long and Barber 2015), an ability to articulate one's expertise is an important part of the professional songwriter's repertoire. However, stories can change over time, so it's also important to be careful about uncritically accepting what we are told about songs. Bennett (2013) confirms that due to their reliance on memory, retrospective interviews can be problematic, and we must not take at face value every story that places a creative person in a good light artistically or personally. After all, in the music industries the ability to conjure a hit song out of the ether is highly prized. The podcast interview therefore presents an opportunity for the professional songwriter to assert, or renew, their status and identity as one of those who can consistently deliver. In her work on signalling expertise, Candace Jones (2002, 213) says: "An identity showcases an individual's aesthetic style and creative skills. Competency is gleaned from a performance history that exhibits requisite skills and commercial viability." Professional songwriters, especially those that are also recognizable performers or celebrities, are well-practised in the art of giving interviews. They construct and tell song stories, and these narratives contribute to our understanding not only of the songs, but also of who they are as professionals. Passionate responses to the work from audiences also help determine the meaning of songs in the wider culture. Over time, these responses often become woven into the narrative that accompanies accounts of the songs' creation.

Depending on context, podcast interviews can also provoke different kinds of responses than those given in other forms of media interview. For example, when compared with a television interview on a news program or mainstream chat show, the long-form audio podcast can be a space to expand and add nuance. If a guest is familiar with the mission and style of the *Sodajerker* podcast, they may share expanded stories about songs that they would normally abbreviate because they know that listeners will appreciate the additional detail. This is apparent in Dan Wilson's account of co-writing Adele's hit song "Someone Like You," in which he describes not only the writing and recording process, but also reactions to the song from family members, record label personnel and Adele's fan base (Barber and O'Connor 2015). Caution is still required though, because in the process of telling a compelling story, the teller may simplify it to convey a more logical chronology of what, in reality, is often a messy set of interactions and processes. *Sodajerker* listeners have reported that they sometimes detect that a guest is giving routine answers to initial questions until they are audibly "unlocked" by a detailed line of questioning about their craft. One such example is episode seventy-two of the *Sodajerker* podcast with singer-songwriter Gilbert O'Sullivan, who comments on the level of research underpinning the conversation, and explains that he is normally asked questions about trivial matters such as his distinctive hair-style (Barber and O'Connor 2015b).

Even when utilizing a semi-structured approach to interviewing, there can be a variety of reasons why certain avenues of inquiry might not be explored at all in the context of a podcast episode. These can include restrictions provided by publicists (though this is rare), time constraints around access to the guest, the limitations of effective follow-up when using video-chat software online, or sensitivity to the artist's privacy. For these reasons, the shaping of song stories (or indeed any narrative-based audio material used in a program) can happen in both direct and indirect ways. This can limit the reliability of the source material as evidence for research unless it is presented and understood within its proper context and as a product of its limitations.

PODCASTING AND LIVE EVENTS

Another important aspect of my podcast making has been the process of recording live podcasts at public events. When the Songwriting Studies Research Network launched in March 2019, Scottish singer-songwriter KT Tunstall attended our inaugural event at the Royal Birmingham Conservatoire to record a live interview. Our second event, which took place at the Ivors Academy, London, in August of the same year, welcomed songwriter and producer Nile Rodgers in conversation about his practice.[4] Unlike our conventional process in which a *Sodajerker* interview is recorded privately and then edited and released, having these esteemed artists present in person for live podcast recordings facilitated the sharing of knowledge directly with members of industry, academia, and the public in a Q & A format. Through this dialogue, the ideas and experiences of audience members were incorporated into the data gathered, helping to bridge the gap between industry and academia.

---

4   The Ivors Academy is a professional association for songwriters and composers in the UK, and is responsible for the annual Ivor Novello Awards.

The subsequent audio recordings were then made available to a global audience via the *Sodajerker* podcast, evincing podcasting's capacity to gather and disseminate knowledge within and beyond the ivory tower of academia.

What is interesting about these events is that it is unlikely that members of our research community would have had the opportunity to put questions to these artists without leveraging the reputation of the *Sodajerker* podcast and the professional relationships it has produced. In that sense, the research network's access to leading professionals is made possible because of the podcast's dual status as a form of popular entertainment. And yet, as indicated in the previous section of this chapter, the fact that the podcast is part of the media infrastructure of the music industries means that outside forces could potentially limit the potential of the data as research. For instance, for personal reasons, a guest may not wish to discuss songs written with a particular co-writer, and the management or publicist for the artist would likely indicate these no-go areas in advance. In this sense, podcast interviews, whether recorded live or not, are no different than any other form of data gathering where one needs to respect ethical boundaries.

The face-to-face interaction that takes place between a guest and audience members in a live recording scenario can make the recorded output seem less significant. However, since there is never likely to be any sort of completely unmediated scenario in which leading professionals will share their experiences at length, even in a live context, value can be extracted from this data by cross-referencing it against the body of knowledge already accumulated. This enables the researcher to observe subtle variations in the descriptions provided and come to an overall understanding about the ways in which this form of creativity works. To a large extent, one must approach the recording of the podcast with the goal of making an engaging piece of media that the audience will connect with, rather than with the aim of meeting one's methodological objectives. The dual status of the podcast as both a piece of entertainment and a repository of information about creative work is facilitated by keeping some distance between those two modes of capture and analysis. The core aim of the *Sodajerker* podcast is to find out as much as possible about the creative process of songwriting, and researchers can use insights from the interviews in a variety of scholarly contexts. As such, there is no fixed line of questioning that serves a particular research agenda. Once again, it is more important to be cognizant of the context in which an interview takes place, the subject's reasons for selecting and telling particular stories over others, and the potential for the editing process to reduce a complex narrative to a simple message.

We must also not forget that the location and context for live events determines much about who attends, the issues lined up for discussion and ultimately what transpires. Situating our second gathering at the Ivors

Academy—an independent trade body representing the interests of songwriters and composers—brought with it a set of connotations about the profile of the event, audience demographics, the issues that were important to the members, and the approaches taken to address them. And so, operating within this liminal space between academia and industry also requires awareness of how social, economic, and political ideas and experiences might interact in different environments. By being sensitive to the needs of all parties and the demands placed upon them, we increase the potential to narrow the divisions between our communities and to enhance the usefulness of podcasting as a tool for data gathering. I've found Wenger's (2010) work on communities of practice to be a useful guide to navigating these kinds of dynamics and potential conflicts of interest:

> The body of knowledge of a profession is not merely a curriculum. It is a whole landscape of practices—involved not only in practising the profession, but also in research, teaching, management, regulation, professional associations, and many other contexts...The composition of such a landscape is dynamic as communities emerge, merge, split, compete, complement each other, and disappear. And the boundaries between the practices involved are not necessarily peaceful or collaborative. What researchers find, what regulators dictate, what management mandates, what clients expect, and what practitioners end up deciding, all these attempts to colonize moments of practice can be in conflict. (Wenger 2010, 183)

When considering the landscape of practices that constitute the nascent field of songwriting studies (whether it be professional practice, research, or teaching), podcasting, and especially podcasting at live events, has been an effective method for engaging audiences from a variety of perspectives and facilitating the creation of a body of knowledge. By enabling close interaction between academics, industry workers, and practitioners, podcasting has enhanced the dynamic nature of the field. And yet, as Wenger indicates, we must remain vigilant about recognizing how different needs and agendas can be in conflict, and when we might be in danger of compromising the integrity of the research to serve a particular audience.

As a result of staging live events incorporating the use of podcasting, the field of songwriting studies has continued to expand. A further four meetings took place online during the COVID-19 pandemic, and these have been distributed online as video content. Through these gatherings, scholars, songwriters, and industry workers made a variety of theoretical and practical contributions to the community. Building on the initial emphasis on professional practice codified through the *Sodajerker* podcast, scholars working in the field are diversifying the scope of work that falls under the umbrella of songwriting studies. For example, researchers are placing an emphasis on exploring non-commercial applications of songwriting established in prior literature, such as work on music therapy (Baker 2015), songwriting as a tool for self-actualization, social change, and well-being (Cobb 2016), and songwriting as a form of protest (Katz-Rosene 2020). The growth of interest in these related areas of practice highlights the effectiveness of podcasting as a vehicle for expanding scholarly initiatives and reaching audiences within and beyond academia.

CONCLUSIONS

My intention with this chapter has been to critically reflect on whether a body of knowledge about songwriting practice, produced through the mediated process of podcast making, and located in the liminal space between practice and theory, could be foundational to the development of an academic field and help galvanize a community. By drawing on broader frameworks from popular music, media, and cultural studies, I've offered a reflexive account of my podcast experiences and its relationship to research. With detailed consideration of the limitations of this proposition, I have shown that a body of knowledge produced by the practice of podcast making can be effectively used, not only as a resource for academic research, but as the basis for theoretical and conceptual development.

The *Sodajerker* podcast was one of the earliest songwriting podcasts to emerge, and because of our awareness of the principles of academic research, we made some specific choices in format and structure that have enabled the podcast to function both as a popular form of entertainment and as a repository for information that researchers can use to study what songwriters say about the creative process. Unlike a podcast like *Song Exploder*, which uses a heavily edited documentary style to construct the narrative of a song's creation, *Sodajerker* is based around long-form conversations with songwriters, utilizing a semi-structured format that allows space to reflect on the process and elucidate the nuances and complexities of how a song came to be. This is not to say that *Sodajerker on Songwriting* is the only podcast that affords songwriters such opportunities; indeed several have emerged that can also be used as a source of data for research. However, the philosophies that underpin the *Sodajerker* podcast are important factors in its success, and have been unwavering since its inception. These principles could therefore be seen as recommendations for best practice when using podcasting to study a creative practice like songwriting. They can be summarized as follows:

1. The podcast should remain independent and non-commercial in an attempt to limit the power of outside forces to shape the content.
2. Interviews should be the product of a detailed research process which is evidenced in the specific kinds of questions asked of the guest. The *Sodajerker* podcast also provides a detailed introduction to the guest as a way to set the context for the interview and to solidify details that might otherwise be overlooked or assumed in conversation.
3. The podcast host(s) should come to the interview from a place of knowledge and expertise. *Sodajerker* is based on the premise that songwriters are talking to fellow songwriters. Guests intuitively or explicitly understand this and can therefore go further creatively and conceptually with their answers than they can in other interview contexts.
4. Post-production processes such as editing should be limited to making the interview as re-listenable as possible in terms of clarity of communication, but should never be about restructuring the content to transform the original meaning or create a new narrative, unless that is the purpose of the overarching research.

Songwriting has an elemental meaning in the lives of artists, industry workers, and scholars around the world. By developing a community around songwriting as research via my own podcast, I've discovered new insights about the craft, its purpose and place in the lives of practitioners, and how it transcends boundaries of geography, language, and culture. As actors in a global network made up of varied perspectives, disciplines, and approaches, we should continue to interrogate podcasting as a methodology for building a body of knowledge so others can access it, use it in their own practice, or expand upon it to enhance a community's understanding. There is still much more to be done to establish and consolidate songwriting studies, and to explore how the affordances of podcasting can draw research and practice closer to each other. I hope that this account of my practice has helped illuminate the value and significance of podcasting in my own work, and of the medium's capacity to disseminate knowledge within and beyond the ivory tower of academia. It is my view that embedding podcast making within academic research initiatives can contribute to the production of new knowledge and shorten the distance between theory and practice, and this bodes well for the future of podcast studies as a field in its own right.

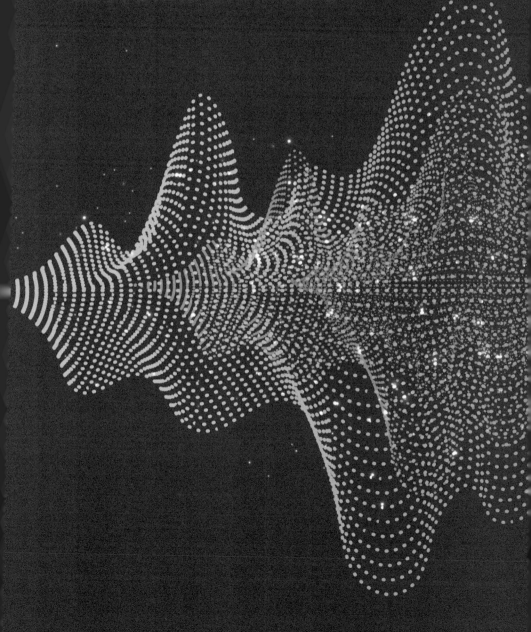

PART TWO

PODCASTING AS
SOCIAL AND
CULTURAL PRACTICE

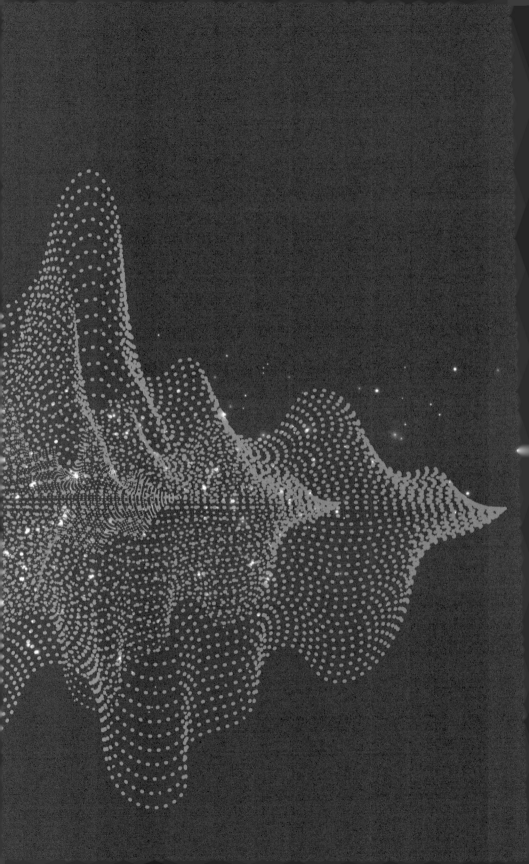

CHAPTER 7

THE KITCHEN TABLE IS ALWAYS WHERE WE ARE

Podcasting as Feminist Self-Reflexive Practice

STACEY COPELAND, HANNAH McGREGOR, and KATHERINE McLEOD

INTRODUCTION: INVITING RESPONSIVENESS

On a Friday afternoon in June, we—Hannah, Stacey, and Katherine—sat down for a Zoom conversation about podcasting as feminist practice. As three feminist scholars and podcasters, this topic—the intersection of our feminism and our podcasting—is something we've often addressed tacitly in our previous collaborations. But this was our first time creating space to explicitly theorize our feminist podcasting practice. We recorded our conversation, ran it through transcription software, and—having talked for over two hours—discovered that we had nearly nineteen thousand words. Seeing the word count reaffirmed what we had felt by the end of the conversation: that we had made something by talking. Our conversation examined how feminist podcasting values process over product, listening as a collective making, and sonic place-making as community building. Our approach, then, to working with the transcription of this conversation foregrounds the fact that our analyses are contingent upon their places within the conversation. In insisting on the importance of context, we are building upon a fundamental principle of standpoint feminism: that knowledge is always situated in relation to the contexts through which it is generated.[1] Our method for presenting this chapter on the page mirrors the dialogic potential within the podcast as a form itself:[2] "The medium's hybridity of thought, sound and text perhaps even fosters a reinvigoration of the dialectic, an exchange of ideas beyond what is possible in purely written form...[with] podcast 'space' engendering a forum for discussion that is not defined by the culture of instantaneous reaction" (Llinares, Fox, and Berry 2018b, 2). With its roots in conversation, our written chapter recreates a dialectic space in which we listen to each other talk about how podcasting *is* a feminist self-reflexive practice. By "feminist self-reflexive practice," we mean a feminist practice that is always in-process. Self-reflexivity demands "the self-conscious *analytical* scrutiny of the self as researcher" (England 1994, 244, emphasis in original), and we argue that podcasting as a feminist practice invites and even requires that self-scrutiny.

While we are resistant to define or limit feminist podcasting as a field or approach, podcast studies as an emergent discipline has been foundational in the study of gender and sound (Copeland 2018a; Hyland Wang 2021; Richardson and Green 2018). This chapter speaks back to this dialogue in an attempt to articulate a feminist politic of podcasting in practice. Resembling a kind of dialogic autotheory (Fournier 2021), our conversation begins with each of us examining the combination of personal and theoretical decisions that have guided our own feminist practices in podcasting. By producing our chapter through a self-reflexive form of feminist collaboration, we position feminist practices within podcasting as being in a state of continual learning, building, listening, and rebuilding sonic spaces that embody feminist politics.[3] In the conversation that follows, we begin by theorizing our own podcasting work in

---

1   We have kept the transcription in its original order for this reason, with each of us editing our own dialogue and then collectively writing the theoretical scaffolds that support each section and that elucidate key concepts. We have also created a playlist (pages 122–24) in which the selected tracks will sonically demonstrate the content being discussed and could be listened to while reading or afterwards.

2   We use the metaphor of the mirror deliberately here, recognizing that a written text by its very nature cannot be identical to a recorded conversation. While the transcription of a podcast is not the same thing as the podcast itself, it also has an undeniable relationship to that podcast, functioning as a kind of representation of the podcast that, like a reflection in a mirror, should not be mistaken for the original, but nonetheless provides vital information about the original. (For more on the complex relationship of transcription to podcasts, see Llinares 2020d.)

3   While we refuse to explicitly prescribe what counts as feminist podcasting or feminist politics, it is critical to note that our collective knowledge on feminist politics is drawn from scholars including Sara Ahmed (*Living a Feminist Life*), bell hooks (*Feminism Is for Everybody: Passionate Politics*), Audre Lorde (*Sister Outsider*), Erin Wunker (*Notes from a Feminist Killjoy: Essays on Everyday Life*), Judith Butler (*Gender Trouble*), Kate Eichhorn, (*The Archival Turn in Feminism: Outrage in Order*), Alexis Pauline Gumbs (*Undrowned: Black Feminist Lessons from Marine Mammals*), and many more.

terms of embodied making, archival listening, and invitations to responsiveness. We then propose some potential feminist articulations of podcasting: as
place-making via the metaphor of the kitchen table, as the enactment of a feminist listening ear, and as the creation of an archive of feminist possibilities.

·ı|ı·ı|ı·ı|ı·

Hannah McGregor: I've suggested that we begin by each outlining our own
case studies, and describing the experience and practice we're bringing into
this conversation. And Stacey, you're the obvious person to start, because this
paper was your idea!

Stacey Copeland: The project I am focusing on for this discussion is the
audio documentary I'm making as part of the methodological process of my
dissertation work [Copeland 2022]. The documentary is tentatively titled
"Lavender Sounds: The Audio Archives." The project takes on an intergenerational dialogue with early lesbian community radio makers here in Canada,
particularly *The Lesbian Show* and *Dykes on Mykes*, which were both on air
for decades—*The Lesbian Show* from the 1970s and *Dykes on Mykes* since the
eighties into the 2010s.[4] I'm bringing my conversations with these audio
makers, their reflections on and personal experiences of making lesbian and
feminist audio into conversation with what's happening today in contemporary queer podcasting.

To do so, I'm talking with feminist activists and makers in the podcast
community—folks like the producers behind *The Heart and Queer Public*[5]—
to ask: How are the ways that we're approaching audio media from a feminist
perspective changing? How are they the same? What might we learn from lesbian radio activist histories to help cultivate our approaches to media making
today and for the future?

Podcast production is a way to keep checks on my own bias. It's a way
to reflect on the actual voice and soundings of my research participants and
their work. One aspect of my reflexive approach, for example, is keeping an
audio diary throughout the research and writing process. So I have little, what
I would call "confessionals" before and after each interview that I conduct.

Hannah: What really stands out to me in your description is how the metaphor

---

4   *The Lesbian Show* was founded in 1979 at Vancouver Co-op Radio, and *Dykes on*
     Mykes was founded at CKUT Montreal in 1987. For more on *The Lesbian Show* and
     Dykes on Mykes see Stacey Copeland (2018b).
5   See playlist tracks (pages 122–24) one and two.

of "putting things into conversation" becomes literal in your methods. We talk a lot about putting things into conversation, but we so rarely—at least in the disciplines in which I'm trained—actually facilitate conversation as part of that practice.

Stacey: Yeah, and I'm trying to get my interviewees to be in conversation with their past selves as well. All of my participants from *The Lesbian Show* and *Dykes on Mykes*, we listen back together to clips in our interview sessions that I've selected from their shows, say thirty years ago. We listen together to bring them back into that space; I ask them to reflect with me on the context surrounding the clip and how it makes them feel. I give them a bit of my reasoning behind why I chose particular clips to listen to together. I then listen to those same show clips with contemporary podcasters. We listen to the same clips I listened to with the folks from, say, *The Lesbian Show*[6] and reflect on what it's like to listen to that from their perspective and their logic as queer audio producers. So that's one of the ways there's a type of intergenerational conversation taking place in my work.

Hannah: I'm just now realizing how much your project is structured around careful listening to archival audio. I hadn't realized how closely tied it is to what Katherine's doing in her *ShortCuts* series, especially in terms of how we engage with feminist histories through the act of careful archival listening, and how reflecting on what we hear can become a way of being in conversation with that historical audio.

Katherine McLeod: That's true. As you are describing that archival listening in your work, Stacey, you've got me thinking about how the historical audio becomes a sonic place. All participants in the dialogue are inhabiting that sonic place for that moment in time when they're listening to it together with you. That means it is a way to sonically bridge generations, to bridge historical moments—and to feel like you are all connected to that moment in time while listening to it. It is like sharing the same text, but in this case it is much more visceral. Do you sit together and listen to it, or do you listen in advance?

Stacey: We sit together and listen. The plan was originally to do it in person before the COVID-19 pandemic meant shifting online. There's a certain reflection I'm going to have to do on how video conferencing factors into that experience of place-making as well. Listening in different spaces,

---

6   See playlist track three.

often our homes, which then amplify and reverberate the same sounds in different ways. There's one clip in particular that I've played for quite a few interviewees,[7] a 1991 audio collage commemorating the one-year anniversary of the Sex Garage raid in Montreal—a familiar story of bathhouse and queer bar raids across North America, where the nightclub known as Sex Garage got raided and a bunch of folks in the queer community got beaten and arrested by police. There were mass protests after that in Montreal, and on the one-year anniversary, *Dykes on Mykes* aired the collage as well as an accompanying audio portrait of a protest kiss-in event. So there are all these sounds of, you know, women and folks smooching, and then making like kissy-face noises and lip-smacking noises; and they're like, "Is that what kissing sounds like?" because they're trying to figure out how to capture the *feel* of the event in sound. I've been listening back to that clip quite a bit with interviewees, especially folks from *The Heart*, a show rooted in playing with the limits of intimacy in audio. What does it mean to listen back to some of those practices, whether we consider them successful or failed? What does it mean to try and bring queer intimacy into the audio space and into our feminist politics?

Hannah: I love the way you're thinking here about the intense isolation of the pandemic, and how the shared practice of listening can become a way of occupying a shared space. Collective listening is a remarkably powerful and affectively charged activity.

Katherine: Yes, collective listening, which can take place in the classroom too as a way of demonstrating that listening functions as an interpretative method.[8]

Hannah: Katherine, since we're on the topic of collective listening and archival audio, would you like to talk a little bit about *ShortCuts*?

Katherine: The story of *ShortCuts* starts with listening collectively to archival audio and with making-as-listening. In 2018–2019, I curated SpokenWeb's Ghost Reading Series at Concordia University, in which we would gather to listen collectively to the entire recording of a poetry reading from the Sir George Williams Poetry Series (1966–1974), and we would make things: we took notes, drew, painted, crafted handmade books made with materials from the events,

---

7   See playlist track four.
8   See Nicole Brittingham Furlonge (2018) on aural pedagogy in *Race Sounds: The Art of Listening in African American Literature*.

and recorded everything.[9] Listening was making, and making was listening. I also was curating clips for SpokenWeb's Audio of the Week for the blog; then, thanks to your generous invitation, Hannah and Stacey, I turned the Audio of the Week blog posts into a short-form podcast on the *SpokenWeb Podcast* feed. That first episode in January 2020 was also the first audio that I had produced, recording it in my closet and editing the rough audio in Hindenburg before sending it over to Stacey.[10] By the time of the second season, I had more formally conceptualized *ShortCuts* as a deep dive—via short "cuts" of archival sound—into the audio collections of SpokenWeb. The "cut" invokes the practices of cutting and splicing tape, reminding listeners of the media history of the recordings.

As *ShortCuts* evolved, as did my audio production skills, I could explore what the series could do as feminist audio. That meant purposefully selecting recordings of feminist poets, and emphasizing in my commentary the embodied elements of their sound or the poems. These embodied aspects could really be brought to the forefront in a close listening to a clip of archival sound.[11]

Stacey: You really have me thinking about how we can come to communicate different modes of feminist podcasting practice that are not just explicitly feminist, but also discreetly feminist, and what that might sound like. It seems the feminist approach to creating *ShortCuts* is less concerned with explicitly naming it as a feminist show, and more about consciously infusing what could otherwise be quite a white male–dominated series with feminist voices and women's embodied experiences from the archives.

Katherine: Yes, and especially since I came to *ShortCuts* with an experimental approach and no particular mandate other than to work with the audio collections that were being processed by *SpokenWeb*. What is accessible to excerpt from the archives determines the sound of *ShortCuts*; but, rather than letting that be a limitation, that selection process is one way in which *ShortCuts* asserts its feminism: through feminist curation. What I'm getting at here is that archives I am cutting sound from are not feminist archives. The Sir George Williams Poetry Series, for example, only had eleven women readers out of the sixty recordings. So, I started out not knowing what *ShortCuts* would be, nor that it would be a feminist series, but what I did know was that

---

9   Aurelio Meza, Ph.D. student and Kodama Cartonera practitioner, brought to SpokenWeb the concept of making small books out of ephemeral event-related objects during the live event.

10   See playlist track five.

11   For more on the relationship between embodiment and sound, see Eidsheim (2015), Voegelin (2021), Cavarero (2015), and Ehrick (2015).

I had a sonic space to work with and I had recordings of women's voices that I wanted to play and replay—on their own and in relation to each other. Then the concept really evolved through the process of making the series, and realizing what you could do—what kinds of critical interventions you could make—with sound.

Hannah: That connection to making is, I think, really key. When reflection is making and making is reflection, reflection becomes a *practice* in a much more material, embodied way. That experience of gathering together to make things in order to reflect on the shared sonic space produced through collective listening—that, for me, is a breeding ground for feminism.

Katherine: Exactly. Podcasting can allow for research to become embodied.[12] For years I have been doing audio-based research about women poets who have read on CBC Radio, but that research hasn't been about making audio until producing *ShortCuts*, and that has been so satisfying, on affective levels, and as to the different kinds of labour put into them. *ShortCuts* enacts the arguments I have been either writing about or trying to write about, and I can see now how *ShortCuts* feeds back into that written work.

Hannah: Yes. I love that. Making as an enactment of your arguments—that's a beautiful way of putting it. When I describe my own podcasting work, I have a tendency to really focus on the process rather than the content. But it's hard for me to prise apart form and content in my work, to articulate anything about the *content* of my work that isn't really fundamentally about how that work is happening.

Stacey: We've had this conversation before: podcasting is process. It's not only the end result. Podcasting is something that you're doing, it's an action. That means there's a particular approach being taken that really needs to be unpacked between practitioners and listeners and within the institution around the process involved in making the podcast. It also brings us back around to my earlier question of explicit versus discreet feminism and feminist practices; Hannah, this might be a great time to talk about your work on *Secret Feminist Agenda*.

---

12   Embodiment within research also underpins the convergence of my creative and scholarly practices when performing dance to archival recordings, as discussed in conversation with Hannah McGregor for *The SpokenWeb Podcast*, "Episode 1.7 The Voice is Intact: Finding the Voice of Gwendolyn MacEwen in the Archive" (6 April 2020). See playlist track six.

Hannah: Ha! There has definitely never been anything discreet about my feminism. I came into podcasting as explicitly a feminist practice, with less interest originally in theorizing podcasting as a medium and more interest in *doing* feminism. I always go back to *Witch, Please* because it's the root of what made podcasting feel like a feminist method to me.[13] *Witch, Please* taught me that we make better ideas when we make them together.

I started *Secret Feminist Agenda* after moving to Vancouver in 2017, and it was really about finding people to talk to, with very little sense of form or structure or intention. As a result, that first season is really formally weird; I was trying to release an interview every week while also minimizing the editing work, so I would just cut the conversations off after thirty minutes, and listeners wanted them to last longer. My solution was to start making what I called "minisodes" every second week.[14] This is where, I think, the self-reflexive process of podcasting became more explicit for me, but it was actually a very practical and labour-based solution to a problem: these interviews needed more space to breathe and I needed more time to edit them. But listeners surprised me by finding the minisodes really engaging. As I reflected on the popularity of the minisodes—which are literally just me thinking out loud about feminism for around twenty minutes—I was reminded that feminism is a fundamentally self-reflexive and embodied practice. It's not an ideology, it's a practice that we do in our daily lives, that we do every day. I think there's a hunger to have collective conversations about what those mundane practices of feminism look and feel and sound like. So the minisodes became a space in which I could materialize that process of reflection in a way that invited responsiveness.

That's something that weaves through all of our projects, I think: that podcasting is a critical practice that invites responsiveness. And I wonder why that is. Is there something about podcasting's own innate media logics, the way as a born-digital medium it has the idea of Web 2.0 interactivity built into it? Is there another reason?

Katherine: It's as though hearing what one version of self-reflexiveness sounds like then invites, somehow, a response, or invites connection. It is vulnerable, and someone hearing this vulnerability feels invited to respond.

---

13   *Witch, Please* originally ran from 2015 to 2018 as an independent podcast, before being rebooted in 2020 and running until 2023, first through podcast network Not Sorry and later through the creation of a feminist production company, Witch, Please Productions. It offered a feminist rereading of the Harry Potter series with a focus on introducing listeners to critical methods that would help them to unpack the books and movies. See playlist track seven.

14   See playlist track eight.

Hannah: You're making me think of the Q & As at conferences after somebody has delivered a twenty minute impermeably argued paper. Everyone's like, "Great job, you did it, I guess let me tell you about my research instead." We blame those question-askers, but when we design our work as authoritative statements with no invitations to respond, what do we expect? Statement invites statement. Reflection invites reflection.

Stacey: Or deflection? I also wonder about listeners that instead actively deflect or oppose invitation into vulnerability and reflection. Our podcast feeds tend to be quite curated to our interests, meaning this sort of deflection is less likely to occur in podcasting than in the traditional mass media space. Still, interest doesn't always equal clear reception of the message as intended. To use an audio metaphor, the podcaster sends out a signal but the listener's ear, like microphones in noise-cancelling headphones, takes in the audio, flips the frequency, and nothing actually gets actually heard.

Hannah: The result is silence.

Stacey: It is something we have to think about when we're talking about explicit versus discreet feminism and the ways that we apply feminist methods to producing media. Who is really listening? We can't always suppose it is another feminist ear or another feminist listener. Right? And so how can we subvert that noise cancellation or coax the ear into resonating with the content that we produce.[15]

Hannah: You can never control for the autonomy of listening as an activity, which is part of its pleasure and its chaos. But minisodes, as reflections without an interlocutor, did seem to invite response in a way that reminds me of how integral self-reflexivity is to feminist practice, particularly in terms of the feminist history of situating oneself. Whether explicitly or implicitly, situating oneself invites response, because you are saying, "I recognize that my view is inherently and always partial." It contains an implicit invitation: now you tell me what you see.

---

15   Doane, McCormick, and Sorce (2017) look to the podcast *Serial* as a potential example of feminist-informed public scholarship when asking a similar question: "How do we 'do' feminist public scholarship without alienating the very audiences that would most benefit from this work?" (119).

THE KITCHEN TABLE: PODCASTING AS SONIC PLACE-MAKING

We assemble ourselves around our own tables, kitchen tables, doing
the work of community as ordinary conversation. Lesbian feminist
world making is nothing extraordinary; I have tried to show how lesbian
feminist world making is quite ordinary. *(Sara Ahmed 2017, 231)*

When Sara Ahmed refers to feminist world making around the kitchen table, she is in part alluding to the Kitchen Table: Women of Color Press, which published a number pivotal works by writers like Audre Lorde, Gloria Anzaldúa, and the Combahee River Collective. In "A Press of Our Own: Kitchen Table: Women of Color Press," Smith (1989) reflects on the significance of the name "Kitchen Table": "We chose our name because the kitchen is the center of the home, the place where women in particular work and communicate with each other" (11). For Smith and Ahmed alike, the kitchen table signifies a distinctly feminist space of organizing: it is domestic but communal, ordinary and yet transformative. They also invite us to understand the kitchen table as a collective site that connects feminists across time and space.

While Ahmed thinks about the work of feminist conversation as "world making," urban geographer and media theorist Fabien Cante (2015) links media creation to place-making, drawing on Ahmed's (2017) concept of orientation as a way of describing how bodies direct themselves towards or away from objects or others as they move through the world. Media practices, such as podcast listening, become a way of orienting oneself differently, or even of developing a collective sonic place, not virtually, but as an embodied and everyday experience. Much as Louise C. Platt (2019) links the "everyday creativity" of crafting to women's collective place-making, we can see how the crafting of sonic space is both an everyday activity (the labour of podcast production being so distinctly banal) and a shared feminist place that invites both creators and listeners to orient ourselves differently. When feminists make media, we also make space—space for ourselves, space for one another, space to sit collectively. For the purposes of our article, that space is the kitchen table.

·ı|ı·ı|ı·ı|ı·

Stacey: As listeners, we aren't actually at a physical kitchen table together. So how does podcasting as a feminist self-reflexive practice invite that imagery or invite that feeling? Personally, interviews are such a key aspect of all of the research I do because I'm craving that interaction and those conversations. I want to sit down over a coffee with my interviewees. I want to sit down with my colleagues in conversation. That's what really draws me to audio production.

You can have such rich conversations in the way *Secret Feminist Agenda* has seen success, but you can also have those conversations and then shape them into a form like an audio documentary, or like Katherine's *ShortCuts* series.

Hannah: As a listener originally, and now as a creator, I find the appeal of podcasting lies in that sense of inviting people to sit around a kitchen table with you. Part of that comes from the original, embodied experience of how I made *Witch, Please* with Marcelle. We were not in a professional sound studio; we were sitting in a domestic space, handing a mic back and forth. I also love listening to conversational, chat-style podcasts, and I often listen to them around my home, as I do everyday activities. If I had a kitchen table, that's where I'd be listening to them. For me, there's a posture with which I create podcasts and listen to podcasts, that regenerates this shared space of the kitchen table. And that doesn't mean there's always some deep feminist conversation happening. Sometimes you're just talking, telling silly jokes to make each other laugh or gossiping about celebrities. But it is a site and a mode of feminist knowledge production.

Stacey: Yeah. I'm interested in the kitchen table perhaps being one of many feminist spaces we are aiming to recreate through our podcast process. Katherine, have you ever thought about *ShortCuts* as a sort of place-making or recreation of feminist space?

Katherine: Well, first, you'll see that I did just move to the kitchen table because construction started up outside, and I thought it would be quieter here. I've had this wood table for a while, so it's a good place for answering this question about *ShortCuts* as place-making and what kind of sound I'm trying to create through that space.

In crafting the sonic experience, especially through these pandemic times, I'm thinking about the body of the listener. I hope that listeners take deep breaths, or stretch, or get pulled into the archival journey. When I listen to the archival recording of Muriel Rukeyser reading the poem "Anemone" [played on *ShortCuts* 2.5, "Connections"], I can't help but take a deep breath in. There's a sense in the poem of breathing in, breathing out—it's a very erotic poem—and I wanted *ShortCuts* to take the time and space to really listen to this, and to breathe with the poem.[16]

Then—back to place-making—I often ask myself, What is the best way to support, or to hold—with care—a recording that is cut out of context? When,

---

16   See playlist track nine.

for example, Phyllis Webb reads from *Naked Poems* on the recording from 1967, she articulates queer intimacy in a public reading that was recorded.[17] I wanted to cut the recording and to bring it out of the archives, but I also wanted whatever I made to hold the recording, sonically, with care. In that recording, Webb reads lines that spoke exactly to that feeling: "the room that holds you / is still here." Even though I've written about Webb for my book and thought about her poetry for a long time, I only learned about what argument I wanted to make and needed to make about that audio by making that *ShortCuts* episode, and I could not have figured that out any other way than by doing it.

Stacey: This is why I love conversation. In hearing Katherine talk about *ShortCuts* as an intimate space for breathing in and breathing out with Muriel Rukeyser across time, I'm now backtracking on my claim that the kitchen table is only one of the many spaces we create through feminist podcasting. I think the kitchen table is *always* where we are. A round kitchen table, like the one Katherine is sitting at right now, but the context and place where the table is located changes. Whether that place is public or private, the table carries with it a sense of closeness and conversation. In the case of *ShortCuts'* "Connections," the table is transported to Rukeyser's live reading where both Rukeyser and Katherine are seated around the table with us. Thinking about the way audio works across time and space, especially when we're engaging with archival audio—we're sitting down at a table that many people have sat at before and are now sitting with us again in our collective listening experience.

THE FEMINIST EMBODIED EAR

> The listening ear...normalizes the aural tastes and standards
> of white elite masculinity as the [default and] singular way
> to interpret sonic information. *(Stoever 2016, 13)*

In their acclaimed work in *The Sonic Color Line*, Jennifer Lynn Stoever (2016) offers us the white patriarchal figure of "the listening ear" to describe what's driving the processes, experiences, and product of racialized sound in American life. A sonic accomplice to Laura Mulvey's "male gaze" theory (1975), the listening ear represents a long history of normative Western listening forms of perception that produce and re-articulate "whiteness" and "blackness." Ultimately, in a white patriarchal capitalist society, the surveilling,

---

17   See playlist track ten.

disciplining, interpretive listening ear decides what is "normal, natural, and right" and filters out the rest (Stoever 2016, 7). The gendered and racialized aspects of the listening ear are similarly brought forward in Dylan Robinson's (2020) conception of hungry listening—or "settler colonial forms of perception" (15)—which superimposes onto our experience of the world a normative positionality grounded in extractivist-colonial violence. In giving name to these oppressive listening practices, Robinson invites us to reflect on hungry listening in our own practices, and on how we might move towards a more self-reflexive listening positionality.

Focusing on audio production as a practice, here we make note of how this listening ear drives the standard disciplines of editing, mixing, and narrative work. To subvert the power of the white elite masculine listening ear and its colonial hungry listening, we must first become aware of complicity in our own listening practices. To counter the listening ear, Stoever's "embodied ear" better represents the nuances of our individual and collective listening practices informed by class, sexuality, gender, and race. As Stoever (2016) writes, "the listening ear is far from the only form of listening" (15). The embodied ear reminds us of the materiality and lived experience that can equally lead us to more subversive and intersectional approaches to listening. In the case of our conversation here, we orient ourselves with a feminist embodied ear.

Learning to listen with a feminist embodied ear also informs how we create podcasts as embodied, feminist producers. In fact, the embodiment of feminist listening and creating blurs what might otherwise seem to be clear lines between those roles, emphasizing the relationality of listening and audio-making as an ongoing dialogue and an evolving lesson in listening otherwise.

·ı|ı·ı|ı·ı|ı·

Hannah: Chatty podcasts may evoke the kitchen table for me, but Katherine, you're making me think about how carefully editing audio can be a deliberate practice of inviting listeners into that shared, embodied space. Which makes me think, Stacey, about what you're doing with your documentary creation. That very careful process of crafting a sonic space can still be about orienting us back to what Ahmed says is quite an ordinary space; you can take great care to invite listeners into that ordinary space.

Stacey: This is why I'm experimenting with the audio diary form. Audio diaries can be personal, contextual, and gritty. They don't have to be recorded in the same way I would traditionally record for radio or podcasting, in an ideal neutral space without reverberations and background noise. I record my audio diaries wherever I just happen to be at the time, whether that's in my living room or in a taxi on my way to take the tapes I just digitized to the archive. You hear the rumblings of me moving through the city and trying to situate myself awkwardly in the car as my arms are piled high with boxes and recording gear.

I try to capture that feeling, that experience I'm going through, for the listener. It's my invitation, saying, "Let's go on this journey together." Audio diaries provide the place-based context so that you have a better sense of where I'm coming from, not only through what I'm saying, but also in the sense of hearing where I am physically and what I'm going through in the process of creating this documentary. For me, it's been a really cathartic experience. There's a certain catharsis involved in self-reflexive practice, in the kinds of pains and failures and successes that we go through in creating these works. Those are processes we need to hear more of.[18] I hear that in listening back to some of your *Secret Feminist Agenda* minisodes, Hannah. They give a sense of that catharsis and process that we don't often hear otherwise.

Hannah: That cathartic process depends on allowing the space for failure, doesn't it? Self-reflexivity involves being willing to fuck up out loud, to think through something without completely protecting yourself from the unpredictability of how others might respond, or from the possibility of making a mistake.[19] You know, we've been talking about taking care of audio clips, and also about using audio as a way to take care of others or to give people a space to take care of themselves by paying attention to their bodies. But I wonder about the relationship between being vulnerable and failing out loud and the kinds of potential harm our failure might cause others, particularly because our failures are often tied up with the inherent limitations of understanding that come with being a white middle-class cis woman.[20] In this sense, part of the practice of self-reflexive feminist podcasting is being willing to return to the work, to be accountable for the work and how it ripples through the world.

Stacey: Yeah. I'm always grappling with how much of my voice should be in my documentary. I want to make sure that my positionality, my experience is there but I have to also consider how much time and airspace is given to voices and experiences different from my own. It's important to be constantly reflecting on and highlighting what voices and experiences are not only

---

18   For more on catharsis and art, see Eldridge (2014). For catharsis in reflexive research, see Pillow (2003).

19   See playlist track eleven.

20   Note from Hannah: This isn't quite how I'm identifying these days, but I meant it at the time.

included but are helping to shape the narrative and overall sound of my work beyond my singular experience.

This ties into the concept of the listening ear from Jennifer Stoever's *The Sonic Color Line* [2016]. I feel like, as someone who was put through the broadcast media production education system, this is something I'm constantly unlearning and trying to negotiate with in the way that I produce work. We can think about feminist self-reflexive podcasting as questioning how dominant audio editing practices, as well as recording choices, might be guided by the white patriarchal ear, from how we emphasize certain aspects of the voice, such as lower tones, to how we mix and master for loudness and remove the actual spaces and sounds of where we're recording.[21] Furthermore, how might we ask our listeners to be okay with hearing things differently? To listen to a podcast that doesn't follow these dominant conventions? This is where the feminist embodied ear comes in. How do we use feminist methods and experiences to rethink the way that we listen?

Hannah: When I think about feminist interventions into listening, I always think back to my first experience of listening to the second season of the audio fiction series *Within the Wires*, which is a queer love story as told through one artist's audio tours of another artist's various gallery shows. There's a moment in episode eight when the narrator becomes so overcome with emotion that she stops talking.[22] She's silent for thirteen solid seconds; I remember checking my phone to see if the episode had stopped playing. That's a bold editorial choice—it demands of me as a listener that I think about the relationship between sound and silence differently.[23] Contemporary audio storytelling is often noisy to the point of being sonically coercive. That kind of sound design feels like it's asking the listener to respond the way the producer is responding, rather than opening up gaps for interpretation and response.

Stacey: There is certainly an internalized industry standard of spoon-feeding ideas in podcasting right now because that's what people expect to hear. It's about familiarity and comfort in repetition. It's how we understand narrative in the sense of audio narrative right now if we listen to top shows like *Invisibilia, Serial,* and *This American Life*; that's what we've come to expect audio storytelling to sound like. So it is a real ask of the listener to rethink the way that they're listening. To ask them to think about feminist

---

21   See Hyland Wang (2021) for more on the gendered politics of professional audio production norms.
22   See playlist track twelve.
23   For more on the deliberate crafting of sonic intimacy in *Within the Wires*, see Euritt (2020).

listening, in the sense of listening to something that maybe doesn't have the music and the voice and the narrative arc structure that they're used to. Will they listen? I don't know.

Hannah: About eight months into making *Witch, Please*, Marcelle had a baby, and we had to make a decision about how we were going to treat baby sounds on the podcast. Neither of us had ever heard a podcast with a baby on it, because you aren't supposed to have "distracting" noise on your podcast. But very quickly we decided, no, feminism means that sometimes you hear a baby.[24] We found out later that our feminist listeners were interpreting the sound of the baby not as "noise" but as a significant sound,[25] one that, to the feminist embodied ear, was making an argument about the place of children and of caretakers within feminist community.[26]

Katherine: We hear the voice of a young child on *ShortCuts* 2.8 (May 2021)[27] and that's so true that, rather than hearing this voice as noise, its sound tells us about the space in which that voice was recorded. It was an unedited recording made at home by poet Alexei Perry Cox, reading along with the sounds of her very vocal eighteen-month-old daughter, Isla. When I first listened, I heard Alexei's reading as a duet—all those little interruptive noises that were not interruptions at all. I noticed that, as she read, Alexei adjusted the cadence of her voice to respond, at times, to Isla and her sounds, as though signalling to the audience that she was comfortable reading in that sonic space, and, to my ear, that was an invitation for us to be comfortable in that sonic space with her too. I thought, what a contrapuntal duet between the two of them, Alexei and Isla. *ShortCuts* was a place to make the argument that this was not noise, this was poetic sound.

Hearing that recording as poetic makes me also think back to Stacey's mention of Stoever and unlearning what we imagine voice to sound like— and to think of unlearning and listening, particularly Dylan Robinson's [2020]

---

24   See playlist track thirteen.

25   Schafer's (1993) definition of noise as "sounds we have learned to ignore" is useful here, especially because that learning has been deeply gendered as it pertains to hearing voice (see Ehrick 2015) and as it controls access to the making of "noisy" sonic spaces (see Rodgers 2010).

26   Since this original conversation took place, baby sounds returned to *Witch, Please*, and interesting conversations ensued about the political importance of leaving them in as significant sounds, and the technical production challenges posed by editing dialogue tracks that contain multiple voices (parent and child). The commitment to leaving the baby in the mix is not an elision of the labour of sound production and editing but rather an invitation to rethink what we consider to be background noise versus meaningful sound.

27   See playlist track fourteen.

Hungry Listening. His conceptualizing of listening positionality in that book is such a helpful way of thinking about unlearning as a listener, or, rather, to ask, How did you learn to listen?

Hannah: I find it really helpful to be reminded that we *learn* to listen; it reminds us not only that how we listen isn't natural or innate, but also that we are always learning (and relearning) how to listen. Part of feminist self-reflexive podcasting is ensuring that we are not always the ones being listened to, but that we are also listening to others, whether through interviewing, engaging with archival audio, or even listening to our listeners.

Katherine: Podcasting as a feminist practice then seems to be about that learning, about undertaking the process knowing that it could change and being open to that change. I think of *ShortCuts* as opening up different possibilities for listening to archival audio in ways that are situated in embodied and affective responses to it. My commentary isn't about offering a definitive interpretation of a clip, but rather it is about listening, and the possibilities within that listening. So integrating conversation has worked well, and that is something I'm planning on doing more often in the third season. Within the making of one episode, you can't change the world—as much as you might wish to—but I still think it's important to understand the work of one episode as an intervention and to ask yourself, What am I going to do in this sonic space that can offer something meaningful? In the making of *ShortCuts* 2.6 "Listening Together,"[28] I recorded a conversation with Mathieu Aubin about encountering unsettling or awkward moments in archival audio, and that conversation ended up being part of the episode. Talking with someone else about what you listened to is a way of talking about what it felt like to hear it. Talking is such a valuable part of the process of podcast production and, especially in the case of that episode, having a chat about messy archives was exactly what needed to happen.

Hannah: I love this idea of "having a chat" as method! The labour of editing and duration is another really interesting aspect of collaborative listening. Sound takes up time in a very particular way; you can't skim it, you have to sit and attend to it. As a result, editing isn't only labour, it's in fact a tedious and time-consuming form of labour that involves a practice of durational listening. And I wonder if we might connect the labour of editing to listening with a feminist embodied ear by also thinking about what it means to produce audio with a feminist embodied ear.

---

28   See playlist track fifteen.

CONCLUSION: AN ARCHIVE OF FEMINIST POSSIBILITIES

I want the generosity and an expansiveness of friendship as a way of life.
I want the worlds that may be possible if we take the feminist killjoy's
multiple versions of friendship as a way of life. *(Wunker 2016, 147)*

In their account of their feminist practice of collaborative editing, scholars Kate Eichhorn and Heather Milne (2016) ask whether the labour of editing tends to be undervalued because it is "affective labour that privilege[s] collaboration and personal relationships over monetary or professional gain" (191), particularly because editing is less concerned with control over meaning than it is with "relationships and proximities" (190). Thinking about editing as affective labour underlines its fundamental relationality as well as its emphasis on listening. It is impossible to edit audio without listening carefully to it—and while the audio industry has developed best practices around how audio *ought* to be edited, feminist self-reflexive podcasting as a practice invites a reconsideration of how this work is done.

This *care-full* reconsideration of podcast editing practices can not only open up new experimentation in how we produce audio, but also help to inform how we approach podcast distribution and archiving practices. As Morris and Hoyt (2021) outline in their work on podcast preservation and historiography, "any act of collection is also an act of power" (8). How we choose to curate or edit podcasts, whether it is an episode or an archive, must be approached with transparency and in collaboration with the communities the work stands to represent. While it is valuable to offer new models and new methods, our goal here is not to create new editorial orthodoxies, but rather to centre the relationality of editing as care work, and to imagine how, through the practice of audio creation, we can imagine new possibilities.

··|··|··|··|··

Stacey: This is what I'm maybe most excited about in thinking about podcasting as feminist practice: How can we rethink the way that we even conceive of audio production? I look to sound art and oral history practices for influences. For example, I'm really inspired by radio producers like the Kitchen Sisters[29] who use oral history methods in dialogue with archival audio. They sit down with their subjects and listen and look through old ephemera together for hours and hours across many different sessions. On the flip side, sound art

---

29   See playlist track sixteen.

and experimental work is an inspiring site for bringing queer theory into my feminist practice.[30]

I think I am going to have to put a disclaimer at the top of my audio documentary, to be honest. To be like, I am inviting you here to listen differently. To listen in a way that thinks through new possibilities of narrative and storytelling and the way that we interact with a podcast or what we understand to be the audio documentary form. We have to start playing with those structures if we want to break down the normative notions of what a podcast sounds like and how we interact with the form.

In addition to the feminist practice of careful editing work that you're talking about, Katherine, when we're editing voices and listening back and also thinking about how we volume-level voices and position voices, we must ask, Where are people placed in the mix? Are we all seated at the kitchen table? How do we invite people to hear those spaces that we're trying to evoke?

Katherine: I keep thinking back, Hannah, to the start of our conversation when you told us about the process of making *Secret Feminist Agenda* and how you were so surprised (pleasantly surprised) by the listeners' responses to the highly self-reflexive minisodes. We've already talked about how your minisodes model a kind of vulnerable self-reflexivity that invites listeners to think with and alongside you. That makes me think about the ways in which sound is shaped by spaces we are imagining when we record and edit a podcast, whether we imagine talking to an audience from a stage or sitting with them at a kitchen table. What we imagine as that shared space ends up shaping what the sound can do.

Hannah: Absolutely. When I ask myself, Where are my favourite spaces to have conversations? I immediately think of my friends Erin and Bart's cabin. Their daughter has gone to bed, and we're out on the front porch so that we won't wake her up by laughing too loud. We all sit facing the window so we can watch the sun slowly set over the salt flats as we drink wine and talk about ideas. I can recall that space and the postures of those conversations with an embodied intensity.

Katherine: We've been using the kitchen table as a shared reference point, but I wonder if what we're really getting at here is that we're trying to create whatever sonic space that, for listeners, is the space in which meaningful

---

30 For an example of sound art, see the sound art exhibit turned podcast series "Resonant Bodies" from Pabani et al. (2019). See playlist track seventeen. For more on queer/feminist approaches to narrative, see Warhol and Lanser (2015).

conversations have taken place. Sound brings listeners to that place—whether that place is the kitchen table or that place is the feeling of being with close friends as you watch the sun set over salt flats.

And I have to add that I thought of you, Hannah, while on a panel with Erin and hearing her speak about archives of feminist friendship (Feminist (Affective) Archive, Wunker 2021). In your making of feminist podcasts, Hannah, you are building an archive of friendship, one that's being built through memorable conversations and lasting connections as much as it is a formal archive of recordings. Friendship is being recorded, not just literally through the conversation, but also in the recordings and even how we remember spaces afterwards as the place-makers of those conversations that then become feminist friendships.

Hannah: We're not just theorizing this, either; we're literally enacting it, right now.

Stacey: Yes. As much as we're sitting around the kitchen table and transporting that kitchen table to different places, we're also creating an archive of feminist possibilities. We're offering up another alternative space, another way of thinking about places and spaces through the work that we're making. A big part of the exciting potentiality that feminist practice can bring to the table is that, regardless of the inequities in our daily lives, we can come here to this archive to listen, and to experience the different possibilities of how the world can be.

Hannah: Mic drop. Done, end of article. Can we write all articles like this from now on? This was a real blast.

PLAYLIST

Track 1: Unter, Phoebe, Nicole Kelly, and Kaitlin Prest. 2020. "Lesbian Separatism Is Inevitable." In *The Heart*. Podcast. MP3 audio, 24:49. https://www.theheartradio.org/solos/2020/1/15/lesbian-separatism-is-inevitable.

Track 2: McGregor, Erin. 2019. "The Atlanta Letters." In *Queer Public*. Podcast. MP3 audio, 40:03. https://www.stitcher.com/show/the-queer-public-podcast/episode/the-atlanta-letters-65523960.

Track 3: Hutchinson, Louise. 1990. "Valentines Day". In *The Lesbian Show*. Vancouver Co-op Radio. Vancouver, Canada: CFRO. Broadcast recording. MP3 audio, 1:01:51. https://alotarchives.org/interview/valentines-day.

Track 4: VanSlet, Deborah. 1991. "Sex Garage 1 Year Anniversary." In *Dykes on Mykes*. Montreal, Canada: CKUT, July 15, 1991. Broadcast recording clip,

MP3 audio, 0:03:10. [Full broadcast recording available at The ArQuives: Canada's LGBTQ+ Archives, Dykes on Mykes fonds, File no. F0195-01-006]

Track 5: McLeod, Katherine. 2020. "Audio of the Month—Daryl Hine's Point Grey." In *ShortCuts*. Podcast. MP3 audio, 06:35. https://spokenweb.ca/podcast/episodes/audio-of-the-month-daryl-hines-point-grey/.

Track 6: McGregor, Hannah. 2020. "The Voice Is Intact: Finding Gwendolyn MacEwen in the Archive." *SpokenWeb Podcast*. Podcast. MP3 audio, 35:54. https://spokenweb.ca/podcast/episodes/the-voice-is-intact-finding-gwendolyn-macewen-in-the-archive/.

Track 7: McGregor, Hannah and Marcelle Kosman. 2015. "Episode 1: The Sorting Ceremony." In *Witch, Please*. Podcast. MP3 audio, 1:01:26. https://play.acast.com/s/oh-witch-please/episode1-sortingceremony.

Track 8: McGregor, Hannah. 2018. "On Being Seen." In *Secret Feminist Agenda*. Podcast. MP3 audio, 20:00. https://secretfeministagenda.com/2018/02/02/episode-2-3-on-being-seen/.

Track 9: McLeod, Katherine. 2021. "Connections." In *ShortCuts*. Podcast. MP3 audio, 13:41. https://spokenweb.ca/podcast/episodes/connections/.

Track 10: McLeod, Katherine. 2021. "Moving." In *ShortCuts*. Podcast. MP3 audio, 13:20. https://spokenweb.ca/podcast/episodes/moving/.

Track 11: McGregor, Hannah. 2018. "Playing, Losing, Failing." In *Secret Feminist Agenda*. Podcast. MP3 audio, 16:54. https://secretfeministagenda.com/2018/03/01/episode-2-7-playing-losing-failing/.

Track 12: Cranor, Jeffrey and Janina Matthewson. 2017. "Season 2, Cassette 8: Ohara Museum of Art (1980)." In *Within the Wires*. PRX. Podcast. MP3 audio, 24:35. https://beta.prx.org/stories/232293.

Track 13: McGregor, Hannah and Marcelle Kosman. 2016. "Episode 13B: Deathly Famous." In *Witch, Please*. Podcast. MP3 audio, 1:18:13. http://ohwitchplease.ca/2016/05/episode-13b-deathly-famous/.

Track 14: McLeod, Katherine. 2021. "Contrapuntal Poetics." In *ShortCuts*. Podcast. MP3 audio, 12:50. https://spokenweb.ca/podcast/episodes/contrapuntal-poetics/.

Track 15: McLeod, Katherine. 2021. "Listening Together." In *ShortCuts*. Podcast. MP3 audio, 16:54. https://spokenweb.ca/podcast/episodes/listening-together/.

Track 16: Nelson, Davia and Nikki Silva. 2015. "WHER: 1000 Beautiful Watts Part 1." In *The Kitchen Sisters Present*. PRX. Podcast. MP3 audio, 24:50. http://www.kitchensisters.org/fugitivewaves/wher-1000-beautiful-watts-part-1/.

Track 17: Pabani, Aliya. 2019. "Singing on the Line." In *Constellations*. Podcast. MP3 audio, 15:51. https://www.constellationsaudio.com/sounds/resonantbodies/pabani.

CHAPTER 8

THE PLAY OF PODCASTING
Liminoid Space and the Ethics of Voice in Collaborative Podcast Practice

ERIN CORY

n early 2020, I began a collaborative research project with Konstkupan (Art Hive), an arts space dedicated to young new arrivals to Sweden. I had been working towards this project for over a year when the COVID-19 pandemic struck. Quickly adapting from an in situ to a digital format, the participants in the resulting *Picturing Home* project met virtually over the spring. This group of individuals, made up of people with various types of migration experience, creatively explored the idea of "home" through pictures, words, music, and homemaking practices, sharing a variety of stories, memories, and traditions with each other. The resulting podcast captures some of the spirit of the larger project. A couple of participants were invited onto the podcast each week, and had a major role in conceptualizing and scripting their episode. We, as researchers, saw in this deeply collaborative ethos a chance to marry research and activism, and in so doing to challenge both the narratives around migrants to Sweden and the academy's claim on knowledge production.

In this chapter, I explore podcasting in the context of the *Picturing Home* research project and problematize the centrality of podcasts to podcasting research more broadly. While interrogating an object's centrality to the literature built around it may seem counterintuitive, I will argue that focusing primarily on the end product of a podcast obscures much of the care work and community building that takes place before and after a podcast is recorded. I am especially concerned with the work done (or not done) around or by histor-ically marginalized communities. In taking up calls by social scientists (e.g., Tuck and Yang 2014a, 2014b; Gordon 2008) to forgo damage-centred narra-tives and to make room for complexity in the stories and voices that form the backbone of research in general, and podcasting research in particular, I link Llinares's (2018) thinking on the possibilities of voice inherent to podcasting's liminal infrastructure to the problematic liminality of border regimes, which routinely silence migrants. Instead, I propose a focus on the liminoid (Turner 1974), the space of play and experimentation *around but outside the podcast-ing moment*, where podcast participants can work through their stories and decide how to best self-represent. I do this by detailing and critiquing the *Picturing Home* project, considering my positionality as a researcher in this collaborative endeavour, and arguing for a more radical decentring of the role of the researcher. Although there is a trend towards thinking about podcast-ing as a method in and of itself, it is crucial that we better theorize the politics not only of voice, but also of silence, and the potentials and perils of the work that leads to and from the podcast as an object of activism and research.

PODCASTING AS ACTIVISM AND RESEARCH PRAXIS

One of podcasting's most alluring—and theorized—attributes is how it harnesses radio's intimacy (Florini 2019; Murray 2019b; Spinelli and Dann 2019), in some cases producing what Richard Berry (2016b) calls a sense of "hyper-intimacy" (666). While a very recent strand of podcast scholarship (e.g., Euritt 2023) has importantly theorized intimacy as a construction that can be wielded towards manipulative ends, a parallel arc in the literature (see, for example, Krishnan and Wallis 2020; Mulki and Ormsby 2021) understands the intimacy afforded by podcasting as important to bolstering the medium's activist potential. The personal narratives around which podcasts are often crafted pave the way for building solidarity between and within marginalized groups (see de los Rios 2020; Florini 2019; Vrikki and Malik 2019). Scholars have argued for podcasting's progressive potential as a pedagogical tool and as a means to building solidarities. Sarah Florini, for example, argues that the affordances of digital media allow for the production of audio "enclaves," listening publics that are "quasi-private spaces" for building "counterhege-monic" knowledges and solidarities (2019, 69, 71, 79). Cati V. de los Rios sees in podcasting a resource that connects the personal experiences of marginalized youth to "broader pressing concerns about immigration, language, racializa-tion processes and resistance" (2020, 2). Listening to shared experiences in these arenas presents these youth with an opportunity for solidarity building in a United-Statesian culture where they are not often heard.

In the context of academia, podcasting has of late been taken up not only as a pedagogical tool (e.g., Oslawski-Lopez and Kordsmeier 2021; Fox, Dowling, and Miller 2020; Wake, Fox, and Strong 2020) and a research object (e.g., Wyld 2020; Pavelko and Myrick 2019; Chan-Olmsted and Wang 2022), but also as a practical vehicle for the dissemination of research to audiences both within and outside the academy (e.g., *AnthroPod*, NPR's *The Academic Minute*, *The Podcast Studies Podcast*), and, less frequently, as a research method in its own right. Furthering earlier work on podcast ethnography (e.g., Lundström and Lundström 2020), Ian M. Cook (2020) has recently argued for podcasting *as* an anthropological method. In his work with and about a podcast on digital cultures in India, Cook examines "interlocutor interview podcasting" as a method. Podcasting's aural intimacy and circulating co-presence might perhaps allow, Cook argues, for "undistracted engagement with the lives of others" (2020, 15). At the same time, Cook acknowledges that podcasting "is not a democratizing magic bullet that enables authentic subaltern voices to emerge from under the anthropologist's pen, but rather a method that offers the possibility to destabilize the typified voices of authority within the discipline by proposing another way of creating such authority" (15). While Cook describes the process of recording a podcast consisting of interviews with interlocutors, he suggests that another avenue of inquiry might be "interlocutor co-produced series" (4), of which *Picturing Home* is an example. Taking to heart Cook's astute observation that "a plurality of voices is not necessarily empowering" (6), in what follows I consider what is at stake in including particular voices in a podcast, particularly when those voices come from marginalized communities—here, migrants to Sweden.

THE SWEDISH CONTEXT AND PICTURING HOME

The *Picturing Home* project began in earnest in 2020, although its roots go further back. In 2017, I began a two-year post-doc position in a Swedish political context in which attitudes to migration were increasingly polarized. This polarization reached a fever pitch in the wake of 2015's migrations, when multiple conflicts—including the Syrian civil war and the war in Afghanistan—prompted the arrival of unprecedented numbers of asylum seekers to Europe (UNHCR 2016). The 2018 Eurobarometer published by the European Commission, in fact, showed that less than 25 percent of Swedes felt the country's approach to integration had been successful. Lund and Voyer (2020), who researched young people in Malmö, refer to a "crisis of meaning" in which Swedes feel their national identity is at a crisis point, and so react by subjecting Swedish residents with histories of migration to everyday racism and exclusion. To combat stigmatization, they write, there must be "a shift from the assimilative mode of incorporation—that there is one way to be Swedish—to the multicultural mode: a recognition of the equal civil status of new groups' cultural characteristics" (Lund and Voyer 2020, 198).

The larger research project for which I received funding in early 2019, as I then imagined it, offered some sort of corrective to the feelings shared by many young migrants I'd interviewed: that they'd been over-researched, and were tired of answering questions at the behest of the state (in both Denmark and Sweden) and of integration protocols that were tantamount to assimilation. I thus sought to refocus my work through a project that would put notions of integration into conversation with one another as a bridge-building tactic. I teamed up with Konstkupan, a creative space for young new arrivals to Sweden, as its activism was rooted precisely in the notion that integration must be two-way, between migrants and the host society, and that creative practice can bring communities into contact and conversation.

Originally, the project was meant to unfold over the spring of 2020. We—organizers at Konstkupan, my Malmö University colleague Hugo Boothby, and myself—had planned a series of in situ arts workshops wherein participants, both new arrivals and autochthonous Swedes in Malmö, would get together weekly to create visual and audio material around the idea of home, and would eventually co-create an exhibition showcasing their artwork. When the pandemic hit, we had to reconfigure our plans while still prioritizing connection, collaboration, and the archiving of stories that might challenge popular ideas about migrants and integration. We scheduled a series of online workshops, and set up a digital image/sound archive in lieu of an exhibition. The iterative process that emerged took place over four fora: Zoom, Instagram, Zencastr, and SoundCloud/iTunes. We began by publicizing the online Zoom workshops on Facebook and Instagram, inviting our networks to share the events with friends and colleagues who might want to join. The idea was to bring together a group of people with a range of experiences, in the spirit of Konstkupan's community-crossing or -building paradigm. We advertised the availability of translation into both Farsi and Arabic, two languages predominant in Sweden's migrant populations. Although the podcast took shape as a last-minute addition, it became the capstone of the project, a space for participants to reflect on the workshops and the image/sound archive, and to preserve their stories on a publicly accessible site.

However, I am less concerned here with the product of the podcast than the larger *process*, of which it was one piece. In focusing on the process—the activities and choices and stories that are ultimately both audible and (intentionally) silent in the podcast itself—I want to consider the ethical charges of deploying podcasting as both a method and a research object, and argue that while podcasting can indeed channel the voices of marginalized people, might bridge communities, and might disrupt academic time-lines that hold sway over the distribution of knowledge, we must still and always—especially when working with over-researched and underrepresented communities, and perhaps *especially* in light of the time-space compression of new media—be mindful of power dynamics that play through all facets of production.

THEORY VS. PRAXIS: PODCASTING AND/ON MIGRATION

Podcasts about migration have flourished of late. Series like *Al Empire* and *Kerning Cultures*, for example, toggle between historical accounts of Arab cultures and "success stories" in Arab diasporas. Others (e.g., *Displaced, Refugees on Air*, and *Refugees' Stories Podcast*) specifically address ongoing migration phenomena by focusing on stories of displacement and resettlement. It is important to note that most examples of this latter sort of podcast are often short-lived, and run by humanitarian institutions and charities. Though few in number, podcasts produced by refugees do exist. *Refugees on Air*, for example, was started by Syrian twins Sarah and Maya Ghassali, who immigrated to Australia during Syria's ongoing civil war. The podcast dubbed itself "The one and only refugee podcast giving refugees from all around Australia a voice to share their stories" ("Refugees on Air" 2023). It is, however, currently inactive (having aired from December 2017 to October 2020), demonstrating the relatively abbreviated runs of such podcasts.

The goal of podcasts documenting the lives of displaced persons is doubtless to humanize the experience of displacement through storytelling. Given the *de*humanizing effects of persistent enumeration and political rhetoric with which displaced populations are beset, the use of the medium to "raise the voice of refugees and asylum seekers," as UK charity Refugee Radio puts it on its website ("About Us" 2022, para. 8), opens up new possibilities for communicating human experience.

Nevertheless, the collection and narration of stories—especially those that pivot around pain, loss, and trauma—however good the intentions, provoke ethical questions about objectification, the politics of voice or speech, and the potentials that reside in refusal. Building on Spivak's central question, "Can the subaltern speak?"(1988), scholars Eve Tuck and K. Wayne Yang build towards other questions they argue must be at the heart of academic research: "*does* the subaltern speak? Can the colonizer/settler *listen*? Can the subaltern *be heard?...What does the academy do? What does social science research do?*" (2014a, 225). The academy has a long history of symbolic violence, a nostalgia and exploitation of Others' pain on which careers are built, as bell hooks writes:

No need to hear your voice when I can talk about you better than you can speak about yourself. No need to hear your voice. Only tell me about your pain. I want to know your story. And then I will tell it back to you in a new way. Tell it back to you in such a way that it has become mine, my own. Re-writing you I write myself anew. I am still author, authority. I am still colonizer the speaking subject and you are now at the center of my talk. (hooks 1990, 334, cited in Tuck and Yang 2014a, 227)

Dario Llinares (2018) suggests that podcasting's deployment of the "resonance of speech" is a means of "nuancing meaning and conveying emotional profundity...injecting a sense of emotional texture to a narrative" (133), which has an important role in public discourse. Llinares considers this nuancing through the lens of a "liminal praxis": podcasting "engenders a move away from authorial, top down dissemination of information to a more conversational, personal and subjective tone" (140–41). I would argue that when researchers work with communities that have been historically marginalized, and to which they do not belong, this "liminality" presents a potentially perilous terrain, wherein the politics of voice and story—what is said and not said, the connections that happen on and off air—must be foregrounded.

ON THE LIMINAL SPACES OF BORDERS AND PODCASTING

In anthropology, the concept of "liminality" denotes the ambiguity that is characteristic of a rite of passage, which may include the subversion of hierarchies, the dissolution of traditions and order, and the feeling—however temporary—of malleability, possibility, and a new order of things (Horváth, Thomassen, and Wydra 2009; Szakolczai 2015). Scholars who have shaped the discourse on liminality have written about it as a productive state, wherein values can be questioned, and new connections forged. Victor Turner (1969) proposed that groups of people experiencing the same liminal state might further experience a feeling of *communitas*, the sense of intimacy and togetherness emanating from shared challenges or rites of passage. And yet, posing liminal states as overwhelmingly positive misses the ways liminality can also provoke anguish and fear (Horváth 2013).

Recent work in border and migration studies takes a more tempered view on the liminal. Scholars have deployed liminality as a particular sort of temporality experienced by migrants, and especially irregular migrants—as, in fact, "the most universal characteristic of the border" (Agier 2016, 36). Jacobsen and Karlsen (2021) argue that traditional, largely positive understandings of "liminality" fail to capture migration experience, in their assumption of a *temporary* in-betweenness which will eventually be resolved (5). In the context of migration, liminality provokes a feeling of alienation (Kirk, Bal, and Janssen 2017), a struggle between bureaucracy and individuals' sense of empowerment (Sutton, Vigneswaran, and Wels 2011), and a loss of the frames of reference through which individuals understand their lives (Genova and Zontini 2020).

Considering liminality under the rubric of border studies, Michel Agier (2016) notes how the border's liminality resides in its ritual aspect, through which a person enters into a different law, and finds oneself, to different degrees and along different timelines, without status, caught in a "moment of exception" that extends in time (35–36). One "becomes" a foreigner in this moment, Agier argues, not only legally and politically, but also socially. The migrant moves into a state of uncertainty about how they will exist socially and be recognized by others. This is a "liminal condition, therefore, which does not have the status of a social category but can sometimes correspond to what is denoted by 'liminal,' that is, a state hardly perceptible, hardly audible and 'voiceless'" (35–36).

At the same time that migration and border studies are working on the concept of liminality and its perils, podcast studies has taken up liminality as something that can *challenge* such voicelessness. Llinares (2018) identifies in the productive in-betweenness of liminality a kinship with the praxis of podcasting, which he argues "offers freedoms from disciplinary regimes and traditions, and from sanctioned modes of communication and knowledge production" (125). Podcasting's liminality resides in its flexibility, boundary crossing between different media, and rejigging of traditional modes of production, distribution, and consumption; and it is this openness that allows podcasting to act as a vector for new modes of thought, identity, and practice to take shape (142).

Writing about the *Picturing Home* podcast in the months after its brief run, Hugo and I argued for the potentiality of podcasting to bring together in community people with different experiences of migration. Theorizing a podcast as a boundary object (Star and Griesemer 1989; Star 2010; Schindler 2020), we argued that podcasting's fruitfulness as a research object, a method, and a mode of activist praxis lies in the multiple ways that multiple individuals can engage with it (Cory and Boothby 2021a). In the work we did on the *Picturing Home* podcast, we saw an opening for dialogue and exploration, in both the process and end product of the podcast, akin to Llinares's theorization of liminal praxis (2018). Still, we recognized the persistence of thresholds, explored below, which we could not honestly say we'd crossed.

EXPLORING THE LIMINOID: PODCASTING'S PRE- AND POST-PRODUCTION PLAYTIME AND/AS REFLEXIVITY

In his later work, Victor Turner (1974) coined the term liminoid, as an addendum to his work on liminal experiences. Understanding the idea of liminal rites as too fixed in results—the transition from one life stage to another, the eventual crossing of a threshold—Turner described instead experiences that do not necessarily offer resolution and are, rather than requisite to social belonging, optional events in which people can participate. Instead of constituting social belonging and cohesion, as in the liminal, the liminoid represents a break with society, an opportunity for play. During these moments of play, norms, rules, and roles are relaxed. These instances of leisure and letting go are defined, according to Turner, by the following:

> *freedom to* enter, even generate new symbolic worlds of entertainment, sports, games, diversions of all kinds...[and]...2) *freedom to* transcend social structural limitations, freedom to *play*—with ideas, with fantasies, with words...with paint...and with social relationships—in friendship, sensitivity training, psychodramas, and in other ways. (Turner 1974, 68)

While liminal processes serve to make the total social process cohere into a complete whole, reinforced by ritual and rite, by inclusion and exclusion, *liminoid* phenomena develop "along the margins, in the interfaces and interstices of central and servicing institutions—they are plural, fragmentary, and experimental in character" (85).

In retrospect, the *Picturing Home* project served as a liminoid site, wherein participants could work on an experiment that was collaborative and multiply construed—a kind of disruption of the bordering practices of Sweden's migration regime, and the persistent racism that colours social life in Swedish urban centres, which are largely segregated along ethnic lines. While we were cautious to assign any overarching meaning or altruistic intent to the podcast, participants were overwhelmingly positive in their responses to the podcast as something edifying and transformational.

It is significant that respondents understood the project holistically. Rather than focusing solely on the podcast, in talking about *Picturing Home*'s relevance to them, respondents understood the whole of the project as an exercise in community building through storytelling. I'd like to consider how this process functioned as a liminoid phenomenon, unfolding along margins and intersections, and in so doing to make an argument for a podcasting method that is not rooted in recording, production, and post-production, but rather is foregrounded in the pleasures of play.

Nearly a quarter of a century before Turner wrote about the liminoid, the Situationists—a group of revolutionary artists and intellectuals—grasped the transformative potential of play, adopting a liminoid "subjunctive mood" (meaning anything can happen) as an approach to the everyday, which could *transform* the everyday and its material conditions (see, for example, Debord

1957, 1958). As Schleiner points out, while the Situationists used play to disrupt the "rotten superstructures" (Debord 1957)—bourgeois culture and fascism chief among them—that haunted postwar Europe, these structures are still at work today, not least of all in the form of neo-imperialism, militarization, and border closures (Schleiner 2011). Certainly, such structures are front and centre in the minds and lived experiences of many *Picturing Home* participants, who have dealt with them in a first-hand manner in their displacement and subsequent efforts to resettle in a new country. While the *Picturing Home* project did not attempt to gamify everyday life as the Situationists did, we were still keen to inspire a sense of play in our initial online workshops. This state of play, I argue, was instrumental to the crafting of the podcast; without this time for participants to interact in an unscripted environment, the podcast would have been deprived of a certain richness that mirrored an inclusivity that still feels out of reach in everyday life in Sweden.

ONLINE WORKSHOPS

Over five weeks, participants met weekly for two to three hours on Zoom to talk about changeable meanings of "home" by sharing the artefacts, photographs, sounds, and practices we associate with the concept, and which we use to "make" it. The themes set for the sessions were: Traveling Objects, Talking Photos, Teaching Home, Sounds Like Home, and Writing Home. Participants were asked to bring to each workshop something related to the theme of the week, a routine we jokingly called our "assignments."

The weekly meeting presented the opportunity for participants to connect with each other and to build trust. As Jasmin, a participant who featured frequently in the podcast, noted in an interview after the project ended, these workshops helped her to feel "safer" sharing publicly in the podcast episodes:

> Having the podcast done in connection with the [online] workshop made it easier. I don't think we would have had as many of the same discussions that we ended up having if we had only had the podcast. Because in a lot of ways the podcast was more about reflecting on what we talked about in the workshop, in a space that was more comfortable, accepting, where people felt safe sharing.

Hugo and I received permission from participants to record the sessions so that we could pull narrative threads and audio content into the podcast with each speaker's permission. However, we also explicitly stated that the online meetings would stay confidential, and no material would be used without consent. We had begun the project around the idea of "home" in order to resist essentializing participants with a recent history of migration. "Home" is something that we each have a relationship to, however problematic or challenging. In the context of the online meetings, these connections emerged in both playful and painful ways, refracted through various experiences of migration.

I would like to claim that we chose the theme of "home" and the format of the workshops to avoid participating in what Tuck (2009) calls "damage-centered research," or "research that operates, even benevolently, from a theory of change that establishes harm or injury in order to achieve reparation" (412). However, I do not believe I can honestly claim that is what we did. We were interested—*I* was interested, as the primary researcher—in conducting an arts-based research project that might build bridges between communities of new arrivals and autochthonous Swedes, something I now understand implicitly foregrounded the experience of displacement.

In assessing the process here, in writing about it for a piece that will at some point end up on my publishing record, I can at least try to move forward ethically in two ways: Firstly, by not only continuing to honour the confidentiality of the conversations that happened during the online workshops, but also by withholding some of the stories that came up outside the context of workshops, Instagram archive, and podcast. Taking further Llinares's observation that podcasting challenges both hierarchies and the academy's push to objective claims, I want to invoke Tuck and Yang's observation that "'objectivity' is code for power" (2014b, 812), and that one way to disrupt this power is to instead practise objection, or refusal. While I can write here about the form our meetings took, I will not tell you what was said in them. There are stories, conversations that are salient to thinking about the intellectual and emotional labour participants put into the project, even the podcast, but I will not tell those stories here. Secondly, I will not identify workshop and podcast participants in this piece by their migration statuses or backgrounds. This may seem disingenuous, as the narratives that constitute the podcast are already public and available, and many of these deal with participants' stories and memories of home, which are often connected to their experiences of migration. As Tuck and Yang remind us,

> the turn toward humanizing the object into a subject—often through the inclusion of people of color, women, youth, and Native researchers—is important work, but not the same as refusal. The goal of refusal is not for objects to become subjects in the academy, but contrarily to *object* to the very processes of objectification/subjection, the making of possessors and possessions, the alchemy of becoming-claims. (2014b, 814)

In this text, at least, I will continue to talk about our group in migration-unspecific terms, to allow space for what Avery Gordon (2008) calls "complex personhood." Gordon notes that it is often the very people who wish to understand and change systemic inequality who "withhold from the very people they are most concerned with the right to complex personhood" (4), which she defines as many things, with the following among them:

> that all people...remember and forget, are beset by contradiction, and recognize and misrecognize themselves and others...that even those called "Other" are never never that...that the stories people tell about themselves, about their troubles, about their social worlds, and about their society's problems are entangled and weave between what is immediately available as a story and what their imaginations are reaching toward...At the very least, complex personhood is about conferring the respect on others that comes from presuming that life and people's lives are simultaneously straightforward and full of enormously subtle meaning. (Gordon 2008, 4–5)

Indeed, in the context of *Picturing Home*'s liminoid, transmedial space (Jenkins 2006), participants wove between different genres of storytelling and between the project's platforms to narrate their lives in multiple ways. We took time to play during the workshops: playing music for each other and telling the stories behind songs we love; sharing photos of our home spaces and the memories they evoke; teaching each other homemaking practices that we have carried between houses, cities, countries, and continents; even performing music individually and together. One thing that became apparent during the workshops was that most of us had some sort of migration background, whether we had moved because we had been forcibly displaced, had moved for economic or personal reasons, or had experienced class migration in our own countries. Some of us had experience with several of these migration routes.

INSTAGRAM ARCHIVE

Between the workshops and the podcast, participants took to Instagram to archive some of these artefacts and practices. Not everyone participated, and not everyone shared their name on their posts.

This was an important aspect of the Instagram archive: all participants had the log-in information to the shared account, which meant they could post and edit as they desired, both to the feed and to the stories section of the app. The shared authorship allowed for anonymity, should participants desire it, and for an entanglement of stories that did not privilege certain voices over others. This audio and visual archive, while small, captures some of the images and sounds that were discussed in the workshops, some of which ended up in the podcast itself. In the posts, everyday objects, practices, and sounds are accompanied by narrative, music, or voice, and are thus relatable as common things (e.g., a coffee cup, pictures of a city, etc.), but also bear the histories and memories unique to the poster. Rather than reinforcing cultural mores and roles, this playful dynamic was conceptualized as foundationally disruptive, challenging the division between researchers and new arrivals by allowing any and all of us to take ownership of the arc of the workshops and the audio-visual content of the Instagram page. In this sense, the work was principally a liminoid, rather than liminal, praxis: while we could not claim any closure to the in-betweenness experienced and expressed by participants, and no apparent threshold was decisively crossed, in this small time-space of the project, participants shared multiple roles (e.g., teachers/students, authors/editors) and expressed their complex subjectivities and histories.

FIG. 8.1. A submission from the Picturing Home Instagram archive. *Source: Instagram*

THE *PICTURING HOME* PODCAST

The final piece of *Picturing Home*'s puzzle was the podcast, which was initially part of the flow of interaction, connection, and production, rather than the project's end goal. Hugo pulled audio material from the recorded workshop sessions, and together we parsed it into a general narrative arc. I wrote some narrative structure around selected sound bites, and used them to frame questions that I planned to pose to the participants taking part in the podcast. We sent this general script to the week's interviewees, both to make sure they were on board with the topic and how their stories were told in the "story" of the podcast, and to give them time to think about answers to the questions. We also sent the selected sound bites to the people whose voices were heard in them, so that we had their consent to use these clips. In this way, *Picturing Home* participants were also responsible for a sizable portion of the scripting and editing that ended up shaping the podcast episodes.

While by and large participants agreed to have the clips used in the podcast and were happy with the arc of the episodes, we left plenty of room for discussion while we recorded. In one particular case, we were recording a bit about artistic practices that are part of homemaking, and one participant brought up a business they had started. The participant was keen to talk about this work, as it was enjoyable and situated them within a creative community in Malmö. The business itself was one that might have seriously challenged stereotypes about migrants with this participant's background. And while this business had its own social media presence, we halted the conversation to discuss the potential perils of including it in the podcast episode. As I knew well from my research (and my own personal experience), speaking about unregistered work—which this was—could have serious consequences for someone in the stage of migration this participant was in. Hugo edited around this conversation, and the resulting episode makes no mention of this participant's pastime turned job.

I mention this here not to celebrate my and Hugo's part in this particular set of decisions, nor to pat ourselves on the back for not exploiting a participant's story, nor to highlight our gatekeeping role (for which we could rightly be criticized), but rather as one example of when we managed to think critically about someone's story, and then, in consultation with them, decided to keep it silent rather than deploy it towards "humanizing" or "triumphant" ends. While in the academy, and especially in qualitative research, the voice has been championed as "true and real" (Jackson and Mazzei 2009, 1, cited in Tuck and Yang 2014a, 229), there is an ethical charge to which stories should be (quite literally) broadcast, and when, and where.

So what does it mean to silence a story in the context of a mode of practice and research in which the actual physical voice is so central?

One of the dangers of podcasting, I would contend, is the "casting" itself— the sort of magic that seems to produce and inhabit any new media platform, as though it had appeared out of the ether, whole and complete and intact. The availability of the technology, moreover, imbues the end product itself with the patina of democracy—anyone can do it, all voices are equal, all stories can be told, and, because this is about storytelling after all, all stories have a resolution. Reality is, of course, quite a bit more complicated, especially when stories are in the process of unfolding, or belong to people with challenging or marginalized positions, or whose telling might have real (legal, political, social) consequences.

To take the metaphor of magic further, the "casting" in podcasting might relate to Avery Gordon's call for a sociology that "conjures social life" (2008, 22). Akin to the Situationists' injunction that play can change material circumstances, Gordon's understanding of this conjuring in the sense of "calling up and calling out the forces that make things what they are in order to fix and transform a troubling situation" (Gordon 2008, 22). I have tried to make it clear that while perhaps there was something of this aim in the *Picturing Home* project as it was originally conceived, I feel decidedly more skeptical about the role of practice-based research in definitively *changing* things, although perhaps this chapter in itself is a form of conjuring, in its merging of "the analytical, the procedural, the imaginative, and the effervescent" (22). It is in the unpacking, in other words, of not only the podcast, but of the play and work around it, that something of the social life of participants, of Sweden at this historical moment, and what we may hope for in the future, can be described and addressed, if not "transformed" or "solved." In her foreword to Gordon's *Ghostly Matters*, Janice Radway notes that Gordon seeks a new way of knowing, "a knowing that is more a listening than a seeing, a practice of being attuned to the echoes and murmurs of that which has been lost but which is still present among us in the form of intimations, hints, suggestions, and portents" (Radway 2008, x). While, to be sure, podcasting offers many opportunities for elevating voices that have not found other fora, as a research method and praxis it demands that we not fall prey to the same perils that have historically plagued social research. In addition to celebrating how podcasting may allow researchers to distribute their work to a larger audience, and more quickly at that, and may serve as a forum for peers in the academy who have previously been silenced, perhaps we should also find ways to attune ourselves to the ephemera, audible and otherwise, about which Gordon writes, and the manner in which they emerge (in part) through the work that happens in building connections, trust, and collaboration *around* podcasting practice.

ON SILENCE AND SLOWNESS:
TOWARDS AN ACTIVIST LIMINOID PRACTICE

This chapter has been, in part, about decentring both podcasting and the researcher in podcast research praxis. At the same time, while the *Picturing Home* project was taking place, I was grappling with one part of my own "complex personhood" that is entangled—in legal and experiential ways—with the same migration systems woven into the stories of *Picturing Home*'s collaborators. Writing this, I feel the visceral compulsion to tell you that I do not pretend my situation is akin to the forced displacement faced by several other *Picturing Home* participants. I feel compelled to tell you that my own strange, uncertain migration status does not give me carte blanche to tell you other people's stories. I feel pressed to tell you that I am part of the academy, and so am part of an institution whose lifeblood is "the generation and swapping of stories," many of which it does not deserve to hear, and should not be entrusted with (Tuck and Yang 2014a, 232), a status which means I am always already bound to channels and relationships of unequal power.

As researchers who have worked, or work still, with communities that have been marginalized, we cannot always leave our own personhood behind, as much as we might like to. Trying to do so belies a reliance on and faith in "objectivity," which remains the academy's imperfect and dehumanizing metric in producing research, and treats even human interlocutors as objects. Also, our own personhood is sometimes deeply connected to our research, in practical and personal ways. We may be led by political conviction, institutional and environmental contexts, and indeed our own stories, to the questions we ask in the world. In podcast work, the challenge as I see it is the same sort of methodological and ethical challenge that has long faced scholars in the social sciences and media studies: Who is represented, and how?

It is easy to assume that podcast technology's expediency and relatively low cost mean it is poised to challenge issues of time and representation that plague academic research. However, looking back at the research project *Picturing Home* with the benefit of hindsight, there are serious shortcomings that I hope to address in future work. The obvious pitfalls include maintaining English as the lingua franca throughout workshopping and podcasting; and the fact that Hugo and I will both benefit from the publication of research on this particular community and the work we did with them, while it is questionable what advantages other participants may have taken away from the experience. While the project was framed as a challenge to Swedish narratives about belonging, identity, and home, in many ways the liminality of the border, and of migration experience, remained as an intact threshold: If the voices that intermingled in the space of the workshops, and were eventually recorded and archived in the form of the podcast, disrupted the silence of the border (Agier 2016), what happens after? What happens now?

This project was also inevitably bound to the timelines of a neoliberal university system, which demands research output at an increasingly rapid pace. To be sure, the affordances of the podcast format, most notably its accessibility and ease of distribution, meant that we could still carry out a practice-based research project delayed by a global health crisis. Yet I wonder what it would mean to marry the potentials of podcasting—its user-friendliness, wide availability and audience potential, and dynamic creative space—to what Mountz et al. (2015) call the "feminist care ethics" of "slow scholarship," which is not only about researchers slowing down "as a means to promote collective action to resist neoliberal and elitist pressures within the academy" (1239), but also central to encouraging the formation and sustainability of caring communities within and beyond the university.

Although the idea of slowness seems to fly in the face of one of the allures of podcasting—its rapid distribution—I would argue that slowness in both producing and *writing about* podcasts should be central to an ethics of care in podcasting work. Tuck (2009) recommends changing out damage-centred narratives for a focus on *desire*, "which is involved with the *not yet* and, at times, the *not anymore*...Desire is about longing, about a present that is enriched by both the past and the future. It is integral to our humanness," and it is fundamentally rooted in the needs and ethics of communities beyond the university (417). Giving over to the liminoid, to an impetus for play and experimentation, without a specific research output in mind, is one way to tap into this desire, to decentre the role of the researcher, and to ultimately short-circuit the academy's hunger for rapidly produced damage-centred research. How do we build our research *with* communities, centring their desires, futures, and ethical concerns? How do we listen to, cultivate, and account for the right to silence and refusal, in a format that is fundamentally about what is *audible*? In its capacity to open up a space for conversation and connection, which only subsequently becomes audible through podcasting, the work around the podcast deserves more theorizing in podcast studies.

CHAPTER 9

PODCASTING RESURGENCE
Indigenizing the Airwaves

TANYA BALL, SHEILA LAROQUE, and KAYLA LAR-SON

Hello everybody, my name is Kayla. I am here with Tanya and Sheila. We are *masinahikan iskwêwak*: the Book Women.

Welcome to the Métis kitchen party! Just like when we were kids, we gathered our supplies from the kitchen (where the adults played cards) and moved the party to the basement. The basement is a ceremonial place of freedom and creativity where Métis children go wild with their cousins. This made it the perfect place for us to begin our podcast. Of course, it was not a professional space, but we made do by imagining ourselves resting from a long day after the buffalo hunt. Instead of encircling ourselves with Red River carts,[1] we placed our teacups around the ceremonial fire, also known as the iPhone, that we used to record our conversation. The visiting was abundant as we traded stories about our plans for the weekend. When it was time to hit record, we sat there...staring at each other for a solid minute...not knowing what to say. There was another guest in the room that we needed to get acquainted with—the audience! This is how it all started. This is how we recorded our first episode of *masinahikan iskwêwak: Book Women Podcast*.

---

1   Red River carts are two-wheeled carts made entirely of wood, developed and used by the Métis from Red River in the late 1800s.

The intentions of our podcast was (and continues to be) our venture into writing, editing, and publishing Indigenous Stories.[2] As three Métis librarians, we had little experience in this world, but through the podcast seasons, we came to learn how the intricacies of Indigenous Storytelling fit into podcasting. Specifically, Métis Ways of Knowing and Being are the centre of everything we say and do.[3] It's about relationality. We have connections to plants, animals, our ancestors, and beyond—they're all our cousins! With these relationships comes responsibility. We must hold ourselves accountable by creating reciprocal relationships. If we do so, life prospers harmoniously outside and within ourselves.

Podcasting is a natural fit for expressing relationality. It comes forth in the stories that we tell and how we hold ourselves accountable to Indigenous communities. More importantly, it provides an intimate, safe space for sharing. Lucasz Swiatek (2018) suggests that podcasting acts as a "bridging medium" (173) as it gives listeners the impression of closeness and closes the gap between spatial and temporal divides. Given that many listeners listen with headphones, we are "literally whispering in people's ears" (Romero as cited in Greene 2016, 91). This creates a sense of belonging to a community of listeners, as well as a relationship with the podcast hosts. This form of relationship between host and listener is called a parasocial interaction, or parasocial relationship. It is "the illusion of being in a reciprocal social interaction" (Hartman 2017, 133). The listener is aware of the one-sided relationship in which they initiate and mediate the interactions. In terms of Indigenous podcasting, the parasocial relationship between host and listener is further enriched by Indigenous community presence. We, as Métis co-hosts, have community relations that we highlight in the show with our conversations and guest speakers. The parasocial relationship nurtures community connections for the listener, which further complements Métis relationality.

In this chapter, we invite you into our circle of Red River carts for a glimpse into Métis Ways of Knowing and Being. We argue that podcasting is a strong medium through which to explore Métis relationality. To accomplish this, we use our podcast *masinahikan iskwêwak: Book Women Podcast* as an entry point. Our podcast demonstrates our relations primarily through Storytelling, reciprocity, and Indigenous resurgence. The chapter is organized into three main sections. The first section introduces the concept of relationality to give a broad sense of Métis ideology and how it is expressed through Storytelling.

---

2   We use the term *Indigenous* to refer to the original inhabitants and stewards of the Lands in what is now known as Canada. Here there are three constitutionally recognized groups of Indigenous Peoples: First Nations, Inuit, and Métis peoples.

3   We follow Greg Younging's advice on capitalization. For further information, please see his work *Elements of Indigenous Style* (2018).

Next, we discuss Indigenous podcasting as a way to share our Stories and experiences. Both sections provide the necessary context that we are working with and against. Finally, the last section provides specific examples of relationality in podcasting using our podcast as an example. So, grab yourself a mug. We'll pour the Red Rose!

MÉTIS STORYTELLING AS A WAY OF EXPRESSING RELATIONALITY

Now that we're properly caffeinated, let's discuss Indigenous Storytelling. Mainstream media is dominated by Western thought, which proves problematic for Indigenous Storytellers. Within modern library systems, for example, Indigenous Stories are classified as Canadian literature (CanLit). Indigenous Stories do not align with Canadian literature. They are not a subgroup of CanLit, but should be treated as their own category of Indigenous literatures (Heath Justice 2018; Younging 2018). The term Indigenous literatures is pluralized to bring attention to the fact that there are many cultures represented in this category. Pluralizing the word also pushes against the stereotype that all Indigenous Peoples are the same. Indigenous Stories stand strongly as their own genre. They encapsulate Indigenous experiences of history, colonization, and contemporary reality as they are created by and for Indigenous Peoples. Essentially, Indigenous Stories have existed long before CanLit and are an extension of Sacred Stories and Oral Traditions (Younging 2018).

Given the misclassifications of Indigenous literatures, it is not surprising that Indigenous podcasting also gets pigeonholed into inappropriate genres. This can largely be attributed to misunderstanding Indigenous Ways of Knowing and Being. In settler-colonial epistemologies and ontologies, knowledge is patriarchal, racialized, possessive, and extractive. Adam J.P. Gaudry (2011) specifically states, "extraction research, rather than affirming and validating Indigenous worldviews, instead judges them by the standards of the dominant culture (often confirming that they are dated and obsolete)" (115). This creates a hierarchy of knowledge which undermines Indigenous Worldviews and enforces Westernized knowledge. Because of this hierarchy, the dominant culture has privilege and power that is used to extract knowledge from Indigenous Peoples. Moreover, it portrays a hierarchy of beings where humans are placed at the top of the pyramid and other life forces came into existence to serve humans (Jobin 2016; Moreton-Robinson 2016; TallBear 2017).

Indigenous conceptions of Knowledge do not follow the same principles. First, Indigenous Peoples do not focus their Knowledge systems in binaries. We see the world as subjective, having multiple perspectives. Knowledge is land-based, personal, experiential, narrative, oral, and holistic. There are multiple perceptions where no single person has the "truth." Rather, Knowledge is an intersection of voices (including our more-than-human relatives) and perspectives that come together in a comprehensive narrative. These Stories are decoded through language and experienced together through ceremony (Castellano 2000; Million 2015). Second, Knowledge evolves from tradition, observation, and intuition (Castellano 2000). Indigenous Knowledges, therefore, are not exclusive to the physical world. They incorporate all aspects of the self: physical, mental, emotional, and spiritual. Third, Indigenous Ways of Being are largely tied to relationality: the interconnectedness of our relations. Our understanding of relationality is greatly influenced by Métis and *nêhiyaw* (Cree) teachings about *wâhkôhtowin* and *miyo-wîcêhtowin*. *Wâhkôhtowin* refers to the interconnectedness of our relationships while *miyo-wîcêhtowin* is "having or possessing good relations" (Cardinal 1973, 14). These connections are rooted in the concept of *pimâtisiwin*, which denotes life. All of these concepts inform how we relate to the Land.[4] This is a crucial relationship because of the wealth of the Land. Within *nêhiyaw* culture, the Land is wealthy but not material. Rather, it is a relation that has the "capacity to provide livelihood" (Cardinal 1973, 43). Relationality, therefore, extends beyond human-to-human relations: it includes more-than-humans (like plants, animals, objects, and ancestors in the Spirit World). Even Stories themselves are considered our relations. Warren Cariou explains, "the story isn't really a thing, at least in that capitalistic way. It's a gift. It's a spirit. It's something that permeates our being in a different way" (Hanson 2020, 78). Viewing Stories as cousins dictates how we interact with them. They must be treated how you would treat your grandmother or cousin: with dignity and respect. These three characteristics of relationality nurture our identity as Indigenous Peoples (Innes 2013).

Storytelling reveals the inner workings of Indigenous communities as living representations of relationality. Stories enhance the relationship between Storyteller and listener as they spend time and share with one another. Each Storyteller is different and adds their own spin on the story, because Indigenous Knowledges have multiple truths depending on a person's individual contexts. Therefore, every Story and every telling is going to have variations. While interacting with a Storyteller, certain Cultural Protocols must be adhered to. In some instances, we offer Tobacco to reflect Traditional Protocol. Tobacco is a sacred medicine for some Indigenous Peoples as it is used in prayer, Ceremony, or to request guidance from Elders. When Tobacco is offered, it is seen as a respectful exchange: an appreciation of the knowledge and experience that comes with each Elder. This is different for every Nation.

---

4   The word *Land* is purposefully capitalized here to denote the fact that the Land is of equal importance to other proper nouns.

Métis, for example, do not always accept Tobacco as Protocol, sometimes they ask for other medicines, like Berries. Whatever the case, the Elder will have a conversation with you before entering into agreements about which Protocol is appropriate.

Indigenous Stories and Storytelling typically come about in Ceremony and through visiting. Ceremonies look different to each Indigenous Nation, but are broadly understood as ways to remember and reconnect (Wall Kimmerer 2013). They can be traditional like Sweat Lodge Ceremonies or more contemporary like mindfulness exercises. For urban Indigenous Peoples, traditional Ceremonies may not be as accessible. In this case, Indigenous Peoples turn to visiting to maintain strong connections to the Land. Visiting overlaps with everything that we do. It is a place for intergenerational learning by swapping Stories (Gaudet 2019). These Stories help us to remember who we are as Indigenous Peoples and how we relate to the Land, and they impart traditional philosophical understandings. Honouring the traditions of Ceremony and visiting ensures the prosperity of future generations (Kermoal and Altamirano-Jiménez 2016).

Outside of Storyteller Protocol, there are Protocols that encourage healthy relationships with the Stories themselves. Like Cultural Protocols, Story Protocols vary. For more Traditional Stories, Storytellers may only tell them to specific audiences. Traditionally, Knowledge is not freely given—it is earned. Therefore, the listener must be in a specific life stage to be deemed ready to receive this certain Knowledge. Cariou explains that stories are "about what somebody's going through in a particular time, and the thing that you hear then, and then later too, the layers come as you remember it" (Hanson 2020, 79). Some Traditional Stories are seasonal or gender specific.

Personal Stories follow separate Protocols. Within Indigenous communities, the person whom the story is about is the owner of the story. As such, they are in charge of how it gets disseminated or forgotten. This contrasts modern-day copyright laws, which claim ownership for the person who collected the data. In other words, if a researcher records an Elder telling a story, once publicly disseminated, the researcher is the owner of the story (Younging 2010, 5). Within Indigenous contexts this is inappropriate because it puts the subjects of the story in a precarious position. It is possible that they do not want their Stories to be publicized or the story is being misrepresented. This is understandable given the trauma that we have experienced as a direct result of colonization. In some of our conversations, we experienced what Stacey Copeland and Lauren Knight (2021) call "wounded vibrations":

Wounded vibrations are not simply pained emotions but also the circulation of memories and felt affect before happy or sad, negative or positive are constituted. They are the vibrations of past, present and future that every sounding natural object from human to bird put out into the world. The ephemeral inexplicable feelings you experience when you visit a former residential school or shake the hand of a survivor are wounded vibrations. (103)

For these reasons, Personal Stories always involve a conversation with the person in the story and how they wish to have their Stories told. Copeland and Knight (2021) further articulate that "we choose to use the term vibration because they can be felt—in the body, in the air, in the land—but not always necessarily seen or heard. Rather vibrations are felt in a way that triggers sensory experience that cannot always be explained" (102–3). We see this as the senses that are there, but are not always directly pointed out. One example of this from our podcast is in season one, episode ten, where we chat with burlesque performer Brittany Johnson about living with pain and chronic illnesses (*masinahikan iskwêwak* 2019). Discussing the physical pain that our bodies might be in can be seen as adding to the vibrations that are felt more than heard. When people who have chronic illnesses discuss their lived realities, there is much that is often left unsaid; either because it cannot be articulated in words or simply doesn't warrant an explanation. Between Brittany and Sheila (and the audience who is listening) there are many things that are understood at an emotional or spiritual level. It is beyond statements like "I have endometriosis too; I understand what it's like." And that's okay! Realistically, it is up to the person how they want their story captured.

With this in mind, we developed a specific Protocol that places our guests in control of the episode. Firstly, we always invite our guests to listen to the recorded podcast before it is released. That way, we have the opportunity to edit out items they do not want in the episode. Secondly, whatever the guests want deleted—we delete it! We do not need justification from them about their decision-making processes. That's not our business. Lastly, we do not release any of our episodes without explicit permission from our guest. If that means we have a delayed release date, it means we have a delayed release date. Scheduling is not what matters here. After the episode is released, we maintain an open conversation with our guest. If they decide that they want their episode removed from our website and podcast archive, we will remove it. By adopting these practices, we transform wounded vibrations into what we call "vibrations of resurgence": from a place where much hurt and trauma can be felt without explicit articulation, to a force that is more empowering and where creativity can be harnessed and further fuelled.

While we recognize the immense value of sharing traumatic experiences and holding space for individuals to heal, it is equally valuable to promote vibrations of resurgence. These vibrations start with the podcast and go beyond. It is a sonic space where we can flip the narrative from victims into survivors. It's a shift in power that uplifts Indigenous voices by providing a space for them to truly be themselves unapologetically. Vibrations of resurgence go out further than we can imagine. They stretch out beyond time and space because they are about recognizing the wounded cries from the past and reverberating back with strength. The vibrations of resurgence begin, continue, and resonate throughout healing processes. Ultimately, we hope to inspire others to feel their own vibrations of resurgence in whatever way makes sense to them.

What makes sense to us right now is refilling our cups as we get ready to explore Indigenous podcasting practices.

INDIGENOUS PODCASTERS IN ACTION: RECOGNIZING THOSE WHO CAME BEFORE US

Bio break over. Back to work! Now let's pause for Kayla's history moment. While traditional radio programming in, by, and for Indigenous communities is still relevant, over the last ten years, we have seen a shift towards the podcasting medium (Avisar 2020). In contrast to traditional radio broadcasts, podcasts can be accessed on demand, providing listeners with control over when, where, and how they listen. In the podcasting space, Indigenous voices are heard, preserved, and shared at minimal cost. With respect to content, podcasting offers a space for sharing all types of Indigenous Stories—traditional, contemporary, and otherworldly—that other gatekept media do not. Indigenous podcasting is thus a unique platform for Indigenous Peoples to express sovereignty and self-determination within the realm of media. Podcasting allows Indigenous Peoples to unapologetically speak their truth, connect with their communities, and share their traditions with a larger audience (Mitchell 2017). Kelly Boutsalis (2021) specifically states, "As a Mohawk woman in an urban setting, hearing Indigenous voices through my earbuds makes me feel like I am back in my community with friends and relatives, telling stories just as we've done for generations" (para. 2). Vibrations of resurgence are amplified through the online communities that podcasting enables and which foster a sense of belonging. In addition, podcasting is an affordable option for Indigenous people to get their ideas out in the world. Podcasting specifically offers a space for the creation of parasocial relationships since Indigenous Peoples can tune in at any given time to hear voices and stories from their community.

Indigenous podcasting is a space for resisting colonial narratives found in mainstream media. In 2015, the Truth and Reconciliation Commission of Canada released its "Calls to Action," including three that specifically relate to the media.[5] The commission highlighted Canadian media as having "a long history of perpetuating negative stereotypes and under-reporting issues of importance to Indigenous communities" (Elliott 2016, 4). Two articles within the *United Nations Declaration on the Rights of Indigenous Peoples* (UNDRIP) outline the Right for Indigenous Peoples to communicate. Elliott (2016) interprets article 16.2 as the state being responsible to ensure that diversity is reflected in state-owned media, and to encourage private companies to also include such measures. Article 16.1 reflects the Rights of Indigenous Peoples to create their own media, in their own languages. Indigenous-owned media that reflects the community's values is an important aspect of resisting negative stereotyping and asserting cultural identity.

Part of this resistance is providing Indigenous programming by Indigenous podcasters that centres Indigenous Ways of Knowing and Being. Being Indigenous is political because of the colonial past that continues into the present. As a result, identifying as such comes with a lot of responsibility. Individually, we are accountable to our communities and the ideologies that they have taught us. It is our responsibility to ensure that our relations are represented in a respectful manner. Respect for our relations comes in the form of reframing the conversation around Indigenous social, political, and economic issues. When we as Indigenous Peoples reframe the conversation we are able to take greater control over the ways in which Indigenous matters and social topics are discussed and handled (Tuhiwai Smith 1999). Traditional media sources tend to be cynical and paternalistic, often framing Indigenous issues as being solely a community problem, failing to acknowledge any historical and contemporary wrongdoings that might be the source of the problem (Tuhiwai Smith 1999). Reframing occurs within Indigenous podcasts when hosts and guests resist being "boxed and labeled into categories that we do not fit" (Tuhiwai Smith 1999, 153), and begin to address Indigenous matters from a place of lived experience and incorporating Indigenous Worldviews. Rick Harp, who left traditional broadcasting to start the Indigenous-focused current affairs podcast *Media Indigena,* says of his decision, "There's obviously a lot of content made by non-Indigenous Peoples about Indigenous issues, there's content made by Indigenous people...about Indigenous issues, but I wanted something that, instead of being a content provider, it was a context provider" (quoted in CBC 2018, para. 5).

Indigenous Peoples have often been presented in mainstream media in negative terms, perpetuating stereotypes and building upon biases. Podcasting

---

5   This commission was formed to address the legacy of Indian Residential Schools in Canada. The "Calls to Action" are suggestions from the committee to promote reconciliation with Indigenous Peoples.

affords the opportunity to be unapologetic as it is not governed by the same media regulations as other forms of communication, such as television or radio. Since there is no governing body that podcast creators and hosts are accountable to, Indigenous communities naturally fill in this space and assert their sovereignty in ways that reflect Indigenous Knowledges. Theoretically, anyone in the world can listen to the conversation, so there is a responsibility on the content creators' part to share only what they know to be true and to adhere to the Cultural Protocol of their respective communities, or that of the community whose Knowledges are being shared. Not all Stories and Traditions are meant to be shared with the general public, and being granted access is a privilege that many take for granted. This is a distinct difference between Indigenous and non-Indigenous communities. Within Indigenous cultures, Knowledge must be earned, and there are specific Protocols on how to earn such knowledge. Aspects such as the clan or family you are from, your age, gender identity, and the current season can determine what Knowledge you are allowed to know and share. Despite these Protocols, there is ample content from which Indigenous creators can pull.

Within the scope of Indigenous podcasting, conversation topics are as numerous and varied as Indigenous communities themselves. There are stories about the relationship between anti-blackness and settler colonialism; Indigenous feminisms and rematriation; Indigenous Storytelling; and Indigi-nerdity (Mitchell 2017). Historically, Indigenous Peoples have not been "passed the mic," when it comes to both speaking on Indigenous matters and being represented in media stories. Due to the lack of Indigenous representation, there is a tendency for anything with Indigenous Peoples to be put into an "Indigenous box." This box is labelled for Indigenous Peoples to only speak on Indigenous topics in a non-threatening, easily digestible way. We are not seen as people who can have interests outside of Indigenous topics, which means we must put forward a great deal of emotional labour in order to be seen as complex and complete human beings. Emotional labour is the act of putting one's emotions to the side in order to fulfill specific requirements of a job. This is hard work because it calls on us to re-traumatize ourselves for the dominant culture. We know that Indigenous Peoples are capable of anything and have a lot to say. Incorporating vibrations of resurgence recognizes us as full human beings with interests outside of Indigenous topics and provides us the space to normalize Indigenous Peoples within the media in the way that they choose to be represented. This can only be possible with a critical mass of Indigenous media creators. To our knowledge, no content analyses of Indigenous podcasts have been published at this time. This might speak to the relatively recent emergence of podcasting, but it might also be due to the lack of presence of Indigenous Peoples in media in general.

Despite these challenges, there are many successful Indigenous podcasts. One of the first Indigenous podcasters to appear on the Canadian scene was Ryan McMahon who found success with his podcast *Red Man Laughing*. He is also the founder of Indian and Cowboy, an all-Indigenous podcasting network in Canada. McMahon led the way and acted as a mentor for many Indigenous podcasters. Other Indigenous podcasts in Canada include *Métis in Space*, about Indigenous Peoples in movies and popular culture; *Who Killed Alberta Williams?* and *Missing and Murdered: Finding Cleo*, both of which investigate the issue of missing and murdered Indigenous women and girls; and *All My Relations*, *Coffee with My Ma*, and *The Henceforward*, which discuss our relations as Indigenous Peoples with one another, the Land, and our ancestors. As well, Indigenous podcasts are now being produced both by broadcasters and independently. Those produced by broadcasters, like *Unreserved* from the Canadian Broadcasting Corporation (CBC), are oftentimes (but not always) released on terrestrial airwaves first, then made available as a podcast. Independently produced podcasts allow their creators and hosts to control the content and resources.

As Indigenous women, we know that we are never alone in our endeavours. We are a part of a larger community. Therefore, In the spirit of relationality, we must pay our respect to Indigenous podcasters of yesterday, today, and tomorrow. Together, they have created a safe space for us to venture into the podcasting world. Without them, we would never have made it to Sheila's basement to create ᒥᔮᐧᒳᐦᑲᐤᐃᐢᑫᐧᐊᐠ *masinahikan iskwêwak: Book Women Podcast*.

CASE STUDY: THREE MÉTIS AUNTIES IN A POD

So how did we end up in Sheila's basement in the first place? Like many good things, this podcast came about due to rejection, common experience, and an undeniable friendship. It began when the organizers of the Writing Stick conference in 2017 planned to create a legacy piece with their leftover funding. The idea of a podcast was brought forth to Tanya who, after careful consideration, reached out to Sheila and Kayla to create and host it together. We all knew each other through our involvement in the Indigenous library internship and residency programs through the University of Alberta Library. Our relationship flourished by virtue of us all being strong-minded, radical Indigenous librarians. Having three Métis women, librarians, and friends was the perfect fit for the podcast, so in summer of 2018, we sat down to begin planning. Together, we decided the intent behind the series was to inspire Indigenous people to pursue writing, editing, and publishing as a career, by interviewing Indigenous people who have done so. Indigenous creators would offer advice and lessons learned during their career. We could feel the vibrations of resurgence throughout Sheila's basement. They got the creative juices flowing. We could see them spilling out into our planning documents. The vibrations were already beginning to change the basement into a podcast studio with our Métis kitchen-party vibe.

Guests invited to the podcast were given a cash honorarium for their time and expertise, which has always been a mandate of the podcast. This was one of many steps towards including Métis relationality in our processes. Knowledge is not freely given in Indigenous cultures, it is earned through relationship development. We acknowledge that Indigenous people are experts in their cultures and deserve to be paid for their time. We never invite a guest onto our podcast without funding to pay them.

Perhaps more importantly, we ensure that our guests are represented in the way that they wish. We are accountable to our guests and they are accountable to their communities. Therefore, it is crucial for all of us to present their interview in a respectful manner. For us, this means that our guest is in control of the content. Because of the casual nature of our interviews, we can get carried away and forget that we are being recorded. Sometimes this means that we can say things that we regret. After we have completed editing the audio, we always send it back to our guests for final approval. If our guest wants us to delete some material, we edit it out and keep it confidential to respect their privacy. As Indigenous podcasters we are highly aware of the relationships that we have with community members and guests of the podcast. At the end of the day, our relationships and our accountability to our relatives are what matter, not a juicy interview.

In creating our podcast we had to consider the name, logo, target audience, and content. Every good podcast has a catchy name that represents what it is all about. As we were all librarians and Métis we went with the *nêhiyawêwin* (Cree-language) word for female librarians *masinahikan iskwêwak*, which translates to "book women," and in syllabics is ᒪᓯᓇᐦᐃᑲᐣ ᐃᐢᑫᐧᐊᐠ. Using *nêhiyawêwin* for the podcast's name not only allowed us to acknowledge Treaty Six Territory and the languages that are spoken there,[6] but also allowed us to reclaim languages that our ancestors would have spoken and engage in language resurgence practices. In giving the podcast a name in *nêhiyawêwin* we are being accountable to our communities by actively resisting giving the podcast a strictly Western name. The *Book Women* logo reflects Indigenous ways of connecting and building relations. Designed by Tanya, the logo is a teacup with a beaded flower

---

6   The podcast is recorded on Treaty Six Territory and Métis Region Four. It is the traditional gathering place for Cree Saulteaux, Blackfoot, Métis, Nakota Sioux, Iroquois, Dene, Ojibway/Saulteaux/Anishinaabe, Inuit, and many others. The treaty boundaries extend across present-day Alberta and Saskatchewan.

sitting beside it. The beaded flower depicts traditional Métis flower bead-work. Métis people are often referred to as the "Flower Beadwork People" because of the vibrant floral designs used. Oftentimes, beadwork includes the flora and fauna of the area to rep-resent our relationship with the Land. The teacup represents the time that we spend with each other visiting, telling Stories, and drinking tea.

FIG. 9.1. The *Book Women* Logo. *Source: Tanya Ball*

The target audience for the pod-cast is Indigenous people who have an interest in Storytelling; however, we welcome audience members from all communities. We aim to inspire Indigenous people to share their Stories in whatever medium that they enjoy by actively seeking Stories outside of the written word. This emphasizes the fact that Stories are kin. They are ever-evolving and must be treated with the respect that we would treat our own auntie. As we know, all aunties possess different qualities: there are cool aunties, empathetic aunties, mean aunties, aunties that cook you food, and aunties that take you to the bar. Treating Stories as aunties, we need to bear in mind that each story is unique and brings its own perspectives to the table. Therefore, when seeking Stories, it is important for us to include different methods of Storytelling, such as illustration, burlesque, beadwork, tattoo art, and improv, along with traditional Indigenous Storytellers and writers. To demonstrate reciprocity, we incorporate any links to their work in our show notes, website, and social media to encourage listeners to continue their rela-tionship with our guests even after listening to the episode. Overall, the goal is to foster relationality and create parasocial relationships by extending our visiting sessions to the listeners, so that they will join the Métis kitchen party and feel like one of the aunties.

For us, it was important to feature a wide range of media that could be considered "Indigenous Storytelling," including Traditional Storytelling, academic research, poetry, illustration, zines, memoirs, podcasting, and bur-lesque. In Western ideology, we are taught that books are the main method of sharing Stories. Ideas presented outside of this form are not validated or seen to have as much value. Validating knowledge in this way is problematic because it puts emphasis on commodification of knowledge and takes other forms of being out of the equation (Hanson 2020). Indigenous Peoples have always told Stories without the written word. While most of this is through oral Storytelling, there are other forms of knowledge gathering that are worth noting. For example, Indigenous people in Peru equipped themselves with quipus, a method of record-keeping using a series of coloured knots and string. A Story is not always just pen to paper; rather, there are countless ways to tell a Story.

Even with our lack of skill and podcasting notoriety, we were able to secure interviews with prominent authors and scholars such as Dr. Norma Dunning, author of *Annie Muktuk and Other Stories*; Marilyn Dumont, author of *A Really Good Brown Girl*; and Dr. Chris Andersen, author of *"Métis": Race, Recognition, and the Struggle for Indigenous Peoplehood.*

We ended the first season with a reflection episode, where we discussed the successes and failures of the series. Self-reflection is a major component of Métis Ways of Knowing and Being. Including this piece encourages our listeners to incorporate these practices into their own lives. Plus, others could learn from our mistakes! In our reflections, we noted that our guests were Métis-centric, being that we relied heavily on our family, friends, and colleagues who were predominantly Métis or had connections with Métis communities. This was something that we wanted to address by expanding who we were including as guests in future episodes. In other words, we needed to expand our circle of relationships to fully represent the territory in which we were recording (Treaty Six and Métis Region Four).

Storytelling and passing down cultural information go hand in hand, so much so that it is difficult to distinguish the difference between where Storytelling ends and cultural dissemination begins. Another prominent theme throughout our podcast is reconnecting with Indigenous culture, discovering aspects of it that have been hidden, or nurturing what might have only been there in small pieces. Finding culture and expressing this through writing and Storytelling can be seen as being synonymous with finding a voice, which is perfectly suited for the podcast medium. The second episode overall, and our first episode with a guest, featured Tammy Ball, Tanya's mother. She is writing a memoir about her life growing up Métis in Saint Ambroise, Manitoba. For Tammy, writing her memoir can be seen as an intentional act that gives meaning to a great deal of why things "were the way they were" while she was growing up, as well as a reclaiming of the past that can lead to transforming the way that we see ourselves in the future.

We were keenly aware of the Cultural Protocols surrounding the Stories and the community members that we interviewed. As previously mentioned, many Indigenous Stories come with particular Protocols. When we interviewed Josh Littlechild, we ran into a problem: the Stories that were told in the episode are only brought out when there is snow on the ground. At the time of recording, it was still winter. Unfortunately, because of our timeline, we did not publish the episode until spring, which left us with a dilemma.

How would we simulate winter to remain respectful of the Stories? We consulted with Josh and reflected back on our own teachings of Story-sharing Protocols and opted to create an illusion of winter by adding the sound of crunching snow. Although we never consulted with an Elder about this decision, it was our hope that the Story would remain in a digital-winter space, no matter the season. In addition, we recorded an extra introduction where we drew attention to the challenge that we faced in editing the audio for that particular episode. In the introduction, we stated that at the time of the recording there was snow on the ground, but we included the sound of footsteps walking through snow over the actual name of the character, so it can be listened to at any time. In doing this, we wanted to have a teaching moment with our listeners where we could discuss the complexities of publishing Indigenous Stories while also being aware of community Protocols.

We step lightly into conversations of a sensitive nature, such as Indigenous sexuality. Specifically, in season three, episode two, we discuss Tanya Tagaq's book *Split Tooth*, which contains triggering content (*masinahikan iskwêwak* 2021). We approached this topic with a trigger warning and mental health check-ins. The check-ins were inspired by the hosts' own experiences of trauma and mental health challenges. For example, we suggested that listeners have a grounding object, an item that one can hold and focus on. It could be a stuffed animal, a rock, a fidget spinner, whatever is special to them. There is power in having something in one's hands while moving through difficult topics. Grounding does not solve the problem, but may prevent emotions from intensifying. It anchors us to the present and distracts our minds enough to tackle these topics with minimal emotion. Other exercises included remaining present by noticing our surroundings: the smells, the sounds, the sights, etc. Of course, we were also able to lighten the mood with humour. We took to uncomfortable topics by including our own stories of vulnerability to ensure that the listeners did not feel like they were alone in the process. Our favourite instance of this is our conversation around chronic illness. Having a negative relationship with our bodies because of pain has seriously affected our lives. Instead of complaining about these experiences, we bring forth fun ideas to solve these problems, like including items like sex wedges in the bedroom! Anything can happen in our recordings. At this point, we've embraced this reality. We know that the recording itself has a life of its own. So we treat it as our honorary fourth auntie.

SIGNING OFF!

Now, we are reminiscing about the times in Sheila's basement. We are no longer in that Red River cart circle, huddled around an iPhone. Instead, there are messy hairdos, pyjamas, and friendly faces on our computer screens. This is a global pandemic, after all. We are sheltering in our new spaces with our mugs and our sass. We include our sashes in the background of our Zoom calls so that our stories stay within the Métis spirit.[7]

The vibrations of resurgence began as a buzz from a cellphone and a wild idea. It now vibrates outside of our circle into the hearts and heads of our listeners. We suspect that as a tool of community connectivity, resistance and indigenization, podcasting will grow more widely and listenerships will expand. Indigenous podcasts continue to tackle topics that allow for communities to tell their truths and share their worldviews in a space that remains community led without settler interruption. As for the future of who will be hosting these podcasts, we suspect that Indigenous youth will be holding the mics, their voices rising alongside Elders on the airwaves, connecting intergenerationally. Indigenous people, Black people, and people of colour (IBPOC) will continue to share their experiences together, while aiding each other in active resistance against injustice and oppression. IBPOC-hosted podcasts can also act as a space to engage in discussions of futurisms.

Well, that's it for this chapter. Although the writing is completed, we're not done yet! You can't get rid of us; there's still a lot to be done. We will continue to advocate for relationality within our practices. We hope to see more Indigenous podcasters following suit. Everyone has their own story to tell. We will uplift you in any way that we can. Together, our vibrations of resurgence will shake the airwaves. Until then, we will let you go in our usual podcast fashion: we are *masinahikan iskwêwak*, the Book Women, signing off until our next episode. Métis aunties *out*!

---

7   Métis sashes are finger-woven belts of various colours. Historically, they were used by voyageurs in the fur trade and taken in by Métis people in Red River. Over time, they have become a symbol of Métis culture.

CHAPTER 10

TALKING THE TALK

A Conversational Cross-Cultural Analysis of a Podcast Story Told to Three Different Audiences

TZLIL SHARON and NICHOLAS JOHN

I n this chapter we explore how one story is told in three different podcasts by two different production teams based in two different countries and in two different languages. The story is about the efforts of a gay Jewish Israeli couple, Tal and Amir, to have children, which they do, in Nepal, with the help of a Ukrainian woman's eggs and two Indian surrogates. The story includes coverage of the powerful 2015 earthquake in Nepal, which happened while Tal and Amir were in Nepal with their three babies, as well as an investigation into how much the surrogates actually earned, following the revelation that they received a lot less than the men were led to believe they would.

The podcasts are produced by *Radiolab*[1] and *Sipur Yisraeli* (Hebrew for *Israel Story*), with the latter creating two versions of the story—one in English (which we shall refer to as the *Israel Story* version)[2] and one in Hebrew (the *Sipur Yisraeli* version).[3] *Radiolab* is a dominant presence in the American (and global) podcast scene. It was first broadcast on NPR in 2002 as a radio show before also being released as a podcast, which is how it is primarily consumed today.[4] It is a leading example of the highly produced long-form

---

1   See playlist (page 179) track one.
2   See playlist track two.
3   See playlist track three.
4   The oldest episode on *Radiolab*'s website is from April 2007 (https://radiolab.org/ episodes). Since 2015, *Radiolab* has been produced by WNYC, a public radio station...

narrative non-fiction podcast (for more on the American podcast delivery style, see Bottomley 2020, pages 174–99; Leonard 2017; McHugh 2016) within the science journalism genre (Spinelli and Dann 2019). Each of its episodes takes a topic, such as morality, vaccinations, or selfhood, and explores it in depth, presenting interviews with experts, stories told by everyday people, and personal reflections from the hosts. *Sipur Yisraeli* is similar in style and format, though its direct inspiration was *This American Life*, another radio show turned podcast that engages with a broad theme each week, usually telling a number of stories that it presents as "acts" in the show. First produced in Hebrew in 2013, *Israel Story* started making shows in English in 2014.

A story produced in three different ways in three podcasts for three different audiences (Americans, Israelis, and American—and other diaspora—Jews) creates a remarkable opportunity to examine the place of podcasts in mediating global flows of culture, the role of the local in shaping the final product, and the imagined podcast audience. In addition, our conversations about these three podcasts—conversations that we recorded and transcribed—enable us to reflect on the importance of language and identity in the creation of podcasts, as well as in the creation of knowledge about podcasts across cultural contexts.

The central questions we tackle are the following: How is the story told differently in the three podcasts? How are the protagonists' and other voices presented to the audiences, in terms of content, accent, and narration? How can we characterize the different soundscapes of the different podcasts? Are there differences in the assumptions the podcasters have about their listeners, consequently resulting in differences in how they are being addressed? And how do our identities as the authors of this chapter shape our analyses? We note that Tzlil is a native-born Israeli and that Nicholas is an English-born migrant to Israel, where he has lived for over twenty-five years. We are both close to bilingual, though we each feel more comfortable talking and writing in our first languages.

In addressing the above questions, we take into account tension between three sometimes intersecting cross-cultural encounters. The first is between the well-resourced and long-running podcast production *Radiolab* and the much younger *Israel Story*, which started out with the support of Israel's army radio station. The second is between the Israeli protagonists, Tal and Amir, and the Indian surrogates with whom they can barely communicate, all of whom we hear talking in their own voices—some with voice-over translation—in the podcasts' episodes. Indeed, the resources of *Radiolab* were

---

...in New York City, and is broadcast on public radio stations in the United States, as well as distributed via RSS as a podcast.

crucial in getting an overheard conversation between one of the surrogates and an agency representative translated into English. The third is between the authors of this chapter, who are differently attuned to Hebrew and English, who write and talk in English and Hebrew with different levels of proficiency, and who approach the story told here with different cultural assumptions.

Because of these tensions—which revolve in different ways around questions of language and identity—we thought it would be important to converse, to talk through this research and to bring this text into being by explicitly confronting these issues of language and understanding that come up when we, the authors, talk and write together. We begin by discussing the very possibility of creating cross-cultural productions through the medium of podcasting, and the methods used to analyze our case study. Then, we offer a comparative analysis of the three versions of the story that shows how the local comes through differently in each podcast, despite what they view as the universal messages of the story and their shared liberal view on the issue of same-sex couples raising children. Finally, we reflect on the process of creating this text—which is part prose and part conversation—as a way of bringing to the fore issues that are usually neglected in more traditional academic writing. Ultimately, our aspiration here is to contribute to novel ways of thinking about developing methodological approaches that might better suit podcast studies (e.g., Bottomley, 2021; Mertens, Hoyt, and Morris 2021; Noh 2021).[5]

HOW IT ALL CAME ABOUT: THE BIRTH STORY OF "BIRTHSTORY" AND THE GLOBALIZING POTENTIAL OF PODCASTING

The starting point for this cross-cultural investigation is, in fact, the background story that eventually led to the three versions of "Birthstory." Hence, before we delve into a more systematic comparison, a short walk-through of the chain of events that brought about the collaboration between the *Israel Story* podcast team and *Radiolab* is in order.

In 2014, about a year before the story told in the three podcasts begins, Maya Kosover, a well-known figure in the Israeli radio scene and a producer of the Hebrew podcast *Sipur Yisraeli*, threw a birthday party. There, she met the protagonists of our story, Tal and Amir, a gay couple who had started a surrogacy process with the hope of bringing children of their own into the world. Since Israeli law at the time prohibited gay male couples from hiring a surrogate in Israel,[6] they were using the international surrogacy agency

---

5   See also chapter seven in this volume by Copeland, McGregor, and McLeod.
6   This law changed on July 11, 2021, when the Israeli Supreme Court authorized surrogacy arrangements for gay men (Library of Congress, n.d.).

Lotus. The process involved implanting embryos created from a Ukrainian woman's eggs and the men's sperm into the wombs of Indian women who would carry their pregnancies to term in Nepal, where surrogacy was permitted (as long as the surrogate was not actually Nepalese herself). When the couple first met Kosover, she was astounded to discover that they were actually expecting three babies (twins from one surrogate, and one child from the other). Kosover decided to follow Tal and Amir's journey to parenthood and to produce it as an investigative long-form storytelling podcast episode for *Sipur Yisraeli*. She provided the couple with audio recording equipment. Tal and Amir in return provided Kosover with over 150 hours of audio journals.

While Tal and Amir were recording their thoughts and experiences for Kosover's production, the *Sipur Yisraeli* team went on an American tour to present their audio work, including a show at a Jewish Community Center (JCC) in New York. During that tour, in which Kosover took a backstage role as she felt insecure about her English, an exciting opportunity came up: a former intern of *Radiolab*, who was now interning with *Sipur Yisraeli*, managed to set up a pitch meeting at *Radiolab* for Kosover and her team.

At this exact time, Tal and Amir were staying at an apartment in Nepal, dealing with the burdensome bureaucracy they had to complete before they could take their three newborn babies home to Israel. On the morning of 25 April 2015, New York time, the day before the *Radiolab* pitch meeting, Kosover woke up to a dramatic voice mail from Tal: sobbing and sounding panicked, he told her that there had been a terrible earthquake in Nepal. Kosover quickly decided that this would be her pitch, and the *Radiolab* team loved it. She played them the voice message, and despite the fact that it was in Hebrew, according to Kosover there was not a dry eye in the room.

Thus the collaboration between *Radiolab* and *Israel Story* was born. With the support of *Radiolab*, Kosover and her team were able to re-record all the interviews with Tal and Amir in English, and the American production—led by producer Molly Webster—was able to track down and collect testimonials from other Indian surrogates in Nepal. As a result, a considerable portion of the *Radiolab* episode (the first to be released) deals with the moral and ethical implications of surrogacy, via the surrogates' voices, whereas the Israeli versions (in both Hebrew and English) include only segments from that *Radiolab* investigation into the surrogates' world, focusing more on the couple's journey to parenthood.

·ı|ıı|ıı|ıı

Tzlil Sharon: Let's begin our conversation by noting that the very possibility of the chain of events that led to the podcasts we're discussing in itself sets up an infrastructure for exploring the notion of the global and the local in podcasting. In fact, I think that one of the motivations for embarking on this project was that the background story presented above is actually only narrated in one of the versions of "Birthstory"—the English-language *Israel Story*. The story of how the two podcast teams met and started working on Tal and Amir's story is told in the beginning of that episode, and described in the show notes as "Prologue: The *Israel Story* team geeks out on *Radiolab*!" I remember us wondering, How come this part of the story was left out in the other versions? Why is it only told to the listeners of the English-language *Israel Story*?

Nicholas John: And also: Why does this prologue begin with a long anecdote about Robert Krulwich, who was then the co-host of *Radiolab*, visiting Israel a few months before this whole chain of events kicked off? The English-language *Israel Story* episode of "Birthstory" stands out in that it is the only one that devotes time to telling us in detail about Krulwich's visit, how he was invited to be the keynote speaker at a conference, how he adored the curtains in his south Tel Aviv boutique hotel, and how he then met the *Israel Story* team for a traditional Shabbat dinner on a Friday night. Why do we, the listeners, need to know about all of that? Why should it interest us? We'll talk more about how this pops up again and again in the episode, but our argument is that this seemingly anecdotal prologue is meant to situate the story within a certain supranational context that has an underlying Jewish connection, that goes beyond the locality of Israel and kind of sets in motion the wheels of the narrative. This Jewish theme is only introduced through the way this narrative is told to the particular audience of this particular podcast: American Jews.

Tzlil: And how do we know this is the audience of this podcast? Well, for one thing, it is fair to assume that the kind of people who would listen to a podcast called *Israel Story* are interested in stories related to Israel or the Jewish people, who perhaps feel connected to Israel in some way, but who don't live here. Or, perhaps, the listeners are American immigrants to Israel who feel more comfortable listening to podcasts in English rather than in Hebrew. This is also evident from the sponsorship ad for the episode, addressing English speakers who want to speak better Hebrew, and offering them on-demand Hebrew courses. It says: "When speaking Hebrew to an Israeli you've only got ten seconds to make an impression: they are listening to the words you choose and the way you sound and if it doesn't feel natural you're marked as a foreigner. With a bit of practice, you can master your Hebrew speech and accent!" It's most likely that the native English speakers who'd be interested in this product are Jewish. So definitely, the framing of the story draws on its Jewish connection. There is this transnational component here that fits with the ethos of the Jewish community being a kind of liminal entity, moving between places, and in this case bringing the two podcast teams together. You know, Nik, I hadn't realized until now how closely tied this case study is to your research into the arrival of the internet in Israel. Could you say more about the role of Jews in mediating the movement of this especially global and globalizing technology, the internet, which of course is also the infrastructure for podcasting?

Nicholas: Sure. Generally speaking, that research showed how important the movement of people between the US and Israel was—be that academics traveling for post-docs and sabbaticals, or Jewish technology experts migrating to Israel—to the spreading of the internet to this particular part of the world [John 2011]. This is interesting because we tend to think about the internet as this sort of borderless and almost magical technology, but actually, its diffusion was very much attached to physical infrastructure, to the actions of specific individuals who crossed the geographical borders between different countries.

Tzlil: That said, we know that those early days of the internet were fuelled by utopian notions about it being a global village that can be navigated at the click of a mouse from anywhere in the world [Fisher and Wright 2001; Katz-Kimchi 2008], which in a way is similar to what we see when we reflect on the first decade of podcasting; how it was perceived in both popular and scholarly discourse as a medium that can bring us together—an argument we made in our study about the imagined ideal podcast listener [Sharon and John 2018]—and overcome institutional barriers due to its open architecture and grassroots nature [Berry 2006; Sullivan 2019]. I wonder, though, can we make the argument that podcasts are inherently more global than radio because of that?

Nicholas: Well, I think so.

Tzlil: Obviously, in the digital age, these distinctions are less valid because radio programs are often listened to via websites, apps, and platforms, which taps into a wider argument about podcasting being simply another manifestation of radio [Bottomley 2020; Sterne et al. 2008]. But historically speaking, for most of its existence, broadcast radio was bound by physical boundaries. When you speak into the ether, you speak to a local community in the sense that you can only reach a certain range of audiences that is limited by the geographical borders of the radio waves' reception. However, the promise embedded in podcasts is that you can potentially spread your message all across the world through RSS enclosures and an internet connection [Berry 2016b;

Bottomley 2015; Menduni 2007]. This mechanism allows the targeting of audiences with shared interests, which again, to me, recalls the early days of the web, when people could gather around shared topics and hobbies in online forums and discussion groups [Baym 2000]. So even before thinking about universal principles of storytelling and how they can, or cannot, overarch the language and the local setting of this story, we could say that the transmission apparatus of podcasts makes them, in a way, agents of globalization.

Nicholas: This is true, but it is worth unpacking the notion of globalization a little. For a while, a commonly held position was that the US was spearheading a process termed "cultural globalization" [Tomlinson 2007], a softer yet still oppressive form of cultural imperialism, embodied in iconic figures such as Mickey Mouse, the Coca-Cola bottle, and the golden arches of McDonald's [see Ritzer 2000]. In the 1990s, though, scholars began theorizing the ways in which local cultures resisted the global flow of American culture, creating new, hybrid cultural forms [Hannerz 1992; Howes 1996; Pieterse 1995]. Concepts were developed, such as hybridization, localization, domestication; the idea being that you bring in something culturally new, and you shape it to fit the local context.

In a similar vein, when I think about these different stories, or rather, about the same story told in different podcasts and different contexts, I wonder how this tension between the global and the local features of the narrative is manifested in each version. I mean, we know that news stories are told from different angles, depending on the cultural context of the journalists and the audience [Lule 2001; Zelizer 2004], and that TV show formats are sold around the world, with local versions expressing local values in different ways [Hetsroni 2004, 2005]. So going back to the outset of this discussion, we can certainly think about the internet as a globalizing technology that enables everyone to surf American websites—or to listen to podcasts like *This American Life* and *Radiolab*, for that matter—but we can also think about different internets in different countries [Abbate 2017], internet borders between different countries, and, more relevant to this study, the limitations faced by non-English podcasts, spreading in this seemingly limitless realm of digital content.

Tzlil: Another question I've been grappling with is this: Did podcasting have a unique role in transmitting this story across the world? I guess this question can be traced back to the very idea of Mishy Harman's initiative to create an Israeli version of *This American Life*. If we operate within the context of the globalization literature, I want to carefully suggest that perhaps *This American Life* has become the McDonald's of podcasting. Not in the sense that it is trying to expand its business enterprise across the globe, but rather in the sense that it has provided a model for a type of podcast storytelling that is widely perceived as the way to tell stories on podcasts across the world, to inject "podcastness" [Berry 2018] into journalistic stories, if you will. Having said that, it is actually based on a specific type of high-brow American radio and might not be the universal language of podcasting that sometimes it appears to be. Moreover, it is fascinating to me that even if Harman learned how to tell a story through the medium of podcasting by listening to This American Life and *Radiolab*, the connection with the *Radiolab* production was only cemented when he and his team were physically present in the US.

Nicholas: Well, I would say this: the way that these three different podcast episodes come about is in itself an instance of the globalization of culture, especially through the movement of people in different spaces.

Tzlil: Good point. Now, before we move on to comparing the different versions of the story, let's explain how we tackle them analytically. This was a tricky endeavour, as analyzing three podcast stories is not the same as analyzing three written stories. We decided to carry out a methodological experiment by approaching this study through a recorded spoken conversation between us. The point of this is to say: When you analyze a podcast story, you have to listen; you can't just read its transcript. Listening makes it impossible to avoid the fact that there are many layers to this so-called audio "text" that cannot be addressed using methods developed before podcasts arrived. Sure, there is the spoken conversation, the speech turn-taking, that can be closely examined using the tool kit of broadcast media conversation analysis [e.g., Hutchby 2006, 17–35; Tolson 2005, 24–53], but then how do we account for sound effects, music, and accents?[7] Also, how do we tackle the editorial decisions of which voices to bring to the story? For instance, when analyzing a written news story from a critical discourse perspective, we ask: Whose voices are represented? Are they brought directly or through reporting? What is the tone and framing of the journalistic storyteller? But with podcasts, when we think about voices we should literally think about the voices. Like, how does the character sound? In what sort of soundscape are they situated?

So we need to work iteratively, moving between the audio and a text. In comparing the three versions, we had to draw up a storyline in order to track all the scenes in every story and see how they compared. I'm saying "scenes,"

---

7   Even within the well-established field of conversation analysis (also known as CA), the recent decade has brought forward the urge to develop more sensitive and complex CA-related approaches that would be able to deal with multimodal aspects of interactions (Deppermann 2013). That said, podcasts have yet to receive significant designated attention from CA researchers.

which is something that comes from a visual world, from movies, but perhaps we should call them auditory pictures. Again, I'm kind of trapped in visual metaphors here. And then we conducted a close listening and started to see the differences. We were basing ourselves on a model that I'm developing in my Ph.D. dissertation [Sharon 2022], which is a tool designed to analyze this sort of content. I have characterized different parameters, and we will touch on five of them.

HOW THE STORY IS TOLD: A COMPARATIVE ANALYSIS OF *RADIOLAB, ISRAEL STORY,* AND *SIPUR YISRAELI'S* "BIRTHSTORY" PODCAST EPISODES

The Openings

Tzlil: We have two ways of looking at the openings. One is to closely listen to how each story begins and examine questions like: Who is the narrator? Which characters are presented to us and what sort of contexts we are provided with? What do the hosts assume we already know, and what needs to be introduced and explained? What voices are brought to the auditory stage? The other way is to look at a paratext that accompanies the podcasts: the show notes.[8] Reading the show notes is fascinating, especially with these carefully crafted narrative podcasts that put a lot of thought into the editing and the conceptual packaging of each episode. The show notes are a significant part of how the story is framed.

Nicholas: Yes, the show notes provide me context and intimate something about what the podcasters think will interest me. With these three podcasts, though, we can't conclude much about the different audiences addressed in each of the versions. What we see is that all three versions' show notes share the framing of: You think you know a thing, but actually, it's much more complicated than you could have imagined.

Tzlil: There's also a shared assumption that two gay men have the right to start a family. It's not something that needs to be justified.

Nicholas: No. None of them feels a need to say that sometimes men love each other and they might want to have a family together, right? For both *Israel Story* (in the two languages) and *Radiolab*, the right of a gay couple to raise a family is not questioned at all.

---

8   For more on the importance of podcast paratexts, see chapter thirteen by Lori Beckstead in this volume.

Tzlil: Moving on to the spoken audio, let's discuss how each episode of "Birthstory" addresses its listeners and sets up the auditory stage for the narrative they're about to hear. If we examine the *Radiolab* version, at the beginning Jad Abumrad says, "the story you're going to hear...is actually one of the best things we've ever done, and I don't think we ever spent so much money and so much effort." Right from the beginning we have a set-up of something that is unique and large-scale. Then there is a conversation between Jad and the other hosts. Robert Krulwich says, "We're calling this 'Birthstory,' because that's what it is. We're gonna tell you about babies, who were very recently born. And who, one day, will turn to their parents and say to them, 'Tell me how I got here. Like, what's my story?'" This is the framing. So for *Radiolab* the story is, in a way, about having a family in today's scientific and technological world. But on the other hand, it's actually a story about a transaction between two parties—the gay couple and the surrogates. And it's also a story about how the surrogates feel, as we later learn.

Nicholas: For the producers of the *Israel Story* version in English, the real challenge is that they have to offer some kind of unique selling point to an English-speaking audience, which may already have heard the *Radiolab* version. So Mishy Harman, the host, who speaks perfect English with an American accent, has to persuade the listener that it's worth their while listening to this particular podcast. One of the ways they do this is by leaning really heavily into a visit Robert Krulwich made to Israel and the time the Israeli Story team spent with him. And we also hear about the *Israel Story* team's trip to New York and their pitch meeting at *Radiolab*. They're star-struck; these are clearly their heroes, and the underlying assumption is that the listeners will be impressed by this rather podcast-geeky interaction too. This is the beginning of the story for the English-language *Israel Story*. This is the set-up.

Tzlil: We should also say that at the very beginning of the episode, Mishy says that this is a story about parenthood and gay rights, that it's about fairness and bodies, and about the differences between the developed and the developing worlds.

I think another interesting part of this intro is when they give us a bit of the conversation that the *Radiolab* team had after the pitch meeting. We hear Jad say, "This is the most bananas story I've heard in a long time. Every single element of it, just to our American ears, felt strange and it just takes something you thought you knew about and flips it, almost twelve different times." So this is in itself a sentence that kind of marks difference. Altogether, I'd say that the opening of the English version of *Israel Story* is very much about the collaboration between the teams and the global flows of people and ideas.

Now let's talk about the opening in *Sipur Yisraeli*, the Hebrew-language version. This is the version with the fewest meta-narrative comments. We don't get a lot of "backstage" snippets here. The story opens with the words, "This is an episode about how unquestioned truths about parenting sometimes turn out to be much more complex than we had imagined," delivered by Mishy Harman, in perfect accentless Hebrew.

Nicholas: Which is kind of how the *Radiolab* version opens as well.

Tzlil: True. However, in this version, the whole episode is called "You Only Get Two Dads," and it has two acts, like the format of *This American Life*. Act one, which is called "Birthstory," is about Tal and Amir and their story, with the earthquake and the surrogates' payment and everything, and then you have a second act, which is a completely different story called "Salt of the Earth." It's an Israeli-based story about a family in which a man marries a woman, they have some kids, then he dies in a war, after which the mother marries his younger brother, and they have some more kids, and they're one big happy family. They tell us a bit about their struggles but they're ultimately a very happy family. So this is another story of two dads, one of whom is dead, and the other alive, which lends itself well in this introductory framing of complex parenting truths.

The Listening Subject

Tzlil: Now let's discuss addressivity. Who is the addressee in each story? Who do the presenters imagine their listeners are?

For *Radiolab*, the audience is American. This is the base. It's a curious, intellectual, and most likely very educated audience, interested in culture and science. And at least some of them are long-time passengers on this ride.

Nicholas: And then we have *Israel Story* in English, which mostly addresses American Jews, but also other diaspora Jews.

Tzlil: We have a few examples to support this. We said that Robert Krulwich was invited to Israel to talk at a conference, and then the whole *Israel Story* crew and Robert went out for a Shabbat dinner together, which is on a Friday night. It's a big deal in Israel. It's something that you do with your family, and you usually don't work on Shabbat, on Friday night or Saturday. So they talk a little bit about that, they kind of joke about not working on Shabbat.

They then talk about how the *Israel Story* team goes on tour, including a performance at a JCC in New York. We could also mention the ads: the opening sponsor is a company that helps Americans speak Hebrew with a better accent, as we discussed earlier. And then at the end, there is a call for sponsors for the show. And they don't say, okay, you can reach a lot of Jews, but they do say that sponsoring an episode is an amazing way of reaching folks in ninety-four countries around the world.

And now some assumptions about the Israeli audience. So obviously *Sipur Yisraeli* addresses an Israeli audience of Hebrew speakers. But this audience is also assumed to speak English well because we have a whole segment in English in the middle of the episode. This is almost twenty minutes of investigative journalism taken from the *Radiolab* episode, where *Radiolab* takes over the story and sends a Nepalese reporter to a shelter in Nepal to speak to Indian surrogates who are waiting to give birth while surrogacy laws in Nepal are going through a dramatic change. This segment is mediated from time to time by Hebrew comments, but most of it is given to us in English, without translation.

Nicholas: Our interviews with Israeli podcast listeners show this assumption, that *Sipur Yisraeli* listeners know English, to be fair enough.[9] Most of the people we spoke to mentioned that they also listen to podcasts in English.

Tzlil: Right. But we should mention that all of these assumptions apply specifically to long-form narrative storytelling podcast audiences. Put differently, the kind of Israeli listeners who are drawn to a podcast known as "the Israeli version of *This American Life*," perhaps have the social and the cultural capital that enables them to listen to podcasts in English.

Voices and Language

Tzlil: The main protagonists in this story are two gay men. They're both Israelis, they're educated, and they're Hebrew speakers. But for the *Radiolab* version, which was the first to be released, they had to record all of their interviews again in English, because their audio journals and the interviews they gave to Maya Kosover were all in Hebrew. I think that the difference between the way their voices come across in the Hebrew version, and then in both English versions, is so different. It completely changes the characters in the story.

Nicholas: To put it more bluntly, their English isn't that good. And when you listen to the Hebrew version, it's clear that they're able to express themselves, but in a foreign language, it's much harder. They sound awkward and clumsy. As a migrant, I know what this is like. And as someone whose professional life

---

9   This is ongoing and as yet unpublished research.

is pretty much carried out in a foreign language, you do too, Tzlil. And what's interesting is that when the surrogates' voices are brought to us, there's no expectation that they will speak English.

Tzlil: If we think about the voices, in the *Radiolab* version the American voice is central; everything is in English, obviously. But you have other voices too. We have the voices of Tal and Amir, who are interviewed about their relationship, how they decided to start the surrogacy process, and how they feel about it in retrospect, knowing that the surrogates didn't get as much money as Tal and Amir thought they would. There's no attempt to keep the original audio-journal bits in, with conversations they had amongst themselves, and then do some kind of voice-over. They're presented to the audience speaking broken English. Maya Kosover is a sort of translator. She gives us more context and information, and kind of mediates the story, protecting her characters. And then when you have the voices of the surrogates, they're presented in their mother tongue, and then you have a voice-over in English with a Hindi accent.

And then we have *Israel Story*, the English version, where again, the characters are speaking in English and do not sound as educated and complex as they sound in Hebrew. But there is also another interesting thing here, to do with Mishy Harman as the narrator of the story. He has a pretty impeccable accent when speaking English; he sounds very American.

And in the Hebrew version, the voices add layers and greater complexity to the stories, which kind of gets lost in both of the English versions. I think the major thing we lose is Tal and Amir's socio-economic background.

Nicholas: Yes, this is a little complicated. Tal and Amir are Mizrahim.[10] Just speaking very generally, in Israel, Mizrahim are disadvantaged compared to Ashkenazim [Cohen, Lewin-Epstein, and Lazarus 2019]. So what the Israeli listener will know is that Amir and Tal are doubly marginalized: they are gay and they are Mizrahim. Also, if they come from Mizrahi families, their families may be closer to religion, they may be more traditional. This turns out to be the case for at least one of them.

We also get the impression that they have both been kind of upwardly mobile, but that they don't have the financial resources both to buy a house and do this expensive surrogacy procedure.

Tzlil: Yes, it's only in the Hebrew version that we learn that they gave up on the idea of buying an apartment in favour of having children. Also, in the

---

10   Mizrahim are Jews of Middle Eastern or Asian descent; Ashkenazim are Jews of European or North American descent.

conversations between them that we hear in the Hebrew version—and this is something that only became very vivid to me once I read the transcript—they use a lot of Mizrahi terms of endearment, like *neshama* ("my soul") and *kapara* (common slang for "sweetheart"). And all of this context is completely gone in the English versions. All the local elements that make the story more complex are flattened out when we hear them in English. But then again, the surrogates' voices remain the same throughout all the versions, because that part was produced exclusively by *Radiolab*: they all have an English voice-over in a voice that sounds educated and articulate, but with an Indian accent that is supposed to convey authenticity.

The Soundscape

Tzlil: Most of the things we've looked at so far can be tackled using conversation analysis or cultural studies paradigms, but there are other things that we don't have a model of analysis for, and one of these is podcast soundscape, a term used in sound studies to describe the environment of voices and sounds [Schafer 1993]. And I think that when you compare the soundscapes of the different versions, you can also pick up a few ideas about the localization of each version.

Something that is shared by all versions is the delivery style, the intonation and the way that the stories are told. They all have the same mode of delivery, right? They speak to us not as if they're speaking to the masses, but as if they're speaking directly to me, sounding emphatic and informal, generously employing pauses, giving a bedtime story feeling to the narrative.[11] This is something that comes across in all languages.

I also find it interesting that in all of the versions we hear two songs in Hebrew. At the beginning of the story, if you remember, Maya, the producer, is throwing a party in Jaffa, a mixed Jewish-Arab neighbourhood in Tel Aviv, and the music is a dance mix of an old Israeli song, an old seventies hit. This dance mix has words in both Hebrew and Arabic. For me, listening to the song that is played right at the beginning sets up the cosmopolitan context of the story. The old and the new are mixed up together, which makes the story even more exotic. The second song is a children's song that Tal and Amir sing to their babies as they arrive home as a family for the first time, "Rutz ben Susi." It was written by Hayim Nahman Bialik, Israel's national poet. I don't think there is a single child in Israel who doesn't know this song. But how does it come across to American ears, do you think?

---

11   This has been described as "NPR voice" (Wayne 2015).

Nicholas: To American ears I think it will come across as exotic, something that emphasizes Israeliness. But for the Israeli listener of *Sipur Yisraeli* it's going to emphasize cultural proximity.

Tzlil: Right. But other than these Hebrew songs, the three episodes have different nuances in their soundscapes. In the *Radiolab* episode, we have a very rich sound production with a lot of inserts and atmosphere music. We hear a lot of contextual sound inserts, like bits from the surrogacy conferences, and we have news broadcasts from right after the earthquake. Most significantly, the communication media themselves are really present: we hear the sound of Skype, and we hear the bad reception of the cellphone. Also, at the end of the episode, the credits are a set of voice mail messages in which Robert, Mishy, and other people from the production are reading out the names. And then you finish with the machine announcing, "No more messages."

Nicholas: What I also found very amusing about that was the way that Jad and Robert destroy the Hebrew names, they can't pronounce them. Which, again, for me emphasizes foreignness.

Tzlil: But why do you think the communication technologies are emphasized?

Nicholas: Like the Skype ringtone? I suppose it emphasizes distance. You're there, we're here.

Tzlil: Also the centrality of the US in mediating the story and kind of being the centre of it all. The communication technologies we hear are signalling to us that this is a story that had to cross a lot of places. It reminds us of the materiality of the media and the time-space relation they mediate.

Now, I don't think that the soundscape in the English-language *Israel Story* is very different from *Radiolab*'s. They are both based on the same English-language interviews and narration with slightly different editing. But the soundscape in the Hebrew version is more distinct. Again, you have the song at Maya's party. And then you have the children's song that Tal and Amir sing to their babies. But then you have other sounds that are unique to the Hebrew version. You have a lot of bits of Tal and Amir talking, their audio journals, which give more depth to their characters. And their segment ends with an Israeli song about the joy of having a child, and the lyrics basically say that once I have a child, a door within me will open up. It's a very pro-children song. In the second act of the episode there are other classic Israeli songs too. However, they finish the whole episode by playing, in its entirety, the song "Daddy Lessons" by Beyoncé, which is interesting in several ways. First, because it's a hit song in English. Second, because it is not a typical Beyoncé song; it's a country song. Everything about it says Americana: it takes place in Texas; the father in the song has a rifle and he acts as a sheriff, protecting his little girl. The choice of ending a two-act podcast story about two sets of Israeli fathers with such an American song is not an obvious one. We recognize here again the assumption that *Sipur Yisraeli* delivers its narratives to an audience familiar with both cultural contexts—the American and Israeli.

The Wrap-Ups

Nicholas: I think this is where it gets really, really interesting. How does each of the versions end? What take-aways are delivered to us by the hosts?

Tzlil: Well, at the end of the *Radiolab* version there is a conversation between Jad and Robert. Jad says, "you can read it as a story about the business of family making." Or, he says, "you can hear it as a story about exploitation, all of these different things are happening in this story." Then he adds that it is also a story about the "inventiveness of people, in some weird way." But then he goes on to say: "I also feel like one of the things that is happening here is a story about dreams, and about aspiring to have a better life. And how in this case, those aspirations meet in this really uncomfortable transaction." So this is a story about dreams, right?

Nicholas: Aspirations and dreams, which is the story of America.

Tzlil: Exactly. And then you have the English Israeli Story version. I think this one is the version that has the most retrospective reflections, because they talk a lot about how the two teams initially met. But then again, you have this conversation between Jad and Molly and Robert, and they talk a lot about the moral implications of Tal and Amir's decision. And then they have another conversation with Mishy at the end of the episode in which Jad says that this is a story that is "primarily about surrogacy, but it's also about women's rights, about gay rights, it's about Jewish culture." This is the only place in the three versions that Jewish culture is mentioned as a theme. And then they talk about the "business of making babies," and this all shifts to a question of whether having children is a good thing or a bad thing. Like, we should put a question mark over whether it is worth pursuing. What price for going after your dreams?

Nicholas: Jad says he would not want to go through what they went through.

Tzlil: And Molly says, "the paperwork alone." For me, this version is a story about globalization and what comes with it. So you have the possibility for production teams to meet and produce a story together, using a lot of communication technologies. But then also, you have a lot of complexities, because you can have babies, like, using one woman's womb and using an egg from a Ukrainian woman. So the subtext for me, listening to this concluding conversation, is: Maybe don't have babies? Or: It's a global world, but make sure you make the right decisions, because maybe bringing more children into this complex world is not the smartest thing.

In the Hebrew version, there aren't many meta-narrative comments from the host, but we do have closure to the stories. Amir and Tal's story ends with Maya explaining, two years later, that the kids are now two years old. They're starting to talk, and their fathers are waiting for the moment that they ask them how they came to the world. And then you hear a giggle and the classic Israeli song about "when I have a child, a door within me opens," and so on. The point of the story—and I don't think that *Sipur Yisraeli*'s team meant for this to be the message—is about the complexities and the beauty of having a family. The subtext is that it is worth it, it is so worth it.

Nicholas: And it's foreshadowed: the very first thing that we hear in the Hebrew version is either Tal or Amir talking about imagining himself being sixty and alone and watching television by himself in his apartment. I think what's also fascinating about this is that in our interview with Maya Kosover she's totally aware and critical of Israeli pro-natalism. But ultimately, the Hebrew version of the podcast comes out as entirely supportive of Tal and Amir's decisions. It was all worth it in the end.

HOW WE ANALYZED IT: REFLECTING ON STUDYING
PODCASTS THROUGH A TALK-RECORD-LISTEN APPROACH

> Storytelling is a tool that comes with a heavy responsibility, responsibility that can be abused...For me it's important to tell stories in a way that is as faithful as possible to the person who told me their story and their experience, and I think that meeting with the person who's telling me their story is hugely important. It doesn't really matter whether it's a life-story for a documentary episode of *Israel Story*, or if it's the story behind a song for *One Song* [a Hebrew podcast about popular music produced by Kosover], the meeting itself is really important. I believe with all my heart that the encounter changes according to the people involved. I mean, if it wasn't me there but someone else, then the story would be different, because every encounter gives birth to a slightly different story, even this meeting with you, I'm telling

you things that I've talked about before in all sorts of places, but something
about the questions or the way you're listening to me brings slightly different
things out of me...do you see what I mean? *(Maya Kosover, producer
and host of the podcast* Sipur Yisraeli, *in interview with the authors)*

Tzlil: We are experimenting with this form of conversational discussion about
the episodes that we're analyzing. As academics analyzing podcasts we want
to be able to touch as many aspects of the phenomenon as possible, and you
can't do this with just the text alone. Talking about podcasting with a specific
audience in mind, and recording that conversation, is actually pretty close to
podcasting. We practise it as a way to reflect on it, arguing this approach can
enrich our methodological tool kit. But why? What do you think are the benefits of holding this conversation between us?

Nicholas: We can start with the connection between conversations and storytelling. The kind of podcasts that we're interested in here are a combination
of spontaneous conversation and tightly written text, and this conversation is
also a bit of a mixture of that.

Tzlil: Yes. There are a lot of similarities, not only in the way we prepared for
this conversation and then worked on its transcription, but also in how we
analyzed the episodes before we recorded our conversation. We used MAXQDA
[software for qualitative analysis] to create a map of all the auditory scenes, to
be able to visualize the similarities and differences between the different versions. We had to rely on visual aids, to use words and codes, because otherwise
there is no way to capture the ephemeral nature of our aural content units. It
makes me think about how similar this analysis process is to the production
workflow of the podcasts we discuss here. In my interview with Maya Kosover,
for another part of my Ph.D. dissertation, she described how she crafts a story
based on hours and hours of audio: she puts together the bits of audio she has
and then she has to allocate codes and break it into segments that will make
sense. She called it going "from the wet [material] to the dry [material]." The
wet is the audio, and the dry is the written word. She has to navigate between
them. And I thought, wow, this is really like reverse-engineering the episodes,
like we did here. In both cases it is very clear that in order to understand the
audio and the speech, you have to go through a text transcription of the podcast episodes, a transcription of our conversation. The audio and the text cannot be separated, they complete each other.

Nicholas: Yes, and even working on this conversation, we've been doing it
with text; we've been looking at notes while we've been talking. The text is

crucially important because the text persists, doesn't it? Whereas sound disappears the moment it's made.

Tzlil: In carrying out this cross-cultural analysis through a speech-to-text method, we pose the questions: What does the conversation bring to the table? What can we learn from articulating our thoughts out loud and listening to each other that we might not see if we were just to write everything down? Maybe it's more obvious for me as a non-native English speaker, but I think that the whole notion of voices and accents is key here. For example, we are having this conversation to get it automatically transcribed, because we have the technology that makes it possible to do that quickly and efficiently. From a blank page to twenty thousand words—this is a revolutionary way of working, and we'll see how it copes, but it also kind of puts me at a disadvantage because of my accent when I speak English. And it reinforces the fact that we have different identities, that I'm a native-born Israeli talking to a British-born immigrant to Israel who speaks English with an English accent. And I think that this made me very aware of the kind of English that I hear when I listen to Tal and Amir talking. This awareness of the voice is significant not only for the podcast listener, but also for the critical podcast researcher. I wouldn't necessarily notice how crucial this is if I were just to analyze the text.

Nicholas: But we're talking...

Tzlil:...in English. We're talking in English.

Nicholas: Yes, well, because we're going to be writing in English, but also because the technology for writing through AI transcription in Hebrew doesn't exist.

Tzlil: It does, but it's not good enough. There is something about, you know, imagining a world in which academics could just podcast their Ph.D.s and deliver their presentations, instead of reading from the page. Creating intellectual contributions through meaningful conversation. But then this would probably give more privilege to the already privileged community of academics, right? Because those conversations would probably be held in English. And when you hear someone's voice, it obviously shapes the impression they make.[12] I mean, when you listen to someone speak and they don't sound very articulate, then presumably you'll listen to their arguments differently. So I

---

12   This commonly held notion is supported by research (see, for example, Giles, Wilson, and Conway 1981; Kalin, Rayko, and Love 1980; Kalin and Rayko 2013).

think this is something that's important to keep in mind when we discuss the differences between the stories and the differences in how the characters are presented to us.

Nicholas: This makes me think of how we actually have much more control over this text than Tal and Amir did over how their story was told. We have obviously edited the transcription, but not only to correct errors; we also removed some of the filler words like *like* and *you know*. We even rewrote some of the text for the sake of clarity, and added text to the transcription as we worked on this text after recording our conversation. If podcasts and podcasting lay some kind of claim to authenticity [e.g., Boling, Hull, and Moscowitz 2021; Fox, Dowling, and Miller 2020; Sullivan 2018], I think this text shows how authenticity can be manufactured, and how sometimes it is not actually that desirable, particularly if we think about how Tal and Amir sound when talking in English.

Tzlil: We sometimes tend to think about barriers that texts can put up, being a linear, visual, and sequential medium that demands certain literacy and suppresses the liberating power of oral culture [McLuhan 1962]. We work really hard to produce publishable academic texts. But in a lot of ways, texts actually help out a lot of people who otherwise wouldn't be able to participate in the conversation. When we speak, we make our geographical and ethnic identities very evident, whereas the written text creates a more even playing field that erases all of these nuanced identity markers manifested by the voice. Listening to the three versions of "Birthstory," and being aware of these aspects, helps us better understand the differences between them, and the meaning of locality as mediated through the relationship between language and power.

Nicholas: And what about your experience in producing a podcast for our department?[13]

Tzlil: For sure, developing and producing *The SIP* (*The Smart Institute Podcast*) has shaped the ways I think about and analyze what I see as the cultural logic of podcast listening, which I argue is strongly rooted in the modes of communication and delivery style of the podcast host, in how they intentionally and unintentionally teach us how to listen to their narratives. Indeed, making podcasts actually helps you to understand how to analyze

---

13   Tzlil Sharon produced *The Smart Institute Podcast* for the department of
     communication and journalism at the Hebrew University of Jerusalem between
     2020 and 2021.

them better, and this may be unique to the field of podcasts. In developing my model of analysis, which we only made partial use of here, I initially tried to build solely on academic literature. But it was ultimately limited, at least in the first decade of podcast studies. A lot has been written about broadcast talk, but podcasting operates in a different socio-technical context, targeting audiences completely differently, and often speaking to individual listeners [Hilmes 2022]. In order to account for the songs and the soundscape there's nothing there that can really help. So I think that one lesson I took from producing *The SIP* is being very aware of the different elements that make a podcast a podcast. For example, I remember myself telling the academics who were having a conversation for these episodes, Don't read from the page. Try to have a more relaxed, casual conversation. And there was a lot of work put into making it sound like a "natural" conversation.

Nicholas: We can think about the style of podcasting that you hear in podcasts like *This American Life* and *Radiolab* and other long-form storytelling podcasts, and I wouldn't say it's trivial, but you can see that it's doable—you can take inspiration from *This American Life* and *Radiolab* and make a podcast called *Israel Story*. And yet, if we're thinking about how the global and the local interact, and this story is full of the global and the local, and you and I talking is also meant to produce something for a book that will be published in Canada for an international audience, but probably mostly an American one. But for me, I love the way that, try as they might, well, they're just not aware of how local their stories ultimately end up being.

Tzlil: And not only for narrative reasons, not only in terms of the structure and the framing, but also because of all of the audio-related things, like the voices and how they're brought out. I want to suggest some conclusions for our analysis. We started by pointing out three cross-cultural encounters that come into play when analyzing our case study: *Radiolab* vs. *Israel Story* at the production level; Tal and Amir vs. the Indian surrogates at the narrative level; and a non-native English speaker (myself) vs. a British immigrant to Israel (you) at the academic level. We tried to cut across, or rather unpack the tension between these encounters by going through five categories: the intros of each podcast; the listening subject (the assumed and/or imagined audience); the voices and language; the soundscape; and the wrap-ups, which is how the podcasts end. These categories allowed us to have a guided conversation about other elements that are crucial for understanding podcasts, such as the show notes, the role of sponsorship ads, and the relation between the front stage of the narrative and the backstage snippets of the production process and afterthoughts.

Nicholas: But what can we say about the local and the global, based on our discussion of these categories and how they operate through the cross-cultural encounters underlying this analysis?

Tzlil: Well, I think our analysis depicts three worlds that I really noticed from carrying out this analysis out loud: The first is the American, or the English-based world, represented by the *Radiolab* presenters. Ultimately, *Radiolab* produced the most critical story, raising moral questions about surrogacy and women's rights, but mainly I think in the very subtly implied idea that maybe we shouldn't have children at all costs. At the same time, this liberal world that seeks to give voice to the disadvantaged and exploited puts the protagonists of the story in a doubly complex position, that not only challenges their decision to use a surrogacy service but also narrows their communicative capital. Tal and Amir don't get an English voice-over. They are expected to be able to express their thoughts, feelings, and opinions in English.

The second is what I call a transatlantic world, one that needs to navigate between local identity and global identity. This represents the Israeli world in the story, the one that's addressed in the *Sipur Yisraeli* episode. It has Hebrew speakers in it, but you can give the audience a twenty-minute segment in English in the middle of a Hebrew podcast and they'll cope. It's probably an audience that's already listening to *Radiolab*. This world wants to be cosmopolitan, but at the same time it's very much rooted in—and limited by—its local context. It wants to tell a story about the complexities of having an untraditional family in Israel in the twenty-first century, but finds itself trapped in the national imperative of having babies at all costs.

And then there is a "third world," represented by the surrogates. This world is mediated to us by the American one, as its voices are brought to our ears through the testimonies of the Indian surrogates in a shelter in Nepal, with an English voice-over, in a journalistic investigation paid for by *Radiolab*. I would be very surprised if any of the surrogates interviewed in the podcast would be able to listen to it one day. I don't think a version of the podcast in their language would ever be produced.

So while you could argue that the casting model of podcasts kind of detaches them from being oriented towards local audiences, and we like to think they have the potential to appeal to different audiences in different places, ultimately the perspective remains local. Local identities always come through spoken language, you know. They kind of can't not. And so podcasts are always already local, which is probably important to remember both as students of podcasters and as people involved in making them.

PLAYLIST

Track 1: *Israel Story*. 2015. "Birthstory." In *Israel Story*. Podcast. MP3 audio. 01:05:55. https://www.israelstory.org/episode/birthstory/.

Track 2: *Radiolab*. 2018. "Birthstory." In *Radiolab*. Podcast. MP3 audio. 01:00:42. https://radiolab.org/episodes/birthstory2018.

Track 3: *Sipur Yisraeli*. 2017. "You Only Get Two Dads." In *Sipur Yisraeli*. Podcast. MP3 audio. 1:12:54. https://tinyurl.com/msyuzp74.

CHAPTER 11

PODCASTING AFRICAN WOMEN
Lived Experiences and Empowerment

YEMISI AKINBOBOLA

H*erMediaDiary*[1] is a podcast that captures the lived experiences of African women working in media industries, using an interview format (African Women in Media, 2024). I did not start the podcast with academic inquiry in mind, but instead to provide a space to share experiences and inspire listeners. This was to keep in line with my international non-governmental organization African Women in Media (AWiM) mantra to "Be Visible to Inspire." The aim of the podcast is to tease out the reflections of interviewees on how their life journey led them to media, and to use this journey to identify what one might interpret as character-building moments: those that led them to take up areas of advocacy, for example, addressing sexual harassment and gender-based violence in the media. As for the listeners, I aim to inspire them through the stories that interviewees share of their barriers and how their histories led them to a career in media.

This chapter is both retrospective and forward-looking. I critically reflect on my past practice of setting up the podcast. I reflect on what I might do differently going forward to be intentional about producing the podcast for academic publishing and as a site for academic reflection, doing so without losing sight of its original goal to inspire others through the stories of the women I interview. This chapter is an exploration of what academic podcasting means

---

1   African Women in Media (2024). *Her Media Diary*. www.linktr.ee/hermediadiary.

to me as an African woman and an academic using podcasting as a digi-tized-audio approach to empower African women.

Had I considered academic inquiry from the start, I might describe the *HerMediaDiary* podcast as a discursive method for capturing the lived expe-riences of African women in media to effect transformative change in its audi-ence. And by this, I posit that the podcast contributes to bringing the stories and voices of African women to audiences, through their perspectives and realities, and in a way that might help listeners in transforming their career trajectory. Therefore, *HerMediaDiary* seeks to use a self-reflective approach to capturing the lived experiences of African women in media industries and how they navigated their journey towards a career in media industries. Their shared stories illustrate both the lack of a singular path to media as a career, successful or otherwise, and a collective narrative that counters a neoliberal and patriarchal construction of what it is and what it means to be an African woman and work in media industries, primarily in Africa, but also elsewhere.

Whilst I did not start *HerMediaDiary* with academic podcasting in mind, it does present an opportunity for me to engage critically with emerging debates on disrupting the sites and nature of academic publishing. This is particularly important for an African podcast, with a primary target of African women, when we consider academic publishing around gender and women's studies in and from Africa, the lack of diversity in perspectives being published in the field, and thus the need to decolonize. Decolonizing gender and women's studies publications means reconsidering the site of publica-tion and the range of scholars and perspectives being published in the field to ensure global representation. Thus, decolonizing the field in terms of pub-lishing necessitates access to a wider range of perspectives and scholars, espe-cially from the Global South, a reimagining of approaches to the study and research of gender and women's studies, and a rethinking of the relationships between scholars and non-Western and Western sites of publishing.

Looking at the representation of scholars from the Global South in lead-ing gender and women's studies journals, Medie and Kang (2018) found that the representation of authors from the Global South ranged from 1–5 percent of articles, with the leading gender studies journal, *Gender & Society*, having only slightly above 1 percent of articles published between 1987 and 2017 pro-duced by scholars in the Global South. Briggs and Weathers (2016) attributed this low representation to the quality of submissions and differences in writ-ing styles, applied theories and methodologies. Africa-based journals, Medie and Kang (2018) found, were more inclusive than publications in the Global North, with *Agenda* having 6 percent of articles published between 2008 and 2017 from the Global North. Established in 1987, *Agenda* is the oldest feminist scholarly journal in Africa. In its efforts to ensure sustainability, it entered a publishing partnership with Taylor & Francis in 2010. Whilst *Agenda* "retains control over the identification of themes, selection of contributions, compilation and editing of the journal," the publisher will create digital versions of back issues and future publications. In consideration of the inequalities of access, Agenda maintaining its editorial leadership is critical, though it raised questions for Tamale (2020) who outlines big Western publishers' colonization of Africa-based gender and women's studies publications. As Tamale puts it, the key issue is capitalism muscling into feminist spaces. The digitalization of *Agenda*'s content will bring great financial benefits and profit to Taylor & Francis. "Ultimately, the relatively small number of big academic publishers will control the development, dissemination, and access of knowledge. This is a good example to illustrate how social movements are institutionalized and legitimated in a colonized context" (Tamale 2020, 55).

The debate on the representation of global perspectives in gender and women's studies, therefore, extends far beyond the site of publication, to include the historic and present-day impact of global economic structures and their consequences for academia in the Global South as a whole. The disruption and decolonization of knowledge production and academic publishing are therefore critical if we are to prevent them from recreating existing global political, economic, and structural inequalities. This has been the concern for critical feminists who highlight the marginalization of scholars in the Global South and the domination of the Global North on the approaches to gender and women's studies scholarship as well as of the perspectives being published (Anyidoho 2006; Crenshaw 1991; Mohanty 1984; Motlafi 2018; Narayan 1997; Okeke 1996; Zeleza and Weare 2002). The casualties of traditional academic structures and broader inequalities of access to academic knowledge production in the Global South are examples that strengthen the argument for alternative academic publishing sites like podcasts. If we are truly invested in decolonizing the curriculum, in access to and production of knowledge, and the democratic approaches to this, then non-traditional sites for academic publishing are a critical need.

That is not to say podcasts themselves do not have barriers to access. For example, whilst the pandemic ignited enthusiasm for online and blended learning—and spaces like the Post-Pandemic University (a collective using magazines, conferences, and podcasts to reflect on the kind of university that will emerge from the pandemic), surfaced to reflect on this—the pandemic also revealed technological advancement gaps, which for many African countries are exacerbated by other levels of inequalities, from financial exclusion to the lack of regular electricity and access to it, as well as digital literacy (Duarte 2021). According to UNESCO, in sub-Saharan Africa "89 per cent of learners do not have access to household computers and 82% lack internet access" ("Startling Digital Divides in Distance Learning Emerge | UNESCO," 2020, para.2). At the same time, many digital initiatives emerged in response to the pandemic demonstrating the capacity for technological innovation on the continent. In Kenya, FabLab created Msafari, a track and trace application. In Morocco, the tracking app Wiqaytna6 was developed. In Rwanda, where, with government investment, 90 percent of the country has access to broadband internet (Broadband Commission 2018), they developed a real-time digital mapping of the spread of COVID-19 and introduced telemedicine and chatbots to support people during the pandemic. The challenges of access are there, but so too are the fast-growing innovations to address these.

Podcasting as a site for academic African feminists, women's rights activists and thinkers embodies the democratic benefits of breaking from the political economy of academic knowledge gatekeeping and the colonial and Western intellectualism frameworks from which modern academic institutions and spaces for intellectual debating stem (Tamale 2020; Mama 2017). Significant to me is the opportunity to bridge conversations between academia, activist sites for women's rights in Africa, and media practice. Tamale (2020, 49) argues that much of African feminism activities in academia are "delinked from civil society and community activism," a problem that podcasting could bridge, for example through its discursive open-forum nature. The accessibility of academic expression is important (that is, how well academic expression, whether written or oral, can be accessed and understood by others), especially in helping activists (practice) understand academia (theory), and vice versa. This can be achieved by bridging the gap between research insights and real-world practice using accessible ways of speaking that the discursive nature of podcasts produces. This speaking culture of podcasts (Cook 2020) further encourages the breaking down of barriers to the use and reception of what is considered academic expression that outsiders may find inaccessible.

Beyond disrupting academic publishing, though, the stories of the women I interview help us towards ambitions of reconstructing transformational feminisms on the continent (Tamale 2020) and speak to calls by African feminists for more empirically grounded theorizing and defining of African feminisms (Akinbobola 2019; Akin-Aina 2011; Oyewunmi 2005; Nnaemeka 2004; Mohanty 1984). For example, through the stories my guests share, might we reconstruct perspectives on gendered barriers in the workplace and more broadly decolonize such perspectives through the podcast's focus on the experiences of African women in Africa and its diaspora? Thus, contributing to a synthesizing of transformative African feminisms is not just about understanding the nature of these barriers and how they appear for African women, but our approaches to navigating our realities within environments where adherence to culture and traditions is often evoked when we advocate for women's human rights. Cultural relativists argue that the pursuit and promotion of women's rights and gender equality are unethical and interfere with traditions and cultures, a position that Msuya (2019) argues is about the protection of cultural diversity. On the other hand, women's rights advocates argue that culture and what it means in many African societies, in how it attributes roles to men and women, has been used to place women in subordinate positions with limitations on freedom and other human rights. Whilst violations of women's rights have often been justified with culture, scholars have on the other hand demonstrated the interdependence of human rights and culture (Nayak 2013; Jivan and Forster 2005; Brems 1997), and the United Nations (2010) has also demonstrated the links between cultural rights and women's rights.

As I discuss later, the feminist label here should not be taken lightly. The rejection of the feminist label by many African women whose work and experiences are clearly about women's rights and equalities makes me pause in labelling *HerMediaDiary* as such, even though I am a feminist, to avoid alienating potential listeners and thus limiting their access to important knowledge sharing from the podcast. Nevertheless, the resistance to the label is why decolonizing feminism is critical. African feminism rejects a particular type of feminism that does not have its roots in the lived experiences of African women and how we navigate patriarchy.

THE POLITICS OF TITLES

HerMediaDiary was not intended originally as a title for the podcast. It was the name for the network that I eventually called African Women in Media (AWiM). It was to be a blog through which I shared my experience (my diary) as an African woman media entrepreneur, serializing my experiences into themed topics. The idea was built on my years of experience running my news media organization, IQ4News. The thought to explore *HerMediaDiary* as a podcast came after the AWiM Facebook group began to grow, and I wanted to capture the stories of the women in the group. I started AWiM in my search for an environment to share my experience and work out what my next move was. I needed an AWiM, so I created one, and instead of sharing my experiences with others, I started the podcast as another extension of this search to discover how others did it. This ethos of sharing experiences to empower and inspire others is the central purpose of *HerMediaDiary* podcast.

I have only published episodes with female guests as I write this chapter. However, I take a moment to reflect on this in the broader context of AWiM— the organization itself and its annual conference—and explore the politics

of labelling and conditions of separatist spaces. This is particularly important if institutional, structural, and societal change are critical requirements
for creating enabling environments for African women in media, and if we
recognize that the decision makers in media organizations are mostly men.
Therefore, what are the pros and cons of separatist spaces, and what consequences do they present for needed reform? The annual AWiM conference is a
women-prioritizing space, and in its early years, we found that men, and even
women who did not identify as African, self-deselected. Following the call for
papers for the first conference in 2017, I received several emails from men asking, "Is this only for women?" and from non-African women (all white) asking, "is this only for African women?" There was an apparent apprehension,
on their part, over their permission to be present and permission to speak in
a space labelled "African Women in Media." During several of the subsequent
conferences, there have been calls for more men in the room, which has led
us to consciously aim for a seventy-thirty ratio of female to male speakers,
and as I write this chapter, having just concluded our seventh annual conference in Kigali, Rwanda, the gender gap in responses to our call for papers has
significantly narrowed, a change that started during the pandemic when we
hosted the conference virtually. Nevertheless, in an environment where allo-
cating capacity-building opportunities through events and training is often
gendered (Akinbobola 2020), women-only and women-prioritizing spaces are
necessary interventions.

The guest lineup of *HerMediaDiary* has so far been women; however, like
the conference, it is not only African women who need to hear their stories,
nor is it only African women who need to take action to address the barriers
and work towards creating equal and enabling environments. This, therefore,
raises a question on recommender algorithms' use of consumption habits like
music preferences and other listening behaviours (Benton et al. 2020; Morris
2021a; Nazari et al. 2020), and demographic data like gender and age, to rec-
ommend podcasts to users. Gender demographics alongside other factors
like cultural backgrounds have also been found to shape music consumption
(Li et al. 2020; Greb, Schlotz, and Steffens 2018). When we consider research
that suggests that our interaction with music can be guided by our gender
(see, for example, Chamorro-Premuzic, Swami, and Cermakova 2010; North
2010), we must consider the impact of this on the discoverability of podcasts
like *HerMediaDiary* for all genders, and for those who hold different cultural
beliefs, where music habits are the primary basis for recommender algorithms on platforms like Spotify, iTunes, and others.

The podcast's objectives are to share the lived experiences of African
women working in media industries, mentor others, and inspire change in
the industry. The open-access nature of the platform allows for others whose

roles make them essential to creating enabling environments for African women in media to join this conversation. The question is the extent to which the labelling, firstly by the podcast itself, and secondly by the podcatchers' recommender algorithms, limits this engagement, and if and how I might deliberately draw the attention of these decision makers by giving them access also to speak on the podcast irrespective of their gender. The dilemma, in other words, is that for the podcast to achieve its aim of highlighting the lived experiences of African women in media in an empowering way for them and others, and yet to address the barriers they face, more decision makers need to partake in the podcast. So, the questions I received in response to the 2017 call for papers and the notions of permission to speak and be present in a space labelled "African Women in Media," and in the case of the podcast, *HerMediaDiary*, again come into play. Additionally, as I consider media and gender researchers as a target audience, how might I ensure the intellectual sophistication of academic output, whilst balancing it with the mentoring and change-effecting objectives of the podcast? *HerMediaDiary*, therefore, has the tall task of inspiring and mentoring others, convincing change makers, and being intellectually robust. All these whilst being mindful of those that self-deselect but are ultimately essential to effecting change. I share later in this chapter how I plan to resolve this conundrum.

My grappling with naming also stems from my scholarship in African feminisms, which has a history of reflecting on the "feminist" label and how or why some African women tend not to want the association, even when their work and experiences align with issues of women's rights and equality. Scholarly debates about distinguishing Western feminism from feminism(s) in African cultures have led to the development of alternative labels like Obioma Nnaemeka's (2004) nego-feminism; Omolara Ogundipe-Leslie's (1994) Stiwanism (Social Transformation Including Women in Africa); Alice Walker's (1983) womanism; and Catherine Acholonu's (1995) motherism among others, theorized on the lived experiences of African women. The late bell hooks was also among feminist theorists who discussed misconceptions of the word, in response to which hooks proposed the definition of feminism as "a movement to end sexism, sexist exploitation and oppression" (2000, viii). Here hooks is emphasizing that women can sometimes be co-conspirators in patriarchy.

I have reflected on the labelling of *HerMediaDiary* in the context of feminist podcasts. I am a feminist, but should I label, and do I have the authority to label *HerMediaDiary* as such? I question my own authority because the stories are not mine, though as producer I am a custodian of the stories and thus protective of those who own their narrative. In associating others' works and experiences with tenets of feminism, care must be taken not to turn labelling into epistemic violence. Spivak (1998, 280) uses epistemic violence to describe "the remotely orchestrated, far-flung, and heterogeneous project to constitute the colonial subject as Other." De Sousa Santos (2015, 237) also speaks of "epistemicide" as a "cognitive injustice" that undervalues other ways of knowing, and the marginalization of knowledge in the Global South through Western domination of knowledge production. Alongside my earlier discussion on the inequalities in academic publishing, I also recognize the potential of epistemic violence in the forced labelling of the podcast as feminist. The rejection of the word is why decolonizing feminism is critical. It is a rejection of a certain type of feminism that doesn't have its starting point in African cultures or in how African women have always navigated patriarchy. The podcast contributes to the decolonization of feminism through the lived experiences of African women in the media industries that it captures.

CHANGING THE NARRATIVE THROUGH DIGITAL AUDIO

It would be remiss to not reflect on the importance of my podcast and African podcasts more broadly and their contributions to the continental agenda to change the narrative of Africa. This agenda stems partly from the history of media framing of Africa from a Western lens, and is championed by the African Union as part of its Agenda 2063 strategic framework. In their neoliberal, free access, easy entry, and decentralized form, podcasts present perhaps a more intimate way to contribute to this agenda. Podcasting bypasses mainstream international media processes and thus the agenda setting of the editorial process to reach an international audience and use the liberating benefits of digital spaces without gatekeepers. For *HerMediaDiary*, this narrative reconstruction through podcasting places the power into the hands of the women whose stories are being told. More poignant still is that they are themselves media workers and their stories of barriers often stem from challenges due to male dominance in their industry and wider lives. My interview style is crucial in considering the most appropriate approach to ease their storytelling in a way that is empowering and that authentically facilitates their stories without fear of the mainstream media reconstruction of their stories to fit a narrative for audience-engagement reasons. Fox, Dowling, and Miller (2020) argue that this kind of community building for marginalized voices is well suited for podcasts.

I am not alone in my quest to capture the lived experiences of African women, nor am I alone in my position as an African female podcaster. In fact, most African podcasters are women (Africa PodFest Report 2021)! Through her podcast *Legally Clueless*, Kenyan media personality and social activist Adelle Onyango "documents her raw human journey as an evolving unapologetically

African woman" and is on a quest to "provide Africans with agency over their own stories and the portrayal of Africa" (2021, para. 2). Zimbabwean Sandra Chuma's podcast *NDINI* is "a collection of the voices, wisdom, witticisms, and truths of African women: women who rock their communities and shape the world with their strength, passion, and vision" (Chuma 2023, para. 1). Zambian Chulu Chansa's *Africana Woman* podcast celebrates African women in their own words and calls on us to "smash the culture of silence on things that hold us back or keep us stuck" (Chansa 2021, para. 1). The central ingredients to these podcasts are sharing women's stories through their own voices, changing the narrative, and empowerment.

The use and uptake of podcasting to capture experiences of minority voices are also explored by Fox, Dowling, and Miller (2020), whose analysis of Black podcasts in the US discusses the rise of diversity in podcast listenership. There was an increase in non-white listenership, going from just over one-third in 2017 to 43 percent in 2019, a percentage made up mainly of African Americans (15 percent) and Hispanics (13 percent; Edison Research and Triton Digital 2019; Winn 2019). Similarly, Fox, Dowling, and Miller (2020) highlight the role of podcasts like *The Read*, launched in 2013, in taking Black podcasts from six shows in 2010 to several hundred five years later. According to them, Black podcasts are used as "discursive cultural guides" to understand the Black experience, with the example of *The New York Times' Still Processing* as mainstream media's attempt to enter the Black podcasting market. Podcasts, they argue, "opened Black discourse on the meaning of blackness in US culture to an audience of unprecedented scope and diversity" (Fox, Dowling, and Miller 2020, 300).

The ease of entry due to the low budget requirement resulted in the first few episodes of *HerMediaDiary* being hard to listen to. The production quality was poor; I relied on my laptop's built-in microphone, though I used the professional podcasting platform Zencastr to record. I later invested in a professional-grade microphone, but I have yet to use it due to my own apprehension of the required technical skills, and I have not had the time to master the new kit. Like many academics who podcast, I do it alongside a full-time and demanding academic job. Instead, I have been using an inexpensive headset mic, which has improved the technical quality and listenability of the podcast compared with when I relied on the laptop's in-built microphone.

Nevertheless, the ease of entry is a critical motivating factor for podcasters. In research on the rise of podcasting in African countries, Africa PodFest found that "accessibility is a key motivator to getting African podcasters started due to [podcasting's] low budget requirements and the accessibility it offers as an audio medium as opposed to, say, visual media" (Africa PodFest Report 2021, 7). While Zencastr is great for making interviews sound like the interviewer and interviewee are in the same room, it can be problematic for interviews in areas of low bandwidth. I have had the experience of loss of data on a few occasions, but the one that I reference here was with an interviewee in South Sudan. We conducted her interview twice and lost data on both occasions due to a drop in her internet connection. I take responsibility: her voice and the voices of other women in media in regions with poor connectivity must not be lost. How then might we work with professional platforms like Zencastr to address this? In the meantime, this is where flexibility is needed by podcasters who aim to capture the voices of those where technology access is a challenge. There are more traditional alternatives that can be employed like the tape sync. Given my target speakers work in media industries for the most part, they will have the technical skills and access to recording equipment to record their end of the conversation, which can subsequently be shared with me via email or a platform like Telegram, WhatsApp, or WeTransfer. This causes the speaker to become part of the production team, and one must consider the ethics around whether this costs them time and data usage. It also changes their experience of the virtual podcast recording process; other guests enjoy the benefit of their commitment to production ending with the "thank you" at the end of the interview. Working with platforms like Zencastr to develop enabling digital environments for guests with limited technological access, therefore, seems to be the most ethical solution in the long term.

THE POLITICS OF VISIBILITY

I started recording *HerMediaDiary* in 2018 after the second African Women in Media conference, held at the University of Ibadan, Nigeria. My training was through listening to other podcasts, mostly those interviewing entrepreneurs on their success stories. I was not entirely new to audio production, though, having produced audio interviews for IQ4News between 2010 and 2014, well before I became familiar with the word podcast. Back then I used Audacity to edit and SoundCloud to publish.

My first interview release for *HerMediaDiary* came after the murder of Hodan Nalayeh, a Somali Canadian journalist killed in a terrorist bombing in Kismayo in 2019. She was due to speak at AWiM's 2019 conference in Nairobi, Kenya. I interviewed Hodan earlier in the year about her organization, Integration TV, and her mission to change the narrative of Somalia. Hodan's death made international news, with many of the reports using her mission to change Somalia's narrative ironically in relation to her death. However unintended, I felt this context was insensitive, and this gave me a sense of urgency to release her episode during the news cycle of her death, because it was her story in her voice. For her, the mission to change the narrative of

Africa, of Somalia, meant being in the country and using media platforms to give the world an alternate view. Hodan Nalayeh was a hero.

Technically, the episode was not the most well produced. I edited her story during a period of personal shock about her death, having exchanged WhatsApp messages with her just two days prior. It was emotionally taxing, and ensuring my editing did her voice justice was fundamental. The interview was one of the last that captured Hodan's voice and memories for the world. I feel a deep sense of privilege to have had that opportunity.

Releasing Hodan's episode motivated me to publish other episodes. Given the lapse of time between recording and publishing, I had to get permission from interviewees to publish their episodes. Two declined, while I could not find the audio file for a third, demonstrating the necessity of organizational structures and file management systems to avoid the loss of content. I recorded new ones too, and as the pandemic hit, I created a special edition called "COVID-19 for Journalists," exploring a host of issues, from data journalism to the mental health of journalists during the pandemic. My reflections on these interviews and how the podcast might proceed with more intellectual robustness started with the consideration of my interviewing style. Was there a systematic method to interviewing the kind of women I was engaging with, for the purpose I was doing so, one that would encourage their stories to emerge to produce audio that would empower my target listeners? My semi-structured interview format took a life chronology approach; that is to say, my interviewing technique facilitated their storytelling to follow their life and career journey sequentially. Upon reflection, while a natural flow of conversation technique worked well, I found that the real-time discovery of their stories during the interview, and on-the-spot decisions on how to navigate the interview, was not always easy.

This reliance on real-time discovery was necessary because researching my guests often only revealed limited information, mostly focused on professional accomplishments and not much on their personal stories or histories. This is exactly why podcasts like *HerMediaDiary* are needed, because cultural barriers, which are in some cases compounded with digital barriers, have limited the visibility of African women online. Thus, we arrive at a broader issue of the politics of speaking and visibility for women from cultures that function in a patriarchal setting in which we find, for example, women having to seek permission from their husbands to do media interviews. Here we also consider locations of agency; that is, the importance of where the interview is taking place in relation to the agency the interviewee has in that location. A woman may find agency in their workplace but not necessarily at home, where their culture and traditional perspectives of their role as a woman and as a wife subordinate them and limit their agency to speak, and therefore limit the extent to which their stories are present in credible sources like news media and platforms like Wikipedia.

In 2019, AWiM partnered with Wikipedia Nigeria Foundation on what we called the Visibility Project. The aim was to train more African women as Wikipedia editors and to increase the number of African women profiled on Wikipedia. Through this project over three hundred African women were trained, and 598 profiles of African women were created and updated on Wikipedia. Yet, the Visibility Project also revealed a lot for the trainees and us about the notion of notability and how Wikimedia defines notability. Many of the women for whom our participants wanted to create profiles were considered notable because we knew them. However, very few of them shared their stories on platforms that Wikipedia considered credible. This lack of visibility has directed my approach to preparing for interviews on the podcast. In the interview I become their friend next door, their confidant, an approach I have found has eased my guests' abilities to speak on the podcast and thus be visible.

In my interviews, the quest for me was to elicit the key events and teachable moments from the guests' journeys and to tease these out so others might learn from them for their own journeys. Moving forward, I wonder if a memoir or themed approach might help focus the episodes better while still leaving room for real-time discoveries or self-reflecting revelations that were not already in the public domain—revelations that the women I speak with might not share if they were not on a podcast recording hosted by another African woman. I began exploring the themed approach in a new season released in November 2022. A monthly theme directed who I invited as guests and what the interview focused on. The themes chosen were not random, but directed by previous research I carried out into the barriers women journalists in sub-Saharan Africa face (Akinbobola 2020). For example, the four episodes released in November were focused on sexual harassment and gender-based violence. My guests were selected because of their work and lived experiences of sexual harassment and/or gender-based violence. So whilst the guests' personal and professional journeys followed that life-chronology approach I mentioned earlier, the month's theme meant that our discussion teased out how this particular topic shaped their journey, and in all cases, how they used their experiences to empower their journeys.

I do not want to underplay or underestimate what visibility, be it in the podcast or on Wikipedia and other platforms, means for the women I interview. The politics of visibility for many African women is fraught with socio-cultural conditions which means parts of the interview may become too personal for some of my guests. On one occasion a guest asked for a whole section of her interview to be deleted due to fear of her family's reaction to how she described her familial structure. Creating enabling environments in which to speak and share lived experiences that they might not otherwise share is not a straightforward proposition. For me as a podcaster, the question is the ethics of being culturally sensitive versus adhering strictly to the legalities of the release form, through which guests give the podcaster, among other things, the editorial rights to the interview.

On the positive side, Fox, Dowling, and Miller (2020, 24) argue that podcasting is an "aural medium not easily intruded upon by trolls," and when we consider this in the context of research showing that women are often reluctant to share their stories online for fear of abuse (Duffy and Hund 2019; Toffoletti et al. 2021; Wilhelm 2021), perhaps podcasting offers a safer alternative to other media for this reason.

For the reasons I have discussed in this chapter, it is an exciting prospect that *HerMediaDiary* presents an opportunity for me to contribute to the disruption of academic publishing. This begs the question, What differentiates an academic podcast, especially one that is produced as practice-based research, from any other podcast? How might I develop *HerMediaDiary* as a proof of concept for academic output?

I start by considering the definition of academic research, which the UK's Arts and Humanities Research Council (AHRC 2023) defines as a process rather than the resulting output. The process consists of defining a set of research questions or problems, objectives, and contexts, applying research methods to explore these, and producing an original contribution to knowledge. The podcast is addressing the following research questions: What are the lived experiences of African women in media industries and how do they navigate the barriers they face? How might the open forum and discursive space of a podcast be used to capture these experiences and inspire others? From this perspective, the podcast is an active piece of practice-based research. Candy (2006, 1) described practice-based research as "an original investigation undertaken in order to gain new knowledge partly by means of practice and the outcomes of that practice." The original contribution to knowledge is demonstrated through the practice output—in this case, a podcast—and supported by writing that provides the "significance and context" of the practice piece. Broadly, though, practice research emphasizes knowing by doing and application (AHRC 2023).

Whilst peer review continues to hold importance in assessing research outputs (AHRC 2023; DORA 2013), research funding bodies, academic institutions, and others recognize that research outcomes can come in various forms of outputs. The San Francisco Declaration on Research Assessment (DORA 2013), drafted by editors and publishers of various journals, calls attention to the flaws in placing importance on the site of publication, and specifically the flaws in using the journal impact factor for research assessment. They argue that the original intention of the impact factor was to help librarians determine which journals to buy, and not intended as a tool for assessing the research outputs themselves. Whilst the primary focus of the DORA is on peer-reviewed research articles, it also acknowledges the declaration's applicability to other forms of research outputs, calling for the importance of online publications to be recognized, and to broaden our valuation of impact to include things like policy and practice impacts.

CONCLUSION

This chapter critically reflects on my past practice of setting up the *HerMediaDiary* podcast, taking both a retrospective and a forward-looking view. In reflecting on podcasting in the context of academic publishing and what academic podcasting means to me as an African woman and academic, I have argued that podcasting embodies democratic benefits, allowing scholars to break from the political economy of academic knowledge gatekeeping, and especially presenting the opportunity to decolonize the Western intellectualism frameworks that guide many modern academic institutions and intellectual forums.

In considering the potential of academic podcasting for decolonizing gender and women's studies publications, podcasts offer a more accessible and inclusive environment in a way that traditional academic journals have been found not to (Briggs and Weathers 2016; Medie and Kang 2018). Equal access to technology does continue to be a barrier (Duarte 2021). Thus, the opportunity here is for academic institutions and funding bodies to support the development and resources of the necessary skills to facilitate academic podcasting. Such programs should form part of a decolonization strategy that aims to ensure that perspectives from the Global South do not continue to be casualties of traditional academic structures within the dominance of heavyweight publishers in the Global North. Virtual podcasting recording platforms also have a role in ensuring that their technology considers technological barriers for those in locations of low bandwidth and thus their ability to contribute their perspectives in podcasts.

Similarly, as the demonstration of impact beyond academia continues to be a critical aspect of academic funding, opportunities presented by the discursive and open-forum nature of podcasts for bridging conversations between academia, activism, practice, and policy is another reason to embrace podcasting as a site for academic publishing.

The *HerMediaDiary* podcast functions in my activism, practice, and research. My sense of responsibility for the stories and the visibility they create for the women individually and collectively means my interview style takes an empowering approach. Similarly, my approach to theming episodes using research findings ensures that we speak to critical issues impacting listeners. As an academic, I envision these stories contributing to various scholarly debates. For example, decolonizing perspectives on workplace practices and policies for women in media, as well as capturing the lived experiences of African women so that African feminist scholars might draw on them in debates that seek to define African feminisms. In contributing to such debates, I am conscious in my approach to ensure I ask interview questions that are both probing and enabling whilst recognizing that some guests may not consider their experiences to be examples of gender inequality due to normalization within their culture and work environments. I am also conscious of their agency and ensure that the agency they exercise, knowingly or not, is apparent in each episode. In many ways, this is me exercising and applying my understanding of the core of what feminism aims to achieve—gender equality—without an explicit expectation that guests align their experiences with feminism. I consider this approach as inclusive, allowing guests to exercise agency in both choosing which parts of their stories to share and deciding how they do so.

For practice and policy, the stories help us to construct and refine transformational leadership approaches for creating enabling environments for African women working in media industries. I have argued that for real transformation and change in this context, the podcast has the task of being a safe space for African women in media to tell their stories and to engage male listeners, given their dominance in media leadership and ownership. All these factors make *HerMediaDiary* an exemplar of podcasting as practice-based research.

Concerning my latter point on industry transformation, recommender algorithms also have some work to do here. Their use of listening behaviour and demographic data like that of gender needs to evolve to consider the gender equality barriers they potentially facilitate by not exposing certain demographics (in this case, men in media leadership) to content that will enlighten their organizational and personal approaches to gender equality. In other words, recommender algorithms need to be more socially aware and conscious towards development goals. Broadly, recommender algorithms need to be smarter in facilitating the impact of academic podcasts to wider audiences who should engage with academic debates in their field to improve practice, policy, and activism.

CHAPTER 12

PODCASTING FANDOM AS PUBLIC PEDAGOGY AND INTERSECTIONAL LITERACY

PARINITA SHETTY and DARIO LLINARES

This chapter is an edited transcript of an interview that Dr. Dario Llinares conducted with Dr. Parinita Shetty focused on how podcasts challenge and expand ideas of what knowledge looks like, who is allowed to create it, and how it's supposed to be shared. For her Ph.D., Dr. Shetty analyzed how fan podcasts act as sites of public pedagogy and intersectional literacy. She used a selection of existing fan podcasts hosted by both non-academic and academic fans as a source of multimodal literature. She also created her own fan podcast called *Marginally Fannish* as part of her research methodology.[1] By doing this, she hoped to include a more diverse range of voices in academic spaces as well as make academic research more accessible to non-academic audiences.

Through the Q & A there is an aim to interrogate the dynamics of fan podcast interactions and offer a collaborative way of doing and presenting research, as well as demonstrate different kinds of analytical processes that balance love and critique. Furthermore, the discussion explores ways in which fan podcasters and audiences use the fictional framework of popular media as a shared language, and how this can help people encounter a more

---

1   Parinita Shetty. *Marginally Fannish*. https://anchor.fm/parinita-shetty.

complex and nuanced understanding of different identities and alternative perspectives. By creating a public space for generative thought, episode conversations bring together multiple ideas, experiences, and insights. They can also make up for some of the gaps in more formal educational spaces by allowing people to be invested in what they're researching, to be in control of what and how they learn, and to create knowledge for an engaged audience of their fellow fans and co-hosts.

·ı|ı·ı|ı·ı|ı·

Dario Llinares: The idea of "process" is the underpinning of this book, particularly within podcast studies and how the discipline is about practice-based research, or the relationship between practice and theory. That's a key crossover in your project, and how that intersects with fandom in podcasting more broadly. Why don't we start by discussing your discovery of podcasts? Where does that fit into your broader cultural consumption? And your fandom?

Parinita Shetty: I had a discovery and then a rediscovery. I first started listening to podcasts when *Serial* and *Welcome to Night Vale* began, around 2012–2014. I also loved *Planet Money,* an NPR podcast that makes information about economics accessible. Then I lost track of podcasts for a little bit until 2019 when I discovered fan podcasts. For my Ph.D., I knew I wanted to study public pedagogy and intersectionality in fan communities. But there are so many online fan communities that I didn't quite know what to focus on. At the time, I had also submitted an abstract for a conference. The conference organizer directed me to an episode of *#WizardTeam*, a Harry Potter fan podcast, because the conference's keynote speaker, Dr. Ebony Elizabeth Thomas, was a guest on it and the organizer thought I'd be interested in it [Davis and Jordan 2017]. That's when I first realized this kind of thing existed—a podcast that specifically dissected Harry Potter through a Black American lens. After some more research, I found *The Gayly Prophet,* which analyzes the series through a queer lens, *Witch, Please,* which studies it through an intersectional feminist lens, and *Harry Potter and the Sacred Text,* which uses a theological lens. I was so excited to discover all these podcasts existed that I fell into a fan podcast–shaped rabbit hole and now podcasts are just my life.

Dario: You write in your thesis and mention it on the podcast as well, about the role of the internet in providing a communal learning space alongside being a kind of open practice tool for you in terms of your immersion into knowledge. You seem to see it differently than classical "educational spaces." So did your consumption of *Doctor Who* or your consumption of Harry Potter, as well as your fandom through the internet, offer you a way of thinking about certain aspects of life such as diversity, inclusion, or racism, say, in a way that more formal practices didn't?

Parinita: It happened quite gradually. I wasn't a critical thinker to start off with; I wasn't analyzing the media's representations of different identities. I started reading Harry Potter when I was ten, and I started participating in its online fandom—fan fiction largely—when I was thirteen. At that time, these conversations about diversity and inclusion weren't really a huge part of the communities I was a part of. But as I grew older and went on other online plat-forms—especially Tumblr and Facebook—I began to discover and appreciate the communal learning aspect. Fans who loved the books as much as I did were critiquing different aspects of the series. Coming across these perspec-tives got me to start thinking more critically about the texts. And I found this with a lot of my co-participants as well, that it's sort of an evolution as a fan. Many people start uncritically loving these things. But then through the inter-net, we have access to these different voices who present alternative view-points. Of course, some fans are not really comfortable with that. You see that a lot—this side of fandom that is aggressively against any opinions that don't mirror their own. But if you're open to them, these diverse interpretations can help expand your imagination. What I have now really become a fan of is these critical perspectives. They're not always critical in the sense of "We hate this." It's more like, "We love this media and we want it to better represent a certain aspect of identity we're invested in or themes we're interested in." And I think many fan podcasts popularize this balance of love and critique.

Dario: Academic fandom does tend to be this negotiation in various ways between the thing that you love, and then what you recognize within it to be problematic, and to have those things situated in conversation. But first of all let's talk a bit about how you came to the subject of your Ph.D. and to the point where, through talking with your supervisors, you decided it would be a good idea for it to become a podcast.

Parinita: I wanted to focus on intersectionality and public pedagogy because, although these were terms I first encountered while researching for my Ph.D., I realized that the academic explanations of these concepts were describing something I had experienced in fandom—even though fans weren't using those terms necessarily. Once I started looking at fan podcasts specifically and had talked to my supervisors about them, we realized there needed to be two sides of my project. One was that I would create my own fan podcast to talk to my co-participants. My podcast itself would create the data that I would then analyze in my thesis. But I was also looking at existing fan podcasts as sources of intersectional literacy and public pedagogy. I cited these podcasts just as I referred to more traditional academic literature. I was drawing attention to these practices that existed even before I started this fan podcast for my Ph.D. I wanted to highlight that these fan podcasts didn't always—if at all—need academic mediators. Many academics don't consider these kinds of podcasts and projects created by non-academics as valuable sources of knowledge—though this is changing. I think creating the podcast really helped me see how other podcasters were engaging with knowledge. A lot of these fan podcasts are created by non-academics. The critical conversations and the kinds of research and analysis that they're doing—the kind that we did on *Marginally Fannish*—may not always resemble how an academic journal article or book does research and critique. But there are still these critical analytical processes going on there. The collaborative process of research and analysis that emerged through conversations in different podcast episodes definitely helped me become a stronger thinker.

Dario: There's so much to unpack about the idea of academic practice, and podcasting as academic practice; what it allows you to do in terms of not conforming to standardized or institutionalized forms of knowledge production, whether it's writing an academic journal or simply sitting in a conference room and listening to a paper for twenty minutes. It's really interesting in your project how you are looking at the fandom podcasts that you're focusing your research on as having an academic quality, even though it perhaps isn't named. It's fascinating then that you create a podcast that you are naming as academic, but also fannish at the same time. So you have to explain and explore quite complicated terminologies, which really, at the end of the day, is just about practices of critical thinking.

When it comes to your own fandom, you chose *Doctor Who* and Harry Potter as your main focuses. Maybe you could talk about the reasoning. Both seem pragmatic but they allow you a critical eye into other podcasts that are very much focused on those particular titles.

Parinita: It was honestly just for logistical convenience that I decided to narrow it down to these two, because I'm a fan of a lot of media. I just figured that Harry Potter and *Doctor Who* are globally popular enough that I would be able to potentially recruit a more diverse group of co-participants from different countries to talk about them. The US and the UK tend to dominate online fandom discourse and I wanted to explore a more diverse range of identities even within these countries. We ended up referring to and recommending a lot of other media in the podcast. Not everybody who wanted to participate wanted to talk about Harry Potter and/or *Doctor Who*. Sometimes we looked at science fiction and fantasy media as a whole, sometimes specific TV shows or books or movies. What I soon realized was that the media itself turned out to be less interesting than what the fans—including me and my co-participants—were doing through their conversations about the media. Popular media like Harry Potter or *Doctor Who* gave us a shared language, which we used as a cultural shorthand to talk about a lot of real-world political and social issues. For example, in 2020, *The Gayly Prophet* co-hosts were doing a reread of *Harry Potter and the Prisoner of Azkaban*, the third book of the Harry Potter series. Both co-hosts are from the US, one of them is Black, and both of them are queer. They used events from that book—specifically the problems with the fictional prison, Azkaban—to talk about prison reform and prison abolition in the US. They raised awareness about these issues that they were personally invested in. I loved that this fictional framework of popular media could be applied to so many different contexts and the issues being explored would keep changing. On *Marginally Fannish*, depending on who I was talking to, we focused on different themes and brought in different examples that were relevant to our diverse social, cultural, political, and geographical contexts. So we brought together multiple knowledges and interests in our episodes.

Dario: One of the great things about your podcast is it acts as a blueprint for listeners being able to discuss both academic ideas and also just what is going on in the world politically right now. I think you demonstrate a kind of methodological bridge across those different approaches to knowledge in a way that academic writing rarely is able to produce and maybe even "allowed" to produce.

Parinita: The methodology of *Marginally Fannish* was very much influenced and inspired by existing fan podcasts. I borrowed elements from the ones that I listened to as a fan. I was especially interested in podcasts that foregrounded conversations with co-hosts. Their conversations were collectively creating this knowledge by drawing on multiple priorities and different kinds of expertise. I only looked at one podcast that has a solo host—*Imaginary Worlds*. Even there, he always invited different guests on his episode and drew on their collective intelligence. The diversity of guests helped expand the diversity of topics being discussed.

Dario: So there you are: you're in your supervision and your supervisor says to you, Okay, so you've got to make a podcast. What immediately goes through your mind? What were the initial challenges? All of us who have become podcasters perhaps almost by mistake, and we're doing it by trial and error, we all go through this journey. So how did that happen for you?

Parinita: When my supervisor first suggested it, I was like, wait, am I even allowed to do that as a Ph.D.? If you don't encounter these ideas in academia, how would you even imagine that this is possible? But then I found some researchers who had submitted their Ph.D.s using different modes, including podcasts. I started looking at the potential of podcasts in making academic research accessible to diverse audiences. I had to educate myself on how to create a podcast. I used a couple of free online learning courses and the first episode acted as a pilot episode of sorts. My two co-hosts and friends Aparna Kapur and Sanjana Kapur were the only co-participants who appeared on multiple episodes; everyone else only came on once. I used what we learned in initial episodes to feed into later episodes. In the pilot episode, for example, it really helped to meet up before the recording to plan the structure of the episode and the themes we wanted to explore. When I look back to earlier episodes, I think maybe I wouldn't have done it that way now. But I really wanted the "trial and error" to be a part of the research process.

One of the biggest challenges was how time-consuming the whole thing was. The podcast recording itself was technically the easiest part of the whole thing—we'd plan and talk on Skype. I was doing the pre-production and the post-production largely by myself, though my partner helped edit most of the episodes. The transcripts especially took a lot of time because I wasn't using any AI software. But typing transcripts for each episode really helped my Ph.D. research. While I was recording episodes, I was mostly focused on being the facilitator as well as a conversation participant. When I went back to transcribe the episode, it unlocked this other part of my brain. When I was typing, I was also thinking about the conversations and making note of themes relevant to my Ph.D. and ideas for blog posts—i.e., my autoethnographic field notes. Some of these actually became focal themes in the final thesis. So this DIY podcasting process did help, even if it wasn't always efficient or convenient.

Dario: How much did that kind of dichotomy between the idea of practice-based research and theoretical research come up in the viva?[2] Did they ask you about the importance of the fact that this is a podcast and not just a written thesis? How does that contribute to the knowledge that you are producing? Were you thinking that they were going to ask you about this relationship

---

2   Viva is another word for "thesis defence."

between theory and practice with regard to issues like knowledge production and rigour, etc.?

Parinita: I was really lucky that my external examiner was Dr. Hannah McGregor. She is both a fan podcaster and an academic who looks at podcasting and public pedagogy as well as how podcasting can be incorporated into academia.

Dario: Yes, she has co-authored a chapter in this book.

Parinita: Oh, that's great! I love her. Apart from *Witch, Please,* she also hosts *Secret Feminist Agenda* in which she talks about the process of podcasting and its role in creating and sharing knowledge. My exposure to these conversations kickstarted this ongoing process of trying to figure out what my ideas are when it comes to practice versus theory. In the beginning, I was just trying to draw attention to what fans are doing. As I mentioned, I think there are fans who may not use the theoretical terms intersectionality or public pedagogy but they are practising these concepts. So I was using theories to translate existing fan practices for academics rather than the other way around. Well, on my podcast, I suppose I was doing a bit of both. This did come up in the viva; where I saw myself—as an academic or as a fan—and the dichotomy there. The practice-theory relationship was something that I was constantly thinking about while writing my thesis. I do believe that the kind of knowledge-making happening in fan podcasts—where they balance love and critique—is really valuable. At the same time, I was sometimes trying to over-justify academic parallels by explaining how fan podcasts research, synthesize, and summarize all these different critical arguments in much the same way academics do. I think there's this tension between what kind of knowledge is considered legitimate within an academic structure, and I'm still trying to unlearn these biases.

Dario: Yes you write in the thesis about impostor syndrome, and mention it on the podcast, and we all have it to a certain degree. It's amazing how many hugely successful people will say, I just feel like I don't know anything. For a podcast scholar, in some ways there is an extra level of impostor syndrome in relation to producing academic work in an audio form. I still carry on writing, obviously. I don't just podcast. But we still feel we have to "guarantee" the knowledge through written texts—to provide evidence there is some sort of knowledge there. And then you add to that, podcasting is a public forum through which you're actually on purpose trying to make your work accessible. In terms of making your podcast, and the use of your actual voice, as well as the sonic materiality of your personality that comes through the voice, did you experience the anxieties of that? All of us seem to have an aversion to what we sound like and, in turn, what we think we portray when we speak. You had to deal with all that on top of the fact that this is a Ph.D.—it's not just a chat with your friends, you know?

Parinita: It's helped that I grew up online and in fandom communities where I've written for digital public audiences. In India, I also write children's books and I've done a lot of events with children and young people. So I'm comfortable talking to people from different backgrounds without thinking too much about how I come across. I'm less comfortable in an academic setting, maybe because of my ingrained ideas about how formal these spaces are supposed to be. I'm more used to informal spaces. While recording the podcast, I identified as more fannish than academic, so I wasn't too worried about the Ph.D. aspect of it. However, I don't think there is necessarily a distinction between being fannish and academic. You can be emotional and critical at the same time—one doesn't cancel out the other. So I was both fannish *and* academic, just like many of the fan podcasts I listen to are.

Like me, many people have specific notions of academic knowledge versus non-academic knowledge because of their experiences with institutionalized education. One of my co-hosts told me that she really struggled with formal education. Her kind of knowledge-making didn't fit into the institutional expectations in Indian primary and secondary schools or in university. In the mainstream education system in India, we weren't really encouraged to learn how to think; we were taught what to think. For me, online communities including fandom played a huge role in learning how to learn in a way that classroom spaces didn't. I wanted to incorporate these practices in the podcast. In *Marginally Fannish* episodes, once we decided on a theme, like disability or social class, we would then go and research the theme to understand it better. We found articles, essays, and podcast episodes that we shared with each other and which informed our ideas and conversation in the episodes. And this co-host realized that she loved this process of public learning. She learned in a way she'd never been able to do in her previous educational experiences because she was invested in the topics she was researching, she could control her own learning, and she could collaboratively create and share knowledge with her fellow co-hosts and fans.

Dario: Thinking about the broader construction of the methodology: you outline a mixed methodology, but at the heart of it is an autoethnographic process. I've written in the past about the "self-reflexive tendency" in podcasting [Llinares 2018], because it's still a newish medium, and arguably still underpinned by independent producers and creators, whether they're academic or not. And therefore there is this tendency to explain what you're doing and why you're doing it, and what the impact you hope it might have is or how it's affecting your life, particularly, of course, in discussion-based podcast formats. Before you placed your thesis within the framework of autoethnography, did you have that sense of wanting to explain the process of what you were doing? And then bring that all together into a structured methodology that could be understood on the outside by an academic?

Parinita: I knew that I wanted to incorporate both my fannish and academic identities in this project. I didn't want to be an "objective" observer of another culture. I wanted to be just as much a participant as a researcher. It was only later when I was researching methodologies that I discovered the term autoethnography. You see a lot of the self-reflexive tendencies you mentioned in fan practices, because they're drawing on their previous experiences, perspectives and priorities and placing them in conversation with the media that they love. So I thought that autoethnography was a helpful way to place that self-reflexivity at the forefront, not just for me but also for my co-participants. We were aware that it's not just an anonymous academic project and we're not just chatting with a fellow fan in private. These episodes would be publicly available. So we would place these different identities and ideas together while reflecting on our own backgrounds and interests. Our conversations were aimed both at fellow fans who weren't academics but who wanted to explore these themes and at academics who maybe hadn't thought about these ideas in the way we were framing them. We were bringing all these different perspectives together by focusing on our personal experiences, our favourite media, and the intersectional discourses we were passionate about highlighting.

Dario: Key to that, as you mention in the pilot episode, are your friends or colleagues, with whom, in some senses, you're just explaining or ruminating on your own ideas of fandom and how it relates to somebody else's fandom. What comes out of that, very obviously, is that whether you're fans of Harry Potter or *Doctor Who* or whatever, the expression and meaning of that fandom is something slightly different for each of you. Rather than it being an interview, the conversation allows a process for generative thought. This is something I've always thought about podcasting, the idea of the production of knowledge instigated with somebody else who can counteract or just spark off something that you've said, or not even said. Not even that it's prescribed, but there's something about the development of the conversation within the formal criteria of a podcast, essentially the apparatus of recording and the presupposed parameters of discussion. It feeds into the idea that this is

doing something different than sitting down and writing ideas that are spontaneously coming into my head on my own, or more than just you and your
mates chatting. There is something kind of unique in framing discussion in
the "conceptual space" of the podcast.

Parinita: That's such an interesting observation because conversation was
a key part of the methodology right from the beginning for exactly the reasons you've outlined. I specifically didn't want it to be an interview because
I thought that my questions would guide the conversation a little too much.
And in some cases, I might not even know what questions to ask when I'm
talking to people from backgrounds that I'm really unfamiliar with. So before
we recorded episodes, my co-participants and I decided on the themes we
wanted to explore in our conversation and then shared fan and media texts
based on that theme. This research and exchange of resources helped us see
where the other person was coming from. After going through each other's
texts, we met to plan what we wanted to talk about. The meeting was also a
good chance for us to get to know each other, because in a lot of cases, these
were people who'd gotten in touch with me on Twitter or via email, and we'd
never spoken to each other before. The pre-recording meeting was a good
opportunity to become more comfortable with each other. The episode itself
was just a chat. It was a structured chat, sure, framed around the themes we
had discussed previously. But like any good conversation, we sparked off of
each other and went in unexpected directions based on the ideas and insights
the other person's points inspired. I'm interested in how this format could be
applied to other contexts. For example, in a classroom, what if both students
and teachers brought in their multiple multimodal resources and ideas based
on a certain theme they were exploring? They could then explore these different perspectives through some sort of structured conversation, the way podcasts do. Instead of relying on the teacher's individual expertise, this kind of
collaborative intelligence could create something new in a way that just one
person may not be able to produce alone.

Dario: The way you've outlined that as well really does speak to what I tried to
explore in chapter one of this book about this notion of conceptual space. But
we use that word space in quite an offhand way, particularly in podcast studies, and we've also mentioned found spaces, academic spaces, and alternative
spaces in this discussion. And it's applied in an abstract way at times, when
really, the specifics of what we mean when it comes to podcasting is really
interesting. For example, we're talking right now on Riverside.fm, which is a
digital space. It is, for all intents and purposes, a practical space that allows us
to talk to each other. But then we're coming, like you say, with a criteria of the

things that we've read, and the things that we want to talk about. So we're setting up our discussion to be within the framework of certain ideas, which provides conceptual parameters for what we can and will talk about. Depending on the type of podcast and the flexibility of it, we might talk about what we did last night, you know: Did we watch a movie? Or did we go out for a drink? Or whatever it might be. And podcasting allows that flexibility. But it seems to me that one of the things that podcasting does, and yours is a key example of this, is it structures the space. Academic podcasts require the input of academic sources, whether they're other podcasts, or research texts, or actual fan podcasts themselves that you've used as primary sources. So this creates the criteria of understanding that you set out as a researcher/producer. But then your discussion hopefully is a kind of accessibility filter through the content and the form of the conversation.

Parinita: Yes. And in terms of what you're saying about structuring the space as well, I realized that I was very much deliberately constructing a space by choosing what media and themes to focus on. In some of the non-academic fan podcasts I listened to, the co-hosts referred to how they did this too. They found and exchanged some articles and media with each other based on the episode theme, they made notes on shared Google Docs, they planned segments there, and they referred to this collaboratively created document while recording. I'd drawn on these practices for *Marginally Fannish*. I had such an interdisciplinary project that I hadn't found any single methodology that quite fit my requirements, so I cobbled together a hybrid methodology. It was very DIY and I borrowed liberally from both academic and podcast sources based on what resonated with me. I really liked the idea of these texts exchanged beforehand prompting or structuring discussions but also leaving enough flexibility that we could go off in different directions during the recording itself. My deliberately curated selection of fan podcasts influenced the space I constructed on *Marginally Fannish* too. Even my co-participants were a self-selecting audience because only people who were interested in talking about different intersectional identities like disability, queerness, race, or religion wanted to participate in the project. Of course, we know from all the academic and online discourse around fandom that not all fans are open to talking about these things. In fact, even bringing up such issues in certain fannish spaces can be really contentious and can lead to a lot of conflict.

Dario: Yeah, let's focus on that for a minute. So, you do self-identify as a fan. It's interesting for me to talk to you, as someone who doesn't really like to identify as a fan, even though there are obviously many things in the world that I like. Maybe you could talk a little about what the affordances of podcasting are in relationship to expressions of fandom, as opposed to, or in the broader context of, say, things like slash fiction, other forms of fan fiction, cosplay, or just online chat forums about *Doctor Who*, or whatever it might be. What has podcasting added to the potential of fan expression?

Parinita: I think that's really interesting. Thank you for sharing your non-fannish-ness as well. I think there is a whole strand of study in fandom studies (that I'm not a part of), which researches anti-fandom. Not that I think you're anti-fandom because that's a very specific identity.

Dario: No, I'm definitely not actively anti-fandom.

Parinita: So obviously, my life experiences have informed me in a different way. I've grown up in online fan communities. Working with children's books and young people has informed my perspectives too. I'm very much in the "everybody can like whatever they want" camp. I think there's something for everyone but not everything needs to be for everyone. What's really interesting about fan podcasts is that it has room for all these different kinds of fan enthusiasms and expressions. Nowadays there are decreasing barriers to creating podcasts. You do need the internet and some basic equipment, but you don't need anything fancy to be able to reach a global audience. It leaves more room for niche topics. I think one of the great things about fan podcasts is that there is nobody setting the rules. People can experiment with formats and subjects and even how long they want to podcast for. There is no set criteria. And the fandom doesn't even need to be about popular media. These conversations can be framed around any kind of shared interest like knitting or hiking or politics. Phoenix C.S. Andrews is a researcher who has theorized that politics acts as a sort of fandom too, and they have written about the intersection of both [Andrews 2017; 2020; 2022]. I like looking at fans through a broader lens. For me, the shared interest itself is not as important as what kind of knowledge the people involved are creating through their interpretations and their conversations. There are a decreasing number of public spaces where you are able to encounter or listen to people who are different. Even online, it's easy to create your own bubble so you only interact with people who are like you and who believe the same things you do. I do this to an extent too. I'm probably not going to hang out in misogynistic or xenophobic online spaces. When it comes to fan podcasts of popular media like Harry Potter or *Doctor Who*, I like that they feature a relatively diverse group of fans that you may not encounter in your everyday offline or online life. At their best, they can expand and open up different conversations for you. The shared framework of this media that you love becomes a way for you to access alternative perspectives and experiences that can help you understand the world—both fictional and real—through a different viewpoint.

Dario: I love your perspective, and that kind of idealism about fandom in many ways, because it's counter to the sense that fan cultures do seem to set out rules. And you can create a fan podcast, for example, that circumvents those rules or challenges those rules. There is a tyranny of that certain kind of fan, relating to the property they love and their assumption that the way they think about this storyline or this character is the only way. Obviously there is conversation around those things, but it's not as if fandom doesn't set up rules of engagement itself that can be quite strictly observed and can lead to ostracization of one form or another.

Parinita: I don't mean to paint an overly utopian conception of fandom because I know it is not. That is precisely why I deliberately curate my fandom—both within and beyond *Marginally Fannish*—because I don't want to engage with the toxic elements. I love the kind of considered critique I studied for the Ph.D. but I don't have time for bad-faith arguments or criticisms born of bigotry. Most of my project focused on the more positive aspects of fandom, but the last two chapters of my thesis challenged this wholly positive view of fandom. That's largely thanks to some of my co-participants who shared their negative experiences. One of my co-participants was a *Doctor Who* fan and he spoke about how he found the online fandom pretty ableist, and described how these spaces marginalized his experiences as a disabled fan [Shetty 2020a]. Another co-participant described the hostility she experienced in a space where Lord of the Rings fandom and academia intersected. You alluded to notions of fan cultures where there is only one specific way to understand canon and there is no room for alternative interpretations. That's what happened here when she ventured beyond the dominant Christian understanding of the series and drew on her own Wiccan background to explore a pagan interpretation of Lord of the Rings. She was hoping to start conversations about diverse religious interpretations but it led to a barrage of comments that criticized and dismissed the suggestion [Shetty 2020b]. And this happens a lot. Not all fan podcasts are intersectional or offer critical counternarratives. Many fan communities are unwelcome spaces for different identities, like racialized fans or older fans or queer fans. Many fans don't like it when their canon expands to include a female time-travelling alien or a Black elf in Middle-Earth. This is all part of a much larger cultural discourse that's happening anyway. Fan podcasts are one more avenue where conversations about the problems in fandom itself can occur.

Dario: Within the context of what you've just laid out, I was wondering whether we should go into some of the obvious critiques of fandom. For example, why do fan obsessions seem to encourage remaining within the cultural and social security of one's childhood? And then there's the critique that these armies of fans are essentially just cultural dupes in the Frankfurt School sense; rather than being autonomous expressions of creativity, fan culture is a process of exploitation by late-capitalist commercial machinery. I don't know if you want to comment on any of that or not. But if we're relating this back to podcasting, one of the issues relates to the idea, as you said, that one of the great things about podcasting is anyone can make one. It's relatively accessible in terms of technology and cost compared to movies or TV or whatever. But then does that offer the opportunity for a kind of self-indulgent navel-gazing, "Let's bury ourselves in the tiniest minutiae of what happened in episode forty-five, season seventeen" kind of thing. The potential that leaning into such overt obsession could actually be detrimental to perhaps growing or even function in broader society. I'm honestly not trying to be very reductive or stereotyping, but I wondered what your response to such critiques is.

Parinita: What is thought of now as the fan studies "canon" started in the early 1990s [Thomas 2011]. Some of the researchers were also fans themselves. Those early researchers grappled with the question of why studying fans and fandom matters. But by the time I discovered fan studies during my master's in 2016, the field was less concerned with justifying its existence. I was also someone who'd grown up in online fandom communities and had gained a valuable education thanks to my exposure to alternative perspectives there. So I drew on my own experiences as well as the state of fan scholarship at the time and didn't bother with justifying fandom and my identity as both a researcher and a fan. I just took it as a given that it's important to some people and I was more interested in seeing what fans did. I may think certain books or movies are terrible because they don't speak to me but I also realize they may resonate with someone else and vice versa. Who decides what you're supposed to like and engage with? I'm not comfortable imposing my judgment of any literature, culture, or art on others. Even if I'm not interested in a particular object of fandom, I really like understanding why people are into it.

When it comes to critiques about fans being cultural dupes, I'm going to turn to public pedagogy scholarship which says that not all people take the messages promoted by popular media or society as a given [Sandlin, Wright, and Clark 2013; Savage 2010]. There are people who critique this and create counternarratives with alternative perspectives. Some scholars believe that there needs to be a facilitator—usually an academic or educator—who creates these public pedagogy conversations and spaces, and helps non-academic people challenge their experience of mainstream messages. But the feminist strand of public pedagogy doesn't think that there needs to be one individual public pedagogue. We believe that multiple people, having these conversations collaboratively, expand and challenge each other's understanding [Sandlin, O'Malley, and Burdick 2011]. I'm looking at how fan podcasts act as these public pedagogical spaces where episode conversations allow people—both participants and audiences—to look at something familiar with a new critical gaze. Obviously, not all fans are like this. I wasn't like this to begin with. But a lot of fans express their fandom by actively looking for what other people have said about the thing they love in ways which might influence their own understanding [Bury 2017]. Hannah McGregor [2019] surveyed Harry Potter fan podcast listeners and some of them reported that they listened to podcasts because they liked having their perspectives challenged so they could understand things in ways they'd never thought of before. This isn't an academic or an educator telling them what to think. Instead, fans who share this love for a certain thing are figuring out how to think together.

Dario: Your outline there about the justification of why someone likes something is something I'm constantly thinking about ever since I got into academia, and particularly reading a lot of cultural studies. I suppose I'm always wrestling with the concept of defining anything as "good" or "bad." Clearly I'm still influenced by my background in an era of didactic education and a certain strand of cultural criticism: that there are art forms along with the processes of their making and the artist's intention and the aesthetic outcome that possess an inherent significance, beauty or ideal within the context and history of the art form they exemplify. And there is a criteria of judgment that relates to the notion of significance and value, and that ultimately taboo idea these days, "quality." But for example, when I make a podcast I want it to be the best it can be. And in my mind there is a criteria of judgment that shapes that. But of course someone could come along and say it's no good. When we say we like something, that's subjective, but always in the back of our mind we secretly, or perhaps not so secretly, think we are objectively right.

Parinita: Conversely, I've been influenced by how I've grown up online and the ideas and conversations I've been exposed to. Pre-internet, people were judging quality in specific spaces, and I wonder how many people agreed or disagreed with this assessment. Most people didn't really have the avenues to be able to contribute to that cultural discussion. What I really love about the fan podcasts and fandom communities I've participated in is the multiplicity of interpretations and opinions. Fans may not always agree with each other; in fact, a lot of the time, they don't. And I love being able to listen to these disagreements and figure out what I think. Just yesterday, I was listening to a podcast and the host received a review asking for the podcast to be edited down so it's much shorter. Her episodes are usually well over an hour. The host spent the segment outlining her rationale for the length and format of her episodes. She explained that this was a deliberate decision that made sense to her requirements but also acknowledged that this may not work for everybody. She even asked people to message her for recommendations for shorter podcasts that explored the same themes her podcast focused on. I like that disagreements can either help change your perspective or help you articulate your contradictory stance. If I make *Marginally Fannish* season two I'll try and learn from my experiences in season one and make a better version, but that will still probably not work for everyone. As long as I know why I'm doing what I'm doing, that's fine.

Dario: And obviously the binary opposition of objective and subjective itself is really problematic. They don't exist as "pure" concepts, especially in their application to how we experience art or culture. But everyone is also applying criteria of judgment to their understanding. As you say, the length of a podcast or a film in the abstract is something that people use. But there is both intention behind that, and at least an aspiration to the notion that length of a show (shorter or longer) might be in keeping with an overall aesthetic coherence, as an aspiration towards creating a "good" piece of work. I'm very much of the view that art that is defined as good or great, or bad, is so depending on historical, political, and social circumstances. Certain types of people and groups have gotten to define this over time—again, related back to the notion of a canon. The open nature of the internet has exploded that. But then I fall back to that problem: so nothing is good and nothing is bad anymore. I'm always struggling with that idea. But that's something we won't solve, so let's move on to talking a little bit about the idea of intersectionality. That is another term that has entered into the popular cultural lexicon from having been an academic term and a certain type of analysis. Can you talk about how that idea is deployed in your work?

Parinita: When Kimberlé Crenshaw first coined the term intersectionality [1989; 1991], she was investigating how race, gender, and social class intersected and impacted the lives of poor Black women in the US. But now she and other scholars look at how intersectionality can be applied to a broader range of contexts [Cho, Crenshaw, and McCall 2013; Choo and Ferree 2010; Collins 2015; Crenshaw 2015; Davis 2008; Jordan-Zachery 2007; Romero 2017]. In India, race is not going to be as relevant as caste or religion, so the intersectional categories being studied there would differ. Ange-Marie Hancock

[2016] proposed that intersectionality has become a viral meme that has travelled beyond academia because of the internet. Online discussions of intersectionality have increased people's awareness and understanding of this concept—and have also led to some people railing against it. I borrowed from both intersectionality scholars as well as non-academic discussions of intersectional identities. There is a lot of debate in intersectionality scholarship about what identities and issues the framework applies to. I'm sure some researchers would be absolutely aghast at my interpretation of it. I'm using fan podcasts to look at the intersection of both privilege and marginalization. The fact that I'm an Indian immigrant in the UK and an Indian fan of Western media very much informed this understanding. I went from being a part of the dominant culture to a marginalized one—though I do have some privileges even here. So I think intersectionality is contextual: you can be privileged in some contexts, oppressed in others.

What I was really interested in was how fan podcasts use the framework of popular media like Harry Potter or *Doctor Who* to build this education of intersectional identities in different contexts. For example, a podcaster in India would have a very different understanding and experience of how race is represented in media compared to a Black fan in the US or an Indian fan in the UK. Both on *Marginally Fannish* and in the fan podcasts I listened to, fans from different backgrounds used the lens of their identities like disability, sexuality, or age to respond to their favourite media. I learned about real-world intersectional experiences, both marginalized and privileged, through these conversations about fictional characters and events. For example, one of my co-participants was an Orthodox Jewish fan from Israel. In our episode, he critiqued the erasure and misrepresentation of religion in mainstream science fiction and fantasy media. He pointed out that as a fan of this genre, he largely had to contend with representations where religious people were hostile forces or villainous plot points rather than their everyday engagements with faith. At the same time, while his culture may be marginalized in the media he loves, he was very aware that he is a part of the dominant culture in the country he lives in [Shetty 2020c]. Many fan podcast episodes grapple with these nuances and complexities within people's identities. So even when people aren't using the term intersectionality, such conversations that use the language of fictional media can help illuminate real-world understandings of diverse experiences.

Dario: Something that I don't think has been done yet is very focused intersectional analysis of the voice in podcasting. It's a non-visual medium and we privilege certain types of listening practices depending on the voice that we're listening to. There's a gender aspect to that, but there's also a racial aspect and even a kind of ethno-nationalist, nationalistic sense to that. There's a cross-over of ethnic and national identities that can come through our voice. I've got quite a broad Yorkshire accent, which I can lean into, but I've definitely clipped it over the years because of teaching in the south of the UK, and even more because of podcasting. You mentioned that you've got a specific accent; was that something you thought about, how you are perceived or how you were listened to, in the making of the podcast?

Parinita: I didn't think about it in terms of how I was perceived, but it was quite a deliberate choice to insert the voices of me and my two Indian co-hosts into a cultural discourse around Western media. In my research before launching *Marginally Fannish*, I read about the politics of voice in audio media, specifically the underrepresentation of certain kinds of voices. This reinforced my commitment to try and recruit as diverse a cohort of participants as possible to be able to feature a broad range of voices and perspectives. They included people from India, England, Scotland, the US, the UAE, Israel, Singapore, the Philippines, Greece, Japan, Bulgaria, and Canada. Apart from this international diversity, they also inhabited a range of identities across the racial, religious, gender, sexuality, ability, and age spectrum. I think it would be interesting to do an intersectional analysis of voice in podcasts—both mine and the fan podcasts I listen to. I don't know if there is research about this in podcast studies, but I found that a lot of fan podcasts emerge from either North America or the UK. Which means that a very specific accent and very specific themes and identities tend to predominate.

Dario: Linking to the importance of decolonization in your work. The idea of decolonization of knowledge is a general principle or agenda in higher education in the West. Obviously, the general idea of opening up to scrutiny the histories of our knowledge and where it comes from should be a vital aim for academia. It's really fascinating that you are an Indian scholar who's studying these UK institutions, *Doctor Who* and Harry Potter, and the irony of that considering British colonial relationship to India. Was there not the potential to look at an Indian podcast that is a fan articulation of Indian popular culture? How did the importance of decolonization inform your project?

Parinita: I hoped that people from formerly colonized countries responding to British media would provide insights and counternarratives. When putting the methodology together, I thought about what texts to focus on and whether I should be looking at Indian media rather than Western media. This may have been because of my own limited searching capabilities but I couldn't find any fan podcasts focusing on Hindi movies at the time. My co-hosts and I love

Bollywood movies and in some of our episodes, we did end up analyzing and critiquing examples based on the intersectional themes we were discussing. But my Indian co-participants and I were also impacted by colonial consequences which means we grew up with a lot of British media. We devoured Enid Blyton books. Aspects of British culture were second nature to us. I realized there were two kinds of decolonization going on in *Marginally Fannish*. First, a more direct form of Asian voices responding to Western media in either a joyful, "Oh, we love this," or "Um, this is a bit suspect" way. For example, we discussed how Arabic, Filipino, and Indian foods, names, and cultures were erased and misrepresented in the British media we loved [Shetty 2022a, 2022b]. Secondly, a collective process of decolonization occurred through our podcast episodes. In our conversations, we unpacked and analyzed things we had otherwise taken for granted which helped us decolonize our own minds. There aren't always spaces or opportunities for us to talk about these things. The podcast framework offered fans a chance to gather around specific media and themes, and enabled us to point out things that were problematic and articulate why we thought that. In one episode, we talked about how our steady diet of Enid Blyton books meant that we used to consider British food aspirational and Indian food inferior [Shetty 2020d]. Another co-participant talked about the failure of imagination when it comes to food in Hogwarts. She pointed out that although this is a British school with some characters of colour, there is no hint of any immigrant influences on what the characters eat. Indian food and Chinese food have influenced Britain for decades but the food in Harry Potter is the same kind of food that you find in Enid Blyton books, which were set fifty or sixty years ago [Shetty 2020e].

Dario: You've talked about the possibility of a second season of *Marginally Fannish*. If you think about the direction that you're planning to go in your academic and podcasting career, have you got any thoughts on the avenues of fan analysis, or looking at fandom or in any particular area that you've covered, through the lens of podcast studies? Where do you see research moving in the future in the context of podcast studies?

Parinita: I would love to see more collaborations between academic and non-academic podcasters so they're both in conversation with each other's practices and cultures. I've listened to academic guests on non-academic podcasts that are aimed at a more general audience and I love them. But I think a more deliberate and sustained partnership where both academics and non-academics come together to co-create a podcast would benefit both the people involved and podcast studies as a whole. There are some things you end up taking for granted within an academic context that you don't even realize until you step outside and talk to different people who are situated beyond these academic bubbles. In *Marginally Fannish*, my non-academic co-participants brought in such a wide range of insights and contributions in the form of both text recommendations and critical ideas, and engaging with them made me such a better thinker and podcaster. I know public engagement is increasingly popular in academia. But I'm less interested in the institutional benefits and more excited to see what kinds of conversations about the politics of knowledge-making such collaborations can open up.

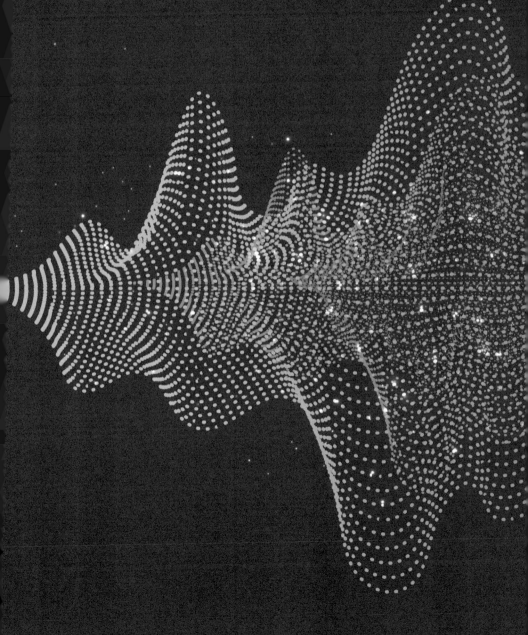

PART THREE

PODCASTING AS PRODUCTION AND PEDAGOGIC PRACTICE

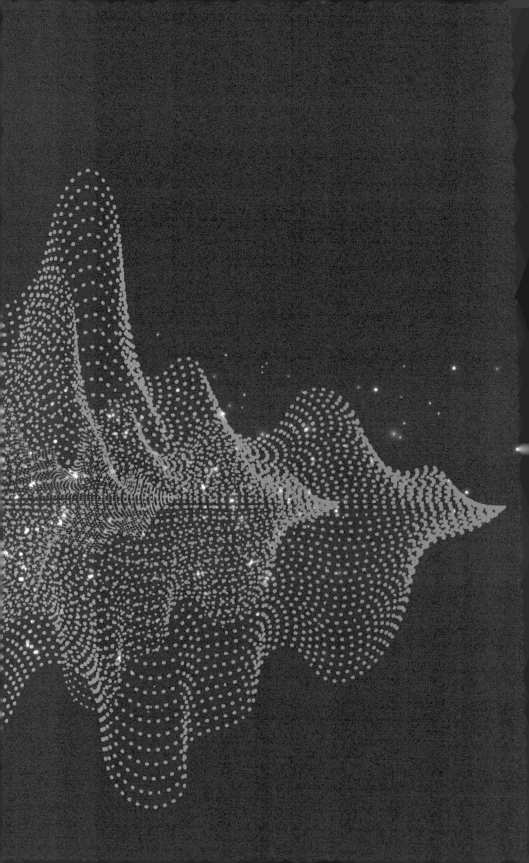

CHAPTER 13

CONTEXT IS KING
Podcast Paratexts

LORI BECKSTEAD

Note to the reader: This chapter was not only peer reviewed via the usual mechanisms (written comments, suggestions, and a recommendation on whether it should be published or not given by one or more unknown peers), it was also peer reviewed via podcast. I invited peers Hannah McGregor and Ian M. Cook to read a draft copy of this chapter, then we recorded an episode of The Podcast Studies Podcast *in which all three of us discussed the strengths and weaknesses of the draft. A second episode was recorded as a follow-up in which we discussed our reactions to and thoughts about the process of doing peer review via podcast.[1]*

Those who make podcasts might be familiar with a scenario something like this: You've just crushed an interview with an articulate and interesting guest. You've designed an introduction and other transitional sonic elements, sourced and placed music to set the tone, and recorded voice-overs, maybe some scripted performances, narration, and other vocal elements. You've sequenced and segued it all to perfection and mixed, equalized, de-essed, compressed, and otherwise polished the sound. Finally, with a feeling of great satisfaction, you bounce it out to a finished audio file. You've finished a podcast episode!

---

1   Look for the episodes entitled "Peer Review Podcasting" parts one and two wherever you access *The Podcast Studies Podcast.*

But hold on a moment while I burst your audio balloon: a bounced audio file does not a podcast make. As podcast blogger Tanner Campbell points out, podcasters—particularly independent ones—don't have the luxury of being good at just one thing. They have to be at least a dozen things: the talent, the social media manager, the audio editor, the audio engineer, the marketing director, the relationship manager, the IT support, the web designer, the writer, the public relations contact, the producer, and the graphic designer (2021, para. 21). Individuals with expertise in any one of these areas know that time, effort, practice, study, and money (naturally) are needed to develop proficiency. Nonetheless these jobs, among others, are required of the independent creator in order not only to produce a podcast but also to make it available and accessible to an audience.

As an independent podcaster myself, I am often frustrated by the need to be good at all those extras. I came to podcasting via radio, to which I came via an interest in sound-based media in general. So for me, working in sound is the pleasure of podcasting.[2] I feel unfettered by constraints of the visual which, for me, impart a certain specificity—here's exactly what this looks like, here's the expression on that person's face—that removes the opportunity for the listener to actively imagine the intent of the artist, contemplate the meaning of the words, or co-create the storyworld. In this sense, sound-based media require more of the audience than visual media do. Indeed, the act of listening to sound media allows for what podcast host Jad Abumrad calls "a deep act of co-authorship." He uses the metaphor of painting a picture "but I'm not holding the brush. You [as the listener] are...we're doing it together because we have to fill this gap of picturelessness together" (2012, 00:44–01:02). Sound media require an intellectual and creative soundmaker-listener co-operation. This, as well as the opportunity for discourse unrestrained by visual prejudice, is what draws me in and makes me happy to revel in the act of pure soundmaking. I admit I dread setting aside the soundwork in order to create all those additional media assets—but they are absolutely necessary if the soundwork is going to exist in the world *as a podcast*. In this chapter I argue that podcasts are therefore not an audio-only medium. While this dismays me as a soundmaker, as a scholar I relish the opportunities this approach presents to further our understanding of the podcast as more than a sound file.

---

2   While a number of podcasters and podcast scholars have, like me, engaged with the medium from the point of view—or point of audition—of sound as the central "text," it is also true that many podcasters come to podcasting rather from a brand-extension approach, wherein the podcast is a way to add value to or promote an existing digital brand. In the latter case, existing logos, websites, and other materials can be leveraged and the additional work for such podcasters may actually be the soundwork itself.

In what follows I examine those extra media assets—the texts that surround and enable a podcast to be a podcast.[3] Using a literary theory lens, I consider them collectively as "podcast paratexts." I argue that podcasts cannot in fact exist without them, and that they must be part of any ontology of the podcast medium itself. We have seen a shift in thinking about podcasts from being paratexts themselves to being primary texts that have their own ecosystem of paratexts. These paratexts not only enable the podcast to exist in the world but also shape how audiences perceive, interact with, and consume the podcast (or don't). As Hoyt argues, if researchers only engage with audio and RSS files, they will miss "important reception environments that are contributing to the rise of podcasting as a vital and important media format" (2021, 237). Similarly, Hansen argues that if podcasts are thought of as audio only, we fail to capture the fact that "podcast feeds can feature everything from videos to PDFs to PowerPoint presentations" (2021, 195). Thus I consider ways in which academics and researchers might engage with podcast paratexts—not only in a broad sense but also particularly with respect to two significant paratexts: cover art and transcripts—as scholarship emerges in this as yet under-examined area of podcast studies.

PARATEXTS

Media and cultural studies scholars have found the concept of paratexts to be a useful framework in understanding how audiences receive, think about, and enter a media-text (Birke and Christ 2013; Desrochers and Apollon 2014; Gray 2010). The term paratext was coined by literary theorist Gérard Genette to describe "what enables a text to become a book and to be offered as such to its readers and, more generally, to the public. More than a boundary or a sealed border, the paratext is, rather, a threshold" (1997, 1). Paratexts, in relation to books as Genette explains them, include title, preface, book cover, illustrations, chapter headings, notes, jacket copy, etc.; they are elements which do not form part of the primary text itself but are necessary to convey the text to its intended audience. Paratexts are the threshold between the outside of the book and the inside. Genette distinguishes two distinct categories of paratext: *peritext*, which exists within the same volume as the primary text, and *epitext* which is located outside of the primary text and includes items generated by the media, such as interviews and conversations, as well as private communications, such as letters and diaries.

---

3   While the word *text* in general refers to a written or published work, I also use it throughout this chapter in the broader academic sense of text as "anything that conveys a set of meanings to the person who examines it" (Burnell et al., n.d.).

Jonathan Gray expands on Genette's work by introducing concepts which, in contrast to Genette's location-based peritext and epitext (i.e., "inside" or "outside" the material text), engage a chronological framework that is useful for examining time-based and digital media texts. Gray's *entryway paratexts* control a viewer's or listener's entrance to the text, framing how they will encounter, react to, and interpret it. A movie poster that depicts explosions and car chases, for example, can be an entryway paratext indicating that a viewer should come to the theatre prepared for thrilling action. Indeed, if the movie does not deliver any car chases or explosions, no matter how good the film might be, a viewer may be disappointed because of the expectations set up by this entryway paratext. Gray's *in medias res paratexts*, true to the introductory phrase's translation from Latin of "in the midst of things," "flow between the gaps" of text and come to the audience during or after the main text (2010, 23). For example, one might encounter an *in medias res paratext*, such as a review or a Twitter thread, during the time between listening to episodes in a podcast series. They can suggest or impose particular reading strategies and interpretations on the audience during the encounter with a text, in between encounters, and afterwards (Gray 2010).

Birke and Christ (2013) propose three ways to categorize the functions of paratexts: interpretive, commercial, and navigational. The interpretive function shares the role of Gray's entryway paratexts in that they suggest specific ways of reading, understanding, and interpreting the text. A modern B movie might use lo-fi production techniques and over-the-top scoring in its paratextual trailer, for example, setting up an understanding among potential viewers that the movie is meant to be understood as campy or interpreted ironically. Birke and Christ's second function, the commercial one, is about promoting and facilitating monetary transactions: advertising the text, indicating the price and how to purchase, etc. Lastly, the navigational function provides a more "mechanical" guidance to the viewer/listener, signposting how to enter the text and providing orientation within it (68). A DVD menu is an obvious example of a paratext that has a navigational function, but other examples might also include a book's table of contents or a website's dropdown menu.

I will use these frameworks to examine specific podcast paratexts, but first let's consider the relationship between podcasts and their paratexts.

A PODCAST BY ANY OTHER PARATEXT...

Can a podcast be considered a podcast unless it is served and supported by paratexts? I argue that a podcast needs to have an audience, or at least be available to a potential audience, in order to actually *be* a podcast. A potential listener could not access a sound file that isn't tied to one or more paratexts which act as a kind of "digital embodiment" of the sound file. At the very least a user interface such as an audio player is required, which itself comprises imagery and text.[4] Podcast archivists recognize that the successful archiving of podcasts must include their paratexts (see, for example, Hansen 2021; Hoyt 2021).

Genette asserts that a text must have paratexts which enable its presentation to the world; they "surround [the main text] and prolong it, precisely in order to *present* it, in the usual sense of this verb, but also in its strongest meaning: to *make it present*, to assure its presence in the world, its 'reception' and its consumption" (1997, 1). In stronger language, he goes on to clarify that "a text without a paratext does not exist and never has existed" (3). It seems the podcast industry also agrees with this premise; a simple survey of writing aimed at podcast producers on the topic of how and why to create paratexts such as cover art, show notes, and show descriptions reveals that one of the assumed primary reasons to create such paratexts is to attract and grow an audience (see, for example, Gray 2020; "7 Reasons You Should Publish Your Podcast Show Notes" 2018; Corbett 2018; "How to Write A Podcast Description That Gets You Listeners" 2021; Logue 2020; and myriad others). Thus, no audience means no podcast. Because audiences cannot access podcasts except through their paratexts, I argue therefore that no paratext means no podcast.

Ironically, the medium of podcasting has spent a good deal of its twenty-year lifespan serving as, or being perceived as, a paratext to radio. Cwynar has argued that the Canadian Broadcasting Corporation's early podcasts were used simply "as promotional paratexts for their source radio programs, the radio service, and the broader CBC brand" (2015, 191). Berry has written similarly about podcasting's evolution at the BBC as "an alternative means of distribution for whole shows or highlights" but which developed into a "distribution route, as well as a space for innovation and remediation—where content can be shared with listeners in a way that linear transmission systems cannot facilitate" (2016b, 665). Both of Berry's characterizations suggest that during this time podcasting was essentially in service to radio. As for National Public Radio (NPR) in the US, its influence on the form and sound of podcasts is difficult to overstate: many of the most popular podcasts of the first ten years of podcasting were NPR radio shows distributed as podcasts. Podcasts

---

4   Digital publishing is built upon, or has at least defaulted to, old paradigms of publishing in which only text (and increasingly imagery) are the means by which a "text" can be accessed. Digital audio is only accessible through graphics and text, giving the impression that it is less tangible than the latter two. In this sense, text and graphics represent what one could say are more solid, or embodied, digital pathways to the arguably "less-embodied" sound.

have also been positioned as paratexts in the context of other media. Hodapp (2020), for example, writes of literary review podcasts as being paratextual, with the books under discussion being the main texts. But over time podcasts have shaken off their ties to radio and have explored and developed their own set of practices, logics, and forms. In tandem, podcast paratexts have established themselves as central to the digital infrastructure and cultural landscape of the medium. The frame of reference has shifted from "podcast as paratext" to "podcasts and their paratexts." These paratexts, however, have been given scant attention by podcast scholars to date.

THE IMPORTANCE OF PARATEXTS

Why study podcasts' paratexts? Gray (2010, 26) makes a case: "paratextual study not only promises to tell us how a text creates meaning for its consumer; it also promises to tell us how a text creates meaning in popular culture and society more generally." In addition, audiences spend a good deal of their time engaging in what Gray calls "speculative consumption": a practice in which a viewer or listener uses paratexts to infer what the text will provide and what effect it might have on them (24). Memes about spending more time browsing Netflix menus than actually watching any given show attest to just how much time audiences inadvertently devote to the practice of speculative consumption, and no doubt the endless scroll of cover art thumbnails and descriptions in a podcatcher have a similar effect on potential podcast listeners. Because a listener cannot possibly listen to every podcast she encounters, speculative consumption may be the only means through which she bases her impression of, and decision to listen to, a show or episode. It is "precisely because paratexts help us decide which texts to consume, we often know many texts *only* at the paratextual level...paratexts, then, become the very stuff upon which much popular interpretation is based" (Gray 2010, 26; emphasis mine). Indeed, I have sometimes deliberately decided not to listen to a podcast based on impressions and expectations gleaned from just one of its paratextual elements. More on that later.

Dan Misener, writing for an audience of podcast producers, points out that "podcast listeners tend to use their *eyes first*, and their *ears second*" (2018b para. 1; emphasis in original). Podcast packaging, as Misener calls what I refer to as podcast paratext, is seen by him and other industry pundits as a paramount consideration for podcast producers if they want to attract and grow their audience (2018a, 2018b).

Audio is notoriously bad for sharing on social media. Viral audio is rare; there are very few examples of audio-only internet memes. The internet is of course a visual medium, but as Zuckerman (2014) points out, it's hard to "glance" at audio. Recent industry discourse recommends that producers post their podcasts to YouTube (a fairly controversial idea, threatening to undermine the widely accepted understanding of podcasting being an audio-only medium), not only to tap YouTube's massive audience, but also because it's a fairly frictionless platform for delivering additional "you might also like" content and for audiences to share its content on social media. Apps like Headliner, Wavve, or Audiogram, which enable podcasters to quickly generate a video to accompany a short audio clip, exist to create a gateway between "unshareable" sound media and potential listeners on social platforms. Audio's viral resistance adds support to the argument that podcast paratexts merit deeper academic scrutiny, underlining the fact that visual, or at the very least text-based paratexts must be created in order to smooth the way for sharing sound-based media.

In short, paratexts—whether they be graphic or text-based—allow access to the main podcast text, shape one's perception of it, enable sharing on social media, and are often the only signifier associated with a podcast that a listener will encounter. These facts point to the importance of cultivating the paratext not only in podcast practice but also in podcast studies.

MAKING SENSE OF PODCAST PARATEXTS

What are the paratexts of podcasts? There is an entire ecosystem of them, many of which I have listed in table 13.1. I classify various podcast paratexts according to Genette, Gray, and Birke and Christ's paratext types and functions.

One of the challenges of identifying podcast paratexts as either peritext (inside the podcast) or epitext (outside the podcast) is that it becomes necessary to define the specific boundaries of the medium. Because the object of Genette's theory was the book—a material object—it is easier to distinguish between what exists inside or outside the text (Birke and Christ 2013). However, in the case of a podcast, which has no material manifestation, this becomes complicated. And despite the fact that co-editor of this volume Dario Llinares and I joked as we began the book that "At least at this stage in podcasting's history we won't need to start with an explanation of what a podcast is," here I go with an attempt to do just that. Many naturally consider podcasts to be an audio-only medium. If this is the case, is the medium's purview limited to just the audio file? Rather, many definitions of podcasting as a medium are predicated on both an audio file *and* an RSS document (Sterne et al. 2008; Farivar as cited in Bottomley 2015). When the *New Oxford American Dictionary* declared *podcast* its word of the year in 2005, it offered this definition: "a digital recording of a radio broadcast or similar program, *made available on the Internet* for downloading to a personal audio player" (Bierma 2005, emphasis mine).

TABLE 13.1. Types and functions of podcast paratexts

	Paratext	Level*	Paratext type (after Genette 1997)	Paratext type (after Gray 2010)	Function (after Birke and Christ 2013)
Intrinsic to the medium (i.e., required parts of RSS feed)	Title	Show	Peritext	Entryway	Interpretive
	Cover art	Show and episode	Peritext or Epitext**	Entryway	Interpretive
	Category	Show	Peritext or Epitext	Entryway	Interpretive
	Description	Show and episode	Peritext or Epitext	Entryway	Interpretive
	Author (producer)	Show	Peritext or Epitext	Entryway	Interpretive
External to the main podcast text	Episode notes (usually referred to as "show notes")	Episode	Epitext	Entryway or In medias res	Interpretive Commercial
	Transcripts	Episode	Epitext or Primary Text†	Entryway or In medias res	Navigational Interpretive Commercial
	Bonus content	Show	Epitext	In medias res	Commercial Interpretive
	Website or homepage	Show	Epitext	Entryway or In medias res	Interpretive Navigational Commercial

External to the main podcast text *(continued)*	Online discussion groups	Show and episode	Epitext	Entryway or In medias res	Interpretive
	Social media posts	Show and episode	Epitext	Entryway or In medias res	Interpretive
	Ratings and reviews	Show	Epitext	Entryway	Interpretive
	Articles, criticism, interviews, etc. about the podcast	Show	Epitext	Entryway or In medias res	Interpretive
	Material goods (e.g., branded T-shirts, gifts, souvenirs, books, etc.)	Show	Epitext	Entryway or In medias res	Commercial Interpretive
	Programmatic ads‡	Episode	Epitext	In medias res	Commercial Interpretive
Internal to the sound file	Host-read ads	Episode	Peritext	In medias res	Commercial Interpretive

*   "Show level" refers to the podcast series as a whole, whereas "episode level" refers to individual episodes (Misener 2018a).

** Whether this is a peritext ("inside" the podcast text) or an epitext ("outside" the podcast text) depends on what one considers the "boundaries" of a podcast to be, as these boundaries are not immutable.

†   A transcript could be interpreted as a primary text rather than a paratext depending on who is accessing it and for what purpose. See section on transcripts in this chapter.

‡   "Programmatic" refers to an automated way of buying or selling ad space, often in real time ("What Is Programmatic Advertising?" 2017). In the podcasting context, programmatic ads are produced outside of the recording/production of the podcast itself, and inserted into the podcast, much like ads on a commercial radio station.

What makes a podcast "available on the Internet" is the RSS document, a text-based document that uses meta tags to point not only to the location of the podcast audio but also to any number of associated paratexts. Major podcast directories such as Apple require that specific meta tags including title, image, description, and URL (where the audio file is located) be present in the RSS document ("Podcast RSS Feed Requirements" 2021; "RSS Feed Guidelines for Google Podcasts—Podcasts Manager Help" 2021). Therefore, it could be argued that these required metadata point to digital assets that are necessary and inherent aspects of the medium. But because RSS documents can theoretically support any number of additional meta tags, and because they currently lack any standardization that is specific to podcasts ("Exploring the New Standard for Podcast RSS Feeds" 2021), the boundaries of the medium can and do shift. For example, a meta tag for a transcript can be included in an RSS document, pointing to the location of a text-based transcript of the podcast's audio. Does this mean that transcripts are inherent to the medium? The necessity of transcripts from an audience perspective is an issue that I will explore later, but they are not required by podcast directories in order to make the podcast available, and furthermore, not all podcasts provide transcripts—and we still call these podcasts. I'm not proposing that just because a meta tag in a podcast's RSS feed points to a related file or paratext that this paratext is therefore an essential part of the medium. But this does problematize the boundaries of the medium, and also, therefore, the ability to categorize podcast paratexts as epitexts or peritexts.

In order to better understand the significance of podcast paratexts, I examine two crucial paratexts below: cover art and transcriptions.

COVER ART

Podcast cover art is one of the most significant paratexts of podcasting. It is an epitext situated outside of the main podcast text, and serves as an entryway paratext with an interpretive function: it indicates the name of the podcast, sometimes what it's about and who is hosting it, and ideally conveys a sense of the tone and feeling of the podcast to potential listeners.

I hope the reader will kindly forgive me for bringing up Joe Rogan. He merits mention here because his podcast *The Joe Rogan Experience* is one of the most popular of all time ("10 Most Downloaded Podcasts of All Time!" 2021). Despite its enduring popularity, I've never listened to it. For someone whose profession it is to know about podcasts and to teach others how to make them, it's basic professional development to keep on top of new and popular shows in the podosphere. But I just haven't been able to bring myself to listen to Joe Rogan's podcast. Sure, I was put off by the broader cultural discourse about

Rogan, particularly since the recent COVID-19 misinformation scandal. But before all that, the initial barrier to listening was the cover art.

For me, the podcast cover art says, rather loudly, "THIS PODCAST IS NOT FOR YOU." The close-up head-on portrait of a man with an exaggerated grin and wide eyes leaning in towards the viewer suggests that "in your face" is the guiding principle of this podcast. As a woman, if that kind of expression were directed at me by a man in person I'd certainly turn and run. The colour scheme of black and muddy brownish orange along with the ALL-CAPS text contribute to the hyper-masculine overtone. There's part of a microphone visible in the foreground, but at first glance I actually perceived it as a gun; perhaps this was my brain automatically associating a threatening-looking man with a weapon rather than a microphone. My aversion to this domineering and confrontational image keeps me from listening to what I assume is a domineering and confrontational podcast. This example illuminates Gray's view that a paratext may be the only way in which a viewer comes to know a text (2010), and exemplifies the interpretive function of paratexts (Birke and Christ 2013).

The visual paratext is a crucial aspect of what is primarily thought of as an audio medium. Podcatching apps and podcast directories make recommendations by displaying podcast cover art and providing a snippet of the textual description of the podcast. While it's possible one may hear a trailer for a podcast while listening to another, or that a listener might access a podcast via an audio-only smart speaker, it's more often the case that the visual elements are the first point of contact one will have with a podcast. In a similar fashion to dating apps, users may be making split-second decisions about whether to "swipe right," i.e., to have a listen, based on a cursory glance at the image presented. As Misener reminds us, like it or not, the first impression a listener will get of a podcast will come from its packaging, not its audio content (2018a). A visual graphic is far likelier to be casually encountered through search engines, in podcatchers, and in archives, and perhaps even likelier than the audio to "survive" beyond the demise of a podcast.

I looked at the cover artwork for *Time* magazine's ten best podcasts of 2021 (Dockterman 2021): *The Just Enough Family, Fighting in the War Room, The Sporkful, 9/12, Sway, Poog, Spectacle: An Unscripted History of Reality TV, StraightioLab, Criticism Is Dead,* and *S***hole Country.*[5] Among these cover art designs, one can quickly detect several commonalities:

- Most are illustrated rather than using photographic elements.

---

5   To view the cover art of these ten podcasts, see time.com/6107375/best-podcasts-2021.

- The chatcasts and interview-based podcasts (e.g., *Straightio Lab*) use photos or illustrations of the hosts as the most prominent feature of the design.
- Of the designs in which the host or hosts are featured, they mostly depict "painterly" versions of the hosts' faces. We can see a similar painterly rendering in *The Joe Rogan Experience* cover art.
- The designs use very limited colour palettes. Six of them use only two to four colours (including black and white). *The Sporkful* and *Fighting in the War Room* employ a simple image over a single colour. *StraightioLab*'s design, employing colour photography, technically may have hundreds of colours in it but the overall effect is nonetheless a limited palette of greys, green, and blue.

It is possible that these impressions, although brief and looking at just a handful of podcasts, speak to wider tropes and trends in podcast cover art. What do we make of the "cartoon rendering of the host(s)" trope that can be seen in myriad examples beyond those above? What does it say about producers' assumptions about listeners (distinguished here from viewers quite deliberately) and their preferences? Why are simple illustrations favoured? What trends and tropes might turn up in an analysis by genre or format? These are some of the possibilities for investigating the role of the visual paratext in podcast studies.

Inspiration for approaching such scholarship can be found in studies of other media paratexts, such as those associated with books and music. Saarinen and Vakkari (2013), for example, found that a book's external appearance was among the top three most common triggers of interest towards a novel while browsing in a library. Similarly, d'Astous, Colbert, and Mbarek (2006) looked into the effect of several variables on a reader's interest in a new book and found that the attractiveness of the book cover had a significant impact. Interestingly, no correlation was found between the representativeness of a book cover—that is, how well the cover design represents the content of the book—and readers' interest in the book. This suggests a possibility that prevailing podcast-industry wisdom, which says cover art should depict at a glance what the podcast is about, might not be entirely helpful. These studies confirm one thing we already know: that despite persistent adages warning against the practice, people do judge books by their covers—and, presumably, podcasts by their cover art. Podcast studies as a discipline has plenty of room for audience-reception studies and analyses of podcast culture and production practices as they relate to visual paratexts.

Music is a natural domain to mine for potential insight about podcasting's relationship with visuals. The connection between podcast cover art and album covers is strong, despite there being sixty-five or so years between the inception of one form and the other.[6] Indeed, podcast cover art's square framework exists because of album art—or, more precisely, because of the iTunes interface. When Apple began including podcasts on the platform in 2005, podcast cover art was also introduced. To fit into the existing interface—designed to showcase square album and CD cover art—podcast cover art needed to be square, and has remained so ever since (Sullivan 2019, 3). This moment in time also represents a "sealing of the deal" that podcasts must have an associated image (a paratext) in order for the podcast audio to be made available to large numbers of potential listeners on prevailing platforms.

In their 2011 paper, Libeks and Turnbull propose that similarity amongst various types of music could be correlated with similarity in music-related images, such as artist photos and album art. For scholars and producers who are frustrated with the very limiting current definitions of "genre" in podcasting—generally narrowly defined based only on the primary topic of a podcast—this represents an interesting possibility: could the characteristics of podcast cover art could be used as a metric for podcast recommendation engines to identify similarities across podcast content that are easily missed by a simple genre-based classification?

Album covers play a similar role to podcast cover art as paratexts, but with several significant differences. An album cover is not always an entryway text. In fact, music-as-text has been accessible to listeners without a visual paratext since the inception of radio. It's quite possible that a music listener may come upon the album art·after experiencing the text (music) on the radio, while podcasts are rarely happened upon through listening.[7] Inqlis (2001) catalogues four functions of an album cover, only one of which is a shared function of podcast cover art: to advertise the recording. Non-shared functions include protecting the material recording (podcasts are immaterial), acting as an accompaniment to the recording (this function is served in podcasting by show notes), and being a commodity in its own right—something to purchase, collect, and display. Unless Rogan devises some kind of non-fungible token for his podcast cover art, this latter function isn't likely to apply to podcasts anytime soon.

Music's visual paratexts have been the subject of less scholarship than one might expect (Butler 2013; Venkatesan, Wang, and Spence 2020). Does this also mean that studies of visual aspects of podcasts are likely to be rare even

---

6   Alex Steinweiss is largely credited with creating the first graphic album cover in 1939 ("Alex Steinweiss and the World's First Record Cover" 2016).
7   An exception would be podcast cross-promotions: listening to a podcast and hearing about, or an excerpt from, another podcast.

as the more general field of podcast studies grows? I argue that podcast cover art considered collectively is a key aspect of a complete understanding of podcasting as a medium. But the conversation about it is only just beginning. At the time of writing there appears to be no specific scholarly analyses of podcast cover art. Perhaps there is a reticence on the part of scholars to examine the visual aspects of a primarily audio medium; those that are attracted to podcasting precisely because it is sound based maybe don't (or prefer not to) recognize the importance of the visual paratext.

PODCAST TRANSCRIPTS

A transcript is a critical aspect of a podcast. Advice around the importance of transcripts has proliferated in online writing aimed at podcast producers in the last few years, most of it focusing on two primary reasons for providing them: accessibility, and better search engine optimization (SEO; see, for example, Terra 2019; *Join the Party Podcast* 2018; The Podcast Host 2020). For the purposes of SEO, this paratext might serve a commercial function in attracting more potential listeners to the podcast, but for the more than 400 million people globally who have "disabling" hearing loss (World Health Organization 2021), a transcript may be more than just a paratext—it may be the only useful text in the entire ecosystem of podcast paratexts. Podcasts lacking transcripts can be completely inaccessible to D/deaf and hard-of-hearing persons. For this reason alone, a transcript should not be considered bonus content (I have seen some podcasts with transcripts behind a paywall) or a premium feature (many hosting platforms reserve the option to add a transcript to the RSS feed for premium subscribers only), but rather a basic human right.

In addition to "making present" (Genette 1997) the podcast to D/deaf and hard-of-hearing persons, transcripts benefit people with other reasons for wanting to "read" a podcast, such as language learners who are not fluent in the language spoken in the podcast, or people who prefer or need to listen and read at the same time. Furthermore, audio can't be quickly scanned by a listener in the way that text can be by a reader. Many podcast apps allow for two-times playback speed, but a sixty-minute episode will still take thirty minutes, while scanning a transcript of that episode may take considerably less time than that. Researchers looking for information and bloggers or reporters looking for quotable material might prefer to use a transcript to find what they need. Like human readers, search engines are good at quickly searching text, but not audio. Podcasters concerned with making the content of their podcasts indexable by web crawlers for SEO purposes therefore need to translate their audio into text. Transcripts allow search engines to find keywords—which may have been spoken aloud in the podcast, but not included in its searchable meta tags such as the title or description. While platforms such as Google Podcasts and Spotify have recently dabbled in auto-transcribing their podcast audio in order to index it (Meyers 2019; "3 Updates on the Spotify Mobile Experience to Help Improve Accessibility" 2021), these transcriptions are neither public facing nor accessible to other platforms (Sullivan 2021b). For now, podcast producers must be responsible for transcribing their own content or subcontracting the work out.

Transcriptions, in their usual form of dense, verbatim lines of words spoken in a podcast, are but a pale depiction of a podcast's content (not to mention no pleasure to read). The way we speak is often very different to how we would write about the same topic; half-finished sentences are abandoned, phrases are started and restarted, and vocal fillers like um, like, and y'know abound in contemporary spoken word. Reading these makes comprehension a challenge as intended meanings can be obscured by these vocal tendencies. Podcaster Evo Terra reflects on the problem with verbatim transcripts:

> When I transcribe this episode, should I strive for a literal word-for-word, accurate representation of the words that come out of my mouth? The obvious answer is yes. Yet, when I've tried that, I don't like the way I *read*. I always listen back to my episodes after they are produced, and I like how I *sound*. I *sound* like I know what I'm talking about. But when I use my eyes to read the exact words that have been accurately preserved as they came out of my mouth, I don't like how I *read*. I *read* kind of like a moron. (2019, para. 9)

It's generally understood that a particular style of writing (or speaking) which works well for one medium does not always translate well into another. "Clean reads," therefore, are sometimes employed by podcasters in order to make a transcript more reader friendly: vocal tics, broken sentences, and other characteristics of spoken word that do not translate well to the written word are removed, and the transcript is presented in a format that is more like a blog post or article. Sometimes additional elements such as images, subheadings, and pull quotes are included to enhance the reader experience (Bussandri 2020). On the other hand, this cleaning up of a transcript potentially alters the intention, meaning, and interpretation of the original podcast text.

Despite the industry spotlight on podcast transcripts and deliberation over how to deploy them, there is a major gap in the scholarly literature on the topic. Pinheiro (2020), in what may be the only scholarship on podcasts and accessibility to date, identifies a more general gap in the literature relating to accessibility in radio and sound media. He proposes that both the semantic and aesthetic aspects of the elements of radio and sound media language—voice, the text (*plavra*), music, sound effects, and silence—must be expressed in a transcript (63). In addition, Pinheiro argues, the physical and emotional characteristics of podcast participants such as hosts, narrators, actors, interviewees, etc. should be accounted for in any truly accessible podcast transcript (55). How this could be done effectively, however, is yet to be determined. Audio fiction podcasts, which often employ complex sound design, are produced from scripts that include cues for sound effects, music, and style of delivery for dialogue. Could that script function as a useful transcript or should there be a post-production "re-encoding" of the audio drama back into a different version of text? And what might that look like? Whereas closed-captioning or subtitling of screen-based dramas easily provide the needed connection between the transcript and the visible action, facial expressions, and body language on screen, an audio fiction or scripted narrative podcast simply cannot bring about the same connection via a verbatim transcript. Unlike "synchresis" in film, in which the sound plus the visual combine to create something with more meaning than the simple sum of its parts (Chion 1994), podcasts so far have not engendered a version of synchresis between sound and transcript.

However, new directions in podcast transcripts are emerging that may change this. Consider, for example, Vox Creative's "immersive transcript" for the branded podcast *More Than This* (Vox Media 2021). It's an illustrated transcript, rich in graphic elements and variations in font and text size, and utilizes a somewhat responsive user interface. Pacing—so important in a storytelling podcast, yet difficult to represent in a transcript—is conveyed with negative space between and around clips of text and other design elements, as well as slight delays in the appearance of the next element as the user scrolls. It's a great, and perhaps the first, attempt to make a transcript as compelling as the podcast itself. Vox worked with engineers, graphic artists, and user experience designers to produce these transcripts for a six-episode season (Scire 2021)—suggesting that this level of transcription is beyond reach for most independent podcasters. But it also raises the prospect that one of podcasting's paratexts is evolving into an entirely new form of media.

As a paratext, a podcast transcript meets the criteria for several different types and functions of paratexts. It could be considered an *in medias res* paratext—one which is accessed while listening to the main podcast text or in between listening to episodes. A listener might follow along in the transcript as they listen to enhance their understanding of the spoken word, for example. However, if someone happens to come upon a transcript through a web search and then proceeds from the transcript to listen to the podcast, the transcript now acts as an entryway paratext. In either case, the transcript's function is also interpretive; it allows users to construct an expectation of what they will hear in the podcast and if it is of interest or use to them. Transcripts furthermore fulfill a navigational function. Space (or place) in an audio file can generally only be indicated by time; a linear bar with a time code is often the only method of finding one's "place" in the audio. This problem can be mitigated with a transcript that acts as a kind of map to help the reader hop through the audio file. Transcripts with time-stamps, or those that are linked directly to the audio file (see, for example, transcripts for *This American Life*), are particularly useful as navigational tools. Finally, for those who only ever engage with a podcast transcript, it can be argued that the transcript is no longer a paratext but rather a primary text in itself.

Because they are so critical to podcasts, transcripts must be given due consideration by podcast scholars. Disciplines such as anthropology, oral history, linguistics, and even law have produced rich scholarship on the use of transcription for the purposes of research, archiving, and communication. This scholarship could be leveraged to assist in exploring questions about podcast transcripts specifically, such as: Who uses podcast transcripts and for what purpose? And how can emotion, tone, intonation, and other subtleties that are expressed in voice, as well as music and sound design, be conveyed in a podcast transcript? Perhaps it will take a medium like podcasting, which relies so heavily on storytelling, emotion, and authenticity, to finally engender a type of transcription that begins to communicate the subtle aspects of these important elements in a visual format.

CONCLUSION

In these first two decades or so of the era of podcasting, inquiry into the medium naturally began with the question, What is it? Early understandings defined podcasts primarily in terms of their format (digital audio) and the means of publishing and distributing them (via RSS, online, mobilely, and asynchronously). The podcast was thought of as either a paratext of radio or as a new distribution mechanism for it. Throughout the evolution of podcast studies, however, little attention has been paid to the entryways to podcasts themselves: the creative and cultural products that present a podcast—and indeed "make it present" (Genette 1997)—to listeners. In this chapter, I have begun a process of parsing out podcast paratexts according to their roles and functions. I have situated one of the most important podcast paratexts, cover art, amongst existing scholarship on similar media, including book covers and album art, and suggested a few directions new scholarship on the visual culture of podcasting could take. Podcast transcripts are an equally important podcast paratext, yet they suffer from a similar dearth of scholarship examining them. I have argued it's possible that new approaches to creating transcripts that serve the various needs of users could come about as a result of the specific affordances of podcasting—a relative newcomer amongst the disciplines for which transcription is critical—which include telling stories with emotion and connecting humans to each other in an authentic way.

"To fully appreciate a text," argues Cronin, "we need to decode the context and engage with the paratext" (2014, xvi). Podcasts do not exist without their paratexts, and because those paratexts are text and image based, podcasting is not an audio-only medium. In light of this, I argue that podcast studies must expand its purview to encompass and engage with podcast paratexts. As the thresholds through which audiences interpret, navigate, and even monetize podcasts, paratexts are as important to an ontology of podcasting as audio content is.

CHAPTER 14

PODCAST DRAMA, HOPE LABOUR, AND BURNOUT

LESLIE GRACE McMURTRY

B y 2017, "podcasting had moved out of its geeky ghetto into an international cultural mainstream" (Spinelli and Dann 2019, 1). Podcast makers expend hundreds of hours of (often unpaid) work on each podcast, which is typical of the cultural industries, where long hours and poor pay are expected in exchange for creative autonomy (Duffy 2016, 453). Given such conditions, it is unsurprising that podcast makers' digital labour can lead to burnout and podfade. Furthermore, despite being one of the most labour- and capital-intensive genres in podcasting, podcast drama is less well-known amongst podcast listeners, podcast makers, and other media creatives than other podcast genres. One reason that podcast drama may be less common than other modes of podcasting is due to its relatively large cost to produce. This is one reason why drama has never inspired commercial radio broadcasters with much confidence—though only a fraction of the cost of making, for example, TV drama. Compare the following figures:

- Episodes of (non-fiction) popular podcast *Radiolab* can cost up to $100,000 to make (Abumrad as cited in Spinelli and Dann 2019, 35).
- An hour of full-cast BBC radio drama costs £22,000 to produce (BBC as cited in Spinelli and Dann 2019, 110).
- Jonathan Mitchell's *The Truth* costs $10,000 per hour to produce (Mitchell as cited in Spinelli and Dann 2019, 110).

- A grant-funded serialized podcast drama, *Blood Culture*, had a budget of £40,000 (Spinelli and Dann 2019, 150).

The specific conditions of drama production combined with a lack of recognition and understanding of the multiple roles they juggle more readily predispose its producers to painful burnout. While supporting this argument with evidence from literature on digital labour and podcast studies, I also use the frame of Practice as Research (PaR) to contribute evidence and interpretations autoethnographically based on my own experience writing and producing a podcast drama series, *Shattered*. Podcast production will be situated within the theoretical lens of hope labour, highlighting how burnout can disproportionately affect those from less privileged positions.

APPROACHES, LITERATURE, AND RESEARCH QUESTIONS

This chapter works within two interrelated traditions of theoretical framing, "cultures of production" and Practice as Research (PaR). The cultures of production approach argues that "*how* media gets made influences *what* media is made" (Herbert, Lotz, and Punathambekar 2020, 50). It investigates cultural norms among media workers by showing "how specific production sites, actors, or activities tell us larger lessons about workers, their practices, and the role of their labors in relation to politics, economics, and culture" (Mayer 2009, 15). This approach assumes that knowledge of modes of production will "alter one's reading not only of the media text, but of the media" (Banks 2009, 87). This marries well with PaR because in both cases the focus is on work practices and the role these have in influencing media, whereas the practice itself in PaR generates theory (Bolt 2010, 33). PaR is a hybrid approach to research that considers creative practice alongside more "traditional" research outputs. Practice is made a "key method of inquiry" to afford "substantial new insights" in a given field (Nelson 2013, 9, 26). Emphasis is concurrent on product, the documentation of process, and complementary writing. This chapter, for example, acts as complementary writing that supports but does not replace the piece of practice (which is far more than simply the digital artefact of the thirteen podcast episodes—it is also the associated paratexts and process). Within podcast studies, PaR has been instrumental to a self-reflexive practice, even if not explicitly articulated as PaR. For example, Lance Dann analyzes and critiques his radio and podcast scripting practice in various chapters of his book with Martin Spinelli (2019) much as a scholar working within PaR would do. Similarly, Wilson (2018) reflects on his performative podcasts within Nelson's framework.

RESEARCH QUESTIONS

Having established the approach, I should now demonstrate why labour is relevant to podcast studies: to put it simply, because of the amount of digital labour that podcast makers put into their productions. Podcast makers expend hundreds of hours of work on each podcast (Spinelli and Dann 2019, 67), whether those hours are paid or not, created within a network framing structure or not, pro-am, hobbyist, or professional. To take a cultures of production approach, *how* podcasts get made influences *what* podcasts are made. If the amount of (unpaid) labour required for podcast drama becomes unsustainable, one of podcasting's most valuable features—its ability to foster voices from outside formal media institutions—could be compromised. This chapter, therefore, poses these broader research questions:

- What are the experiences of indie drama podcasters who aspire to professional standards?
- What are their material work conditions like?
- What factors lead to burnout and podfade?

To answer these questions, I will first provide some background literature on the experiences of indie drama podcasters, then I will define *burnout* and *podfade*, and then through PaR I will make some remarks, based on my own experience of podcast drama production, on material work conditions as well as the factors that lead to burnout.

DIGITAL LABOUR

"Low pay and long hours" (Duffy 2016, 453) have long been considered the price to pay for creative autonomy in the cultural industries. At the same time, the cultural industries present "fashionable sectors with low entry barriers that attract young entrepreneurs" (Leadbeater and Oakley 1999, 41). Replace the word *cultural* with *podcasting*, and the example still stands, even though Leadbeater and Oakley were writing more than twenty years ago. Podcasting encompasses a new kind of digital labour unknown to Leadbeater and Oakley and their independent British cultural entrepreneurs of the late 1990s. The digital labour of pro-am producers is fraught with the ambivalence of precarity and instability while "individualist appeals to passion and entrepreneurialism temporally reroute employment concerns" (Duffy 2016, 452–53).

Like the independent cultural entrepreneurs of Britain as described by Leadbeater and Oakley (1999), podcast drama makers in particular can often be "producers, designers, retailers and promoters all at the same time" (11).

In terms of values, many are "highly individualistic: they prize freedom, autonomy, and choice...in a spirit of self-exploration and self-fulfillment" (15). While some makers advocate delegating some of these roles, such as podcast drama producer Paul Sating (Golding and Thraille 2017a), others, such as Wireless Theatre Company drama producer Mariele Runacre-Temple, work "obsessively" at website design at the potential expense of producing the drama (Golding and Thraille 2017b). As put by McLean,

> You're actually trying to master two different arts: writing and sound production. Even to master one of these alone takes years of patience and is very lonely, very solitary, work, just to get one of them right (McLean and Cudmore 2015, 04:56).

The demands placed upon podcast drama producers are many and wide-ranging.

HOPE LABOUR

If we accept the parallels between the British regional cultural entrepreneurs of the 1990s as described by Leadbeater and Oakley and podcast drama makers of today, we have to examine the latter within conditions of capitalism and the monetization not only of the internet but of podcasts. The values of the early web of openness, sharing, and collaboration (Jaffe 2021; Kuehn and Corrigan 2013; Duffy 2016) run counter to the monetized, private internet. In podcasting terms, this is "[t]he slow transformation of an amateur medium into a new vehicle for commercial media content" (Sullivan 2018, 35). Within wider podcasting ecosystems, as Jorgensen describes, increasing monetization has nevertheless been rejected by "a diminishing minority" who are "uninterested in using their podcasts to generate income" (2021, 144). This is framed within the so-called free labour debate,

> wherein uncompensated digital media activities—commenting on a TV show review board, creating a YouTube parody or participating in a user-generated ad contest—are conceptualized as digitally enabled forms of creative expression or, alternatively, as free labour exploited by the machinations of capitalism. (Duffy 2016, 442)

The former is epitomized by Adam Bein's (2021) argument that making podcast dramas is "a more intellectual, newer version of being in a band, doing poetry slam, being in a drum circle or volunteering," emphasizing the inherently hobbyist nature of the venture. Participants in Jorgensen's study rejected the label of "hobby" or "passion project" (2021, 150), however, which I would argue to be the case for many independent podcast drama producers.

The motivations for making podcasts have been previously studied, with exploratory work by Markman in 2012 suggesting six key motivators: interest in technology/media, desire to share content, interpersonal, personal, process, and financial (economic) reasons. Markman and Sawyer's findings in 2014 were similar, though they stressed the importance of community and continual improvement to podcasters. All of these motivations are consistent with Scott's (2012) figure of the cultural entrepreneur, which he characterizes by the following motivations:

- creative autonomy (rejecting economic capital);
- skill-building (building cultural capital);
- proving oneself (building symbolic and social capital); and
- trying to subvert the field (acting as change agents within the field).

These are quite similar to motivations I would identify for volunteer podcast drama productions, based on my own production insights and a section of the global audio drama community, a number of mainly anglophone audio drama enthusiasts and tastemakers active on Facebook from the 2010s (Audio Drama Hub), and the *Audio Drama Production Podcast* (2015–19). Based on this group, between approximately 2008 and 2018, most in the audio drama community participated on a voluntary basis. The drama was freely available online, and everyone (writers, mixers, editors, producers, actors, composers, sound designers) provided their labour on a voluntary basis. What motivated these creators if not economic gain?

- art for art's sake (self-expression, legacy), as per Cudmore (McLean and Cudmore 2015)
- a belief in the utopian ethos of the early internet, with media freely shared across social, geographic, and economic boundaries
- a kind of barter system: you do the score for me in this drama, I'll act in your next drama in kind

I would also characterize the motivations as "hope labour" (Kuehn and Corrigan 2013), similar to "aspirational labour" (Duffy 2016). Hope labour is termed thus because "specific plans are rare" as opposed to vague hopes (Kuehn and Corrigan 2013, 14). This refers to un- or under-compensated work carried out "in the hope that future employment opportunities may follow" (10). According to Kuehn and Corrigan, hope labour is predicated on digital labour and perceived online opportunity.

"Hope" is generally characterized as a positive concept, but in hope labour, it seemingly takes on connotations of accidental or deliberate deception—or in Jorgensen's words, "a distorted myth" (2021, 158). Jorgensen discovered through interviews with independent podcast producers in Australia that "they did not think it was possible to make any significant amount of money from podcasts in Australia but that many new producers or non-producers mistakenly thought it was" (2021, 149). This contrasts significantly with Sullivan's (2018) experiences from participant observation at the Podcast Movement convention in Chicago in 2016, in which entrepreneurial striving for success galvanized every motivational presentation. This suggests something more sinister or negative in tone than "hope." Nevertheless, all participants in Jorgensen's study were characterized by hope or aspirational labour, "all hoping their podcast would help them find future employment in the industry" (2021, 150). Hope labour is a familiar aspect of digital labour in general, with Patricia Hernandez (2018a) describing how popular and profitable influencers on platforms like YouTube and Twitch have "made the idea of being an online influencer aspirational" without exposing the seamy underbelly of loneliness and exploitation.

BURNOUT

Despite the lack of institutional support and the considerable barriers to podcast drama production, countless hours of work are needed to "give each podcast the life and energy they need to survive and be noticed" (Spinelli and Dann 2019, 67). This leads to burnout for potentially all podcast producers but, arguably, certain kinds of podcasts require more labour than others. For example, Jorgensen argues that "the production of narrative podcasts requires a more significant time investment and skill level than studio chat-based podcasts" (2021, 148). Given the unique demands of drama production, I would argue drama podcasts require an equivalent or greater time investment and skill level. If we collapse Hesmondhalgh's terms of *primary creative personnel, technical craft workers, creative managers,* and *owners and executives* (2002, 52–53) into potentially one person, the podcast drama creator, this person often works alone as the equivalent to TV's head writer, showrunner, executive producer, director, casting director, sound designer, marketing director, social media manager, accountant, and possibly the mixer or engineer as well (it's not unknown for podcast drama makers to serve as composers, actors, and cover image artists as well on their own productions). While the work of non-fiction podcast makers is undisputed, the number of roles to juggle, the number of people to manage, and the multi-tasking to handle in drama podcasting exceeds all but the most complex non-fiction podcasts. The logistics involved with managing actors, for example, incorporates many of the skill sets and time that would go into chatcast/chumcast podcast makers' management of guest speakers, but amplified. Chatcast or chumcast guests need to be scheduled and coached on how to interact for the best-sounding recording, but podcast drama actors need to be cast, directed, and, depending on the mode of recording, may need to be managed for multiple retakes. If they are lucky, podcast drama makers may be able to share some of this burden with a few others willing to take on this (unpaid, largely invisible) labour as co-writers or co-producers, but this only increases the number of drama makers on the road to burnout.

Pascal Chabot, in his book *Global Burnout*, argues that those affected by burnout are conscientious, passionate, and devoted to their work, but through burnout experience feelings of "fatigue, anxiety, unmanageable stress, depersonalization" (2018, 4). It is unlikely we would find any podcast drama makers who have actually succeeded in making something who are not conscientious and passionate, because the barriers are so high to accomplishing a finished product that only the most conscientious and devoted will persist. Within the context of podcast drama, I would characterize burnout with feelings of cynicism, increased mental distance, and reduced professional efficacy (Chabot 2018, 12–13). Burnout can have severe repercussions for creators' mental health, sometimes leading to spirals of depression and anxiety that can culminate in suicidal ideation. In short, the desire that fuelled making podcast drama is replaced by fatigue, cynicism, disenchantment, depression, and podfade.

"Podfade" is the consequence of an inability to keep up with the disciplined and relentless schedule of podcast releases, so that episodes are released more and more sporadically and eventually cease entirely ("What is Podfade?" 2020). According to Steve Goldstein, industry veterans "report that many podcasts 'podfade' by their seventh episode" (2018). Statistically, podfade proves to be a surprisingly prevalent issue within podcasting, with an estimated 75 percent of the roughly 540,000 podcasts in existence in 2017 having ceased production by 2020 (Kidd, Nguyen, and Titkemeyer 2020, 169). Although focused on metadata preservation issues, the Preserve This Podcast project coincidentally highlighted the cumulative podfade that has taken place since 2005, finding that the affiliated websites of 87 percent of podcasts published in 2005 are no longer available online and 98 percent of the sample are no longer available on Apple Podcasts (Kidd, Nguyen, and Titkemeyer 2020, 169). Patricia Hernandez argues that "Streaming and vlogging careers on YouTube and Twitch are new enough that we can't yet see how sustainable they truly are in the long term" (2018b), but clearly, podcasting has had enough longevity to demonstrate the unmistakable prevalence of podfade over a long-term period. Clearly, podfade can affect all podcast makers, regardless of genre. However, it is extremely noticeable if a podcast drama series is planned and only one or two episodes are ever released. This is almost never laziness or lack of enthusiasm; this is almost certainly burnout leading to podfade.

CASE STUDY: *SHATTERED*

The *Shattered* podcast is a thirteen-part drama podcast that I wrote, directed, produced, and promoted. The writing took place between 2018 and 2020 and production between 2020 and 2022 (impacted unsurprisingly by the COVID-19 pandemic). A loose adaptation of *The Phantom of the Opera* (1910) framed as a non-fiction true crime podcast, *Shattered* responded to research inquiries (RIs) as part of a practice as research (PaR) project.

Funding

The labour implications—or the *how* of the media work to dictate *what* media was made—begin with how *Shattered* was funded. Producing, disseminating, and marketing a podcast requires funding. The funding needed for forms like drama can be considerable, as explained by Lex Noteboom (Fernández Collins 2021) and Golding and Thraille (2017b), where more voices, more music, more SFX (sound effects) are often required than for non-fiction podcasts. A number of funding models have been explored to resolve the seeming contradiction between the DIY, accessible nature of podcasting and the desire for makers to be economic successes (or just break even).

Ultimately, *Shattered* was funded by a small bursary from the City of London Phonograph and Gramophone Society and through crowdfunding (a Kickstarter campaign). Crowdfunding is an interesting funding model that absorbs some aspects of public service broadcasting and the purely commercial. For example, what Spinelli and Dann call the "pleas and begging messages that launch shows" are very similar to the chronic exhortations for money heard on NPR and the like, and "the impetus for an audience to make crowdfunding contributions is essentially altruistic, with rewards serving as markers of support that are not commensurate with the value of donation given" (2019, 45, 44). Crowdfunding is seen on platforms such as Kickstarter[1] and GoFundMe where creations can be funded in varying degrees by supporters, usually with rewards offered as compensation (similar to the pledge-drive model in US-style public service broadcasting). Possibly the highest-profile example of the freemium model is *Welcome to Night Vale* (WTNV). Initially

---

1   It should be noted that all Kickstarter creators can be subject to legal action from their backers if they don't produce and release the media piece that they pledge to make.

made on freeware and available for free, *WTNV* survives due to its comprehensive freemium content, special content only available to funders/supporters.

Most of my previous radio and audio dramas have been volunteer productions, for which no one was paid.[2] I made the conscious choice with *Shattered* to seek funding in order to pay the actors, composers, and website designers; *Shattered* would also be freely available online. I did not consider commercial sponsorship, due to a belief that commercial imperatives are often incompatible with artistic practice—Jorgensen refers to this as "rejecting economic capital as 'profane'" (2021, 151)—and also because attracting an advertiser would be too time-consuming. It was not particularly important for me to monetize this project, partially because I made it using resources (a subscription to Adobe Audition, access to LinkedIn Learning videos) provided by my employer, the University of Salford, partially because it was a loose adaptation of a (copyright-expired) novel, partially due to my adherence to the utopian ideals of the early internet as previously detailed, and partially due to an instinct (later supported by data) that the project might not get off the ground if I inflated the budget to include paying for my own labour.

Also, importantly, I had financial security due to the fact I was able to work intensively on *Shattered* during the period of a (paid) research sabbatical (the sabbatical covered a period of five months while the actual production period was more than twice that). I recognize that many aspiring audio drama makers are not as fortunate. They have not only to fit in the drama making around full-time jobs, caring responsibilities, and other situations (McLean and Cudmore 2015; Golding and Thraille 2017a), but do not have the financial independence that I, as an employed academic, do (Wilson 2018; Spinelli and Dann 2019). Furthermore, as Collins notes, an economic digital divide "still prevents the availability of even relatively low-cost technology for everyone" (2018, 242). Class intersectionalities are key here (Duffy and Pruchniewska 2017); I possess "a degree of cultural capital" that I am able to channel into my "pursuits and aspirations" (Duffy 2016, 448). I was also fortunate in that my family and friends—often important early backers of crowdfunding projects (Spinelli and Dann 2019)—had the financial wherewithal to generously support the Kickstarter. Furthermore, "technologies of production not only require economic capital, but also the leisure time to learn to use them effectively" (Duffy 2016, 448), which I possessed. That is to say, I was not prevented from learning these technologies because I had to go into paid work in order to survive.

---

2   By contrast, I was paid by a (US) radio station for my first professionally produced radio drama, *The Mesmerist* (2010). The actors and directors/producers were also paid by the radio station.

Learning by Doing

With *Shattered*, my perspective as a practitioner/academic informs not only my practice, as per the tenets of PaR, but also my teaching. I can say from my current vantage point that *making* a podcast drama is vastly different from the theoretical "thinking" about it. During the first English national COVID-19 lockdown, I had to rapidly develop proficiency with a number of technologies and processes. The amount of work involved was considerable—between June 2020 and January 2021, I organized a call for auditions; created a variety of social media accounts; created the website; recorded and mixed a trailer; supervised the Kickstarter campaign; learned how to use content creation apps, such as Headliner, Wavve, and Canva; organized recording sessions across five time zones and four countries; and fulfilled orders for physical merchandise as part of the Kickstarter rewards, all in addition to the production, direction, and mixing of the episodes. All of these areas involved steep learning curves and a variety of learning moments that could not have been obtained by imitating someone else, reading how-to guides, or imagining the processes. Some skills—editing in DAWs (digital audio workstations), social media management, scriptwriting, directing, producing, composing, recording, Foley—are learned in formal education but many are learned "from experience and peers rather than in a classroom" (Leadbeater and Oakley 1999, 18) or, indeed, self-taught. As a very rough estimate, during the five-month sabbatical I invested over one thousand hours into *Shattered* (not including writing the script) plus a further unpaid five hundred hours in the period leading up to the launch.

My conclusion from the praxis of making podcast drama is that, as argued by Spinelli and Dann, "independently producing a podcast is not just a job" (2019, 216). As noted by Mariele Runacre-Temple (Golding and Thraille 2017b), Austin Beach, and Paul Sating (Golding and Thraille 2017a), it consumes your life. Such feelings or interpretations chime with so-called presence bleed, the blurring line between work and leisure increasingly obvious in digital labour economies (Duffy and Hund 2015). The mythologies about work in the age of social media, that it's "fun," not work, and that one suffers through long hours for the reward of creative freedom (Duffy and Wissinger 2017, 4653) apply to podcast drama producing. Indeed, I experienced presence bleed in a way I am still struggling to fully process. For example, to increase the believability of my production company, Lesser of 2 Weevils, releasing a non-fiction podcast after all my previous titles had been drama, I decided to script, record, and edit a non-fiction chatcast, or chumcast, with my husband, released between the end of the *Shattered* Kickstarter campaign and the release of *Shattered*. This was the Christmas-themed podcast *Yes, Virginia, This Is a Podcast* (2020–21). With the sabbatical project of *Shattered* taking up my "workday," *YVTIAP* was made on evenings and weekends, though there was considerable workflow and skill set merging of the two podcasts. Where did "work" end and "leisure" begin, particularly as working on *YVTIAP* was spending time with my husband? Four years later, I am inclined to qualify making *YVTIAP* as useful experience, even though it represented an enormous output of time (approximately two thousand hours) and skill for no monetary reward. Despite Bein's (2021) reduction of podcasting to a hobby, in labour terms, what makes me comfortable with classifying *YVTIAP* as hope labour yet makes me bristle at the same for *Shattered*?

Why Did I Do It?

Considering that the official monetary cost of *Shattered* is equivalent to 0.4 percent of the budget of some episodes of *Radiolab*, 11 percent of the cost of one hour of BBC radio drama, 40 percent of the cost of an episode of *The Truth*, and 6 percent of the budget for serialized podcast drama *Blood Cultures*, why did I do it? Granted, I didn't fully understand the implications at the outset—hence why the project is PaR and generates theory through praxis. Nevertheless, as a consumer of audio drama for over a decade and an academic studying podcasting, I should have had a fairly informed notion of what I was getting myself into.

A body of work on podcast producer motivations is growing (Markman 2012; Markman and Sawyer 2014); however, more work could be done on the motivations of podcast drama producers. Some producers, such as Cudmore (McLean and Cudmore 2015), cite the rewarding and fun aspect of making the dramas as well as a sense of self-realization. As a self-reflexive practitioner who also happens to be an academic, I have been drawn to making audio drama since 2018 for the following reasons:

- Potentially new voices can be heard by bypassing traditional gatekeeping structures, as per Brian Mock (McLean and Cudmore 2016).
- It would allow me to have a large canvas, or tell a large story, with inversely proportional resources (McLean and Cudmore 2014, 2015).
- The entry threshold for audio drama is relatively low (McLean and Cudmore 2014).
- Podcasting appeals to me because of my interest in interdisciplinarity, as per Beckstead (Llinares 2020b; McLean and Cudmore 2014, 2015).
- It's important to me to retain relatively high creative control of my work (McLean and Cudmore 2014), similarly to Anna Ashitey (Llinares 2020b) and Lex Noteboom (Fernández Collins 2021).

Indeed, as Spinelli and Dann argue, "the freedom to work with an audience who can choose when and where to listen" in podcasting allows "for complex plotting and intricate storytelling" (2019, 120).

I must add to this list a further three specific objectives for *Shattered* as a PaR project:

1. To make podcast drama that succeeds within the medium's "podcastness" (Berry 2016a); an explicit response to the Gothic narrative frame story inherent in Leroux's original text
2. To attempt to dramatize *Phantom of the Opera* in audio form, pushing the boundaries of the dramatizable
3. To increase the public understanding and appreciation of the lasting importance of recorded sound

In order to fulfill the first objective, and in emulation of *The Black Tapes* and *The Message*, my most immediate models, I felt I had to preserve the ambiguity of *Shattered* as fiction and as a spinoff of *The Phantom of the Opera*. This meant I felt compelled to be very careful about revealing details at all stages of production. This approach was in fact extremely limiting, as I could not participate in the creative milieu of the audio drama community for support, both emotional and technical. This would have been invaluable; it would have mitigated some of the aspects of burnout and perhaps prevented the toll the production took on my mental health. This also caused me considerable problems with my release schedule. Indeed, the podcast was finally released in August 2022, having been delayed for nearly eighteen months by, among other factors, COVID-19–related impacts upon the music production. One's digital reputation becomes a form of currency (Duffy and Wissinger 2017), and success or lack of it can influence future work.

Was It Worth It?

Is it any wonder that many podcast dramas experience podfade (McMurtry 2019)? Such conditions can easily lead to burnout. My commitment to paying others but not myself starts to seem self-defeating. With the boundaries of work and pleasure or play collapsed (as with presence bleed), exploitation has become endemic in the digital economy. Duffy (2016) notes the narratives of "empowerment" are at odds with Marxian models of exploitation and alienation (443). From a Marxian standpoint, hope labourers "undermine the very labor market they aspire to enter by continually supplying it with individuals who are willing to work for nothing" (Kuehn and Corrigan 2013, 20). Thus do the economics of podcasting "lead to creative burn-out" (Spinelli and Dann 2019, 216). Even the payment received by collaborators may not be particularly rewarding; one of the leads in *Shattered* joked that he worked on the project because he admired the writing, not because of "the vast fee."

The experience of making *Shattered* was, of course, meaningful. Kuehn and Corrigan argue that the motivations for working for free, in addition to hope labour, have to do with self-realization and a desire for the community to recognize the labourers' good work. By self-realization, they mean "autonomy, mastery, and connectedness" which provides for "compelling experiences" (2013, 17). I have been involved virtually with the audio drama community through Facebook groups, Zoom listening groups, Twitter accounts, and other venues for nearly a decade. While this community is generally very supportive of producers, everyone is concentrating on their own productions. Because, as we've established, so much energy and time is expended in the myriad jobs related to podcast drama production, there is little left over to engage with, and recognize, the work of others. This is not confined merely to podcast drama or even podcasts in general, but is prevalent within ecosystems of digital labour: "But when seemingly everyone wants to record footage or live stream, who ends up watching the content?" (Hernandez 2018a). The practice is even more noticeable on YouTube, with successful YouTubers feeling "compelled to make nonstop videos for an ever-hungry audience, afraid to take breaks for fear of losing momentum, or worse, being reprimanded by the algorithm that decides what videos people see" (Hernandez 2018b). The emotional labour of commenting (on social media), for example, is very time-consuming but arguably necessary to podcast promotion as it allows one to build up networks and get noticed (Duffy 2016). On YouTube, for example, "Once a video is up, creators are expected to continue to engage viewers via comments, social media, live streams, and more—only to start the process all over again the next day, and the next day, and the next" (Hernandez 2018b).

It is extremely difficult to perform this emotional labour when expending all resources on the production of one's own show. Leadbeater and Oakley describe a cultural milieu as "like a public good. No single cultural entrepreneur or institution can hope to create, manage or control it" (1999, 32). Similarly, based on interviews with ten fans of his podcast drama *Blood Culture*, Lance Dann discovered that those interviewed

> related to audio drama not just as fans of a genre, but as members of a community. They made judgments about the aesthetic and technical qualities of other shows, they were aware of their deficiencies, but they still listened to them...A sense of criticality toward these works was suspended, and instead they were encouraging and supportive of their peers' efforts. (Spinelli and Dann 2019, 170)

Despite this general level of support, the cultural milieu of the audio drama community is therefore implicated through the continued normalization of hope labour and burnout.

Of those they surveyed for their work on hope labour, Kuehn and Corrigan found that creators hope to one day "be compensated for the same or related work" (2013, 17). My motivation in the form of hope labour on *Shattered* referred to a vague hope that the success of the podcast might translate further down the line into paid work for some drama-producing network. For all aspirational podcast drama makers within the audio drama cultural milieu, a meritocratic idea is at work, forcing us to come to terms with the fact that if we don't succeed, it's because of our own lack of talent or hard work (Kuehn and Corrigan 2013, 18; Duffy and Pruchniewska 2017, 844; Duffy and Wissinger 2017, 4653).

Is there—can there be—a solution? While Hesmondhalgh argues that for artists (or as he calls them, symbol creators), "great sacrifices have to be made to achieve even limited autonomy," the underemployment or underpayment of creative workers "should not be seen as a natural phenomenon: it is a result of specific economic and cultural conditions" (2002, 70, 57). If every podcast drama maker burned out, we'd be left with no podcast drama at all. There does, however, seem to be an everlasting stream of new podcast drama makers to enable this situation to continue indefinitely. With regards to burnout on YouTube, Hernandez recognizes that it's a complex issue:

> Admitting that you're human, you have limits, and need a break takes a lot of courage, let alone admitting that you need help with your mental health. Most creators who show that kind of vulnerability often have to be pushed to their breaking point, where they have no choice but to talk about the thing eating them alive. (2018b)

However, she places at least some of the blame on the platform, which, she argued in 2018, was doing "virtually nothing to create a culture that makes creators feel safe enough to take a break, or to create audiences who don't expect a constant stream of content" (2018b). She further posits that even if YouTube fundamentally changed the way the platform works, the pervasive culture would be much harder to change (2018b). If this culture change were possible, what would it look like? Clearly, (genuine) accountability for platforms would be a reasonable start. More ways of accessing audiences for podcast producers without using the platforms might be another. Difficult but important steps to take are educating would-be makers on podfade as well as better self-reflexivity when it comes to hope labour.

Jorgensen makes nuanced and essential distinctions with regards to the unsustainability of hope labour and the value of unpaid work on podcasts:

"[r]ecognizing the contribution of unpaid work should not be conflated with a finding or argument that this work should be unpaid. This is an unsustainable approach for podcast producers" (2021, 159). I, too, want to clarify that the early utopian ideals of audio drama should not be conflated with an excuse not to fairly compensate creatives. The shift that, in my experience, occurred around 2019 in the audio drama community encapsulated this, as it was then becoming increasingly common for independent audio drama productions to offer payment, principally to actors. This was reflected by more calls for auditions on Facebook and Slack groups that promised payment. To meet such costs requires capital from some source. To further clarify, I believe, like Jorgensen, that "pursuing economic capital that does not exist is also (and likely more) unsustainable" (2021, 159). The research of Jorgensen, Hernandez, and Sullivan on burnout and exploitation, and the pervasiveness of podfade in the industry, suggests that, truthfully, most independent audio drama makers are pursuing "economic capital that does not exist." Jorgensen argues that the educational and self-reflexive aspect is valuable for making a case for

> independently funding the production of this type of work and as a starting point for gaining a more complex understanding of how to untangle this work from a pure means of generating economic capital, particularly in an increasingly money and audience-driven industry. (2021, 159)

Along these lines, could a solution perhaps consist of cultural intermediary incubators of the kind discussed by Leadbeater and Oakley? Spinelli and Dann argue that currently there are "no commissioners to oversee and nurture the development of [podcasters'] work, no unions to protect their rights, and minimal funding to offset commercial pressures" (2019, 200). Pillsbury (2021) likewise notes the lack of a podcasting union, suggesting one could be modelled after the way SAG-AFTRA supports the TV and film industries in the US.

CONCLUSION

Within the approach of cultures of production, "the meanings and values that shape the people who shape the media" are explored (Herbert, Lotz, and Punathambekar 2020, 50), which has been the intention of this chapter. Within the framework of Practice as Research, this case study is necessarily reflective of my own experience. The theory generated from this practice can nevertheless be applied more generally. There are, undoubtedly, podcast drama creators who have produced series in much more difficult circumstances than I did and who may not have experienced burnout, or may have had a very different experience than I did. Nevertheless, indie drama producers aspiring to professional standards in the last ten years have either survived—somehow—on hope labour or have been podfaded out. Barriers are considerable; it takes enormous energy to sustain podcasts. As argued by Goldstein, " if good audio is hard to create and sustain, it stands to reason that while they are still available on Apple Podcasts and other aggregators, many podcasts have come and gone," for even after getting a podcast released, creators face the fact that "once a podcast has been published, it can be frustratingly hard to attract an audience" (2018). Funding through grants and public service broadcasters is extremely competitive to the point of being unachievable for most. Crowdfunding is precarious and characterized by a phenomenal amount of invisible (digital) labour. By contrast, commercial funding is lucrative and relatively secure once obtained, but requires convincing advertisers of the saleability of your product, which can be especially difficult to do with resource-intensive drama. This leads to material work conditions for drama producers that are precarious and unsustainable, which in turn can lead to burnout for the producers and podfade for the productions. Some potential drama makers may not even make it beyond considering the idea, because they don't possess the cultural capital and economic security of an academic like myself. Research demonstrates that intersectionality can influence who rises to the top in digital labour (Duffy and Pruchniewska 2017). This severely limits us in terms of the new voices we could be hearing.

Recognition gives meaning and staves off burnout (Chabot 2018), and for podcast drama makers toiling away in obscurity, this is important. Podcasters are motivated in part by "feedback to help them improve their skills" (Markman and Sawyer 2014, 32). The cultural intermediaries could provide "productive constraint, allowing for creativity and imagination within a certain set of boundaries and for enhanced understanding between audiences and producers" (Hesmondhalgh 2002, 71). This could enhance the existing culture of reciprocity (Duffy 2016). More generally for podcasts of all kinds, invisible digital labour needs to be recognized. Podcast makers and podcast studies should consider presence bleed and question whether it is empowering or exploitative.

That any podcast drama is made at all is testament to motivations more complex than hope labour alone. Nevertheless, podfade is undeniably prevalent, with Goldstein (2018) claiming that most podcasts fade by their seventh episode. Podfade is a kind of burnout, characterized by fatigue, cynicism, and disenchantment. Podfade can be the end result of hope labour, which has long-reaching consequences; as argued by Kuehn and Corrigan, hope labour "undermines. the very labor market" that producers aspire to, "supplying it with individuals who are willing to work for nothing" (2013, 20). Podcast platforms and many podcast networks demonstrate minimal concern about podfade and creator burnout, because they recognize there will always be a steady stream of new makers to replace the previous ones after burnout; economically, they are hardly affected. For independent podcast drama producers, self-realization and creative autonomy frequently fuel their aspirations into this market, but at what cost? For Jorgensen, her findings into Australian indie podcast producers demonstrated that there *is* value in podcasts made for reasons other than generating income. Making it easier for such podcasts to be sustainable is a complex issue requiring a culture change, platform accountability, more ways for audiences to access productions outside the platforms, education on podfade or better self-reflexivity on hope labour, and unionization or the creation of cultural intermediaries.

Future directions for research include examining cultures of production specific to podcasts and podcast drama, and more primary research (qualitative and quantitative) on burnout and podfade. While I cannot make claims here for my specific experience with regard to gender as a woman drama podcaster and "the masculine-coded nature of entrepreneurship and its markers of success, which require women to assume additional risk and engage in unpaid, largely invisible labor" (Duffy and Pruchniewska 2017, 845), I do believe that the roles of gender and labour in podcast production should be further explored. This ultimately leaves us with a question, which has relevance for all podcasters: Who (or what) guarantees avenues for art? If creating podcast drama in the short term and ending with burnout and podfade is the fate of indie makers, do we as a society of podcasters find that acceptable? If we do, I predict an ever greater proportion of podfade and a vast homogenization of the voices we hear in podcasting.

CHAPTER 15

PODCASTING AS A CONTEMPORARY CURATION PRACTICE

A Conversation with *Projections Podcast's* Mary Wild and Sarah Cleaver

NEIL FOX

P odcasting as a space is malleable and open to a variety of readings, engagements, and practices. Its "hybridity of thought, sound and text… fosters a reinvigoration of the dialectic" (Llinares, Fox, and Berry 2018b, 2) that creates a space for conversation to be cultivated and new, emerging voices to be heard and embraced. While this dialectic reinvigoration is evident in the work of audio creators whose background in traditional media (such as radio) affords them the gatekeeping privilege of historical power, there is also cause for optimism that podcasting is emerging as a democratic space populated by a diverse range of voices. Many of those voices, ones traditionally marginalized within traditional media spaces if represented at all, have found a home in podcasting. Via a conversation with the hosts of the psychoanalytic film podcast *Projections*, Mary Wild and Sarah Cleaver, this chapter explores the potentiality of podcasting for developing new, previously underserved audiences, and examines the capacities of audio curation as a mechanism for prompting audiences to discover or revisit undervalued texts, voices, and narratives.

As the medium of podcasting and its subsequent academic study grows it is vital to expand existing ideas around podcasting to incorporate different contexts. The role played by curation—how audiences and podcast producers think through and enact the cultural play and labour of not just listening, but collecting, sorting, sharing, and reflecting on their podcasting practice—is an under-theorized strand of podcast studies. By situating podcasting as a curatorial practice, or "collection-making" as curator Hans Ulrich Obrist (2015, 39), a renowned curator and someone responsible for detailing and engaging with the term and its shifts in the twenty-first century, describes it, we can conceptualize how the dynamics of the medium engender curation and archival assemblage that can be placed in the context of both commercial and nostalgic consumer needs. However, as a largely democratic medium, for the time being at least, podcasters can also use and create archives to address historical and cultural erasures through what Maura Reilly terms "curatorial activism" (2018, 22).

Podcasting can animate already-existing archives and create new ones, and by doing so address historical oversight in terms of the cultural spaces they are in dialogue with. This "narrative correction," as Ashley Clark calls contemporary film curation practice (2019, 09:05), creates the opportunity for previously unheard voices to engage with previously underserved audiences. In this vein, this chapter considers podcast curation a potentially political act. Podcasts often contain, consciously or not, an enunciation of ideological positioning or critique through the content and form of their work. I begin by unpacking some key insights regarding the aims and possibilities of curatorial activism within the broader context of curation, and its potential applications to the medium of podcasting. This is followed by the transcription of an interview with the hosts of *Projections Podcast*, in which the potential enactments of curatorial activism within their podcasting practice is explored.

CURATION

Hans Ulrich Obrist defines curating as "connecting cultures, bringing their elements into proximity with each other" (2015, 1). Most commonly, curating is associated with museum and gallery spaces where cultures are connected through both shared and coexisting collections, as well as with visitors. In podcasting, there is the potential for different cultures to connect through listening, and this connection is enhanced through the ability to connect intimately with different cultures as represented by podcast creators, not only in content but also through the voices of those creators. *Curating* is a word that gets thrown around a lot in cultural spaces, particularly online and digital ones, and has come to have negative connotations not dissimilar to those associated with the word *creator*. There exists the idea that digital technology has made everyone a creator. Terry Smith writes that "the title of curator is assumed by anyone who has a more than minimal role in bringing about a situation in which something creative might be done" (2012, 18). Curating and curators have become ubiquitous, identified by brands and corporations eager to create experiences that are meaningful, and self-identified by people online in various forms on multiple platforms curating their own lives. Additionally, the sharing culture of social media implies something productive in the act of sharing—that this often spontaneous and ephemeral gesture of moving "content" from one digital space to another online, makes us curators.

This is, in some ways, merely the elevation of participation to the level of active creativity and gatekeeping through language. In *Ways of Curating*, Obrist quotes a conversation with Stewart Brand in which Brand claims curating "has been democratised by the net, so, in one sense, everybody is curating. If you're writing a blog, it's curating. So, we're becoming editors and curators and those two are blending online" (Obrist 2015, 169). These are ideas that will be familiar to anyone with even a cursory engagement with media commentary. However, they fail to a certain degree to engage with how curation in Obrist's idea of "collection-making," through digital spaces such as those occupied by podcasting, is embraced and used with positive disruption in mind.

The democratized mode of dissemination that is a significant part of podcasting's appeal has resulted in some breaking down of the racialized and gendered gatekeeping of past curatorial practices. The medium is part of a revolution of practice in which the born-online generation not only actively reject the traditional structures of media gatekeeping, but challenge the very boundaries and practices that engender cultural hierarchies. Obrist (2015) writes that

> A new generation of younger individuals is beginning to contribute to contemporary art and culture. Born in the age of digitization, this group... shares an irreverence for traditional notions of authorship and cultural heritage, something that is manifested in their work. They have instant knowledge and technological know-how at their fingertips, and they rely on digital social platforms to showcase their new ideas and culturally iconoclastic approaches. (169–71)

It is clear that the technological affordances of the podcast, through the online structures of production, distribution, and exhibition, have manifested an independent and in many ways experimental aural culture, which exists in constellation with many other forms of digital creativity. For Obrist,

> We are already starting to witness visionary acts of digital curating, and curating will surely change as a generation native to digital tools begins to develop new formats. This generation has grown up in an entirely new

world. Perhaps by learning from them, we can learn something about our future. (171)

It is instructive to think of podcasts as "visionary acts of digital curation," perhaps because of how their technological apparatus carves out a particular kind of cultural space within a tumult of digital information. The negative result of the explosion of content creation on the internet is so much content. "Noise"—an ironic term in an audio-medium context—is the difficulty of making sense of it all. How does one find the "meaningful" or "worthwhile" in the limitless cultural experiences? Jennifer Lynn Stoever claims that "noise" is "sound's loud and unruly 'Other'" (2016, 12). It is important to consider the act of curation as a vital, active endeavour that helps parse from the "noise," leading audiences to work that is driven by a desire to provide those meaningful cultural experiences. The activation of the idea of curation, turning it from something passive to something active, is necessary to maximize the potential of podcasting as outlined in this piece. Erica Lehrer says that curating "creates an opportunity for a kind of rarefied contemplative encounter" (Abell 2015, 589) and podcasting as a practice is most often, but not exclusively, engaged with through solitary encounters and thus is a potentially rewarding contemplative space. Obrist describes the role of the curator as follows:

> To create free space, not occupy existing space...the curator has to bridge gaps and build bridges between artists, the public institutions and other types of communities. The crux of this work is to build temporary communities by connecting different people and practices and creating the conditions for triggering sparks between them. (2015, 154)

The temporary nature of the community is a pointed insight within Obrist's ideas about curation in the art world. He adds, beautifully, that "curating after all produces ephemeral constellations with their own limited career span" (2015, 58). The internet, the space where podcasting exists, is a space where the temporary is inherent, albeit with the paradox that it also contains permanence. People listen, read, watch, then move on. There's a beauty in this, in the multitude of experiences available to listeners and users. But the internet is a record, and through the publishing of podcasts there is the chance to create an archive that is politically representative of a diverse listenership and by extension citizenry. Charles Fairchild writes that "there is little doubt that popular culture has what we should call a 'politics,' if only because it is a source of tremendous power, influence and learning" (2012, 1). In the next section of this chapter I attempt to bring together the political and the curatorial by discussing curatorial activism.

CURATORIAL ACTIVISM

For Hannah McGregor, podcasting offers opportunities for "feminist inter-ventions"; she claims that podcasting spits "straight in the eye of mainstream media in a very pleasurable way" (2020, 01:15:10). This echoes ideas—though McGregor admittedly uses more directness and "spitting" in her framing—that have taken shape in the field of curation, particularly regarding what Maura Reilly terms "curatorial activism." Reilly writes:

> "Curatorial activist"—[is] a term I use to describe people who have...com-mitted themselves to initiatives that are levelling hierarchies, challenging assumptions, countering erasure, promoting the margins over the centre, the minority over the majority, inspiring intelligent debate, disseminat-ing new knowledge, and encouraging strategies of resistance—all of which offers hope and affirmation. (2018, 22)

Podcasting, if we accept its possibility as a democratic space in terms of the means of production and dissemination, at least by traditional media metrics and signifiers, offers space for creators to challenge existing canonical ideas and practices. Dario Llinares writes that the technological changes that have come with the territory of podcasting have "forged new creative possibil-ities of production, distribution and exhibition which, in turn, has given rise to an independent cadre of producer/consumers who have arguably forged a new sound media culture" (2018, 126). Some of these producer/consumers have embraced the technological opportunities and used them to approach the building of that culture in a way that directly challenges pre-existing cul-tural problems and inherent biases lagging over from traditional media.

Werner et al. write that "podcasts have power. They carry economic weight, and they can influence our thinking in the public sphere...the voices we hear matter, and gender diversity is imperative for representing a breadth of viewpoints and experiences" (2020, 1). Therefore, an idea such as curato-rial activism is useful to explore podcasting's social and political use in this context. It activates and politicizes how podcasting as a mode of curational practice activates political discourse through making and listening. Despite its comparatively short lifespan, podcasting has, like other media, become a space dominated by white males, with women particularly expected to ful-fill certain roles. This is why I chose to interview the hosts of the *Projections Podcast*: their podcast doesn't fulfill those expected roles. Julia Hoydis writes that it "is especially the engagement with marginalized voices, devi-ant opinions, or what we might deem narrative transgressions, that reveals podcasting's socio-cultural potential. It lies in the decentering and thus reopening for exploration of relations between text, image and sound" (2020, 8). Commenting on their own podcast work Tiffe and Hoffmann (2016) write:

> Our podcast was created in the spirit of Do It Yourself ("DIY") punk communities that made their own culture instead of consuming what was made for them…and we are not alone. Thousands of podcasts are hosted on the internet, with more and more of them being hosted by a woman or multiple women. This is significant in a world that teaches us to take up less space and be quiet. (116)

In the *Projections Podcast* many of these ideas are evident, inherently if not explicitly. *Projections* represents new and emerging conceptions of curation, listening, and podcasting that align to provide audiences with material that approaches a concerted redressing of historical erasure, which marries podcasting to key intellectual battles in the era of its emergence, be it diversity and representation, decolonization or open access.

Obrist writes that "the task of curating is to make junctions, to allow different elements to touch" (2015, 1). The type of impact that is possible when this curatorial activity occurs is discernible in both the direct address of podcasters stating the activist and corrective intentions of their work, and the indirect associations that can be gleaned by listeners from the associations thrown up by podcast curators—even when, as the interview below suggests, programming is instinctive and the activist intentions are more discreetly embedded in creators' personalities than overtly stated. It would be overly simplistic to suggest that just because a podcast focuses on previously overlooked or marginalized works or voices that it is an example of curatorial activism. While podcasting provides a valid space for people who may not have had a voice previously to speak, not everyone is, in bell hooks's formulation, "talking back" (1989, 8). That is, not everyone is explicitly addressing marginalization or erasure and attacking dominant ideological structures. Writing about the role of the curatorial activist, Reilly posits key questions that should be asked, including those relevant to this discussion, such as "How can each of us act to guarantee that more voices are included? How can we re-envision the historical definition of 'greatness,' to include all Other artists?" (2018, 217). Reilly capitalizes "Other" intentionally to suggest those alienated or marginalized from the centre. These questions feed into the aforementioned idea of "narrative correction" and form the basis for a significant number of podcasts that include a focus on ideas such as race, gender, and sexuality in relation to cinema.

To keep the focus aligned with the interview, I will briefly look at feminist and female-led film podcasts to start a discussion on how some podcasters may engage with Obrist's ideas around curation and some of what Reilly is concerned with, but how only some, including *Projections*, could be classed as curatorial activism. One of the most significant and popular film podcasts to emerge in recent years is Anna Smith's *Girls on Film*. The podcast is an accessible, female-led review show. It focuses on discussions of films directed by women, and these discussions feature female filmmakers, critics, programmers, and other industry figures. It is resolutely feminist in this regard, with very scant dispensation made for work directed by men. For example, in episode ten, director of *Eighth Grade* (2018) Bo Burnham became the first non-female contributor, and, as such, was labelled an honorary "girl on film" (Smith 2018). Discussions on the podcast frequently cover contexts such as repressive industry practices regarding women historically and contemporarily, and curation is evident in that films are largely chosen based on a criteria of female authorship. However, the focus is generally on mainstream cinema releases directed by women, giving a valuable voice to such works, but operating mostly at the level of the existing industry infrastructures and adding voice to the growing demand in the mainstream for female voices on and behind the screen.

What distinguishes a podcast like *Projections*, and also a podcast such as *Sentimental Garbage*, which looks at the politics of female fandom through the prickly lens of the "guilty pleasure," is how the hosts are aware of discourses around their chosen field and create work that defies, critiques, opposes, or challenges the dominant discourse. This is represented by often choosing to discuss work historically considered "bad" or "trashy," for example, through a rigorous intellectual engagement with such work that is often reserved for "deserving" or "good" art. This is combined with a knowledge that such an approach goes against perceived ideological understandings regarding what women consume and how they consume it. *Sentimental Garbage* challenges, in similar ways that a podcast like *Black Men Can't Jump (in Hollywood)* does with race, what gets to be discussed, who gets to discuss it, and how that discussion should take place. This combination of who is talking, what they are talking about, how they are talking about it, and how that represents a new form of discourse in opposition to existing structures, marks out the work as potentially curatorial activism, even if, as the interview that follows now suggests, the makers themselves may not specifically align with that terminology.

SHIFTING PERCEPTIONS:
THE CURATORIAL WORK OF THE *PROJECTIONS* PODCAST

Griselda Pollock writes that "versions of the past ratify a present order, producing 'a predisposed continuity'" (1999, 10). The *Projections* film podcast is a "dialogue about film and psychoanalysis" (Cleaver and Wild n.d.) created and hosted by Sarah Cleaver and Mary Wild in 2018, and still running at the time of writing, that disrupts the presupposed continuity of the past. The podcast takes the form of series of episodes that focus on different themes, genres, and ideas, such as women in horror, cults, fashion, mental illness, work and labour, all discussed through the lens of psychoanalysis. What is fascinating about this podcast is the way it reframes the cinematic past, creating new juxtapositions, new mini canons through new critical alignments that form the basis of discussions. The hosts challenge long-standing patriarchal ideas in film studies about what interests female scholars in the field. This is particularly interesting in the contexts of current debates about the validity of certain auteurs, and the morality of studying and discussing their work. Cleaver and Wild unashamedly announce on their website, for example, that they are drawn to the work of the directors Lars von Trier and Roman Polanski. These two filmmakers have long been considered controversial for both on- and off-screen behaviour, opinions, and representation. They are considered "problematic faves" in the post-#MeToo era, in reference to their treatment of women onscreen and during production (von Trier) and long-standing statutory rape offences (Polanski). Projections disrupts the complexities around the relationship in cinema between art and artist by using psychoanalysis and, by dint of that perspective, the impact of the work itself on the viewer. The challenges posed, in terms of addressing perceptions of the role of women in the film-podcast space, are present in the content but also in the way the hosts address and show understanding of that perspective. Projections achieves what Hogan (2008) refers to when she says that "new means of communication have thus afforded otherwise invisible and marginalized...communities the means with which to re-represent community, challenge dominant representations, highlight the importance of minority representation itself, and archive the results of their activity and activism."

In episode five (January 2020) of the Women in Horror season, the hosts were joined by horror writer Zoe Rose Smith (known online and via her website as Zobo with a Shotgun). The episode focuses on extremity and extreme horror. The discussion that the three women have covers both why extreme horror cinema may be a space for women to work through trauma safely and the impact on them as women when discussing with other people the fact that they not only watch extreme horror but that they like it, and how they are then perceived. The podcast gives space to the nuances of such positions: the complexities of owning that fan position and articulating intellectually what draws women to something that is commonly perceived as having nothing to offer them due to the often terrifyingly horrific portrayals of violence against women. Pollock writes that "the maternal haunts the culture that the modernist sons attempted to create" (1999, 35), and the long discussions in the

Projections Podcast add to the work of pronouncing the long-known but rarely so publicly admitted complexities of female audiences and scholars. It is part of a body of work that brings a new perspective to not only those audiences and scholars as objects of interest, but also to the films being discussed, as the hosts create critical positions that are rarely considered in such long-ranging, accessible depth. It is an example of podcasting as a space where difference can coexist, cross-fertilize, and challenge, be acknowledged, confronted, celebrated, and not remain destructive of the other in an expanded but shared cultural space.

Using quotes from Obrist on curation and from Reilly on curatorial activism as impetus, I spoke with Mary and Sarah from *Projections* over email in early 2022 about their work, and how it could fulfill some of the curatorial aspects of podcasting outlined in this piece so far. The quotes I used to frame the interview are featured, in part or in whole, earlier in this chapter as part of the sections on curation and curatorial activism. I share them in full again, here, to frame the interview for readers as it was framed for the participants.

Obrist defines *curating* as "connecting cultures, bringing their elements into proximity with each other." He also calls curation "collection-making," which he defines thusly:

> To make a collection is to find, acquire, organise and store items...It is also, inevitably, a way of thinking about the world—the connections and principles that produce a collection contain assumptions, juxtapositions, findings, experimental possibilities and associations. Collection-making, you could say, is a method of producing knowledge. (2015, 39)

Reilly defined the term *curatorial activism*. She says that

> "curatorial activist" [is] a term I use to describe people who have...committed themselves to initiatives that are levelling hierarchies, challenging assumptions, countering erasure, promoting the margins over the centre, the minority over the majority, inspiring intelligent debate, disseminating new knowledge, and encouraging strategies of resistance—all of which offers hope and affirmation. (2018, 22)

·ı|ı·ı|ı·ı|ı·

Neil Fox: Do you see yourselves as curators or curatorial activists? If not, would you see yourselves as curators or curatorial activists after reading the quotes above? In what ways do you see your work as fulfilling the descriptions quoted above? In what ways do you think your work is not doing the above? What is it doing in addition or instead?

Sarah Cleaver: I like the Hans Ulrich Obrist quote, about collection-making being a method of producing knowledge, because sometimes I feel so entrenched in the collecting process. I feel like I don't know anything. I think that the way he describes curating, as a group of assumptions, juxtapositions, findings, experimental possibilities, and associations that suddenly produce meaning sounds very psychoanalytic and close to what happens when we podcast together. The two elements that come into proximity are both of us, and the podcast is the result. I don't know about Mary, but I don't see us as engaged in any form of activism. If we do achieve any of those things, it's a side effect of what we're concentrating on, which is quite an instinctive exploration of themes we find interesting. I do hope our listeners find hope and affirmation in listening to us though.

Mary Wild: The Hans Ulrich Obrist quote is relatable—I've been a collector since I was a kid, and always enjoyed making collages. It's not just the accumulation of content that is pleasing, it's the assembling process, exploring how things might connect and synthesize, even if at first it seems like there's only a tenuous link. I would not categorize any work that I do, whether individually or with Sarah on the podcast, as "activism"—certainly not consciously, anyway. I guess I am a politically motivated person, and very curious about political discourses online, but this doesn't enter into film analysis for me. If anything, I'd rather keep these things separate, because an unmediated and "uncivilized" primal response to cinema is more interesting to me. The political virtue I'm most attached to is liberty, and I often bang on about ensuring that artists have total freedom to do whatever they want. I don't know whether any of this makes listeners feel affirmed or hopeful, but in a way, I would rather make them feel provoked, or uncomfortable enough that they would want to introspect and think more deeply about these things.

Neil: Your film selections often go against the expected in terms of film history, critical acclaim, the canon, and other long-established ideas of what makes "good" cinema—What was your original thought process for the films you wanted to cover on your podcast, and were you aware, or did you discuss, what that collection of films would look like to your expected audience and a potential audience?

Sarah: I think we have this interesting position in the film industry. We're both cinephiles but we came at the industry from unexpected angles. So we've never really worried about prevailing ideas of "good cinema" because both our entries into film came from this very joyful, escapist, deep-seated place. I think this is very deeply rooted in both of us and would be impossible to change. I can't speak for Mary, but going in, I never had an agenda in championing any particular type of cinema. The simple fact that a film sparks my interest and holds it makes it worthy of analysis in my book. And even with films that don't appeal to me, the fact that Mary's interested is enough to bring me round to it. We're both Scorpios so we're drawn to taboo and shadows, so maybe the fact that a film sparks strong dislike or is overlooked makes us interested. We do sometimes notice that more well-known films or figures get higher listener rates, but I don't think either of us want that to dictate what we discuss. Also, I don't think that the films we're discussing fall very far outside the realms of what is considered "good." The people who are really out there are discussing things like extreme cinema or lifetime movies, things that a lot of people have a real resistance to. I think "good" is a fluid idea, and often tied up with profitability and publicity, or else the approved identity politics of the time. I think it helps that we look at films a certain amount of time after their release. I personally find it easier to think about a film when it's not surrounded by discourse.

Mary: Being perceived as going against the expected in any capacity makes me happy, so thanks for the compliment. If I happen to enjoy a film that's been panned by the great and the good, then it makes me appreciate it even more. I have a mistrust of authority and see myself as more aligned with the figures of the "guttersnipe" and "edgelord"—my film tastes reflect this. Hopefully I don't get squashed underneath the persona of a contrarian, but I would like to be thought of as an enjoyer of "bad" cinema, actually. Bad in terms of what it stirs in us: something dangerous, forbidden, unwanted, confused, trashy, illicit, outlandish, illogical, and weird. Our thought process on the podcast is primarily to choose films that illustrate some sort of psychoanalytic function, so we often select titles that produce a feeling of discomfort in the audience; it just goes with the territory. Our process is seamless because we seem to have similar taste, so it's easy to write a program together.

Neil: I love the confidence you have in your curation of titles to discuss. You seem very assured in justifying your choices and wanting to engage with unexpected texts. Where do you think that confidence comes from? How much of your selection process is wanting your choices to engage audiences in wider ideas about film and film history and culture? To what extent are you picking titles to discover what you think about them, rather than affirming pre-existing ideas, and can you give an example of a film that defied any pre-expectations you had and why?

Sarah: I think for me, the confidence comes from the fact that it's just us in the room, and we're having a good time. I've never felt like we must justify anything we talk about. Perhaps I've been lucky; I grew up in a culturally confident house, and I've always attracted like-minded compatriots (most notably Mary). I also think we're both lucky to have the capacity for obsession. When you're obsessed, you're happy to go it alone, and no one else's opinion really matters. I think we pick films based on our pre-existing ideas, and then we're often surprised about what comes out in the discussion.

Mary: If I'm sounding confident it's because I trust in the process Sarah and I have created together: a designated space for free-associating about films through dialogue. We are essentially treating cinema as a projective test (e.g., Rorschach inkblot), hence why we call our podcast *Projections*. There is no assumed "correct" reading of a given film; we're simply responding spontaneously, and only very loosely guided by psychoanalytic theory. We're relying on the cinematic arts to access, work through, and hopefully articulate what's going on for us unconsciously. Uncovering repressed material is difficult, and we might never fully resolve subjective problems while recording, but just having a space for this practice and continually returning to it leads to a stronger analytical approach in all the projects we take on, whether separately or together. Following the raw data of the films we choose purely for exploration purposes, rather than affirming pre-set ideas, feels more authentic to me.

Neil: Your podcast has been going for some time now. What are your reflections when you look back at the collection of episodes you've built? Do you feel that you have done any work in addressing the historical canon, and how do you feel about your own collection being seen as a canon of sorts?

Sarah: It's nice to think we're building an archive of psychoanalytic cinema, and that in itself being a genre. I'm not sure the canon really matters in a post-internet world.

Mary: Judging by the series we've covered so far, I think our podcast is providing plenty of support for François Truffaut's claim that film lovers are sick people. Ha ha. I'm really proud that there is a structural integrity to our show, that we never try to overcome our subjectivity by performing "normality." I think this rings as truthful to our listeners. I don't believe that addressing the historical canon has really been a priority for us, but because our approach is unique, perhaps what we're building over time might help to inform the broader canon of psychoanalytically oriented cinema.

Neil: Your podcast uses the lens of psychoanalysis to discuss the films you choose. What other ways would you define your work? Is it feminist? Is it engaging with, or in dialogue with feminism? Does that matter? To what extent, and if not, why not?

Sarah: When we started, we were aware that most of the dominant voices in film criticism were male, something that has changed a lot over the years we've been podcasting. But we also felt that there was more to women's point of view than feminist readings (not that we don't enjoy many feminist writers and cultural critics). I don't think that either of us particularly want our work to fall into a "feminist" category, purely because that feels a bit limiting. However, if our listeners see us as feminist, I'd be interested in hearing more about that.

Mary: I guess "philosophy" is another way I would define the work we're doing on the podcast. Feminism and psychoanalysis are awkward bedfellows, and I hesitate to call myself a feminist because I believe all genders ultimately wrestle with subjectivity and alienation, and the gender war feels like a false struggle compared to that (in my opinion). I'm a liberationist feminist, I guess, since I want women to feel free to enjoy whatever is available to men, etc. But to quote a personal hero of mine, Timothy Leary, "Women who seek to be equal with men lack ambition." In all seriousness, I have a lot of sympathy for men in modern times, and I often find myself sticking up for them. For reasons unknown to me, my desiring gaze is perhaps more male than female, even though I'm a heterosexual cis woman who performs femininity in conventional ways. My misgivings about feminism don't make me feel conflicted in my discussions with Sarah, however—it's not something that is at odds with the dialogues we have, so that's cool.

Neil: How has your process of and criteria for selecting films changed over time, and do you see it evolving further? How much of your selection process is instinct, and how much is reflected upon and researched?

Sarah: Back in the early days, we used to each pick one of the two titles that featured in each episode. Now it's a process of designing the whole series at once, and often one of us will lead on the choices and the other will fill in the gaps and make suggestions. I see it as quite instinctive. And often it's not totally clear to us why we've selected something until we start to discuss it. Once or twice, we've made choices that we haven't been able to come to a clear reading of, but that's rare.

Mary: I would qualify what Sarah and I do as "stream-of-consciousness pro-gramming"; it's pure instinct on my part, like following a path set out in a dream and feeling compelled by unknown psychological processes. But then, in conversation with Sarah, something gets clarified and clicks into place. I've had so many aha moments on the podcast through exchanging ideas with my co-host. The research is in formulating the theoretical framework and pro-viding an accurate reading of Freudian or Lacanian concepts; the selection process feels more fluid, decisions made on a hunch, and difficult to explain in objective terms.

CONCLUSION

Reading Sarah and Mary's responses I am struck by how instinctual their approach to podcasting is, how trusting they are in their taste and complex cultural identities, and how comfortable they are with each other in exploring cinema on their show. On the one hand, it potentially negates my claim that podcasting is a curative practice born of active engagement with issues such as "narrative correction." However, it reveals to me that much of what drives contemporary curation and curatorial activism is present in their work albeit in possibly less declarative and more process-driven ways, which is exciting to consider in terms of what a specific definition of podcast curation could be. A definition tied to traditional ideas of curation and activism, but also separate, something that uses the podcast form's immediacy of broadcast as a tool for instinctively addressing erasures and gaps in culture. So what of the relation-ship between curation and podcasting as a unique melding? What marks out podcasting as a special opportunity to reconsider ideas around curation in an age of multitudinous digital and internet possibilities for the dissemination of ideas? I would argue that it is the following interlocked ways. There is the potential for boundaries regarding serialization or "collection-making," with defined start and end points much like a film season, that are more clearly understood and approached than a YouTube channel offers. A podcast series has more intentionality than a playlist in its presentation of a set of ideas to an audience. It is a space where discernment is still, presently, and for the most part, valued. In addition—and this is something that marks it out from written film criticism—podcasting offers a space for an intimate dialogue, for hearing people think through meaning making. If many selections are instinctive, as my interview subjects suggest they may be, podcasting offers an opportunity to validate those instincts by providing a space for people to work through their curatorial choices. Podcasting offers the opportunity to reveal both the curatorial impulse and latent activism, things that are present in the choices and conversations found on the *Projections Podcast* and they provide vital examples of how to engage with podcasting through the nascent lens of curatorial activism. The *Projections* seasons, like many similar podcasts, group together in a discrete block a set of texts that the curators then set about critiquing, unpacking, justifying, and making meaning with, as individual films and a collection of representative ideas, through the process of podcasting. Podcasting as curatorial activism, then, may be something born of "stream-of-consciousness programming," but it is being done by people who have sensed an open space and entered it, changing perceptions about culture, historical positions, and taste along the way.

CHAPTER 16

PODCASTING PEDAGOGY
The Power of Sound, Participation, and Marginalized Voices in a Virtual Classroom

KELLI S. BOLING

I n January 2020, the world began to follow news of a rapidly spreading virus with no known cure and alarming death rates. Countries began closing their borders to travelers and cities initiated mandatory lockdowns, including for universities. We were all scrambling, attempting to finish the semester while battling an invisible virus that had isolated us from what we knew as "life." I was in my third semester teaching Women and Minorities in the Mass Media, a large lecture class of 135 students at a large southeastern university in the United States. The syllabus included entire weeks devoted to in-class discussions of homophobia, Islamophobia, racism, and sexism. Leading these discussions was life-giving for me every semester. The discussions often included difficult conversations in which we would confront our prejudices by examining mass-media representation of traditionally marginalized groups. The COVID-19 virus brought everything to a screeching halt and forced academia to change plans for the remainder of spring 2020. Narrated PowerPoints were not how I intended to finish the semester, and I also saw weekly mass Zoom calls as unfeasible for a group that large. I turned to the only place I knew critical conversations about these topics existed—podcasts.

As an avid podcast listener, I regularly consume podcasts like *1619* by *The New York Times*, *Ear Hustle* and *The Stoop*, both by Radiotopia, and *In the Dark* by American Public Media. These podcasts challenge not only my prejudices but also my beliefs regarding inequities in our society (Boling 2019).

I knew (or at least had hope) that podcasts were a space where I could finish the semester on my terms, and approach the topics in a way that was accessible and convenient but still challenging for everyone involved.

In this chapter, I am going to revisit academia in the spring of 2020 to walk through the pedagogical decisions that I made amid a global pandemic. While I was forced to take my instruction online, I had free rein to adjust the content in any way I felt necessary. Because of my love for podcasts, I made a series of decisions to convert the course content into a weekly podcast for my students while trying to remain true to my initial plans for critical pedagogy. In this chapter, I show that critical pedagogy is possible in a virtual classroom and that podcasts can be used effectively for student engagement, even during a global pandemic.

PODCASTING: A VIRTUAL CLASSROOM

A June 2020 study of 7,070 students, administrators, and faculty across thirteen different countries found that 75 percent of US respondents, 62 percent of Europe, Middle East, and Africa respondents, and 78 percent of Asia-Pacific respondents felt that COVID-19 had negatively impacted student engagement. Socio-economic factors were a significant indicator of students feeling connected to class, coursework, and campus relationships (Canvas 2020). During the pandemic, a primary concern in higher education was student access to course material due to limitations in technology or unreliable internet (Wong 2020; Dennon 2020; Levin 2020; Canvas 2020). One issue often cited in news reports was that smart phones were many students' only access to the internet (Dennon 2020; Levin 2020). Since podcasts are audio media that can be accessed easily with smart phones, they addressed most of my logistical concerns.

A global pandemic may not have been the ideal place or time to completely overhaul my approach to the semester. Still, I did not want my students to become disengaged statistical examples of education during a crisis, like the 80 percent of students who reported difficulty concentrating during remote lectures (Ezarik 2021). I also felt like the material was important, timely, and deserving of the commitment it would take to produce a weekly podcast. Since prior research had shown podcasts to be a unique form of media with active, engaged audiences (Florini 2015; Markman 2015; Salvati 2015; Wrather 2016), I hoped that would extend to active and engaged students. Or, more accurately, I was hoping my students would become an active, engaged audience.

My idea was not novel. Researchers have been studying podcasts in education, and professors have been using podcasts as supplemental material successfully for years (Carvalho et al. 2009; Chung and Kim 2015; Edirisingha and Salmon 2007; Huntsberger and Stavitsky 2007; McKinney, Dyck, and

Luber 2009; Moryl 2013; O'Bannon et al. 2011). While scholars have found measurable benefits for students, I had never created a podcast, so I felt like this venture was experimental at best. However, I was convinced that producing a weekly podcast would make the class asynchronous, easy to access, and convenient. In addition to my concern for student engagement during a global pandemic, I was also doing this for myself. Creating the podcast each week gave me a pandemic diversion and allowed me to participate in creating something I already loved.

While podcast usage in higher education is not new, research on the motivations of educators is scant (Carvalho et al. 2009; Fernandez, Sallan, and Simo 2015). Most research focuses on the benefits for students (Carvalho et al. 2009; Chung and Kim 2015; O'Bannon et al. 2011; Edirisingha and Salmon 2007; Gunderson and Cumming 2022; Huntsberger and Stavitsky 2007; McKinney, Dyck, and Luber 2009), and fails to address the logistics of creation or the motivations behind incorporating podcasts into a college-level course. I was admittedly doing this because of my own interest and because there were essentially no restrictions on how to convert my course into an online format. In my mind, I had nothing to lose, and I thought it would be fun. My motivations as an instructor using podcasts during a global pandemic are notably different from others'. I am also analyzing this with the benefit of hindsight. Unlike the other research published on podcast usage in higher education, I did not enter into "podagogy" (Huntsberger and Stavitsky 2007) with research in mind. Reflecting on my pedagogical choices has afforded me the ability to critically analyze my own decisions as well as the experience of my students. Connecting virtually with 135 students solely via sound was exciting, motivating, and upon reflection, successful.

Sound scholar Brian Kane argues that sound is a relationship between listeners and their own history, space, and time (2014). Essentially, I would be creating sound that I found relevant and insightful, but what my students would hear would be completely dependent on their own history and experiences, as well as the current space and time that they are occupying. Incorporating this idea into the environment of a global pandemic, the lived experiences of each student varied greatly. They were no longer living on campus. Many had returned home and become caregivers for younger siblings while their parents worked or returned home to the distractions of a full house during a lockdown and poor or inconsistent internet connection. The students were expected to be engaged in courses, and I was asking them to be an active audience, interpreting polarizing content on a weekly basis.

Critical cultural media scholars have argued for decades that the audience determines how the media gets interpreted (Kellner 2011; Radway 1984; Parameswaran 1999). However, in most studies, the audience's environment does not shift dramatically mid-engagement as it did when COVID-19 hit. The environment we were all living in was a notable threat to critical pedagogy. In an in-class lecture, there are visuals: an enthusiastically gesticulating professor presenting slides summarizing essential points and engaging classmates. There is also consistent Wi-Fi, a focused educational environment, and peer feedback. I wanted to create an engaged listening audience for my podcast, where they were not just listening to the material as a virtual classroom of students, but interpreting the material and incorporating it into their lives just as they would have if we had been meeting in person.

PEDAGOGY OF AUDIENCE RECEPTION

Research supports the implementation of "flipped" classrooms in higher education, where students learn outside of class and then do group work in class to solidify concepts (Låg and Grøm Sæle 2019). Specifically for large lecture classes, instructors are encouraged to avoid being a "sage on the stage" and instead become a "guide on the side" (King 1993). Both of these methods involve hands-on interaction with students; they are not a passive listening audience, but an actively engaged group of adults taking control of their own learning. Considering that, it may be controversial to consider students as a media audience, but that is precisely what I am proposing.

Henry Jenkins describes audiences as active participants who are "engaged in a process of making, rather than simply absorbing, meanings" (Jenkins 2000, para. 8). When I turned my in-class lectures into produced podcasts, I created media. My students consumed the media and engaged in making meaning from the content instead of simply absorbing what I had created. I will support this argument and address it directly in the following section. Still, I want to emphasize that while the idea of students as an audience might be controversial, studying how audiences interpret and make meaning from the media they consume is not. It is a critical practice in understanding how audiences receive and apply media to their lives. The podcast I created was media, and it was consumed by an interpretive community, a group of people with "shared patterns of meanings or shared strategies of interpretation" (Jenkins 2000, para. 11). While every student may understand the material differently because of their own history, space, and time, they are all students in the same class, at the same university, attempting to get a good grade and progress towards completing their college degree while broadening their understanding of the world around them.

Schrøder argues that "people—at least those who have turned themselves into digital natives, who are online accessible during all their waking hours—are audiences all the time; they are never not audiences" (2018, 160). Since several of my students were international and had returned home for quarantine, my class became a global audience of the media I produced each week. Because we were no longer in a classroom setting, my role as professor turned into that of a producer/host, and their role as students turned into that of audience members. I was producing media with the audience in mind. Like other media producers, I needed to understand my audience and create a product they wanted to consume. This venture into "podagogy" would have implications for both myself and my students, producer and audience. Examining only the impact on students leaves out a critical component of analysis. For "podagogy" to be successful, I argue that it needs to benefit both the instructor and the student, or both the producer and the audience, similar to traditional media.

CRITICAL PEDAGOGY IN COMMUNICATIONS EDUCATION

The only way to understand how the audience interprets the media is to engage in discussions with the audience and allow them to describe how they understand and make meaning from what was produced (Kellner 2011). This is a core concept of critical pedagogy—that students, by discussing concepts with others, are able to reach a more critical view of the world (Freire 2002). Revisiting my earlier point about audience reception work, my students as a participatory audience were making meaning by discussing the concepts with others via online discussion forums and actively participating in the creation of the weekly podcast.

I wanted to create knowledge *with* the audience while challenging predominant ideology about media representation of traditionally marginalized groups to encourage a critical understanding in these future media producers. Freire refers to this process as "learning to perceive social, political, and economic contradictions, and to take action against the oppressive elements of reality" (2002, 35). Other researchers have argued that through this critical engagement of material, "instructors are able to create a sense of purpose for both themselves and for the creation of critical knowledge" (Rodriguez and Huemmer 2019, 3).

Critical pedagogy is particularly important in intercultural communication classes (Lawless and Chen 2020). My course was structured to examine media representation of racialized and ethnic populations in the United States. We examined depictions and industry representation of Asian Americans, Arab Americans, African Americans, Latinxs, and LGBTQIA Americans. Anecdotally, the classroom was made up of approximately 70 percent white students and 30 percent racialized or minoritized ethnic students. Many of the classroom discussions were meant to help students better understand those that are different from themselves. Knowing how to navigate the media industry or cover stories about diverse populations is critical for these students as future media producers. Chen asserts that communication professors have a responsibility for critical pedagogy to "provide methods of thinking and the tools of reflection to direct students' lives and action" (2013, 437).

WOMEN AND MINORITIES IN MASS MEDIA: FROM LARGE LECTURE TO PODCAST

The stated goals for the semester were (1) to demonstrate historical knowledge of the topic, (2) to think critically and write clearly about the topic, (3) to apply specific mass communication theories to the topic, (4) to value and understand the diversity of audiences, and (5) to be critical observers of media representation.

We began the semester by establishing a theoretical base. We discussed several mass communication theories: social cognitive theory (Bandura 1971), cultivation theory (Gerbner and Gross 1976), agenda setting (McCombs and Shaw 1972), framing (Goffman 1974), symbolic annihilation (Gerbner and Gross 1976), and gatekeeping (Shoemaker and Reese 1996). We also linked the following critical cultural theories to mass communication scholarship: feminist theory (Butler 1990b; hooks 2000), feminist standpoint theory (Hartsock 1998), intersectionality (Crenshaw 1995), and critical race theory (Bell 1992). Each of these theories was presented in conjunction with published communication research as a case study so that students could see how the theories help us understand society and media audiences.

After we understood the theories behind the research, we began to cover media representation of specific subsets of the US population, such as women, LGBTQIA people, Asian Americans, and African Americans. Each of these groups was presented and discussed using this basic format: (1) historical stereotypes seen in the media, (2) demographic and industry research from organizations studying that specific group,[1] (3) a case study of recent research on the topic, and (4) media pioneers that identify as members of the group.[2] If

---

1   This research was meant to show how mass media depicts the group, and statistics on employment in mass media roles. For example, GLAD regularly produces reports about media representation of the LGBTQIA population, the Latino Media Gap produces reports on Latinx media representation, and institutions like USC Annenburg and non-profits like the Norman Lear Center or the Center for the Study of Ethnicity and Race at Columbia University produce research on gender, race, and age of those employed in mass media roles. Research was gathered based on what was available for each topic. Most research examined in class had been produced in the last two to five years.
2   For example, Oprah as a media pioneer for African American women and Hoda Kotb as a media pioneer for Arab Americans. Each week, five pioneers were presented and then students discussed who might be missing from the list. The term pioneer...

there was any terminology that needed to be covered for the week, I covered that at the beginning before the historical stereotypes.[3]

The first decision that I made when moving to a podcast format for the class was to include student voices, feedback, and interviews in each episode. We had an ongoing conversation in class, and I wanted to continue that in a virtual environment. This meant I could not just speak into a microphone and push my podcast out into the digital ether. To do this material justice and continue the critical pedagogy that had begun in person, there must be real, honest interactions.

I regularly assigned podcast episodes, TEDx presentations, and YouTube videos instead of readings, so in some ways, the transition from in-person to podcast felt natural. I turned towards something I knew would at least get a few students interested—extra credit. For the first episode, I offered extra credit to any student willing to be interviewed discussing LGBTQIA representation in the media. These conversations got much more personal than I had expected, and the student response was immediate. They were more than willing to be interviewed anonymously for the podcast, and their classmates loved hearing the voices of other students while in social isolation. This mirrors findings from a previous study on college students' podcast usage motivations which found that students often listened to podcasts for social interaction and companionship (Chung and Kim 2015). Hearing their classmates' voices brought some level of solace during a time of social isolation.

For the second class on Arab Americans and the media, I leaned heavily on research conducted by the Arab American Institute Foundation for statistics regarding Arab Americans ("Quick Facts about Arab Americans" 2018). I also used Jack Shaheen's research on Arab American representation in movies to ground the historical stereotype discussion (Shaheen 2001). And finally, I cited research on *Aladdin* (Lacroix 2004), the physiological impact of racism on Arab Americans (Lauderdale 2006), and detailed research by *The Washington Post* regarding Arab American representation in news articles (Bleich et al. 2018; Bleich and van der Veen 2018; Hatuqa 2021).

For the podcast, I used the same basic in-class format. I uploaded the PowerPoint presentations that I would have used in class as supplemental material. I structured the podcast episode to begin with terminology and stereotypes, moved to demographic and industry research, case studies, and

---

...is defined as someone who was the first to do something like win an Oscar or host a morning television show.

3   In LGBTQIA week, we reviewed proper terminology for journalists to use, as well as the difference between sexual orientation and gender identity. For Arab American week, we discussed the terms *Arab*, *Islam*, *Muslim*, *Indian*, and *Asian* and how they each may be included in coverage of Arab Americans.

finally, media pioneers. Specifically for the Arab Americans and the media class, I also interviewed one of my best friends from my Ph.D. program. Noura, an Arab living in America finishing her degree, who identifies as hijabi, Arab, and Kuwaiti. While Noura does not identify as an Arab American, I knew her experiences living in the US as an Arab would offer insight to the students, who would most likely be hearing a Muslim woman discuss her religion and life experiences in the US for the first time. As a media scholar, Noura is also well-versed in the research regarding Arab American representation in the media, as well as her own anecdotal experience seeing Arab American media representation in the US. As a friend, I knew Noura and I could have a candid conversation and that she would be open and honest with my students.[4] For these reasons, I will be using the episode I created on Arab Americans in the media as the basis for this critical pedagogy examination and a focus for the remainder of this article.

MAKING THE "ARAB AMERICANS AND THE MEDIA" EPISODE

For the episode on Arab Americans and the media, I wanted to hear all the students' voices. The only assignment for the week was to call a toll-free number and leave an anonymous voice mail with an answer to the question, "What word or phrase comes to mind when you think of Arab Americans?" I downloaded every response and compiled an audio file using the students' voices. In total, 79 percent of students (107 in total) left a voice mail. I downloaded and categorized each message to identify salience. The most prominent category was "religion" (twenty-five students, or 23 percent). This included terms such as *Muslim, Islam*, and *religious*. The second most prominent category (nineteen students, or 18 percent) was "misunderstood." This included terms such as *persecuted, marginalized, stereotyped, standoffish*, and *misunderstood*. "Terrorist," "foreign," and "hijab/turban," were the three most negative categories, and they combined for 40 percent of the messages (43 students). These categories included terms such as *foreign, immigration, exotic, dirty, hijab, turban, beard, brown skin, wealthy, 9/11, terrorists, dangerous*, and *Osama*. The remaining voice mails combined for a total of twenty (19 percent) of the messages and included terms like *Aladdin, human*, and *neighbour*. Quantifying these results added depth to my discussion with Noura, but I also incorporated them into the episode so the students could have insight into their peers when listening to the podcast and posting on the discussion board.

---

4   This was not the first time that Noura and I had discussed racism, her experiences in the US, or media representation of Arabs and Islam. This was an ongoing conversation between us and several other international students.

There was only one student in my classroom that was visibly Muslim and identified as an Arab American. She wore her hijab proudly as she walked into class each day. It was not difficult to recognize her voice message: "When I think of Arab Americans, I think of my family." While I was not making the podcast just for her, I found myself motivated to educate the other students, not just on Arab American representation in the media, but also on the lived experiences of Arab Americans in our society due to distorted media representations (Stelter, Manji, and Bernstein 2016; Bleich et al. 2018; Bleich and van der Veen 2018; Hatuqa 2021; Shaheen 2001). Suddenly, in my mind, this episode became a plea for marginalized Arab Americans in the US.

To be clear, the material I was teaching would have been the same if we were meeting in class. However, in the podcasting environment, I felt that I had the freedom to teach the material in a way that would resonate best in an audio format. I had the freedom to include the voice of a friend that I knew could connect with the entire class while supporting the hijabi student. I had the freedom to bring this material to life in a way that I had never done in a lecture format, and I was excited to take advantage of this opportunity.

The episode was created in GarageBand and launched via Anchor.fm on 4 April 2020, lasting one hour and four seconds. There were 159 downloads in a class of 135 students by 8 April 2020. The average listening time was fifty-nine minutes and fourteen seconds. While best practices of online instruction suggest videos no longer than three to five minutes ("Best Practices: Online Pedagogy" 2020), my weekly podcasts were between forty-five and sixty minutes. A basic outline for the podcast appears in this chapter's appendix.

CRITICAL PODCAST PEDAGOGY AND AUDIENCE RECEPTION IN ACTION

As defined, critical pedagogy must involve a participatory audience—students given a chance to critically discuss the material and come to a more critical view of the world (Freire 2002). In a podcast environment, this was presented in two different ways. First, the students had an online discussion forum where they were required to discuss the content and engage with others for class credit. Second, most of the podcast consisted of my conversation with Noura using terms that the students had contributed. While not an active discussion in real time, the final, produced podcast did include me, Noura, and the 107 students that contributed via voice mail. They were able to hear their own voices and their classmates' voices in the podcast. So, while it may not have been an active or engaged conversation during the making of the podcast, the final product combined our voices to create a cohesive conversation.

Arguably, this both supports and challenges Freire's concept of critical pedagogy. Instead of face-to-face group discussions, we were consuming, interpreting, and applying the material simultaneously by listening to an audio collage of voices, including our own. Instead of a real-time discussion, our individual contributions to the podcast resulted in a mediated discussion that allowed us, on our own terms, to come to a more critical view of the world. The end result is what Freire described, but the digital, audio-only format takes the pedagogy beyond the bounds of in-person learning into a natural space for "digital natives" who are constantly connected digital "audiences all the time" (Schrøder 2018, 160).

"HASHTAG SIGH"

There were four critical moments in the podcast that students mentioned in their online discussion. The first was the conversation about the animated movie *Aladdin*. While several of the students mentioned *Aladdin* as the first thing they think of when they hear the term *Arab American*, Noura said, "*Aladdin*, for us, he was a fictional character in a fictional place. He was not Arab." She continued with, "When I saw the movie, it did not represent...for me it does not represent Arabs and Muslims. Real Arabs, real people, do not have flying carpets. This is not real." She also pointed out the theme of female oppression: "this Arab girl Jasmine...she's sad, and she wants to be liberated and fly on the cloud with this Prince Charming."

We discussed a few of the blatant racist issues with the movie, then concluded that everyone understands it is a cartoon, but that cartoon could be the only depiction of "Arabs" that some children in the US may have seen in (or since) 1992. In addition to the limited fictional representation, we discussed a public policy poll from 2015. It found that 30 percent of Republicans and 19 percent of Democrats said they would vote to bomb Agrabah (the fictional city from *Aladdin*; Kasperkevic 2015). To this, Noura replied simply, "Hashtag sigh."

Online, the students agreed. One student said,

> The part that I found the most interesting was when Nora [*sic*] was talking about how it hadn't even registered with her that *Aladdin* was depicting Arabs and that she always viewed it as a made-up magical place. It was so far-fetched and unrealistic she didn't even think twice about it. It just goes to show how misrepresented this population truly is.

Another student applied it to their own beliefs, saying

I found it super interesting that when Noura watched the original *Aladdin* movie, she did not relate or associate herself to the characters or setting of the movie. She said it did not represent Arabs or Muslims, nor did she feel it had any significance towards the Western Asia region. To Noura, the movie was all fictional, but to regular Americans, including myself, the movie creates a real depiction and representation that created the basis of our narratives of Arabs and/or Muslims.

And finally, a third student found the conversation "a little shocking":

I thought the overall conversation with Noura was extremely interesting. A few moments that stood out to me was her lack of opinion on the cartoon *Aladdin*. It is a little shocking that the culture was so misrepresented within the film that she, as a young Arab American, couldn't even relate or feel offended because she clearly didn't associate it with her culture.

Examining this exchange (before, during, and after the podcast) demonstrates that the students were presented with data and a personal experience explaining why *Aladdin* is not a representation of Arabs. They were willing to discuss it and embrace that this new information might challenge their current paradigm. Revisiting Freire's outline for critical pedagogy, listening to this discussion on *Aladdin*, and reflectively posting in the online discussion allowed the students to come to a more critical view of the world by seeing the media through the eyes of someone other than themselves.

"IT'S US"

The second critical moment in the podcast was our discussion of how media depictions of Arab Americans create biases and prejudices that we may not consciously support but often assume to be true. Noura described the typical Arab children portrayed: "Children of Arab immigrants, they are... suffocated by their parents, by their culture, by their customs. And they're lacking liberation, the American liberation, the western liberation." She described a change she has noticed while living in the US: "these are subtle, negative portrayals of Arabs, Arab Americans and Muslims. They're not terrorists. They're not backward. They're not idiots anymore, but they're not liberated. They're not enjoying life. They are 'other' in a different way." She went on to say,

We want representation, good representations...you put a Muslim or an Arab woman in the show and call it diversity...it's just like a Muslim hijabi woman walking in the back...It's not working. It's not shifting the discourse. What will shift the discourse is good representation, balanced representation.

She recommended that the students watch the movie *Amreeka* (Copyright Collection 2009), which she described as follows: "It's just, it's us. It's what happens in our living rooms and in our houses."

The students responded online:

> she felt like people around her were trying to get her to admit that the hijab she wears as a choice, was not one. But rather a sign of oppression she was forced on by her religion and culture. And I agreed completely because this is exactly what I see and hear from older family members as their reasoning for being cruel. "Well, they're oppressed. This and that and this is why we hate Muslims blah blah blah." It's terrible, and ignorant and really frustrates me that people won't even take a second to get educated before being so prejudiced toward a single group of people, especially when that group of people is actually so massive and all different.

Another student addressed the shift in media coverage that Noura discussed:

> The thing that I found most interesting in this podcast was when Nora [*sic*] explained how yes, representation of Arab Americans in the media has changed to be not so blatantly racist. It is still racist. I found this interesting because I think before hearing that, I would have assumed if a show didn't portray an Arab American as a bad guy, terrorist, over-the-top Muslim, etc. then they had fixed the problem and were probably having good portrayals. However, after hearing Nora explain that they are just showing racist representation in a different way, I realized that there is a lot more to look out for in the media.

A third student related the comments to their media use:

> The media archetype of the Muslim girl who falls in love with a white man and is liberated by finally taking off her hijab and presenting herself in a more Western way is still perpetuated to this day. The criticism of the *Aladdin* remake, and physical browning of characters specifically is mind-boggling that this happened recently where they had the chance to be progressive and finally correct their previous mistakes.

Again, the students directly quoted Noura and showed how this information had changed or impacted their beliefs regarding Arab American media representation. Statements like "I think before hearing that, I would have assumed..." and "it's terrible, it's ignorant, and really frustrates me" show continued student engagement on the topic and demonstrate how the material challenged current beliefs. These statements show an active and engaged audience reflecting on their beliefs before the information was presented, as well as the impact that this discussion had on their view of media representation.

"GOD, I HOPE IT'S NOT MUSLIM BECAUSE ALL OF US WILL BE JUDGED"

This conversation about media representation led to a review of *The Washington Post* study about how Islam and Muslims are represented in news media (Bleich et al. 2018; Bleich and van der Veen 2018). One of the key findings in this global study is that Islam has the most negative coverage of any religion worldwide, even when controlling for articles about terrorism, and there has been no change in this coverage from before the 11 September 2001 terrorist attack on the US to over twenty years after the attack. Noura shared a moment when she got a notification on her phone of a terrorist attack in London while living in the US. She said her immediate thought was, "God, I hope it's not Muslim because all of us will be judged." She explained, "We don't want those people to do this in our names, but we're really more terrified of like, the more hate that our people are going to receive based on these maniac individualist acts."

The students discussed Noura's lived experiences as well as *The Washington Post* data. One student posted:

I found it particularly interesting when you explained that the media's portrayal of Arab Americans and Arabic culture was negative even before 9/11. In my mind, I always considered that to be a turning point in the way people perceived this nationality. The podcast made me think of a few of my friends and colleagues who are Arab American as well as those who still live in the middle east. In one of my classes abroad, my classmate was from Iraq. Getting to know him was very eye-opening and helped me rethink the way I perceived his culture. Just as your friend said on the podcast, everyone deserves respect and to be treated like a human. You can learn a lot about yourself and the world by learning about others.

Another student quoted Noura and specifically cited the incident she mentioned:

What I found most interesting in the podcast was when Noura was saying how one time she was at your house and she checked her phone for the news and saw that there was a stabbing in London and the first thing she thinks when there's an attack is, "God, I hope it's not Muslim because then all of us will be judged." I found this so heartbreaking because like you said, terrorist attacks receive [five times] more coverage if the perpetrator is Muslim *and* even though Muslims perpetrated 12.4% of attacks, they received 41.1% of the coverage, and that was *before* 9/11.

Once again, students quoting Noura directly and citing the statistics from one of the studies discussed shows active engagement with the material and an ability and desire to apply the material to their own lives. The keyword is *desire*. Freire's plan for critical pedagogy simply affords the students a chance to critically discuss the material and a choice to apply it. These comments show that the podcast presented that chance, and the content created the desire to come to a more critical view of the world.

"SHE'S ONE OF THE GOOD ONES. THEY'RE STILL BAD"

The podcast culminated with more discussion of Noura's lived experiences in the US and a general conversation on Islamophobia. Noura discussed how she prepares herself for the perception of others: "I occupy a place before I enter this place. So, when I enter the place, I see I'm already there as a Muslim, as a hijabi woman, and the perception of people." This particular comment resonated with my hijabi student, who wrote, "People have their perceptions and judgments made up before you meet them. As visibly Muslim women, we do *not* want to be known as 'one of the good ones.'"

That student was also referencing Noura's comments on what happens after Americans get to know her: "What they do is they like me, they like Noura, but they still hate Arabs and Muslims. She's one of the good ones. They're still bad." Noura went on to say, "It's very sensitive for me like, it's because it's my identity. And it's who I am. And if you like me, just me, but you really do not appreciate the whole package and the places that I come from, you're not really helping."

We concluded by directly addressing Islamophobia. When asked where she thinks Islamophobia comes from, Noura said, "Does it come from ignorance that results in hate? Or hate that sustains ignorance with your selective biases? Does it come from fear of other? I really do not know. I don't understand this. I'm disgusted." Noura further discussed how she does not understand the Islamophobic mindset: "I don't understand that you really believe that you're better and more human and more loving and more generous, just because of your skin colour or because of your religion or because of where you were raised." She also said it makes no sense to hate 1.7 billion Muslims because twenty or thirty commit horrible attacks; "Radicalization happens, but we should not judge the belief itself."

This really resonated with the students precisely because they heard it directly from Noura. One student posted, "I think your friend really summed it up nicely when she said that she just didn't understand. There is no rational comprehension for hate and oppression. It is now just our duty as allies to *all* people to be kind and treat everyone with respect." Another posted, "What I found most interesting about this podcast was Nora's [*sic*] personal experiences. I've never actually thought deeply about what Arab Americans go through so to hear her first-hand account was an eye-opener." A third commented:

> Another moment that I found interesting was the discussion of those who had a strong negative opinion of Arab Americans, then got to know Nora [*sic*]. I would have thought that getting to know the person that Nora is and accepting her would change many people's feelings. However, this is often not the case and many consider Nora the "exception." This was difficult to hear, and my heart goes out to those perpetuating this type of mindset.

I asked Noura to wrap things up with whatever she would like to say to undergraduates learning about media representation of traditionally marginalized groups. She said, "Do not judge an entire group of people based on a small representation....Just search, 'Are there lovely Muslims?' Look for a different discourse than the mainstream discourse."

CONCLUSION

While these key points in the conversation appear to have resonated with the students, it is possible that students were responding with what they thought I wanted to hear. The fact that 40 percent of the voice mails left were negative shows that anonymity allowed the students freedom to say what they wanted without retribution. An online discussion board does not offer that same degree of freedom. Based on Freire's definition of critical pedagogy, the podcast gave the students a chance to come to a more critical view of the world. Critical pedagogy does not guarantee changed hearts and minds, just a chance for change. In that regard, I consider the podcast a success.

The podcast also offered the added benefit of reflection. In a classroom environment, students hear, discuss, and process material in an hour and fifteen minutes. The podcast allowed students to listen to the episode more than once, take notes if they desired, and even discuss the content with others before posting on the discussion board. There was no pressure to comment; comments simply counted as attendance. Given the polarizing topics that were discussed, the podcast served as a mediator to allow consumption of the material on students' own terms and application if they chose to do so.

When I began the spring 2020 semester, I had no idea what the future held for academia. In hindsight, having to get creative with how I delivered the material to students and keeping us all in an ongoing conversation was a gift. So many different opportunities and challenges had to merge to create this experience for my students and me. I am honoured to have been able to interview my friend for the podcast and grateful for the students that participated. We all learned to listen better, become critically aware of the media we consume, and be mindful of the lived experiences of those around us. Through critical pedagogy, I presented information to the students and engaged with a conversation online and in the podcast each week. The classroom community that we had built pre-pandemic became a global audience of learners, and the podcast format allowed us to continue learning and engaging with each other each week.

While this is one case study from a time of global uncertainty, several key lessons can be applied post-pandemic. First, instructors can easily incorporate podcasts into their curriculum in place of readings to engage students in the material outside of class. Because podcasts are portable and easily accessible, I argue that they may engage more students on a weekly basis. Second, instructors can use podcasts in an engaging way as a conversation. Some students may not be comfortable sharing in class but might be willing to contribute their voice on a podcast anonymously. Podcasts also include many different formats, so it doesn't have to be "talking at" the students; it can be "engaging with." Finally, it is possible to engage in critical pedagogy in a virtual setting using podcasts as the primary medium. Again, many students may prefer this because the portability of podcasts makes it easy to listen to the material more than once and quickly share it with others.

While some educators may scoff at the idea of considering their students as an audience, I believe that was a critical component to the success of this podcast. Cultivating the mindset of engaging with a global audience, using technology that could easily keep us connected, such as toll-free numbers for voice mails and an online discussion forum, directly mirrors audience interaction techniques used by many successful podcasters who discuss controversial topics. In *Death, Sex and Money*, Anna Sale and her production team regularly incorporate audience voice mails into their podcast content. *Terrible, Thanks for Asking* also includes both voice mails and audience interviews in their weekly podcast. As Schrøder argues, since many college students are constantly on their phones, they are constantly an audience (2018). For instructors, using technology that makes it easy for students to engage on their phones seems like a natural way to connect outside of the classroom.

Considering students as an audience creates a mindset of, "How can I best connect with my audience?" instead of thinking of them as students and expecting engagement with traditional course materials.

This concept of asynchronous critical pedagogy with students as an audience directly impacts podcasting pedagogy because it extends both theories beyond their current boundaries, taking critical pedagogy into podcasting and taking audience reception into the classroom. This combines these two theories in a unique way to offer insights and tactics on using podcasts in classrooms beyond production classes and into classes across disciplines, campuses, cultures, and technological boundaries. While many instructors became competent in online learning because of the pandemic, we can now embrace online technology for classes post-pandemic to boost student engagement with the material. A post-pandemic study conducted by Canvas found that 50 percent of students and 62 percent of administrators now have a more favourable opinion towards online learning (Canvas 2020). As instructors, we must meet the needs of the students and present the material in an engaging and challenging way. This case study shows that while there are challenges in podcasting pedagogy, there are also rewarding benefits for both the students and the instructor, and that podcasts have a place in the future of critical pedagogy that thrives on interaction and discussion.

APPENDIX:
OUTLINE OF "ARAB AMERICANS AND THE MEDIA" PODCAST

Introduction
- Updates from last week and responses to online chat/discussion board
- Media examples: Three examples of racist Arab American portrayals in recent media
  - Busta Rhymes's 2009 "Arab Money"
  - *Sex in the City 2* scene in Dubai
  - Trailer for the Sacha Baron Cohen film *The Dictator*

Terminology
- Map of Asia: Review of countries in Asia
- Arab Americans: Arabs living in the United States who identify as being of Arab descent
- Review of different Arab states
- Define and discuss Arabs, Asians, Islam, Indians, Muslim

Demographic Statistics
- Percent of population, religious affiliation, citizenship, education

- Introduction to Noura: Arab, woman, hijabi, Kuwaiti
  - Discuss most prominent terms from student voice mails—what Noura expected versus what the students said
  - Voice mail statistics summary
  - Concept of perpetual foreigner

Discussion of Arab American Media Portrayals

- Women are oppressed, in need of a white saviour
- Women in hijabs can't be pretty until they take the hijabs off
- Not idiots, but they're not liberated, and they're not enjoying life
- Tokenism is not the answer. What kind of media representation is needed?
- Noura movie recommendation: *Amreeka* (2009)

Discussion on *Aladdin*

- Noura's thoughts
- Case study on *Aladdin* with research
- Whitewashing

Arab American Media Pioneers

- Rami Malek
- Rashida Tlaib
- Hoda Kotb
- Sanjay Gupta

Islamophobia

- Noura's experiences
- Media/news representation of Muslims
- Radicalization and terrorist attacks
- *Washington Post* research on Islam and Muslim news coverage
- The physiological impact of racism

Moving Forward

- Critically examine the mainstream discourse; depictions of Arab Americans as "forever foreign"
- Hate, ignorance
- Accurate representation

CHAPTER 17

RETHINKING KNOWLEDGE AND BECOMING PODCASTERS

Three Assignments as Pedagogical Tools to Decolonize College Classrooms

JASMINE L. HARRIS

As a Black woman faculty member who used to be a Black woman student in predominantly white undergraduate and graduate classrooms, I understand first-hand the disorientating experience of being in classrooms shaped almost entirely via white perspectives and frameworks. I've experienced the self-doubt that comes with difficulty comprehending assignments and meeting faculty expectations for written and spoken engagement with assigned course materials. I also see how easily white supremacist frameworks seeped into my own teaching. These experiences have led to my continued work, which seeks to actively disengage from white-centric pedagogy in the classroom, as I attempt to create more equal classrooms than historically seen in North American higher education. Podcasts, both as assigned information content and in the practice of podcast production, have become a tool in the pursuit of equality because of their ability to circumvent traditional course assessments in higher education and therefore challenge the white supremacist frameworks on which they're built.

In the United States, higher education privileges whiteness as part of its foundational structure. Created for white men as gatekeeping tools to upper-class membership, colleges and universities perpetuate a white supremacist culture despite the demographic makeup of the campus community

(Brunsma, Brown, and Placier 2012; Harris 2019; Moore 2008). In the class-room, this manifests as course content, like readings and videos, and assess-ments, like exams, essays, and research papers, that privilege standard English and white American histories and perspectives, derived from expectations of "typical" learning styles (Jones, Reichard, and Mokhtari 2003). This impacts how students understand what constitutes knowledge and who creates it. For white students, their belonging is then ingrained into the very fabric of their post-secondary learning experience, but for Black and brown students, non-belonging is conversely solidified by the absence of people and ideas that correlate to their own experiences and identities (Cabrera et al. 1999; Fischer 2007; Hausmann et al. 2009).

Decolonizing higher-education classrooms means identifying and remov-ing pedagogical practices that utilize and perpetuate colonial knowledges (Villanueva 2013; Karen Buenavista Hanna 2019) and maintain oppression of non-white students (Freire 2002). Decolonization starts with the recognition of Indigenous sovereignty, and acknowledgment of the settler colonization of lands on which many higher education courses take place. Colonial knowl-edges are those of white settlers who privilege their language, culture, beliefs, and values as "right" in comparison to natives of that land, and name them-selves at the top of the racial and ethnic hierarchies in their communities (Espinoza-Gonzalez et al. 2014). In white supremacist classrooms, pedagog-ical practices favour positivism (Green 2016), a lasting vestige of colonization that standardizes human behaviour, and requires explicit distance between researcher and participant (Acton 1951), and subsequently teacher and stu-dent, to establish legitimacy. A long-standing philosophy of science that argues that objective accounts of the real world are possible, positivism relies solely on traditional scientific method and deductive reasoning to answer questions about the world around us (Acton 1951; Clark 1998). Such a staunch reliance on objective Western sciences leaves little room for qualitative data and subjective accounts in scientific inquiry, and limits the inclusion of non-white voices and experiences in analysis of the social world (Weston 2013).

Positivist classrooms teaching colonial knowledges are inherently incom-patible with the increasingly diverse campus communities they serve because they focus on a singular "traditional" type of learning, and assessments which privilege colonial knowledges (Hill Collins 2009). When course readings and discussions suggest "standard" cultural understandings and demographic perspectives, "standard" becomes a placeholder for white as the power-holding majority in the US. And when whiteness is established as a baseline for understanding the world, then the experiences of non-white people are "othered," existing outside of the norm. This type of classroom construction facilitates white students' success over that of other students.

Black social scientists like Mary Church Terrell and W.E.B. Du Bois responded to positivism in social science research via constructivist approaches which reject the attempted standardization of human life, instead using deep qualitative work within communities under study (Wright 2009, 2016). Born in the image of constructivist approaches to research, constructivist classrooms help decolonize higher education by allowing students to actively construct knowledges, in part, with their own experiences, rather than simply absorbing and regurgitating information from oppressive and colonial forces. Constructivism also prioritizes a diversity of cultural understandings and perspectives (Charmaz 2003) building on students' current conceptions rather than expecting standard baseline understandings. To create a constructivist classroom requires assessments and materials that encourage learning beyond the traditional, beyond the basic tools of the "master" (Lorde 1984). Discussions must welcome dialogue in a variety of forms, acknowledge diverse perspectives, and accept their useful and necessary contributions to public discourse on social issues.

The distinction between positivist and constructivist classrooms is important in higher education because classrooms shape our understanding of who are true "citizens," participating in the shaping of American life, and who are not (Hill Collins 2009). Positivist classrooms, because they rely on objective and "normal" perspectives, can be assumed to justify white students' roles as true citizens while alienating non-white students. Constructivist classrooms, on the other hand, are designed to offer citizenship to all participants. Inclusion is built into the very structure and culture of constructivist classrooms because engagement activities purposefully reject the racialized hierarchy of normative versus non-normative perspectives (Hill Collins 2009).

Podcasts, episodic audio (and increasingly video) files dedicated to conversation on specific issues are useful media for creating constructivist classrooms because the wide range of styles, language use, and formats expand expectations of learning dynamics, offering a practical mechanism for rejecting settler frameworks.

Both as course content and course assessments, podcast studies research has examined the medium's potential as a tool to help in the effort to decolonize higher-education classrooms, offering content that potentially shifts away from standard experiences and traditional modes of learning (Harris 2019; Tam 2012; Saeed, Yang, and Sinnappan 2009). Furthermore, the number and diverse types of podcast formats makes them malleable enough to be used to deconstruct colonizer-created traditions in higher education (Durrani, Gotkin, and Laughlin 2015). The disruption of the traditional classroom via a format that, in my experience, is not a medium with which many students actively engage on their own, can thus become a pedagogical tool in itself

(Bolick, Glazier, and Stutts 2020). In this chapter I explore the potential of podcasts to encourage deep learning in an inclusive group of students using a constructivist approach. I argue that podcasting assignments help decolonize students' perceptions of critical thinking and public discourse participation by legitimizing the non-traditional language use, argument construction, and background knowledge used across the medium. Assignments like this level the playing field between privileged and marginalized students in the classroom because they don't rely on old school assessment practices, which historically maintain advantages and disadvantages among students across racial lines. Podcasting assignments don't inherently decentre whiteness in this way, but when implemented with the goal of replacing existing colonizer frameworks, they are more than just innovative, they are part of a larger project to help decolonize college course syllabi; a pedagogical tool that collapses who produces knowledge, and in what format.

PODCASTS AND LEARNING STYLES IN THE CLASSROOM

As a medium, podcasts were disruptive when first introduced in the mid-2000s because they expanded who has the power to share ideas in public discourse, and who has the ability to choose what ideas and topics are important to discuss (Fox, Dowling, and Miller 2020). Prior to the introduction of podcast technology, public discourse was dominated by mainstream media controlled by power structures that privileged white men above all (Heider 2014; Pritchard and Stonbely 2007). Literature on the use of podcasts in higher education and their potential role in changing pedagogies goes back more than fifteen years (Campbell 2005) including faculty creating their own podcasts to support classroom content (Carvalho et al. 2009), podcasts as informational content (Richardson 2006), or as lectures themselves (Lane 2006). Throughout the literature, podcasts are suggested as a pedagogical tool that can fundamentally transform students' perceptions about school, learning, and their participation in public discourse at both the local and global levels (Carvalho et al. 2009, Fryer 2005, Harris 2019; Lane 2006, Tam 2012; Richardson 2006; Saeed, Yang, and Sinnappan 2009). As such, podcasts allow faculty to engage a diverse range of students without explicitly focusing on specific learning styles, and their limitations, to encourage learning.

The existence of learning styles has been rebuked in social psychological research (Reiner and Willingham 2010), yet their conceptual use as part of pedagogical approaches in higher education remains (Newton 2015). We, as educators, understand that students are unique learners and as such their success using traditional assessments will vary; therefore, trying to fit traditional pedagogical styles neatly across a diverse array of potential student needs is an impossible task, especially as class sizes increase. However, relying on a singular "traditional" learning style in perpetuity limits teaching effectiveness to specific students. Decolonizing higher-education classrooms does not mean trying to transform faculty teaching to address specific learning styles. Instead, we should strip assignments and assessments of appeals to any distinct set of learning styles.

Because higher-education classrooms in North America are built with white supremacist foundations, students come to expect course content and assessments to come in a limited set of predetermined formats that reward particular types of learning. Rather than create assignments or require content that privileges "visual learners" over "auditory learners," for example, as a way to instigate diverse pedagogy, faculty should focus on the end goals or achievements they envision for students at the conclusion of the course. Instead of trying to fit into those existing learning-style frameworks, the use of podcasting can expand what *kind* of learners students believe they are, or faculty expect them to be. In fact, across the educational research landscape, the use of audiovisual materials in the classroom improves student interest (Ofodu and Oso 2015), student achievement (Fakeye, Adebile, and Eyengho 2015; Olagbaju and Popoola 2020), and overall learning (Fauzi, Komalasari, and Malik 2017), especially among students with learning disabilities (Knoop van Campion et al. 2020; Olagbaju and Popoola 2020). A 2016 project studying the usefulness of audio and visual resources to learning outcomes among undergraduate medical students found that students perceived such resources as responsible for improving their preparation for and learning from the course topics (Choi-Lundberg, Cuellar, and Williams 2016).

Podcasts centre on listening and speaking, rather than reading and writing, the latter of which is usually the focus of course assessments (Vandenberg 2018). Their unique role as a "bridging medium," enables podcasts to blur the boundaries of knowledge and context (Swiatek 2018) by expanding the sense of connection students feel to the material and the knowledge producers on the microphone, hearing individual voices rather than reading and comprehending written words. Traditionally, when narratives are introduced into the Western classroom, whether told by family, teachers, or the media, they centre whiteness—white identities, perspectives, and theories (Elson 1964). White students have an advantage in both comprehension and skill (Swartz 1992) compared to non-white students. Because course content skews towards concepts and experiences they understand, white students have more direct potential for academic success, an advantage faculty often support without conscious critique (Mills 2011).

The combination of improved connection to and comprehension of course material positions podcasts as tools for improving student learning.

For example, mass incarceration can be explained by asking students to read Michelle Alexander's *The New Jim Crow*, a complicated text about the history of slavery and its transmutation to a system of mass incarceration in the US, but listening to *Ear Hustle*, a podcast whose guests include currently imprisoned inmates, expands Alexander's ideas and makes them palatable for a diverse set of learners by explaining the everyday real-world impacts of the system. The former relies solely on students' reading comprehension to achieve learning goals; the latter expands to include narrative storytelling to reach the same end. Only one levels the playing field for all students—podcasts.

PEDAGOGICAL EXAMPLES

If we're concerned with the work of decolonizing college classrooms beyond the confines of learning styles and the privilege they perpetuate, podcasts are a useful tool in this endeavour. Podcasts' audio (and sometimes video) presentation, colloquial tone, flexible social/political relevance, and ability to influence larger public discourse on a variety of topics can disrupt traditional classrooms because of their power to transmediate information into more widely accessible language and issues. Podcasts can be used as course content and as course assessments, depending on the predetermined goals and learning outcomes faculty are trying to accomplish with their students. Podcasts can mitigate disparities in reading comprehension skills among students. Producing a podcast requires students to develop new skills as a group, minimizing disproportionate levels of educational capital between white and non-white students. This is possible because podcasts can be, and are increasingly, produced by people from marginalized non-white cultures and communities (Fox, Dowling, and Miller 2020), are delivered in a language familiar to non-white students, and address issues familiar to non-white students—an important, but often missing piece in increasingly diverse higher-education classrooms (Yosso 2005). Increased accessibility, comprehension, and topical interest among students can, and often do, lead to increased success in the classroom.

The assignments suggested below are examples of best practices for integrating podcasts into college-level courses. Each suggested assignment is but one of many iterations that are possible using the pedagogical frameworks explained here. As such, the pedagogical goal of each assignment is discussed to provide foundations for adjustments as necessary. These approaches are based on my own understanding of pedagogical practices that I've developed and refined over a decade in higher-education classrooms and grounded in pedagogical research. Students are first asked to learn about podcasts and the variety of podcast formats. Then students will begin to understand podcasting as a medium for knowledge production and dissemination via a semester-long assignment in which they propose a podcast series. Lastly, I ask students to become podcasters, creating and producing their own series and formally joining public discourse. Scaffolding in this way gives students time to adjust to unfamiliar formats and to develop their skills.

Assignment 1: Discovering New Knowledges (for Introductory Courses)

For this assignment choose at least eight podcast episodes as required listening content over the course of the semester. The podcasts should span *at least* four different formats to ensure that you're acknowledging variations in how knowledge is delivered. The syllabus example in table 17.1 shows a breakdown of this assignment over the course of the semester. For this assignment, both faculty and students are on a mission to learn about podcasts as a medium.

Podcasts are constantly available, which is part of what makes them such a flexible pedagogical tool. The first assignment purposefully leans into podcasting's flexible nature and offers content in formats and from perspectives with which students are likely unfamiliar. At least 50 percent of the podcast selections provided should offer perspectives distinct from mainstream whiteness because, as argued earlier, white-centric conceptions of knowledge can lead to disadvantages in academic engagement among non-white students. This assignment asks students to consider podcasts as sources of knowledge via discussions of their content, including what information podcasts employ in their discussions, who produced it, when, and where, what perspectives are privileged and why.

I have found that assigning podcasts as course content to listen to in introductory-level college courses where students are then tasked to think critically about the content is a better fit than asking students to produce podcasts because I have found students are less familiar with podcasts as listeners (and potential producers) than the faculty assigning them (Harris 2019). In fact, the unknown element of podcasts can make them a useful pedagogical tool, in that new, unfamiliar content can be novel and interesting for all students.

This assignment asks students to critically examine how they engage with each podcast's content. The goal of this assignment is to challenge how students think about the information faculty offer them. Here faculty should consider the following questions about how students respond to this new material.

- How does the non-traditional format (existing outside of the usual academic texts, videos, and audio created explicitly for higher education classrooms) impact students' engagement with the information?
- Do they consider it knowledge, and what is shaping those considerations?
- How does information in this format make them *feel*?

TABLE 17.1. Podcast Content Assignment Syllabus Example

Week	Podcast Format	Podcast Episode	Learning Goal
Week 2	Personal narrative	*Ear Hustle*	Redefine *expert*
Week 4	Cultural critique	*The Read*	Unpack critique
Week 6	Current event analysis	*Louder than a Riot* or *Code Switch*	Apply theory
Week 8	Non-fiction narrative	*Through the Cracks* or *1619*	Expand historical knowledge
Week 10	Scientific exploration	*You're Wrong About*	Redefine *facts*
Week 12	Docuseries	*30 for 30*	Expand historical knowledge
Week 14	Social change	*Incredible Women* or *Pod Save the People*	Learn productive discourse

When making decisions about which podcasts to assign in this first stage of introduction to the medium, faculty should provide examples in a variety of formats. Using my personal familiarity with podcasts, and discussions with podcast producers, I have created a list of podcast format types that I use to diversify those assigned in class (table 17.2). Some, like those whose hosts are limited to white cis-het men, or those who have reputations for spreading misinformation, are not useful for this project. Other podcasts may not fit with the intellectual pursuits of the course; however, there is room for creativity here— another opportunity to think beyond what fits nicely in our expectations of higher education course content (Durrani, Gotkin, and Laughlin 2015).

Assessments for this assignment include small and large group discussions about the podcasts' main points, reflections on what emotions were instigated during listening, and responses to arguments made within. I guide students through a three-step engagement process to facilitate learning from assigned podcasts. First, I ask them to spend ten minutes at the beginning of class free-writing or webbing their thoughts and feelings about the podcast episode. These exercises are not turned in, but simply an opportunity for students to gather their thoughts in preparation for sharing. Second, I break students into small groups for discussions about their perspectives and feelings regarding the podcast. This gets students in the habit of talking to one another, sharing ideas, and building on each other's thoughts. Then, students take the conversation public (to their fellow classmates, at least) by recording short "faux-casts," audio of small group discussions outside of the classroom.

These are shared on the course page of our online learning system for fellow students to listen to and engage with on our discussion board.

TABLE 17.2. Podcast Types

Podcast Focus	Podcast Format	Description	Example
Personal Narrative	Storytelling	Story-driven, centres hosts' experiences, often stream of consciousness	*Gettin' Grown*
Cultural Critique	Round Table	Focused on specific cultural issues, multiple voices, personal opinions and support	*The Friend Zone*
Current Event Analysis	Interviewing	Modelled on local/ cable news, highlights important "facts"	*Pod Save America*
Non-fiction Narrative	Storytelling	Story-driven, centres specific individuals (often historic), heavily edited, narrated in the past tense	*Slow Burn*
Scientific Exploration	Interviewing	Explores compelling research, relies on experts	*Houston, We Have a Podcast*
Docuseries	Storytelling	Follows story of important social issues or agents of change, heavily edited	*Gangster Capitalism*
Social Change	Round Table	Focused on relaying convincing arguments, often on political topics and ideologies	*Nonprofit Lowdown*

Grading (or ungrading[1]) assessments for podcast content are based on shifts in students' understanding of knowledge and knowledge producers, rather than regurgitation of the information provided. Evaluation of assessments should focus on enhanced critical-thinking skills, asking how consuming this type of informational content impacts students' understanding of complex social issues. Ask students to use assigned podcast content as part of

---

1   Ungrading is the process of decentring grades from a course and instead focusing on self-evaluation to remove students' fixation on metrics rather than learning outcomes (Blum 2020).

everyday conversation. Get them to identify where it fits into their own lives, even if it's from a perspective previously unknown to them. Ask students which assigned content they've encountered in college is more "academic": podcast discussions or empirical texts. Help them to unpack the colonial framing of such distinctions and the impact on what they typically learn and how they typically learn it. Encourage students to challenge conceptions of knowledge along the way. If my presumptions associated with this assignment are correct, that white-centric conceptions of knowledge lead to disadvantages in academic engagement between white and non-white students, then podcasts as content can reimagine knowledge and knowledge producers for students simply by virtue of faculty including "non-traditional" voices in "non-academic" formats.

Assignment 2: Critical Creating: Developing Critical Thinking in Unfamiliar Territory (For Mid-Level Courses)

For this assignment, students work in groups to develop a production proposal for a podcast series. Groups are responsible for developing all facets of the series (theme, title, content, hosts, guests, visuals, sound cues, artwork, and more). A curated podcast series proposal is a semester-long active learning exercise that encourages students to become knowledge creators outside of the "traditional" scholarly method and jargon often expected in college courses.

The perpetual dominance of white perspectives and knowledges in the classroom not only dictates what knowledge is, and who has the power to create knowledge, but also influences students' comfort participating in discussions centring such content. Positivist frameworks create distance between students and course materials, encouraging passive learning. Assignments that focus on memorization and regurgitation, but very little critical thought, are the result of positivist frameworks in the classroom (Weston 2013), and perpetuate such passivity among students. Beyond differences in comprehension of and cultural connections to course content, a sense of belonging in class discussions goes a long way to encourage participation. But increased participation isn't instigated by simply changing the kind of course content faculty provide students; first students must learn what it means to join the conversation. This assignment forces students to become knowledge producers, active participants in public discourse on important social issues as they attempt to answer these questions. The goal of this assignment is to expand their understanding of the layers of knowledge and knowledge production in public discourse.

Thinking about how to potentially participate in public discourse strengthens the rhetorical muscles for students' own participation. Instead of simply using podcasts as content, asking students to think critically about public discourse participation requires an alternative approach. As such, this assignment works best in mid-level courses—preferably those that follow an introductory level course utilizing podcasts assignments like the one in the previous section. This assignment asks students to use the skills they've learned in vetting podcast-created knowledge and knowledge producers to imagine an entire podcast series dedicated to exploring social issues. Students are tasked to try podcasting by learning how to create a podcast series and experiencing the decisions made therein.

Podcasts, because they are discursive and conversational, make the complexities of knowledge production more accessible to students. They challenge students' socialization around academic success in higher education because assessment measures improvements in critical thinking and expanded understandings of diverse perspectives in public discourse knowledge-making. Below is a sample description of this project for the course syllabus.

> Over the semester students will work in groups to create podcasts series proposals. Proposals will not be in traditional essay format. Groups will create pitches to potential media company investors about the format, tone, voice, and audience for the series. Students will work together to pitch weekly podcast content. All proposals must pitch a ten-episode series. Weekly class meetings will act as listening sessions for groups to pitch episode themes, guests etc. and to solicit advice from peers in different groups.
>
> Participation in the development of the podcast series pitch is required by every group member. You have the freedom to create your series as you see fit in terms of theme, format, length, and voice. The only requirement is that the series theme connects to the overall course topic and theme. Every podcast episode must grapple with current events and discourse on social issues in the US. Groups should include guest speakers and additional content as part of each episode's description.

Assessments for this assignment measure whether students can construct information on topics of interest that reflect public discourse, via various perspectives and conversations, and if they can understand ideas counter to their own. How are students trying to shape the conversation? What perspectives does their podcast series reflect when analyzed as a whole? Have their own perspectives shifted over the semester, and how is that illustrated in the series proposal? These questions should be at the centre of any formal or informal assessments of students' podcast series proposals. Instead of asking a question about students' perspectives, this assignment challenges students to become knowledge producers in ways previously not expected of them. If traditional assignments limit students' learning because familiarity allows for formulaic completion (Hadwan 2018; Orlin 2013; Towler 2014), then the development of a podcast series proposal forces students to be present and think critically of the process in ways unfamiliar to them. It requires them to take control of and responsibility for shaping potential discourse in ways generally unavailable in college classrooms.

Lastly, the addition of working in teams to create cohesive series proposals, in both flow of episodes and ideas presented, improves verbal and social learning by encouraging a change in understanding among students that occurs through discourse among them, but also extends beyond the classroom and into their broader social networks (Reed et al. 2010). It also drives home the point that siloed ideas are not always representative of the majority of perspectives, and therefore are not the only valid knowledges useful in academic pursuits. Having to justify the inclusion of specific voices and perspectives will force students to reflect on their own perspectives, hopefully expanding their understanding of others, and on the power implicit in making decisions about what people *should* know.

Assignment 3: Learning a New Language (For Upper-Level Courses)

For this assignment students take the final step to join public discourse by becoming podcasters themselves. Students will first work in teams to construct podcast series proposals, then after voting on the series they're most interested in producing, they'll work together in one group to record and host a podcast series over the semester.

Language use is a big part of judgments about intellect and worthiness in the classroom (Guay, Marsh, and Boivin 2003; Lippi-Green 2012, Tang et al. 2013), both among faculty and among students. Teaching students from an early age that standard English denotes a socio-economic status and level of intelligence that is higher than those whose cultural language style differs also establishes belonging in those classrooms (Hill Collins 2009). This is an issue that intensifies as students make their way in their educational journeys. If course materials skew towards white perspectives and white narratives, framing whiteness as the default, then the dominant language of white people is the literal standard. Even after mastering disciplinary-specific topics, students—especially non-white students—fear they will fail to meet language-use expectations, which stops them from participating fully in class discussions (Baker-Bell 2020a, 2020b). Utilizing podcasts as a tool to teach alternative conceptions of knowledge and knowledge production is useful to expanding students' beliefs about the connections between knowledge and language, but does not teach them *how* to join the public discourse of knowledge producers in their own right.

Privileging "standard" English and academic jargon in higher-education classrooms means course assignments and grading expectations also privilege this "standard" language use (Inoue 2015 and 2019). This disadvantages dialect speakers and those whose first language is not English, most often nonwhite students. Feeling confident in one's linguistic abilities is directly related to one's comfort level speaking in public contexts, including the classroom (Baker-Bell 2020b). More importantly, one's positive self-concept and internal perceptions of one's behaviours, abilities, and personality characteristics are constructed by responses to language use in various settings. Responses to their language use in the classroom then shape how capable and intellectual students feel there. If expectations of standard English in the classroom make white students feel more capable of engaging with their peers and their teachers, then they're better positioned for academic success, rendering the space inherently racialized (Ray 2019). In podcast production, language that sounds too formal is often eschewed by audiences looking for personal and cultural connections to both the podcast hosts and the material. Encouraging students to speak in their own voices in this assignment teaches them to synthesize information and repackage it in ways more comfortable or natural to them than speaking in classrooms may feel.

Every student must do every job associated with the series production (see table 17.3), including acting as the episode host, at least once. Students may hold a role more than once, or more than one role for the same episode, during the semester as the size of the class and length of the semester (quarter, trimester, summer session, etc.) will determine the number of opportunities to play each role. All podcast episodes will be hosted on public mainstream hosting platforms like Apple Podcasts, Spotify, and Stitcher. Making podcasts public is important to the assignment because it means there are potential social consequences (positive or negative) to the work beyond the classroom. The goal of this assignment is to teach each student to be confident in their own "voice" as part of public discourse. Participation in the production of a podcast series helps students develop their own voices by providing unique opportunities to learn how to articulate their ideas and arguments beyond the traditional essay format they expect.

Assessments for this assignment should evaluate how each student develops their unique voice over time. Keeping in mind that this assignment forces students' dialogue-based engagement with complicated issues, faculty should focus on shifts in language use and expectations of language in academic contexts over time. These shifts might include how students insert their first-person narratives into discussions of larger social issues in a conversational tone and how they are able to develop and articulate well-supported arguments using existing data and theory. Do they understand the variety of audiences and diversity of ideas in public discourse, and are they able to communicate their arguments regardless? As faculty, we should hope to see an improvement in confidence about their ideas, positions, and subsequent argument development. At the conclusion of this assignment faculty should consider how, if at all, students come to understand themselves as intellectuals, and what students think it means to contribute to public discourse on important social issues without being "experts."

TABLE 17.3. Podcast Series Production Responsibilities for Each Episode

Job Title	Job Description	Production Relevance
Host	Acts as "on-air" personality	Public-facing voice
Showrunner	Schedules/makes decisions for episode	Taskmaster and organizer
Writer	Decides episode topic, creates episode outline	Content creator
Editor	Produces final episode audio	Final eyes and ears before public release
Producer	Creates production plan	Coherer of distinct episode production activity
Tech Support	Troubleshoots episode production	Roaming helper to eliminate mistakes

Podcasts teach discourse participation without the boundaries of "standard" expert language. Podcasting forces students into the public discourse they usually avoid. Instead of the expected rhetorical or research-based writing perspective, this semester-long active-learning exercise encourages critical thinking and argument development from a conversational perspective and with a real audience in mind. It is a culmination of the work of beginning the decolonization of higher-education classrooms using podcasts. As such, this assignment works best in upper-level courses where it is the final course in a sequence using the aforementioned assignments as scaffolding, building skills in anticipation of this final project. It dips into aural, verbal, social, and physical learning, and asks students to stretch their understanding of learning practices in higher education beyond that to which they expect to be exposed.

CONCLUSIONS AND REFLECTIONS

The ability to revamp classrooms, shift perspectives, and expand critical thinking starts with an acknowledgment that existing higher-education structures and cultures privilege whiteness in a variety of ways, via white perspectives, white language use, and white-centric knowledges. I argue that as a pedagog-ical tool, podcasts are uniquely suited to expand positive student outcomes in college classrooms because they provide opportunities to expand students' conceptions of knowledge and develop their own voice for participation in public discourse. But to do this, faculty must integrate podcasts into their syl-labi deliberately, strategically, and while explicitly decentring whiteness.

Scaffolding podcast pedagogy in multiple sequential courses, from intro-ductory to advanced, takes what might be a nebulous notion of podcasts and podcasting and breaks it into digestible assignments, simultaneously teach-ing what podcasts are and how they can be used. As students are asked to first become familiar with podcasts as a medium (what they are and what they can be), then to plan a podcast series, and finally to become podcasters, faculty must introduce, and therefore identify, content, materials, and topics which centre non-white knowledges and perspectives. Podcasts can only do the work of helping to decolonize higher-education classrooms if students and faculty both engage in the reflexive practice of identifying how colonization limits what we define as knowledge and who gets to produce knowledge in higher education.

Like all new pedagogical tools, there is an element of trial and error to successful implementation in the pursuit of achieving specific learning goals and student outcomes. Since I began experimenting with podcasts in my courses in 2014, podcast production and access have been radically simpli-fied, and podcast formats and language have expanded. These changes have significantly impacted what assignments I use and how I structure them. Students are offered multiple opportunities throughout the semester to offer comments and critiques on their experiences with podcast assignments, both publicly in in-class focus group–style discussions, and anonymously via qualitative surveys I provide and institutional semester-end course eval-uations. Students' responses were used to adjust and readjust podcast assign-ments as necessary. The assignments described here are constructed from the many failures and few successes I've experienced as I have worked to decol-onize my classrooms. They are not perfect, and represent my experiences in conversation with literature on barriers to success in higher-education classrooms for non-white students.

Engaging with innovative pedagogical tools is generally met with resis-tance from at least a few students, in my experience. But rather than be dis-couraged, I meet their reluctance to accept these unfamiliar assignments by positioning the use of podcasts as ongoing learning experiences shared by both faculty and students. Expecting pushback and meeting it empathetically helps begin the process of decolonization in higher education. It may feel uncomfortable and disorienting, much like the disorientation felt generally by non-white students in white-centric classrooms, but the discomfort is part of the work. If it doesn't feel uncomfortable, you're not instigating enough change to create equal spaces.

For too long faculty have tried to tweak "traditional" course content and assessments to account for the increased student diversity on campus, rather than acknowledging the old styles may no longer fit and seeking new pedagogical tools to address this long-developing reality. Even when we try new tools, there is often little innovation in how they're integrated into the classroom. This means rather than creating fairer, more egalitarian and inclusive spaces, we simply find new ways to perpetuate white supremacy and encourage positivist understandings of the social world. Instead, the podcast assignments detailed here attempt to avoid all aspects of traditional content and assessments, challenging both faculty and students to move outside of their comfort zones in the pursuit of knowledge.

We're nearing the twenty-year anniversary of the beginnings of the podcast medium, and podcasts have been used in higher education for nearly as long. It's time for podcast studies to be more seriously considered, cited in pedagogical journals, and referenced as it pertains to interdisciplinary application in the classroom. Diversity of format, content, tone, and social relevance make podcasts a malleable tool for creating equity across student populations. Students' ability to comprehend, engage with, and learn from podcasts in more effective ways than written material alone is a topic that requires long-term dedicated study. As people become more familiar with the usefulness of podcasts and podcasting in providing more equitable opportunities for student learning, innovative imaginings of their pedagogical potential demand documentation, especially regarding their ability to reduce some of the disadvantages created by white supremacy. Podcast studies may be an emergent discipline, but it's ripe for expansion.

CHAPTER 18

TEACHING PODCASTING IN THE CONTEXT OF PODCAST STUDIES

LORI BECKSTEAD in conversation
with RICHARD BERRY and KIM FOX

The first body of scholarship to emerge about podcasts and podcasting was rooted in pedagogy. Because of their asynchronicity, mobility, and the relative ease with which they could be recorded, podcasts were of interest to educators as an alternative means of presenting material to students. Teachers and professors, particularly those involved in online learning, found them a useful medium for recording lessons and lectures—what McGarr (2009) identifies in his review of podcast use in higher education as "substitutional," i.e., acting as a substitute for an in-person lecture. Students found them to be a handy way to increase their understanding of course material on their own schedule (Bryans Bongey, Cizadlo, and Kalnbach 2006; Copley 2007), and even while accomplishing other things such as commuting (Walls et al. 2010). Because podcasts circumvented the gatekept boundaries of traditional broadcasting, which needs to appeal to a broad audience to be commercially viable, podcasts could speak to a niche audience. Thus podcasts emerged that dealt with niche topics that might be relevant to coursework, providing a rich source for what McGarr identifies as the "supplementary" use of podcasts. For example, the Wright brothers and the birth of flight technology, or how trees affect the weather, or why toothpaste makes orange juice taste bad (all examples drawn from *Stuff You Should Know*) might make for interesting and useful complementary material in physics, environmental science, biology, or culinary classes, respectively. Verma (2021) refers to this supplementary use of podcasts in education as "podagogy 1.0." Perhaps most importantly, podcasting's DIY ethos and the relative ease of access to simple production tools meant that educators could assign podcasts as a way for students to engage actively, and often collectively, with course content (what McGarr identifies as the "creative" use of podcasting in education and Verma identifies as "podagogy 2.0"). It makes sense, then, that educators were early adopters of podcasting and that much scholarly discourse about podcasts hinged on this innovation in pedagogy.

Using podcasts and podcasting as tools that enhance teaching and learning activities is not the whole story for podcast pedagogy, however, particularly for professors in media studies, media production, journalism, or similar programs. For them, not only are they teaching *with* podcasts, but also *about* podcasts and podcasting, as well as *how to* podcast. In this chapter Lori Beckstead is in conversation with Kim Fox and Richard Berry, all three of whom are podcast teachers, practitioners, and scholars. Kim Fox is a professor of practice in the department of journalism and mass communication in the School of Global Affairs and Public Policy at the American University in Cairo, Egypt. Richard Berry is a senior lecturer in radio and podcasting at the University of Sunderland, United Kingdom. Lori Beckstead is associate professor of radio, podcasting, and sound media at the RTA School of Media at Toronto Metropolitan University in Canada. Here we reflect on the opportunities and challenges of teaching both about podcasting as a medium as well as how to do podcasting, and what implications our experiences might have for podcast studies as an emergent discipline.

·¦|··¦|··¦|··

Lori Beckstead: I think that the three of us are in a bit of a unique position. There's all kinds of scholarly literature on podcasts for education—since the get-go, that was the bulk of the podcasting literature out there. And that's focused how to use podcasts in the classroom. Oliver McGarr [2009] classifies podcasts as being used three ways in the classroom: one, "substitutional" (so they could be a replacement for a lecture); two, "supplementary," as additional material to the lecture; or three, they could be what he calls "creative," which is student generated—a way to assess the learning of students. And the three of us definitely do that last one in our classes. But I think what makes what we do unique is that there's another level to it, which is that we also teach students *how* to podcast, because our students are potential future podcast professionals, and we also teach them *about* podcasting as a medium. I think if you're using podcasts to teach art history or something like that you're not necessarily delving into those aspects. I think that puts us in a good position to unpack what it means to *teach podcasting*, as opposed to teaching *with* podcasts. So let's talk about how we're currently using podcasts and podcasting in our teaching.

Kim Fox: I'm using it in a couple of ways. And it's different now than when I started teaching in Cairo thirteen years ago. Back then we were just kind of creating audio for radio-ish purposes, and sharing that content online. So it's not necessarily what we're considering to be a podcast today, with that dedicated RSS feed (though it did have an RSS feed). And then it was just a matter of sharing with students the steps: "Here are the steps we take—we pitch the idea, we do the interview, we edit the audio, we do the narration," that kind of thing. Now I'm doing it more as a collaborative effort. We still have those same steps. But at every step, there is a lot of feedback, which comes from the students. It's good for them to be doing that kind of peer feedback. The feedback also comes from the teaching assistant, and it also comes from me. So those three tiers are really useful for the students at those different benchmarks in the production process. They also have to do reflections. So they're trying to consider, What am I learning, and what's difficult, and what kinds of challenges am I overcoming as a part of this process? That's pretty much the condensed version of how my general teaching of audio content is working right now.

Lori: It sounds like your approach is both iterative and reflective. And also that instead of just targeting individual learning, it's more of a collective learning experience. They're learning from each other's productions, and from giving and hearing feedback on all of them.

Richard Berry: At my university we've got a long-standing heritage in radio, radio broadcasting, and radio production. And obviously, I'm here, and I've had this long-standing interest in podcasting. What we've gone through here is quite an iterative process over a number of years in terms of how we integrate podcasting into our wider radio curriculum. The first thing is we've integrated podcasts within project modules. Over the past couple of years, we've been adding the words "and podcasting," or "podcast" into the definition of what students could do. So if you're making a radio piece, it could be a classical radio documentary for BBC Radio 4, or it could be a podcast in style. We've a three-year undergraduate program and in the second year we have an option in podcasting, which is a theory-practice module. And about a year ago, we rewrote our master's program, so it's now an M.A. in radio, audio and podcasting. So we've integrated podcasting there, again, giving students that additional scope to make podcasts. So a bit like you were saying, Lori, it's sort of giving students the theory, so introducing students to podcast studies, getting them to get the concept of what a podcast is, and then to make some podcasts. And I don't follow the Siobhán McHugh[1] kind of crafted, polished audio-documentary format; what I want them to do is come up with great ideas that can only work as podcasts, make them, and get them online. So thinking more about the entrepreneurial side of that. And we have a new module that will run in the third year in narrative documentary production. So getting students to make narrative documentaries, for podcasting, rather than thinking about documentaries for radio.

Lori: One thing you mentioned that I want to touch on, Richard, is this idea that the students need to understand the medium, and that they have to produce something that could *only* be a podcast. And Kim, you can jump in on this too, because I find this a difficult thing to tackle in the classroom, especially given that you've only got twelve weeks. I'm not sure how long your semesters are, ours are twelve weeks. My course is called the Art of Podcasting, and my students have a background in some basic audio production, but this may be the first course they've taken about podcasting at all. I've always found it a bit of a challenge, how to get the students to understand the medium fairly quickly, so they can begin production pretty soon. Do either of you struggle with that? How do you teach students about the medium before they dive into creating a podcast?

Kim: I kind of give them two versions at the same time, two ways to figure this out. One is by listening to a lot of podcasts. I send them an email the week before classes begin to say, "Hey, here's some stuff to listen to." How many people listen, I don't know.[2] But I feel like that's a way to get them started

---

1   Siobhán McHugh is an audio storyteller and the author of *The Power of Podcasting: Telling Stories Through Sound* (2022).

2   A tip from Lori for getting students to listen: I draw up a list of podcasts divided roughly into five categories: chatcast, narrative non-fiction, audio fiction, news and current affairs, and "other," and assign students to choose one podcast from each category and listen to one episode from each podcast. Then I have them fill in a Google Form in which they rate each podcast on characteristics such as timeliness (Is it current or evergreen?); to what extent storytelling, celebrity, humour, authenticity, etc. is a factor; whether it's niche or general interest; and so on, using a Likert scale. The point is that while the form only takes a minute or two to fill in, the characteristics they're asked to rate will help them think about and understand what makes the medium unique. I give a grade of 100 percent for filling in five forms for five different podcasts, 80 for filling in four, and so on, so that the student can decide how many they can or want to listen to for which grade. It's very easy to grade because Google Forms gives you a spreadsheet of all the input to see at a glance. Making this due before the next class ensures that any class discussion about podcasts and podcasting is very rich and well-informed because almost all students choose to earn 100 percent and have therefore listened to five different podcasts.

listening at least. Listening to some content that students have made and to some content that is just, you know, content they should be listening to that's well produced. The second thing is immersion. Because after the first week of classes, I get them to start making a podcast. It's a chatcast—but it's like a round table, three of them in a group, here's the topic, go talk about it—so that they can start to learn, and we can start to critique and refine as they go along. So it is quick and fast. But in the past I used to start that project much later in the semester. And now I just feel like throwing them in there and getting them started is a better option, because they learn by doing and it's much quicker.

Lori: And just to clarify, Kim, what is it you're teaching? Are you a journalism professor? Or are you teaching podcast production? What kind of course is this?

Kim: I do both. The course that's been around the longest is the audio production course, and it is in the journalism department so that gives it a journalism-centric focus. We are doing narrative non-fiction but we also do those round-table discussions. So I'm giving them a chance to get comfortable in the studio talking to each other, then they have an interview component as a part of that radio show that they're producing. Well, we used to call it a radio show and now we call it a podcast because we don't have a radio station. So it's a hybrid. Basically, the course is focused on the chatcast and the narrative non-fiction piece, which are the two pieces that they mostly produce. And everything else is scaffolded to work on that narrative piece.

Lori: It's so interesting to me that you say it's a hybrid between radio and podcasting. Many of us, I think, work in that hybrid space; certainly my background is in radio. And of course, I was teaching radio production long before I was teaching podcast production. So I'm curious what your thoughts are in terms of what the difference is. And I don't want to get into the obvious differences between these two media that we're all familiar with. But when we're teaching students, is it necessary for us to really demarcate podcasting from radio? Or is there enough overlap that it's okay, and they can kind of figure out as they go along what the differences are? Because some people are purists: they say podcasting is absolutely not radio, that they are very clearly and distinctly different. And others think along the lines of, you know, podcasting really just evolved from radio, so it pretty much *is* radio, with some differences. I'm curious to hear both your perspectives on that.

Kim: I don't make a big lecture out of what the difference between the two is. I give them a small mention of the RSS feed as a technical difference. But even then, I usually draw back from that. Years ago, when I taught audio and radio in Ohio, I was hard on technical, all of the specs of the technicality of audio. But what I found is that it alienates some of the students, those who aren't necessarily interested in doing that. And so now I focus mostly on the storytelling, which really works well in a journalism department. When I say hybrid, I mean, yes, these are certainly, in my opinion, both. That content that's a chatcast could easily be a round-table discussion on a morning show. And the narrative non-fiction pieces could be a part of an NPR or a BBC broadcast. So I don't know that I need to make that distinction to confuse them at that point in their life.

Lori: Got it. And we're talking about undergrads, right?

Kim: Exactly.

Richard: I do actually kind of get them to try and think about the difference. I want them to think about how a podcast might be different from radio and therefore the scope that gives them in terms of content, because the lines are different. In terms of how niche they can make it, how focused they can make it.

Lori: I have a somewhat different experience in that students don't necessarily come into my podcasting class having a background in radio. In fact, many of them have not listened to the radio at all. I used to start with radio as the thing that they were already familiar with, so it was like, "let's compare this new podcasting thing with radio so that we can figure it out." And I realized a number of years ago that it was falling completely flat when I did that because the students were like, "I don't know. What's radio in the first place?" So I began approaching it as, okay, we're not even dealing with radio, we're dealing with podcasting as its own thing.

Richard: I think our students have a similar experience. I've seen that listening to radio has gone down and down and down over the years to the point where you ask a group of first-year undergraduates if they listen to the radio, and even coming into a media production course, most of them don't. But they are familiar with digital media, they are familiar with podcasts, they are familiar with YouTubers. So they kind of innately understand that form of media of which podcasting is a part. But if anything, in this last year the challenge has been separating podcasting from YouTube, and that *"Hey, guys!"* style of YouTubing, you know?

Lori: Kim is holding her head in pain [laughs]. She knows where you're coming from.

Richard: Yeah, Kim is shaking her head. On YouTube a "documentary" is someone talking to you for thirty minutes about things that they've read on Wikipedia. Students, and how we teach podcasting, are going to change over time, because we're dealing with different students who have different reference points to us. It might be that in our radio classes we now need to explain the difference between podcasts and radio rather than the other way around, because they listen to Joe Rogan, but they don't listen to their public service broadcaster.

Kim: Some of my students think that podcasts are just anything, any audio, so I have to make some sort of distinction for them. But they do listen to a really popular radio station called Nile FM, which is very much like any other CHR³ pop station that's out there in the US, or perhaps in Canada as well, so they have that as a reference. Often I will refer to the morning team on that radio show because I know they listened to that and that they'll get it. So it's interesting that I have to reverse things—that I know they get the radio reference, but they really still don't know what a podcast is.

Lori: How much does "podcast studies" as an academic discipline come into your classrooms? Does it, for example, simply inform your own approaches? As in, you're reading the literature and getting new ideas from that? Or is it something your students actually study?

Richard: For us, it's something that students actually study. I have a module in second-year undergraduate in which everybody writes an essay about podcasting. We have a list of essay titles, and about half of those are podcast studies based.

Lori: And how far do you find the students are delving into the literature? I find if I don't specify what to read, where to look, and how to look, that they'll come back with a lot of industry-based punditry from the web. Or they cite you, Richard, because that's the thing that comes up first in the Google results. Which is great! You're one of the earliest and maybe most-cited podcast scholars [Berry 2006]. But what do you find they're coming back with when you assign those essays?

Richard: Yeah, they're coming back with the same thing. As with listening, we're giving prescribed reading and saying, "Right, here's an article connected

---

3   CHR stands for Current or Contemporary Hits Radio.

to this essay, read this." We have reading lists. So some of them do a great job and come up with things where you think, "Yes, I'd expect you to be referencing these people," like Dario Llinares or Andrew Bottomley or other people where you think, "Yes, I would expect you to be looking at their work." And then some that don't. But that's the global nature of students, isn't it?

Lori: Yeah, certainly undergrads. Kim, how much does podcast studies as an academic discipline come into your classroom? Are you using it to inform yourself? Are you assigning it to students? Is it important for undergrads to be cognizant of the literature?

Kim: I'm definitely using that literature to help inform my pedagogy as it relates to radio, audio, and podcasting. In terms of my students, in my podcasting class we also have students who are non-majors, so we've structured it in a way that students don't have to get into podcast studies necessarily. So you're right, when I ask them to do readings they will come back with that industry content. I do one assignment called Ignite, where I ask three or four students to give a two-minute presentation with audio to explain, for example, what an audio fiction podcast is, because some of them just don't know what that is. So instead of me lecturing to them, I have them do short speeches to their colleagues. Often the reference material in those short presentations just comes from that random Google search. So I kind of grapple with "Should I give them this list of more academic material?" because I feel like it might be alienating, that they won't read a twenty-page article that might be really useful. I feel like we need something that's more their speed. They want snappy, they want fast. They're doing that Google search, they want those results in like ten seconds. And it's just chop, chop, chop.

Lori: Kim, you said students need "something more their speed" in terms of academic sources. If podcasting is a very practical field (certainly in undergraduate education), but the literature about it seems to be a million miles away from that, is there some way we could "do" podcast academia differently? I mean, if the theory is supposed to inform the practice, and vice versa, we should probably find ways to make the literature more accessible to the students.

Kim: I think that one workaround for that right now is *The Conversation*[4] (though there's not enough podcast content on it) because that is exactly what

---

4   *The Conversation* is "an independent source of news and views from the academic and research community," that works "with experts to unlock their knowledge for use by the wider public" ("About *The Conversation*" n.d.).

The Conversation does. It's scholarship for the public. You need to remove all of the academic speak, and make it shorter and make it more concise and all of that. So I think that is one workaround to get people to read because it just looks like you're reading a short article.

Lori: It's a good idea. Richard, do you have any thoughts on this?

Richard: I came into teaching as a practitioner, so I teach practice. And there's always that gap between theory and practice. It's difficult bringing it closer together, particularly for practice students who perhaps don't see the need to do theory. But I always think that if they do, and it's the right kind of theory, it helps them understand because it frames what they do, you know, just the same as learning the history of media frames the practice, because you can now understand why we have these processes. I think having an element of theory somewhere is important, but we know what academic journal articles are like, and some theoretical work is like driving into a brick wall sometimes because it's so dense and it's so complicated. So I think that there's a definite case for scholarship within practice to be accessible. There's always that pressure from our old friend Reviewer 2 to be more theoretical, to link to the great theorists and Raymond Williams and whomever it may be. But at the same time you want to make students understand it, because otherwise what's the point?

Lori: It seems to me that, because there's this tension between practice and theory, that we've identified a gap in podcast studies that needs to be filled, that this halfway point between the professional industrial perspective and the academic perspective can be useful to both parties, including students who want to be professionals and those that might want to pursue scholarship.

Richard: Yeah, absolutely. I think that podcast studies has to be—because we're at this early stage—it can be more contemporary, it can take a different perspective. I think that when we get to have a podcast studies journal, it's got to be not only written articles but it's got to be podcasts as well. And that scholarship has to bridge that divide, because, you know, are students going to thank us for giving them really dense, turgid, academic work? Or are we going to give them things that they go, "Oh, wow, that's really interesting!" and it lights a fuse in them that makes them want to research and makes them want to read?

Lori: And then there's going to be some Grumpy Pants in the ivory tower that's like, [mimics a deep male voice] "That's just dumbing down school!"

Kim: I think invariably without teaching them podcast studies, we're teaching them podcast studies. At least I feel like I am by the examples that I give. We usually do a listening session at the start of every class and then we do a bit of a discussion, like, "What was really working in that piece?" and it usually leads to a theory of some sort. Students often want to talk about their delivery and invariably vocal fry comes up. So that ends up being a discussion which drifts into podcast studies. I think it's about how we frame it so that the students really get it. It's the same thing with pedagogy: I'm doing scaffolding but they don't realize that that's what it's called. I'm breaking apart their big assignment into smaller assignments and smaller chunks so that they can complete it. And it's really good content in the end. So I think we have, again, a mixture of the two, it is just a matter of how that content is then streamed to the students. And who are those students? Because if they're graduate students, sure, they can take all of that literature because they have to and they should. But for the undergrads, I don't know that that approach is necessary for a production course specifically.

Richard: I use Listen Notes with students, where you can build playlists. So there's a weekly playlist that might relate to a theme. But there's a thread, you know, that when you listen to that and you go, "That could only be a podcast." Listen to the structure, listen to the presentation. The fact is they might be quite raw, or they're speaking in a particular way to a particular audience, you know? And then we ask, Well, why is that popular? Why is that show successful? By looking at these examples, we can then think about what we might want to do in terms of the techniques we're going to use. Through listening, you can then pull out the qualities you want students to be aware of. Why does this work? Why is this interesting? What can we learn from listening to this? And there are so many different podcasts and so many different approaches to it—that's the key thing.

Lori: It strikes me that what we're saying here is that podcasts themselves are the primary texts that are being studied in these courses. So the scholarship itself is not necessarily principal here, it's the podcast-as-text that's the important thing.

Richard: Yeah I think so.

Kim: Scholarship is principal for us as the educators. And then it's up to us to siphon that to the students through what we are listening to and how it can demonstrate whatever thing that we want students to incorporate into their work. And then for me, the scholarship is also important in how I design the course—that's also how it's interwoven into the course and into the projects that we work on.

Lori: I want to circle back to the idea of podcast genre. You mentioned, Kim, that your students do narrative non-fiction and chatcasts, for example. I'm curious, does the genre or the format of the podcast play into how it can be used in pedagogy? Whether you're using it as a text to be studied, or if students are generating the podcasts, how does genre or format play into that?

Kim: If I'm trying to demonstrate interviewing skills, then I'll give them a playlist of some really good interviewers. And the same thing if I'm trying to highlight how music is used, or how the nat sounds and ambient sounds are used, I'll point that out for them. That may not be genre specific. But for me, it often comes from narrative non-fiction. I remember playing a piece from *Radiolab* in class one time and *Radiolab*, as we know, is high in terms of production and how they produce their content. And one of my students came back with her idea. She's like, "Yeah, I want to produce it like that *Radiolab* piece we listened to," and I was like, "Oh, well, that's ambitious! How are we going to do that?" But when you listen to her piece you would hear the influence. And so again, it wasn't necessarily a genre kind of thing, but it's the storytelling approach. She wanted to have this really tightly cut part like *Radiolab* does. And it really worked for her piece.

Lori: It's interesting how you say that narrative non-fiction is where you start with the students, because in the hierarchy of how difficult a podcast is to make, a chumcast is pretty low-hanging fruit, but narrative non-fiction is like *way up here*. So do you find sometimes the students are overwhelmed, or they find it too difficult?

Kim: I think in the beginning, the answer is yes. But again, that's where the scaffolding comes in. The students do interviews in their chatcast. And then they do longer oral history-type interviews for their narrative non-fiction piece. So it is kind of a walk-through. It's a bit of a slow walk, but what we call the semester walk, right?

Lori: Yes, I think scaffolding is really the only way to teach how to podcast. You have to scaffold that. Richard, I'll give you a chance to answer a question about whether genre or format plays a role in how it can be used in pedagogy.

Richard: You know, I think there's a definite grammar and a DNA to podcasting where a lot of those things could cross all kinds of formats. So you might be listening to a chatcast, but a lot of the same phrasing and editing and tonal qualities are there in narrative documentaries as well. I think in some ways, thinking about genres within podcasting can be risky because you risk putting walls up between these things when actually you want students to think across these genres and formats.

Lori: Yes, I think students sometimes come with a certain idea that a podcast is something that sounds like NPR, or it's *Serial*, or it's whatever very popular podcast they're aware of. So one of the things I really love to hear from them is, once they've done the initial listening exercise in my class where they have to listen to a variety of podcasts from different genres and formats that they say, "I didn't know a podcast could be *this*," or "Really? You can do *that* as a podcast?" So for me the idea of genre and format comes into it in terms of just making sure they understand how much podcasting cuts across many of those categories. And I agree, Richard, that trying to silo them too much can be dangerous—you don't want to try to fit them into boxes necessarily. And as you say, the podcasts that fall outside of the well-known genres and formats often really inspire the students. They're like, "Oh, that's super cool that you could do something like that!" because they're the ones that don't want to be constrained by convention.

Kim: I'll just build on that: I feel like I'm often telling the students this is the medium that you can disrupt. You don't have to follow what you hear on the radio. I mean, radio's a good starting point, but the key is to do something unique and different and be niche. That is what makes it really a podcast.

Richard: Absolutely. That's the thing for the students to know, that there are no rules here. *I* make the rules. *I* decide what my podcast is. Because that's ultimately what draws the listener to the podcast, right? If they listen and think, "Wow, this is the only place I can hear something like this," either because the content *is them*, or because it's just an incredible thing to listen to, because it's beautifully edited, or it's funny, or whatever it is. For our students, a lot of the radio they make is going to go on our radio station. So they know what that sounds like. It has a sound, it has a format, it has an audience, it has a geography. A podcast doesn't have that. So for them to go completely wild and just really think about what it could be, I think that's important.

Lori: Not to be Debbie Downer here, but the flip side of that is if a podcast can be anything, and the students are in charge of it, when you have a student who hands in a podcast that's definitely not good, but it's like, "Well, I did what I wanted to do," how do you handle that?

Kim: It comes up in that scaffolding phase. So you're walking with them and you can kind of see the train wreck happening. And it's up to us as the professor, as the coach, to help them make it into something that's more coordinated, that's better produced. Where is the error and why is it not good? We have to have those conversations, and of course present it to them in a way that helps them make it better. So on the final submission I'm not getting something that I've never heard before. I'm getting something that should be tweaked. And it should have taken into account some of the feedback that they got over the past few weeks on the project.

Richard: Yeah, I've had work where you think, "Really?" But there's got to be some glimmer in there that they've understood something. And often it comes down to listening: Have you listened to enough to really do this? Or are you sounding like a YouTuber? Which might not be a bad thing, you know, but it's a challenge. I always find that difficult when I'm marking student podcasts and they've *made* a podcast, but it's just not a *great* podcast.

Kim: I'm finding that when this scenario comes up—and invariably it happens for all of us, right?—this is when reflection comes into play. What is the student saying about that awful podcast after it's produced? And what are they learning from that? I mean, we know that the deep learning comes from life lessons: it comes from failure, that something didn't go right. And so if the student thinks it was amazing, then we have to gently let them down, right? [laughs]

Lori: But that doesn't often happen, does it—often in the reflection they *know* they didn't quite make it right, don't you find?

Kim: Thankfully, yes, they do realize.

Lori: But that's a great point, the idea of reflecting on it, because we don't always get it right the first time we try to produce something. And the reflection element allows students to still demonstrate what they learned, even if they couldn't show it through the physical manifestation of the podcast they produced. Scaffolding and reflection are really important when you're teaching *how* to podcast, right? If you're just asking students to produce a podcast as a way to assess what they've learned about whatever topic in whatever discipline, then scaffolding isn't as important because you're not that worried about how the podcast turns out—as in, Is it technically professional? Did they get this genre thing right? etc. It's really just a way of letting them express their learning orally instead of in written format.

Richard: Yes, I think so, because we've got different aims. I know there are colleagues in this university, probably in yours, too, who are giving podcasting as an assignment: you can write an essay, or you can do a poster, or you can make a podcast. And the students turn up in our studios and say, "Hey, can we use the studio? We need to record a podcast for this class." And we're like, "Yeah, do you need us to help you?" "No, no, no, we're just gonna go in and record." Because what those professors and those tutors are looking for is the thinking. And for us as audio practitioners, we're looking for the idea, but we're looking for the craft as well.

Lori: The book that this chapter is going to end up in is focused on how academics who podcast are turning podcast practice into podcast theory. So I'm curious about how that idea of "practice into theory" has informed what you do in the classroom and in your academic practice.

Kim: It's twofold for me. I have turned my pedagogy into research content. I have a couple of articles out there on the topic of teaching podcasting [see, for example, Wake, Fox, and Strong 2020]. And usually my pedagogy is based on two theories: active learning and project-based learning. That's the simple response.

Richard: Yeah, I haven't applied my teaching into published scholarship. We've got this thing in the UK for accrediting tutors called the Higher Education Academy, which we're supposed to be fellows of. So I use some of my scholarship within podcasting for that accreditation. Teaching hasn't fed back into my wider publishing yet, although my publishing feeds through into my teaching. This kind of research into practice thing has been a big driver at the university for a couple of years. But in terms of, you know, you talk to students, you teach it, you listen to things, I think that that does inform your thinking, because you're thinking about, well, How does this stuff stitch together? What do students know? What do they understand? Because I think you think by doing, don't you? You think, Well, how do these things work? And with podcasting, because it's so open, the rules haven't really been written yet. At least we're hoping they haven't.

Kim: Yeah, I agree with you on that for sure, Richard. And I just wanted to mention a research article that I recently published on Egyptian female podcasters [Fox and Ebada 2022], which really was based on my students. I was working with these students to produce these pieces, and it dawned on me at some point that there was a running theme in some of the podcasts that the women were producing, and the theme was digital advocacy or feminism.

So then I thought this should be a research article, and started the process of writing it up. I really thought it was interesting because this article comes years after they've graduated and produced this piece. So also having them reflect on something they produced years ago in interviewing them about it was so revealing in so many ways. So yeah, it was quite exciting.

Lori: That's awesome. I love that they come back to think about it several years later. That's very insightful, I'm sure. And I think that's great advice for any professor who's on the tenure track, or beyond, who teaches podcasting: that there are ways in which you can consider your pedagogy or the outcome of a class project, and incorporate that into your scholarship. We can turn our classroom practice into scholarship. For example, I have my students rate podcasts based on questions I provide for them as part of a class assignment. The point of the assignment is to get them familiar with different podcasts. But every year I get that feedback and it goes into a database, which I can use in my research. So I think it's good advice for anyone who's in the "publish or perish" situation.

Okay, so now let me ask you to get your crystal ball out now—Have you got one? [laughs] What will podcast pedagogy look like in the future? How do you see this evolving, based on where it's been, and what it looks like now?

Richard: I think it's exploding, that's the first thing. I'm seeing more and more universities and professors saying, "Hey, I'm doing a course in podcasting!"—Henry Jenkins has a course in podcasting. If that doesn't make it mainstream then I don't know what does.

Lori: He finally caught up to us, that laggard! [laughs]

Richard: I think for all of these universities and academics, whether they're in radio, or digital media, or journalism, we'll see that actually this is something that students are engaging with and that industry is engaging with. And that in terms of resources, it's not huge, necessarily; you don't need to spend tens of thousands of dollars on studios. (You can if you want, but you don't need to.) So I think in terms of where scholarship is going, I think we'll find more and more people coming in, we'll find more and more students doing it. Whether they're from media programs, or journalism programs, or even broad humanities or film students who think, I can use this as a way of making a documentary for less money; I can use this as a way of testing ideas; I can use this as a way of exploring formats; and so on. So I think we'll find more and more people coming in and the scholarship will then develop and we'll see more people like Kim, who are writing their experiences and sharing those through those traditional modes of publication. I think that's got to be a good thing. It's got to be a good thing that more students are learning podcasting, and more people want to teach it.

Lori: Kim, what do you see in your crystal ball?

Kim: I totally agree with that. And I appreciate the fact that Richard was ahead of this so many years ago [with his publications on podcasting]. But in terms of the pedagogy, and in academia, I see two things that I'm hoping will come to fruition: that we aren't so dependent on the written word for our research and output. That we will see podcasts as theses and as dissertations. And—

Lori: Hallelujah! Preach! [laughs]

Kim: Yes! [laughs] And not just as a sub-genre of the text—it should be right there in the forefront. So I'm looking forward to encouraging that from graduate students and from undergraduates to pursue that in their graduate studies. And I'm also looking at universities to be tapping into this, because of having studio access on campus and the ability to monetize the studio and the content. So we've also got to get in front of that advertising component of this, because that is also a teaching tool for our universities. At my university, I have a colleague who teaches entrepreneurship and the students produce podcasts. In our rhetoric department, they produce podcasts. More and more people outside of media and journalism departments are producing podcasts. So we need to make sure we're providing everyone with the resources to really produce that good content, as opposed to saying, "Hey, our podcasts are nested inside of Blackboard[5] because they're not that good for the public." I'm like, no, let's try to encourage students to produce public-facing scholarship.

Lori: Yes, universities want to encourage public-facing scholarship and this is one way to do it.

Kim: I think that what we're doing here is also a really good example of having scholars come together to talk about their experiences. But also to say, like, the only barrier we really have is the time zone. Like we're in different countries, and we're still able to do this and come out with good-quality audio. So I think that's a very important factor to share with others when they're considering doing podcasting, having discussions about it. It's doable.

---

5   Blackboard is a web-based course management system.

Lori: And doing podcasting *as scholarship*, as you pointed out earlier. I couldn't agree more that we're going to see more and more of that. I'm definitely behind that 100 percent [see Beckstead, Cook, and McGregor 2024].

Richard: We get requests from colleagues that are thinking of doing podcasts, because more and more people are thinking about podcasting as scholarship, as a way of delivering content, as a way of assessing students, or as a tool for whatever it might be. I'd say I use a podcast as a tool for getting students engaging and getting them "out of the building," so to speak. And I think that as you make it accessible it's even better.

Kim: I agree about making it accessible and making it better. I was just at the AEJMC [Association for Education in Journalism and Mass Communication] conference, and there just weren't enough podcast presentations. I say this because AEJMC is a relatively big conference with a lot of different interest divisions, so I think I'm expecting more, and the fact that it's not there?—I don't know what to say about that. I went to ICA [the International Communication Association's conference] in May, and it was a similar situation. I know that we're publishing and you all are working with edited volumes and things like that, but what we also know is that often the scholarship comes from the conference and starts to make its way into publications.

Lori: Yes! So can we maybe cut off that very long peer review/publication process to get the scholarship out there via digital media, such as, you know, *podcasts*?

Kim: I love that! Yes!

·ı|ı·ı|ı·ı|ı·

Much of podcast pedagogy scholarship to date has focused on teaching *with* podcasts: using them in place of lectures, to supplement lectures, or as a means of assessment by having students produce podcasts. Often the latter is employed under the assumption that it is simple enough for today's tech-savvy students to produce a rudimentary podcast without formal instruction on how to do so. Podcast educators, however, teach not only with podcasts but also *about* podcasting and *how to* podcast. Through our conversation, Kim, Richard and I have strengthened our understanding of what it means to do this. We know that listening to podcasts, particularly structured listening using frameworks provided by the instructor, offers opportunities for students to deconstruct and critically evaluate how podcasts are created.

Through scaffolding—an approach in which instructors begin with assignments that help students master basic skills and increasingly assign more complex tasks that build upon the previous ones—we can guide students to successfully complete a detailed podcast concept document or produce a pilot episode. And reflection is an important meta-cognitive activity in which students examine their own learning and unpack how well they did and what they might need to do to improve.

Listening, creation/production, and reflection are the primary ways we as educators have approached "teaching podcasting" as a medium. Finding the right scholarly sources to underpin this learning is often a challenge for podcast educators. The three of us agree that it is the podcast-as-text that is being studied in our courses, rather than podcast scholarship per se. We acknowledge the need for scholarship that broadly addresses podcasting as a medium, is at least somewhat oriented towards practice and production, and is accessible to an undergraduate audience. The answer could be a podcast series created by podcast scholars who are also podcast practitioners and understand the needs of undergraduate students of media production.

PODCAST STUDIES: NOW AND NEXT

LORI BECKSTEAD and DARIO LLINARES

As the editorial process for this book moved towards its conclusion, we sat down in our respective spaces, separated by a five-hour time difference but present together in the digital ether, to record a conversation reflecting upon the eclectic range of work in the book and some of the key connecting strands pointing towards the further development of podcast studies. A conversation, we thought, would be the appropriate way to conclude, as the method of transcribing and editing a recorded dialogue has been so fruitfully deployed in several of the chapters. It offers the ephemeral advantages of thinking in the moment, but with the possibility of shaping ideas after the fact to hone and clarify. With these concluding thoughts we reflect on the intentions we set out with and how the authors, both implicitly and explicitly, point towards the future development of podcast studies.

·ı|ı·ı|ı·ı|ı·

THE QUESTION OF PRACTICE INTO THEORY

Lori Beckstead: Dario, as we think about the connecting threads through the chapters of the book under the guiding of idea of podcasting as practice into theory, one of the questions we posed at the beginning, or maybe it was more of a provocation, was: Is there an onus on podcast studies researchers to actually be podcasters themselves? And how closely intertwined is podcast studies and academic podcasting?

Dario Llinares: Well, initially, when we sent the call out, we had an intention that "practice" should have a broad interpretation. That has manifested itself in the chapters through the various approaches to the podcast process. It's telling that many of the writers did take a very direct approach to theorizing their own practice almost retrospectively, in a sense that the "doing" of podcasting came first. For most of the authors there wasn't initially a kind of classical or traditional theoretical approach or methodology that set out a framework for research. No hypothesis or research question, literature review, the discussion with outcomes or conclusions. These all might be there, but it's much more implicit in their podcasting work, and only unpacked retrospectively. The form of podcasting requires a more holistic or organic sense of knowledge production within what we still might call research or scholarship.

With that said, any sense of an "onus" on scholars to podcast is more of an acknowledgement that practice then creates ways of thinking. So rather than saying didactically that podcast studies scholars must podcast, maybe the nuance is this: there's an onus to acknowledge that podcasting as a form of communication, expression, or even creative practice manifests its own epistemological conditions and even ontological experiences. Therefore, any research outcomes are defined through the form as much as the content. But this is not to exclude the fact that there can be research and study into podcasting without making a podcast. But advocating for the specificity of the form, and the many ways that scholars deploy it, makes a difference to the intention and the reception of knowledge.

Lori: In terms of the form of podcasting and how sound is the raw material, those things naturally dictate a certain approach—well, not necessarily dictate—but sound offers certain affordances and properties, which include conversation and discourse. These are creative and messy and imprecise, just as I struggle to find the words that I want to use here [laughs]. So that does invite a certain methodological approach or way of thinking, a certain way of coming to an understanding with other people. So podcasting affords a lot of opportunities for knowledge to be created, discussed, and even peer-reviewed.

Dario: There's also a difference between the stasis of a piece of text, which is immovable, and the dynamism of a podcast, which is conversational. That's not to say that all academic podcasts are just academics talking with each other, or they're presenting in an academic style. I think one of the interesting things about this book is the different styles in writing. The authors have transposed a sense of their podcast voice to the written page. But as well as they've done that elementality of sound, the materiality of sound imbued within the spoken voice kind of stands in for the person in an emotional sense.

So, it's very difficult in podcasting to aspire towards that notion of formalized academic objectivity and consider knowledge as a "neutral" thing. When you are podcasting as an academic, you're emotionally invested and consciously considering your relationship to knowledge and what your role might be in the production and shaping of that.

Lori: Yes, the *presence* of the researcher, scholar, or academic is inevitable in podcasting. And so it definitely provides a context for the work, beyond the types of contexts we're used to providing in written work. We embody the knowledge that we're speaking of, through our own voices, with all of the associated benefits and even drawbacks. Perhaps we don't feel our voice conveys authority, for example, or we might be embarrassed that we are being imprecise or vulnerable, especially in an academic situation. All of this is implicit in speech, but generally not present in writing.

Dario: And academic podcasting, at its best, can be taken up by scholars who do actually feel those kinds of experiences in the institution of academia more directly. Academics of colour, or women, or those of any background or identity that might find these spaces quite difficult. And that's not to say that podcast studies doesn't have work to do, or podcasting doesn't have work to do in that sense—it's still very white, still very English. We've discussed the intention we had from the start to bring on as diverse an array of authors as possible, but how difficult this was for ingrained structural reasons. But I think that at its best, podcasting is a medium of voice in a literal, symbolic, and political sense.

Lori: Exactly. And it allows people to re-evaluate what their assumptions are about who has an "authoritative" voice, not only in terms of the physical voice but also the metaphorical voice. As we hear various voices in podcasting, it helps us to change our preconceived notions of the voice of authority as the bearded old white man lecturing with a posh British accent.

I wanted to talk about the aspect of seriality of podcasting and how that helps us with the idea of practising podcasting and turning that into theory. The serialized nature of podcasts allows us to be more reflexive: So "What did we talk about last time and how will we address that next time?" can become a framing mechanism. So, there's a continual re-addressing of what's been said and done. That also happens, obviously, in written scholarship. If I'm writing a paper, I'm building on someone else's thoughts and ideas. But of course, that happens at a much slower pace because of the publication timelines and so on. So the serialized aspect of podcasting allows that to happen much more quickly.

Dario: Yes. And I think imbued in that is a requirement for some kind of good faith on the part of the person that you're talking to. So if you write a paper and present at an academic conference there is an implicit sense that you're going to be confronted over what your claims are, because you've set them down. And all of this has a very formalized rigidity to it. But there's something about podcast conversations. I've written previously about the notion of conditionality, borrowed from Malcolm Gladwell who I heard on a podcast talking about it [Gladwell in Llinares 2018]—that there is this conditionality to what anybody says. With a discursive intercourse between two people, there's a sense that one person is listening, reacting, and maybe even disagreeing, but not disagreeing in a sense that there is an immediate jump to adversarialism. They're trying to figure out why and how that person has got to the point that they've made. And therefore, they're also thinking about how they've got to their own point that they've made. There's always an acceptance and hopefully a feeling that nobody has been closed down. That's academic podcasting in its best sense, I think.

Lori: Exactly. If it's a published paper, there's a sense that it's written in stone, if you will, so it's a lot harder to say to someone who's questioning what you've written, "I just didn't even think of that." Whereas when we're having a conversation in a podcast, it seems far more natural to be able to say that and then to build on that space between ideas.

POINTS OF SELF-REFLECTION

Lori: Let's talk about what the chapters have taught us about the relationship between practice and theory. One of the things that I've noticed throughout the chapters is the prevalence of what you have called podcasting's self-reflexive tendency. That podcasting just kind of lights up that centre in our brain where we want to think about what is it I'm doing and why am I doing it and how did I do it. An autoethnographic approach, of course, becomes an important methodology that we've seen used in some of the chapters. Although in many of the chapters autoethnography is not specifically defined. But that's not always necessary, is it? In podcasting there is that sense of an informal self-reflection, but I think this is just as important.

Dario: This is the most difficult question, I think, to answer in a coherent sense. There is that fundamental question: What is theory? What does that actually mean? Also, there is an incredible diversity of motivation, practice, and outcomes across the chapters in this book. One of the core connecting theorizations I see, whether it's implicitly or explicitly, is around the situational or environmental aspect of podcasting. I don't mean in the global-warming sense. I could talk about the dynamism between physical, social, and cognitive environments and experience manifested through podcasting. In my chapter I've theorized the "podcast space" so that's why it's at the forefront of my thinking, but I do think it is reflected throughout the book. Whether it's the feminist space discussed by Stacey, Hannah, and Katherine in their chapter [see chapter seven], whether it's Martin Feld's eventful spaces [chapter two], whether it's a space for calming down and idleness as proposed by Sam Clevenger [chapter three], or whether it's Parinita Shetty and fan spaces [chapter twelve]...

Lori: Or spaces for learning, as both Kelli Boling and Jasmine Harris wrote about [chapters sixteen and seventeen], or spaces for community gathering and activism [see chapters eight, nine, and eleven for example]...

Dario: Exactly. The common denominator there is the idea of a safe space, which I realize is overused to the point of cliché. But podcasting seems to be a kind of sanctuary for engagement with ideas and people in a way that's paradoxically both apart from digital noise, while completely embedded in digital culture. In making podcasts, one is carving out a protective forum to be able to think, reflect, maybe even argue, without somebody on Twitter, for example, saying you're wrong and you're evil at the same time.

Lori: It's also a place where academics can exist outside of some of the neoliberal pressures of academia. I think that's maybe part of where you're going with the idea of it being a sanctuary. Many people I know who are podcast scholars took up podcasting specifically because it mostly exists outside of the norms of academia.

Dario: But again, as Leslie Grace McMurtry pointed out in her chapter [chapter fourteen], there is that sense of burnout. And there is a sense that academics feel compelled, I think, to be part of the zeitgeist. Every institution now wants academics to podcast in order to advertise the institution, but then academics start to feel like they need to podcast—maybe just to distribute their work to a broader audience, but also to use podcasting in a much more direct way as part of their scholarship or research. So there's that sense of the work that's being done. The labour itself takes a lot more time and difficulty than people realize. I still speak to a lot of people who think you just sit down, press record, and away you go.

(RE)ESTABLISHING PODCAST STUDIES

Lori: The idea for this book, and most of the work that went into it, happened during the very lengthy period of on-again, off-again COVID-19 lockdowns. So I'm thinking about the ways in which podcasting and specifically academic podcasting is, or has been influenced by that. In my experience, academic podcasting was enhanced by the situation of lockdown. Lockdowns meant no more going to conferences, no more being physically in the university environment. For me, that gave me space and time to reach out to the podcast studies community, whether they were in New Zealand or England or Egypt or wherever. And suddenly, I had a community of like-minded scholars who were interested and excited about the same things that I was. I feel like the lockdown for me engendered a lot of new connections and collaborations internationally. I recognize that this was not true for everyone, especially where people had small children at home or other burdens of care [see, for example, chapter five by Liz Giuffre]. But overall, I think it maybe even sped up the adoption of podcasting as a tool for academics and scholars to connect across disciplines and across borders.

Dario: I think that's true. And it's interesting then to see the last two or three years when things have gotten back to so-called normal. They haven't. Do you remember how academia moved its entire mode of operation online in about a month, when they'd been talking about how impossible it was for the last ten years? And suddenly, we just did it in a month. And on the back of that, everybody was exhausted and panicking about what lockdown was going to be. But in the midst of that there was a sort of moment of utopian hope. A lot of the systems that we had taken for granted were no longer usable, so all bets were off about what academia could be and could do. Podcasting then functioned beautifully as a "bridging mechanism," to quote Lukasz Swiatek [2018]. It allowed connections and conversations to take place. I think that's a valuable legacy. It's something that podcast studies should continue to champion because academia wants to go back to business as usual. And so does most of the neoliberal world. It's important as a political agenda that we remember that podcasting is useful as an accessibility tool across the board, whether it's at conferences or whether it's just, for example, allowing students to listen to podcasts rather than having to read really lengthy tech texts. So it's that sense of podcasting as a tool to circumvent those things that we took for granted which has been a positive legacy that came out of COVID-19.

Lori: This is the direction in which podcast studies needs to go. Podcasting itself has been a space for niche communities, for marginalized communities to come together, for counterpublics, etc. We need to be aware how the study of podcasts has been, and perhaps continues to be, largely the domain of white Western scholars. In terms of podcast studies going forward, it's a matter of how we ensure that it doesn't continue to be just that. Are there ways in which we can, because it's a fairly new field, establish or really *re*-establish the canon? I'm not sure that a canon is always useful, because it's often the reason why we always go back a hundred years ago when some man said *this*, and that becomes the accepted framework for all further scholarship. But if there is going to be a canon in podcast studies, how can we ensure that it isn't reproducing Eurocentric ways of thinking?

Dario: But I think this is something that underpins the political ethos of podcast studies, that you are always battling against wider structural forces. Our intention with this book, and it was at the forefront of the call for chapters, was to set a benchmark with the diversity of the work. We had two rounds of calls and then directly approached many media scholars to offer the opportunity to contribute directly. Perhaps we still didn't reach out to the right people in the right places. Or the call itself might not have had the right appeal. And we were very conscious of not simply asking non-white, non-Western scholars to contribute as a box-ticking exercise. It had to be inherent to the ethos of the book. But rather than it being the problem of podcasting or podcast studies, I think it's the problem of wider academia and the problem of wider society. For instance, the number of ethnically diverse scholars at the professor or senior-lecturer level is not there. And of course, this is systemic in terms of the university, but also intersects with structures of class, education, social expectation. So, it's a case of continuing to make sure, particularly within podcast studies rather than podcasting—and I'll make that distinction because the "studies" part has some control over itself—that "we" create mechanisms for inclusion wherever possible, reflect on our own practices, challenge the sense of a right and only way of academic podcasting. Not in the sense that there is a central political voice of podcast studies, but we are in the networks, as are the authors in this book. So those networks need to be constantly self-reflexive about how they are working to not only advocate for but proactively expand different voices and ways of thinking.

AND FINALLY...WHY PODCAST?

Lori: As we wrap up this book, let's reflect on why we continue to practise podcasting. For me, there's a bunch of reasons. It's a way for me to stay current as someone who teaches podcast production. So, similar to staying up to date on the latest scholarship or keeping up to date on emerging technologies as a media professor, I stay up to date on what it is to be a creator and a producer. I gain insights about that that I can share with my students. And that's all important, but primarily I just really enjoy the experience of podcasting.

Dario: Core to my own central motivation is the sense of committing to the podcast as a scholarly act. Not to reject or abstain from writing journal articles or books. But I'm less and less afraid to stick my neck out and say, I'm a podcast studies scholar and I make podcasts because of that. I don't want to say that this is how everybody should feel and every scholar should do this. But for me, academic podcasting is explicitly embracing the fact that the medium is doing something that the journal article can't do, or other forms of academic output can't do, and therefore, you're leaning into its formal possibilities. Because of that there is an onus of experimentation in approach and methodology, something I think many of the chapters touch on in their theoretical reflections on practice. I'm interested in deconstructing my own ways of thinking as well doing it on a systemic level. The podcast is a tool for that, for putting a lens on academia, to challenge its systems and hierarchies, its ways of doing and its ways of being.

Lori: Let's also not forget the sheer joy of podcasting. I think that all of the scholars we've spoken to and who've written pieces in this book wouldn't be doing it if there wasn't joy in it for them. We have talked about the labour involved and whether there is the required recognition, academically speaking, for podcasting. So, there obviously has to be further impetus for scholars in terms of their motivation to do it. And it often comes back to the sheer joy of it. I mean, here we are, you and I, sitting here speaking about what we've learned from putting together this book and where we think podcast studies is headed or should head. And it's quite a pleasure in that I keep gaining new insights. Even though we've edited this book together and we've read every chapter from start to finish, I'm still gaining new insights. As I hear you speak and we react to each other, I'm able to add nuance to my understanding of things, if not completely blow my mind open. There's everything on that spectrum of possibility when I have a conversation with other people through podcasting. So that's really beneficial to the academy in terms of knowledge production and sharing that with the world, of course. But it's also hugely beneficial just to me, because I just love it. Simple as that! I love it.

Dario: That's exactly the same for me in terms of the primary reason I continue to podcast. That sense of communication and that sense of conversation. There's that lovely, awful phrase I used in my chapter, "productive collaborative dialogue," and I stand by it. I know it's a long-winded academic phrase, but it hopefully reflects that sense that there is a specificity to the situation where we know we're going to talk about something. And it's going to be informed by a common ground of interest and even expertise. But there's an informality and a sense that we are there for the enjoyment of the conversation as much as for the outcome of the conversation. And as much as we want to put podcasting through the academic mincer, which requires questioning such as, How do I turn this into an "output"? Or where is the rigour? It's the pleasure that remains foremost as my motivation too. And it's a pleasure akin to that which any two podcasters get when they talk to each other about, say, football or Marvel movies or cooking or whatever it might be. There's a pleasure in understanding and it's always interesting to listen to somebody else be interested. We exist in a very cynical world, and it can be very uncool to be enthusiastic. But when people go out of their way to create in this environment, then it almost gives them licence to be enthusiastic. And in our own often very measured, formalized academic ways, it allows that freedom of enthusiasm. And perhaps even a sanctuary from getting beaten down with the day-to-day grind of academia. I've said to Neil, who I've co-produced *The Cinematologists* with for eight years, if it becomes a chore we will stop. And I will stop because actually I don't *have* to do it. But I still do.

Lori: You still do it because you love it.

Dario: Yes, exactly.

Lori: Well, that seems like a great place to wrap up this conversation, and indeed, this whole book!

References

Abbate, Janet. 2017. "What and Where Is the Internet? (Re)defining Internet Histories." *Internet Histories* 1, nos. 1–2: 8–14.

Abell, Jane. L. 2015. "Curating Ambivalence: An Interview with Erica Lehrer, Concordia University." *American Anthropologist* 117, no. 3: 587–98.

"About *The Conversation*." n.d. *The Conversation*. Accessed August 11, 2022. https://theconversation.com/ca/who-we-are.

"About Us." 2022. Refugee Radio. 2022. https://refugeeradio.org.uk/about-us/.

Abumrad, Jad. 2012. *How Radio Creates Empathy*. Big Think. https://bigthink.com/videos/how-radio-creates-empathy.

Acholonu, Catherine O. 1995. *Motherism: The Afrocentric Alternative to Feminism*. Owerri, Nigeria: Afa Publications.

Ackerman, Drew. 2022. "1043—Baking Bread Week | Great British Bake You Off to Sleep C5/S8—E3." *Sleep With Me*. January 26, 2022. Podcast. MP3 audio, 70:11. https://www.sleepwithmepodcast.com/1043-baking-bread-week-great-british-bake-you-off-to-sleep-c5-s8-e3/.

Acton, H. B. 1951. "Comte's Positivism and the Science of Society." *Philosophy* 26, no. 99: 291–310.

Adams, David. 2021. "'We Are an Industry in Crisis': Australian Live Music Giants Call for Urgent Extension to JobKeeper in Open Letter to Federal Government." *Business Insider* (online), February 17, 2021. https://www.businessinsider.com.au/live-music-industry-jobkeeper-open-letter-2021-2.

Adler Berg, Freja S. 2022. "Podcasting About Yourself and Challenging Norms: An Investigation of Independent Women Podcasters in Denmark." *Nordicom Review* 43, no. 1: 94-110. https://doi.org/10.2478/nor-2022-0006.

Adorno, T. W. 2001. *The Culture Industry: Selected Essays on Mass Culture*. New York: Routledge.

Africa Podfest Report. 2021. "'IS THIS MIC ON?' Exploring how podcasting is taking root across Africa." Africa Podfest. Accessed February 2023. https://www.podcasting.africa/s/Is-this-mic-on-A-2021-Africa-Podfest-report-December-2021c.pdf.

Agier, Michel. 2016. *Borderlands: Towards an Anthropology of the Cosmopolitan Condition*. Cambridge: Polity Press.

Akinbobola, Yemisi. 2019. "Neoliberal Feminism in Africa." *Soundings* 71: 50–61.

———. 2020. "Barriers to Women Journalists in Sub-Saharan Africa." *Fojo: Media Institute*. https://fojo.se/wp-content/uploads/2020/12/Barriers-to-Women-Journalists-In-Sub-Saharan-Africa5.pdf.

"Alex Steinweiss and the World's First Record Cover." 2016. *Illustration Chronicles* (blog). July 12, 2016. https://illustrationchronicles.com/alex-steinweiss-and-the-world-s-first-record-cover.

Ahmed, Sara. 2017. *Living a Feminist Life*. North Carolina, USA: Duke University Press.

AHRC (Arts and Humanities Research Council). 2023. *Research Funding Guide*. Arts and Humanities Research Council. Accessed February 2023. http://www.ukri.org/wp-content/uploads/2021/08/AHRC-010223-ResearchFundingGuide.pdf.

Akin-Aina S. 2011. "Beyond an Epistemology of Bread, Butter, Culture and Power: Mapping the African Feminist Movement." *Nokoko* 2: 65–89.

Ames, Kate. 2016. "Talk Vs Chat-Based Radio: A Case for Distinction." *Radio Journal* 14, no. 2: 177–91.

Andrews, Phoenix C. S. 2017. "Every Day Can Be Ed Balls Day in UK Politics Fandom." *Discover Society* 46.

———. 2020. "Choose Your Fighter: Loyalty and Fandom in the Free Speech Culture Wars." In *The Free Speech Wars: How Did We Get Here And Why Does It Matter?*, edited by Charlotte Lydia Riley, 251–60. Manchester: Manchester University Press.

———. 2022. "Publications." Politics Fandom. https://www.politicsfandom.com/publications/.

Anyidoho, Nana Akua. 2006. "Identity and Knowledge in the Fourth Generation." In *Intellectuals and African Development: Pretension and Resistance in African Politics*, edited by Björn Beckman and Gbemisola Adeoti, 156–69. London: Zed Books.

Arendt, Hannah. 1998. *The Human Condition*. Chicago: The University of Chicago Press.

Arment, Marco. 2016. "Apple's Actual Role in Podcasting: Be Careful What You Wish For." Marco.org, May 7, 2016. https://marco.org/2016/05/07/apple-role-in-podcasting.

Arment, Marco, Casey Liss, and John Siracusa. 2022. *Accidental Tech Podcast*. Podcast, Website. https://atp.fm.

Avisar, Claire. 2020. "Is Podcasting the Future of Indigenous Storytelling?" Vocal Fry Studios, December 16, 2020. https://www.vocalfrystudios.com/blog/2020/12/11/sonic-sovereignties-podcasting-and-the-future-of-indigenous-storytelling-in-canada.

Baker, Felicity A. 2015. *Therapeutic Songwriting: Developments in Theory, Methods, and Practice*. Hampshire: Palgrave Macmillan.

Baker-Bell, April. 2020a. "'We been known': Toward an Antiracist Language and Literacy Education." *Journal of Language and Literacy Education* 16, no. 1: 1–12.

———. 2020b. *Linguistic Justice: Black Language, Literacy, Identity, and Pedagogy*. New York: Routledge.

Bandura, Albert. 1971. *Psychological Modeling: Conflicting Theories*. Chicago: Aldine Atherton.

Banks, Miranda J. 2009. "Gender Below-the-Line: Defining Feminist Production Studies." In *Production Studies: Cultural Studies of Media Industries*, edited by Vicki Mayer, Miranda J. Banks, and John T. Caldwell, 87–98. New York: Routledge.

Barber, Simon. 2016. "The Brill Building and the Creative Labor of the Professional Songwriter." In *The Cambridge Companion to the Singer-Songwriter*, edited by Justin Williams and Katherine Williams, 67–77. Cambridge: Cambridge University Press.

———. 2017. "Professional Songwriting Techniques: A Range of Views Summarized from the *Sodajerker* Interviews." In *The Singer-Songwriter Handbook*, edited by Justin Williams and Katherine Williams, 51–68. London: Bloomsbury.

———. 2020. "Songwriting in the Studio." In *The Bloomsbury Handbook of Music Production*, edited by Simon Zagorski-Thomas and Andrew Bourbon, 189–203. London: Bloomsbury.

Barber, Simon, and Brian O'Connor. 2015a. "Dan Wilson." *Sodajerker on Songwriting*. January 7, 2015. https://www.sodajerker.com/episode-65-dan-wilson.

———. 2015b. "Gilbert O'Sullivan." *Sodajerker on Songwriting*. June 8, 2015. https://www.sodajerker.com/episode-72-gilbert-osullivan.

———. 2018. "Scroobius Pip." *Sodajerker on Songwriting*. January 16, 2018. https://www.sodajerker.com/episode-83-scroobius-pip/.

Barker, Philip W., Suzanne M. Chod, and William J. Muck. 2020. "Political Science, Public Intellectualism, and Podcasting." *PS: Political Science & Politics* 53, no. 2: 326–27.

Barnard, Stephen. 2000. *Studying Radio*. London: Arnold.

Barrios-O'Neill, Danielle. 2018. "Wild Listening: Ecology of a Science Podcast." In *Podcasting: New Aural Cultures and Digital Media*, edited by Dario Llinares, Neil Fox, and Richard Berry, 147–72. London: Palgrave Macmillan.

Bastian, H. 2015. "Weighing Up Anonymity and Openness in Publication Peer Review." *PLOS Blogs: Absolutely Maybe* (blog), May 13, 2015. https://absolutelymaybe.plos.org/2015/05/13/weighing-up-anonymity-and-openness-in-publication-peer-review/.

Baym, Nancy K. 2000. *Tune In, Log On: Soaps, Fandom, and Online Community*. Thousand Oaks: Sage.

Beckstead, Lori. 2020. *Open Peer Review Podcast*. Podcast. MP3 audio. https://oprpodcast.ca.

Beckstead, Lori, Ian M. Cook, and Hannah McGregor. 2024. *Podcast or Perish: Peer Review and Knowledge Creation in the 21st Century*. New York: Bloomsbury Academic.

Beckwith, Jamie, and Leslie McMurtry. 2020. *Yes, Virginia, This Is a Podcast*, produced by Lesser of 2 Weevils. Podcast. MP3 audio. https://soundcloud.com/user-420543381/001-yvtiap-101-while-shepherds-watched-their-flocks.

Beer, Tommy. 2021. "Women of Color Rise to Major Media Leadership Roles." *Forbes*. April 15, 2021. https://www.forbes.com/sites/tommybeer/2021/04/15/women-of-color-rise-to-top-us-newsroom-positions/.

Bein, Adam. 2021. Comment. Audio Drama Facebook group. https://www.facebook.com/groups/AudioDramaHub/permalink/4068970813170824.

Bell, Derrick. 1992. *Faces at the Bottom of the Well: The Permanence of Racism*. New York: Basic Books.

Bennett, Joe. 2011. "Collaborative Songwriting: The Ontology of Negotiated Creativity in Popular Music Studio Practice." *Journal on the Art of Record Production* 5. https://www.arpjournal.com/asarpwp/collaborative-songwriting---the-ontology-of-negotiated-creativity-in-popular-music-studio-practice.

———. 2013. "Constraint, Collaboration and Creativity in Popular Songwriting Teams." In *The Act of Musical Composition: Studies in the Creative Process*, edited by Dave Collins, 139–69. Abingdon, Oxon: Ashgate.

Bentley Singer, Jonathan. 2019. "Podcasting as Social Scholarship: A Tool to Increase the Public Impact of Scholarship and Research." *Journal of the Society for Social Work and Research* 10, no. 4: 571–90.

Benton, Greg, Ghazal Fazelnia, Alice Wang, and Ben Carterette. 2020. "Trajectory Based Podcast Recommendation." *Arxiv*. https://arxiv.org/pdf/2009.03859.

Berkowitz, Daniel A. 2011. *Cultural Meanings of News: A Text Reader*. Thousand Oaks: Sage.

Berr, Jonathan. 2021. "Amazon Signs Multi-Million Dollar Deal for 'SmartLess' Podcast." *Forbes*, June 30, 2021. https://www.forbes.com/sites/jonathanberr/2021/06/30/amazon-signs-multi-million-dollar-deal-for-smartless-podcast/?sh=35a1f8826ca9.

Berry, Mike, Inaki Garcia-Blanco, and Kerry Moore. 2016. *Press Coverage of the Refugee and Migrant Crisis in the EU: A Content Analysis of Five European Countries*. Project report. Geneva: United Nations High Commissioner for Refugees. http://www.unhcr.org/56bb369c9.html.

Berry, Richard. 2006. "Will the iPod kill the Radio Star? Profiling Podcasting as Radio." *Convergence* 12, no. 2: 143–62.

———. 2015. "A Golden Age of Podcasting? Evaluating Serial in the Context of Podcast Histories." *Journal of Radio & Audio Media* 22, no. 2: 170–78.

———. 2016a. "Podcasting: Considering the Evolution of the Medium and Its Association with the Word 'Radio.'" *Radio Journal* 14, no.1: 7–22. https://doi.org/10.1386/rjao.14.1.7_1.

———. 2016b. "Part of the Establishment: Reflecting on 10 Years of Podcasting as an Audio Medium." *Convergence* 22, no. 6: 661–71.

———. 2018. "'Just Because You Play a Guitar and Are from Nashville Doesn't Mean You Are a Country Singer': The Emergence of Medium Identities in Podcasting." In *Podcasting: New Aural Cultures and Digital Media*, edited by Dario Llinares, Neil Fox, and Richard Berry, 15–33. London: Palgrave Macmillan.

Berry, Richard. 2022. "What is a Podcast? Mapping the Technical, Cultural, and Sonic Boundaries Between Radio and Podcasting". In *Routledge Companion to Radio and Podcast Studies*, edited by Mia Lindgren and Jason Loviglio, 399-407. Oxford and New York: Routledge.

Besser, Erin D., Lauren E. Blackwell, and Matthew Saenz. 2021. "Engaging Students through Educational Podcasting: Three Stories of Implementation." *Technology, Knowledge and Learning* 27: 749–64. https://doi.org/10.1007/s10758-021-09503-8.

"Best Practices: Online Pedagogy." 2020. Harvard University. Accessed July 7, 2021. https://teachremotely.harvard.edu/best-practices.

Bierma, Nathan. 2005. "'Podcast' Is Lexicon's Word of the Year." Chicago Tribune. December 28, 2005. https://www.chicagotribune.com/news/ct-xpm-2005-12-28-0512270256-story.html.

Birke, Dorothee, and Birte Christ. 2013. "Paratext and Digitized Narrative: Mapping the Field." *Narrative* 21, no. 1: 65–87.

Katie Bishop and Anna Sale, "Death, Sex & Money," 2014-2021, in *Death, Sex, and Money*, produced by WNYC Studios, podcast, MP3 audio, https://www.wnycstudios.org/podcasts/deathsexmoney

Bjørnholt, Margunn, and Gunhild R. Farstad. 2014. "'Am I rambling?': On the Advantages of Interviewing Couples Together." *Qualitative Research* 14, no. 1: 3–19.

Bleich, Erik, Julien Souffrant, Emily Stabler, and A. Maurits van der Veen. 2018. "Most News Coverage of Muslims Is Negative. But Not When It's about Devotion." *The Washington Post*, October 17, 2018. https://www.washingtonpost.com/news/monkey-cage/wp/2018/10/17/most-news-coverage-of-muslims-is-negative-but-not-when-its-about-devotion/.

Bleich, Erik, and A. Maurits van der Veen. 2018. "Newspaper Coverage of Muslims Is Negative. And It's Not Because of Terrorism." *The Washington Post*, December 20, 2018. https://www.washingtonpost.com/news/monkey-cage/wp/2018/12/20/newspaper-coverage-of-muslims-is-negative-and-its-not-because-of-terrorism/.

Blum, Susan, ed. 2020. *Ungrading: Why Rating Students Undermines Learning (and What to Do Instead)*. Morgantown: West Virginia University Press.

Bolick, Cheryl M., Jocelyn Glazier, and Christoph Stutts. 2020. "Disruptive Experiences as Tools for Teacher Education: Unearthing the Potential of Experiential Education." *Journal of Experiential Education* 43, no. 1 (spring): 21–36.

Boling, Kelli S. 2019. "True Crime Podcasting: Journalism, Justice or Entertainment?" *Radio Journal* 17, no. 2: 161–78.

Boling, Kelli. 2020. "Arab Americans in the Media." Podcast, MP3 audio. URL https://open.spotify.com/episode/5oUYHNYoKn2AkoamImKBYF?si=dBLsXBp3SNWNjMqMpOaoFw

Boling, Kelli S. and Kevin Hull. 2018. "Undisclosed Information—*Serial* Is *My Favorite Murder*: Examining Motivations in the True Crime Podcast Audience." *Journal of Radio & Audio Media* 25, no. 1: 92–108.

Boling, Kelli S., Kevin Hull, and Leigh M. Moscowitz. 2021. "Missing, or Just Missed? Mediating Loss in the Missing Richard Simmons Podcast." *Journal of Radio & Audio Media* 28, no. 2: 254–74.

Bolt, Barbara. 2010. "The Magic is in the Handling." In *Practice as Research: Approaches to Creative Arts Enquiry*, edited by Estelle Barrett and Barbara Bolt, 27–34. London: I.B. Tauris.

Bonini, Tiziano. 2015. "The 'Second Age' of Podcasting: Reframing Podcasting as a New Digital Mass Medium." Quaderns del CAC 41, no. 18: 21–30.

———. 2022. "Podcasting as a Hybrid Cultural Form between Old and New Media." In *The Routledge Companion to Radio and Podcast Studies*, edited by Mia Lindgren and Jason Loviglio, 19–29. London and New York: Routledge.

Borges-Rey, Eddy. 2020. "Towards an Epistemology of Data Journalism in the Devolved Nations of the United Kingdom: Changes and Continuities in Materiality, Performativity and Reflexivity." *Journalism* 21, no. 7: 915–32.

Bossetta, Michael. 2020. "The Professional Benefits of Podcasting Politics." *PS: Political Science & Politics* 53, no. 2: 328–29.

Bottomley, Andrew J. 2015. "Podcasting: A Decade in the Life of a 'New' Audio Medium: Introduction." *Journal of Radio & Audio Media* 22, no. 2: 164–69.

———. 2020. *Sound Streams: A Cultural History of Radio-Internet Convergence*. Ann Arbor: University of Michigan Press.

———. 2021. "Podcast Archaeology: Researching Proto-Podcasts and Early Born-Digital Audio Formats." In *Saving New Sounds: Podcast Preservation and Historiography*, edited by Jeremy Wade Morris and Eric Hoyt, 29–50. Ann Arbor: University of Michigan Press.

Boutsalis, Kelly. 2021. "12 Great Podcasts Hosted by Indigenous Women." *Chatelaine*, July 6, 2021. https://www.chatelaine.com/living/indigenous-podcasts-hosted-by-women.

Boyd, Ashley S. 2017. *Social Justice Literacies in the English Classroom: Teaching Practice in Action*. New York: Teachers College Press.

Boyer, Ernest L. 1996. "The Scholarship of Engagement." *Bulletin of the American Academy of Arts and Sciences* 49, no. 7: 15–27.

Brabazon, Tara. 2019. "The DIY Phd Student Doctoral Education and Punking the Podcast." *International Journal of Social Sciences & Educational Studies* 5, no. 4. https://doi.org/10.23918/ijsses.v5i4p22.

Brajković, Jelena, and Lidija Dokić. 2014. "Identity of New Media Spaces." In *Places and Technologies 2014: Proceedings of the First International Academic Conference on Places and Technologies*. 388–99. Belgrade: University of Belgrade.

Braylock, Jonathan, Jarah Milligan, and James III. 2015–Present. *Black Men Can't Jump (In Hollywood)*. Podcast. MP3 audio. https://foreverdogpodcasts.com/podcasts/black-men-cant-jump-in-hollywood/.

Brems, Eva. 1997. "Enemies or Allies? Feminism and Cultural Relativism as Dissident Voices in Human Rights Discourse." *Human Rights Quarterly* 19, no. 1: 136–64.

Briggs, Ryan C., and Scott Weathers. 2016. "Gender and Location in African Politics Scholarship: The Other White Man's Burden?" *African Affairs* 115, no. 460: 466–89.

Broadband Commission. 2018. *The State of Broadband 2016: Broadband Catalyzing Sustainable Development*. Geneva Switzerland: Broadband Commission for Sustainable Development.

Brown, Wendy. 2015. *Undoing the Demos: Neoliberalism's Stealth Revolution*. New York: Zone Books.

Brunsma, David L., Eric S. Brown, and Peggy Placier. 2012. "Teaching Race at Historically White Colleges and Universities: Identifying and Dismantling the Walls of Whiteness." *Critical Sociology* 39, no. 5: 717–38.

Brunt, Shelley. 2021. "Our 'Stay Home' Music Video: The Collision of Academic Research and Family Life During COVID-19 Lockdown in Melbourne, Australia." *Journal of Children and Media* 15, no. 1: 21–24. https://doi.org/10.1080/17482798.2020.1858436.

Brunt, Shelley, and Liz Giuffre. 2020a. "Nardi Simpson." *Music Mothers and Others*. October 19, 2020. Podcast. MP3 Audio, 30:03, https://musicmothersandothers.com/nardi-simpson/.

———. 2020b. "Something For Kate—Stephanie Ashworth and Paul Dempsey." *Music Mothers and Others*. December 1, 2020. Podcast. MP3 audio, 26:03. https://musicmothersandothers.com/something-for-kate-stephanie-ashworth-and-paul-dempsey/.

———. 2020c. "Heidi Braithwaite." *Music Mothers and Others*. November 9, 2020. Podcast. MP3 audio, 28:47. https://musicmothersandothers.com/heidi-braithwaite-2/.

———. 2020d. "Virginia Hanlon Grohl – Archive Special." *Music Mothers and Others*. November 17, 2020. Podcast, MP3 audio. https://musicmothersandothers.com/virginia-hanlon-grohl/.

———. 2020e. "Alexandra Plim – Hot Dub Time Machine." *Music Mothers and Others*. September 27, 2020. Podcast, MP3 audio. https://musicmothersandothers.com/alexandra-plim-hot-dub-time-machine/.

———. 2020f. "Andrew P Street." *Music Mothers and Others*. September 20, 2020f. Podcast, MP3 audio. https://musicmothersandothers.com/andrew-p-street.

———. 2020g. "Koko – Regurgitator's Pogogoshow." *Music Mothers and Others*. October 11, 2020. Podcast, MP3 audio. https://musicmothersandothers.com/koko-from-regurgitators-pogogoshow.

———. 2020h. "Chris Carey." *Music Mothers and Others*. December 20, 2020. Podcast, MP3 audio. https://musicmothersandothers.com/chris-carey/.

———. 2021a. "The Soul Movers—Lizzie Mack and Murray Cook." *Music Mothers and Others*. June 29, 2021. Podcast. MP3 audio, 26:42. https://musicmothersandothers.com/soul-movers-lizzie-mack-and-murray-cook/.

———. 2021b. "Shevonne Hunt." *Music Mothers and Others*. May 3, 2021. Podcast. MP3 audio, 2:30. https://musicmothersandothers.com/shevonne-hunt/.

———. 2023. *Popular Music and Parenting*. London: Routledge.

Bryans Bongey, Sarah, Gerald Cizadlo, and Lynn Kalnbach. 2006. "Explorations in Coursecasting: Podcasts in Higher Education." *Campus-Wide Information Systems* 23, no. 5: 350–67. https://doi.org/10.1108/10650740610714107.

Burnell, Carol, Jaime Wood, Monique Babin, Susan Pesznecker, and Nicole Rosevear. n.d. "What Is a Text?" Accessed December 7, 2021. https://openoregon.pressbooks.pub/wrd/chapter/what-is-a-text/.

Bury, Rhiannon. 2017. "'We're not there': Fans, Fan Studies, and the Participatory Continuum." In *The Routledge Companion to Media Fandom*, edited by Mia Lindgren and Jason Loviglio, 123–31. London and New York: Routledge.

Bussandri, Sara. 2020. "Why Publishing Your Podcast Transcripts Is *bad* Customer Experience." *Digital Content Writer* (blog). February 14, 2020. https://sarabussandri.com/publishing-your-podcast-transcripts-is-bad-customer-service/.

Butler, Jan. 2013. "Album Art and Posters: Psychedelic Interplay of Rock Art and Art Rock." In *The Routledge Companion to Music and Visual Culture*, edited by Tim Shephard and Anne Leonard. London, United Kingdom: Taylor & Francis Group. http://ebookcentral.proquest.com/lib/ryerson/detail.action?docID=1331856.

Butler, Judith. 1990a. *Gender Trouble: Feminism and the Subversion of Identity*. New York: Routledge.

———. 1990b. "Gender trouble, feminist theory, and psychoanalytic discourse." *Feminism/Postmodernism* 327: x.

Buzzsprout. 2022. "Podcast Statistics and Data [January 2022]." Buzzsprout. Accessed January 27, 2022. https://www.buzzsprout.com/blog/podcast-statistics.

Cabrera, Alberto F., Amaury Nora, Patrick T. Terenzini, Ernest Pascarella, and Linda Serra Hagedorn. 1999. "Campus Racial Climate and the Adjustment of Students to College: A Comparison Between White Students and African-American Students." *Journal of Higher Education* 70, no. 2: 134–60.

Callison, Candis, and Mary Lynn Young. 2019. *Reckoning: Journalism's Limits and Possibilities*. Oxford: Oxford University Press.

Campbell, Gardner. 2005. "There's Something in the Air: Podcasting in Education." *Educause Review* 40, no. 6: 32–47.

Campbell, Tanner. 2021. "Using RSS to Solve the Problems Facing Podcasters Today Is Like Using HTML to Catch a Fish." Medium. July 13, 2021. https://medium.com/tannerhelps/using-rss-to-solve-the-problems-facing-podcasters-today-is-like-using-html-to-catch-a-fish-a674fc0317c7.

Candy, Linda. 2006. "Practice Based Research: A Guide." *CCS Report* 1, no. 2: 1–19.

Cante, Fabien. 2015. "Place-Making, Media Practices and Orientations. Exploratory Connections Between Communication Geography and Sara Ahmed's Critical Phenomenology." *Sociologica*, no. 3 (2015). https://doi.org/10.2383/82479.

Canvas. 2020. "State of Student Success and Engagement in Higher Education." Canvas. Accessed June 29, 2021. https://www.instructure.com/canvas/resources/ebooks/student-success-engagement-higher-education-research-study-trends.

Caplan-Bricker, Nora. 2016. "The Podcast That Tells Ingeniously Boring Bedtime Stories to Help You Fall Asleep." *The New Yorker*, June 11, 2016. https://www.newyorker.com/culture/culture-desk/the-podcast-that-tells-ingeniously-boring-bedtime-stories-to-help-you-fall-asleep.

Cardinal, Harold and Walter Hildebrand. *Treaty Elders of Saskatchewan: Our Dream Is That Our Peoples Will One Day Be Clearly Recognized As Nations*. Calgary, AB: University of Calgary Press, 1973.

Carpenter, Julia. 2017. "This Podcast Is So Boring It Puts People to Sleep. And That's Why Insomniacs Love It." *Washington Post*, February 14, 2017. https://www.washingtonpost.com/news/the-intersect/wp/2017/02/14/this-podcast-is-so-boring-it-puts-people-to-sleep-and-thats-why-insomniacs-love-it/.

Carvalho, Ana A., Cristina Aguiar, Henrique Santos, Lia Oliveira, Aldina Marques, and Romana Maciel. 2009. "Podcasts in Higher Education: Students' and Lecturers' Perspectives." In *Education and Technology for a Better World. WCCE 2009. IFIP Advances in Information and Communication Technology* 302. Berlin: Springer. https://link.springer.com/chapter/10.1007/978-3-642-03115-1_44.

Castellano, Marlene Brant. 2000. "Updating Aboriginal Traditions of Knowledge." In *Indigenous Knowledges in Global Contexts*, edited by George J. Sefa Dei, Dorothy Goldin Rosenberg, and Budd L. Hall, 21–36. Toronto: University of Toronto Press.

Cavarero, Adriana. 2015. *For More Than One Voice: Toward a Philosophy of Vocal Expression*. Redwood City: Stanford University Press.

CBC. 2018. "Indigenous Perspective: Podcast Created to Fill Gaps in Mainstream Media." CBC News. September 28, 2018. https://www.cbc.ca/radio/unreserved/on-the-mic-indigenous-podcasters-taking-space-and-sharing-stories-1.4841296/indigenous-perspective-podcast-created-to-fill-gaps-in-mainstream-media-1.4841297.

Chabot, Pascal. 2018. *Global Burnout*. Translated by Aliza Krefetz. London: Bloomsbury.

Chakravartty, Paula, Rachel Kuo, Victoria Grubbs, and Charlton McIlwain. 2018. "#CommunicationSoWhite." *Journal of Communication* 68, no. 2: 254–66.

Chamorro-Premuzic, Tomas, Viren Swami, and Blanka Cermakova. 2010. "Individual Differences in Music Consumption Are Predicted by Uses of Music and Age Rather than Emotional Intelligence, Neuroticism, Extraversion or Openness." *Psychology of Music* 40, no. 3: 285–300.

Chan-Olmsted, Sylvia, and Rang Wang. 2022. "Understanding Podcast Users: Consumption Motives and Behaviors." *New Media & Society* 24, no. 3: 684–704. https://doi-org.ezproxy.lib.torontomu.ca/10.1177/1461444820963776.

Chang, Grace. 2007. "Where's the Violence? The Promise and Perils of Teaching Women of Color Studies." *Black Women, Gender Families* 1, no. 1: 46–73.

Chansa, Chulu. 2021. Africana Woman Podcast. Podcast. MP3 audio. www.africanawoman.com/podcast2.

Charmaz, Kathy. 2003. "Grounded Theory: Objectivist and Constructivist Methods." In *Strategies for Qualitative Research*, Second Edition, edited by Norman K. Denzin and Yvonna S. Lincoln, 249–91. Thousand Oaks: Sage Books.

Chartable. "Sodajerker On Songwriting Podcast - Listen, Reviews, Charts." n.d. Accessed March 18, 2022. https://chartable.com/podcasts/sodajerker-on-songwriting.

Chen, Shihua. 2013. "The Responsibilities of Communication Scholars: A Political Economy Perspective." *Cultural Studies ↔ Critical Methodologies* 13, no. 5: 432–40. https://doi.org/10.1177/1532708613495802.

Chion, Michel. 1994. *Audio-Vision: Sound on Screen*. New York: Columbia University Press.

Cho, Sumi, Kimberlé Williams Crenshaw, and Leslie McCall. 2013. "Toward a Field of Intersectionality Studies: Theory, Applications, and Praxis." *Signs: Journal of Women in Culture and Society* 38, no. 4: 785–810.

Choi-Lundberg, Derek L., William A. Cuellar, and Anne-Marie M. Williams. 2016. "Online Dissection Audio-Visual Resources for Human Anatomy: Undergraduate Medical Students' Usage and Learning Outcomes." *Anatomical Sciences Education* 9, no. 6: 545–54.

Choo, Hae Yeon, and Myra Marx Ferree. 2010. "Practicing Intersectionality in Sociological Research: A Critical Analysis of Inclusions, Interactions, and Institutions in the Study of Inequalities." *Sociological Theory* 28, no. 2: 129–49.

Christidis, Yiannis, and Nico Carpentier. 2017. "Translating an Academic Text into Sound Art: An Experiment with a Communication Studies Text on Participation." In *Present Scenarios of Media Production and Engagement*, edited by Simone Tosoni et al., 207–24. Bremen: Edition Lumière.

Chuma, Sandra. 2023. "About NDINI." NDINI. www.ndini.com/about-ndini.

Chung, Mun-Young, and Hyang-Sook Kim. 2015. "College Students' Motivations for Using Podcasts." *Journal of Media Literacy Education* 7, no. 3: 13–28.

Clandinin, D. Jean, and F. Michael Connelly. 2000. *Narrative Inquiry: Experience and Story in Qualitative Research*. San Francisco: Jossey-Bass.

Clark, Alexander M. 1998. "The Qualitative-Quantitative Debate: Moving from Positivism and Confrontation to Post-Positivism and Reconciliation." *Journal of Advanced Nursing* 27, no. 6: 1242–49. https://doi.org/10.1046/j.1365-2648.1998.00651.x.

Clark, Ashley. 2019. "The Rep Report #7: Black '90s at BAM." *Film Comment Podcast*. May 1, 2019. Podcast. MP3 audio, 38:13. https://www.filmcomment.com/blog/the-film-comment-podcast-the-rep-report-7. Accessed 5/7/22.

Cleaver, Kathryn, and Mary Wild. n.d. "About." Projections Podcast. Accessed March 26, 2022. https://www.projectionspodcast.com/about-1.

Cleaver, Sarah, and Mary Wild. 2022. Email Interview. February 17, 2022.

Clevenger, Samuel M., and Oliver J. C. Rick. 2021. "The Uses of Imperfections: Communicating Affect Through the Lo Fi Podcast." *Participations: Journal of Audience & Reception Studies* 18, no. 1: 323–38.

Cobb, Maggie Colleen. 2016. "'When I Feel a Song in Me': Exploring Emotions through the Creative Songwriting Process." *Studies in Symbolic Interaction* 47: 61–79.

Cohen, Yinon, Noah Lewin-Epstein, and Amit Lazarus. 2019. "Mizrahi-Ashkenazi Educational Gaps in the Third Generation." *Research in Social Stratification and Mobility* 59: 25–33. https://doi.org/10.1016/j.rssm.2019.01.001.

Cole, Johnnetta B., and Beverly Guy-Sheftall. 2003. *Gender Talk: The Struggle for Women's Equality in African American Communities*. New York: One World.

Collins, Kathleen. 2018. "Comedian Hosts and the Demotic Turn." In *Podcasting: New Aural Cultures and Digital Media*, edited by Dario Llinares, Neil Fox, and Richard Berry, 227–50. London: Palgrave Macmillan.

Collins, Patricia Hill. 2015. "Intersectionality's Definitional Dilemmas." *Annual Review of Sociology* 41, no. 1: 1–20.

Cook, Ian M. 2020. "Critique of Podcasting as an Anthropological Method." *Ethnography*, October 20, 2020. https://doi.org/10.1177/1466138120967039.

———. 2023. *Scholarly Podcasting: Why, What, How?* London and New York: Routledge.

Copeland, Stacey. 2018a. "A Feminist Materialisation of Amplified Voice: Queering Identity and Affect in *The Heart*." In *Podcasting: New Aural Cultures and Digital Media*, edited by Dario Llinares, Neil Fox, and Richard Berry, 209–26. London: Palgrave Macmillan.

———. 2018b. "Broadcasting Queer Feminisms: Lesbian and Queer Women Programming in Transnational, Local, and Community Radio." *Journal of Radio & Audio Media* 25, no. 2: 209–23. https://doi.org/10.1080/19376529.2018.1482899.

———. 2022. "Lesbian Radio Radicals and the Queer Podcast Revolution: A Political Phenomenology of Soundwork." Ph.D. dissertation, Simon Fraser University. https://summit.sfu.ca/item/35760.

Copeland, Stacey, and Lauren Knight. 2021. "Indigenizing the National Broadcast Soundscape—CBC Podcast: *Missing and Murdered: Finding Cleo*." *Radio Journal* 19, no. 1: 101–16.

Copley, Jonathan. 2007. "Audio and Video Podcasts of Lectures for Campus-Based Students: Production and Evaluation of Student Use." *Innovations in Education and Teaching International* 44, no. 4: 387–99. https://doi.org/10.1080/14703290701602805.

Copyright Collection (Library of Congress). 2009. *Amreeka*. (Film).

Corbett, Rachel. 2018. "What Are Podcast Show Notes and Do You Need Them?" Rachel Corbett (blog). April 2, 2018. https://rachelcorbett.com.au/blog/podcast-show-notes/.

Cory, Erin, and Hugo Boothby. 2021a. *Picturing Home*. Podcast. MP3 audio. https://soundcloud.com/picturinghome.

———. 2021b. "Sounds Like 'Home': The Synchrony and Dissonance of Podcasting as Boundary Object." *Radio Journal* 19, no. 1: 117–36.

Crang, Michael, and Nigel Thrift. 2000. *Thinking Space*. London: Routledge. https://doi.org/10.4324/9780203411148

Crenshaw, Kimberlé. 1989. "Demarginalizing the Intersection of Race and Sex: A Black Feminist Critique of Antidiscrimination Doctrine, Feminist Theory and Antiracist Politics." *University of Chicago Legal Forum* 1: 139–67.

———. 1991. "Mapping the Margins: Intersectionality, Identity Politics, and Violence Against Women of Color." *Stanford Law Review* 43, no. 6: 1241–99.

———. 1995. *Critical Race Theory: The Key Writings That Formed the Movement*. New York: New Press.

———. 2015. "Why Intersectionality Can't Wait." *Washington Post*. September 24, 2015. https://www.washingtonpost.com/news/in-theory/wp/2015/09/24/why-intersectionality-cant-wait/.

Crider, David. 2023. "A Public Sphere, On-Demand: An Assessment of Local Podcasting."

Popular Communication 21, no. 1, 43–56. https://doi.org/10.1080/15405702.2022.2028157.

Crittenden, Letrell, and Antoine Haywood. 2020. "Revising Legacy Media Practices to Serve Hyperlocal Information Needs of Marginalized Populations." *Journalism Practice* 14, no. 5: 608–25.

Cronin, Blaise. 2014. "Foreword: The Penumbral World of the Paratext." In *Examining Paratextual Theory and Its Applications in Digital Culture*, by Nadine Desrochers and Daniel Apollon, xv–xix. Hershey: IGI Global. https://www.igi-global.com/pdf.aspx?tid=122526&ptid=97342&ctid=15&t=Foreword&isxn=9781466660021.

Csikszentmihalyi, Mihaly. 1990. *Flow: The Psychology of Optimal Experience*. New York: Harper & Row.

Cwynar, Christopher. 2015. "More Than a 'VCR for Radio': The CBC, the Radio 3 Podcast, and the Uses of an Emerging Medium." *Journal of Radio & Audio Media* 22, no. 2: 190–99. https://doi.org/10.1080/19376529.2015.1083371.

———. 2019. "Self-Service Media: Public Radio Personalities, Reality Podcasting, and Entrepreneurial Culture." *Popular Communication* 17, no. 4, 317–32. https://doi.org/10.1080/15405702.2019.1634811.

d'Astous, Alain, Francois Colbert, and Imene Mbarek. 2006. "Factors Influencing Readers' Interest in New Book Releases: An Experimental Study." *Poetics* 34, no. 2: 134–47. https://doi.org/10.1016/j.poetic.2005.12.001.

Davis, Bayana, and Robyn Jordan. 2017. "Episode 115 and 7/8—Dr. Ebony Elizabeth Thomas." *#WizardTeam*, produced by Black Nerds Create. November 10, 2017. Podcast. MP3 audio, 1:14:00. https://anchor.fm/wizardteam/episodes/Episode-115-and-78---Dr--Ebony-Elizabeth-Thomas-e28at9.

Davis, Julie Hirschfeld. 2018. "Trump Calls Some Unauthorized Immigrants 'Animals' in Rant." *The New York Times*, May 16, 2018. https://www.nytimes.com/2018/05/16/us/politics/trump-undocumented-immigrants-animals.html.

Davis, Kathy. 2008. "Intersectionality as Buzzword: A Sociology of Science Perspective on What Makes a Feminist Theory Successful." *Feminist Theory* 9, no. 1: 67–85.

Debord, Guy. 1957. "Report on the Construction of Situations and on the International Situationist Tendency's Conditions of Organization and Action." *Situationist International Online*, 1957. Accessed 18 June 2021. http://www.cddc.vt.edu/sionline/si/report.html.

———. 1958. "Contribution to Situationist Definition of Play." *Internationale Situationniste* 1, June 1958. *Situationist International Online*. Accessed 18 June 2021. http://www.cddc.vt.edu/sionline/si/play.html.

Dekker, Rianne, and Godfried Engbersen. 2013. "How Social Media Transform Migrant Networks and Facilitate Migration." *Global Networks* 14, no. 4: 401–18. https://doi.org/10.1111/glob.12040.

de los Ríos, Cati V. 2020. "Translingual Youth Podcasts as Acoustic Allies: Writing and Negotiating Identities at the Intersection of Literacies, Language and Racialization." *Journal of Language, Identity & Education* 21, no. 6: 378–92.

Dembo, Myron H., and Keith Howard. 2007. "Advice about the Use of Learning Styles: A Major Myth in Education." *Journal of College Reading and Learning* 37, no. 2 (Spring): 101–9.

den Drijver, Robin, and Erik Hitters. 2017. "The Business Of DIY. Characteristics, Motives and Ideologies of Micro-Independent Record Labels." *Cadernos de Arte e Antropologia* 6, no. 1: 17–35.

Dennon, Anne. 2020. "Coronavirus Deepens the Digital Divide for College Students." Best Colleges. Accessed July 6, 2021. https://www.bestcolleges.com/blog/coronavirus-deepens-the-digital-divide/.

Denzin, Norman K. 2003. *Performance Ethnography: Critical Pedagogy and the Politics of Culture*. Thousand Oaks: Sage.

Deppermann, Arnulf. 2013. "Multimodal Interaction from a Conversation Analytic Perspective." *Journal of Pragmatics* 46, no. 1: 1–7. https://doi.org/10.1016/j.pragma.2012.11.014.

de Sousa Santos, Boaventura. 2015. *Epistemologies of the South: Justice Against Epistemicide*. London and New York: Routledge.

Desrochers, Nadine, and Daniel Apollon. 2014. *Examining Paratextual Theory and Its Applications in Digital Culture*. Hershey: IGI Global. https://doi.org/10.4018/978-1-4666-6002-1.

de Wolfe, Danielle. 2020. "Best Mindfulness Podcasts 2020: Chill Out with These De-Stressing Words." ShortList. November 9, 2020. https://www.shortlist.com/lists/best-mindfulness-podcasts-402159.

Dibdin, Emma. 2021. "7 Podcasts to Soothe Your Back-to-Normal Anxiety." *The New York Times*, May 28, 2021. https://www.nytimes.com/2021/05/28/arts/podcasts-anxiety-covid.html.

Doane, Bethany, Kaitlin McCormick, and Giuliana Sorce. 2017. "Changing Methods for Feminist Public Scholarship: Lessons from Sarah Koenig's Podcast *Serial*." *Feminist Media Studies* 17, no. 1: 119–21. https://doi.org/10.1080/14680777.2017.1261465.

Dockterman, Eliana. 2021. "The 10 Best Podcasts of 2021." *Time*, December 2, 2021. https://time.com/6107375/best-podcasts-2021/.

DORA. 2013. "The Declaration on Research Assessment (DORA)." DORA. https://sfdora.org/read/.

Duarte, C. 2021. Africa Goes Digital. 2021. *Finance & Development*. March 2021. https://www.imf.org/en/Publications/fandd/issues/2021/03/africas-digital-future-after-COVID19-duarte.

Duffy, Brooke Erin. 2016. "The Romance of Work: Gender and Aspirational Labour in the Digital Culture Industries." *International Journal of Cultural Studies* 19, no. 4: 441–57.

Duffy, Brooke Erin, and Emily Hund. 2015. "'Having It All' on Social Media: Entrepreneurial Femininity and Self-Branding Among Fashion Bloggers." *Social Media and Society* 1, no. 11: 1–11.

———. 2019. "Gendered Visibility on Social Media: Navigating Instagram's Authenticity Bind." *International Journal of Communication* 13: 4983–5002. https://ijoc.org/index.php/ijoc/article/view/11729/2821.

Duffy, Brooke Erin, and Urszula Pruchniewska. 2017. "Gender and Self-Enterprise in the Social Media Age: A Digital Double Bind." *Information, Communication, and Society* 20, no. 6: 843–59.

Duffy, Brooke Erin, and Elizabeth Wissinger. 2017. "Mythologies of Creative Work in the Social Media Age: Fun, Free, and 'Just Being Me.'" *International Journal of Communication* 11: 4652–71.

Durrani, Mariam, Kevin Gotkin, and Corrina Laughlin. 2015. "*Serial*, Seriality, and the Possibilities for the Podcast Format: Visual Anthropology." *American Anthropologist* 117, no. 3: 1–4.

Edgerly, Stephanie. 2022. "Audience Sensemaking: A Mapping Approach." *Digital Journalism* 10, no. 1: 165–87.

Edirisingha, Palitha, and Gilly Salmon. 2007. "Pedagogical Models for Podcasts in Higher Education." Paper presented at the Beyond Distance Research Alliance Conference, University of Leicester.

Edison Research. 2020. "Super Listeners 2020." Edison Research. https://www.edisonresearch.com/super-listeners-2020/.

———. 2022. "Super Listeners 2021." Edison Research. https://www.edisonresearch.com/wp-content/uploads/2022/02/Super-Listeners-from-Edison-Research-and-Ad-Results-Media-2-16-22.pdf.

Edison Research and Triton Digital. 2019. "The Infinite Dial 2019." http://www.edisonresearch.com/wp-content/uploads/2019/03/Infinite-Dial-2019-PDF-1.pdf.

Ehrick, Christine. 2015. *Radio and the Gendered Soundscape: Women and Broadcasting in Argentina and Uruguay, 1930–1950*. New York: Cambridge University Press.

Eichhorn, Kate, and Heather Milne. 2016. "Labours of Love and Cutting Remarks: The Affective Economies of Editing." In *Editing as Cultural Practice in Canada*, edited by Dean Irvine, 189–98. Waterloo: Wilfrid Laurier University Press.

Eidsheim, Nina Sun. 2015. *Sensing Sound: Singing and Listening as Vibrational Practice*. Durham: Duke University Press.

Eldridge, Richard. 2014. "Art and Emotion." In *An Introduction to the Philosophy of Art*, 200–24. Cambridge: Cambridge University Press.

Elliott, Patricia W. 2016. *Decolonizing the Media: Challenges and Obstacles on the Road to Reconciliation*. Ottawa: Canadian Centre for Policy Alternatives.

Ellis, Carolyn, and Arthur P. Bochner. 2000. "Autoethnography, Personal Narrative, Reflexivity: Researcher as Subject." *Handbook of Qualitative Research*, 2nd edition, edited by Norman K. Denzin and Yvonne S. Lincoln, 733–69. Thousand Oaks: Sage.

Elson, Ruth Miller. 1964. *Guardians of Tradition: American Schoolbooks of the Nineteenth Century*. Lincoln: University of Nebraska Press.

England, Kim. 1994. "Getting Personal: Reflexivity, Positionality, and Feminist Research." *The Professional Geographer* 46, no. 1: 80–89.

Espinoza-Gonzalez, Daniel, Kristen B. French, Stephanie Gallardo, Ethan Glemaker, Saraswati Noel, Michelle Marsura, Elaine Mehary, Nadia Saldaña-Spiegle, Brendan Schimpf, and Chelsea Thaw. 2014. "Decolonizing the Classroom through Critical Consciousness: Navigating Solidarity *En La Lucha* for Mexican American Studies." *The Educational Forum* 78, no. 1 (winter): 54–67.

Euritt, Alyn. 2020. "*Within the Wires*' Intimate Fan-Based Publics." *Gender Forum* 77: 34–50.

———. 2023. *Podcasting as an Intimate Medium*. Oxfordshire: Taylor & Francis.

Evans, Adrienne, and Mafalda Stasi. 2014. "Desperately Seeking Methodology: New Directions in Fan Studies Research." *Participations: Journal of Audience & Reception Studies* 11, no. 2: 4–23.

"Exploring the New Standard for Podcast RSS Feeds." 2021. Podcastpage.io. April 8, 2021. https://podcastpage.io/exploring-the-new-standard-for-podcast-rss-feeds/.

Ezarik, M. 2021. "How COVID-19 Damaged Student Success." Inside Higher Education. June 21, 2021. https://www.insidehighered.com/news/2021/06/21/what-worked-and-what-didn%E2%80%99t-college-students-learning-through-covid-19

Fairchild, Charles. 2012. *Music, Radio and the Public Sphere*. London: Palgrave Macmillan.

Fakeye, D. O., R. F. Adebile, and T. Eyengho. 2015. "Participation in Literary Club Activities and Literature Instruction in a Dynamic and Evolving Society." *International Journal of Educational Research Technology* 6, no. 3: 65–69.

Fannin, Mike. 2020. "The Truth in Black and White: An Apology from the *Kansas City Star*." *The Kansas City Star*. December 22, 2020. https://www.kansascity.com/news/local/article247928045.html.

Fariello, Megan. 2019. "Mediating the 'Upside Down': the Techno-Historical Acoustic in Netflix's *Stranger Things* and *The Black Tapes* podcast." *Sound Studies* 5, no. 2, 122–39. https://doi.org/10.1080/20551940.2019.1587581.

Fauzi, H. A., K. Komalasari, and Y. Malik. 2017. Utilization of Audio Visual Media to Improve Student Learning Result in IPS Learning (Classroom Action Research in Class VII C SMP Negeri 7 Bandung). Social Science Education Studies Program, FPIPS, Indonesian University of Education.

Feld, Martin. 2019. "1. Indexed Five Ways!" *Lounge Ruminator*. September 24, 2019. Podcast. MP3 audio, 08:05. https://loungeruminator.net/2019/09/24/1-indexed-five-ways/.

———. 2020. "45. A Ticking Clock." *Lounge Ruminator*. September 27, 2020. Podcast. MP3 audio, 14:04. https://loungeruminator.net/2020/09/27/45-a-ticking-clock/.

Fendler, Rachel. 2013. "Becoming-Learner: Coordinates for Mapping the Space and Subject of Nomadic Pedagogy." *Qualitative Inquiry* 19, no. 10: 786–93. https://doi.org/10.1177/1077800413503797.

Fernandez, V., J. M. Sallan and P. Simo. 2015. "Past, Present, and Future of Podcasting in Higher Education." In *Exploring Learning & Teaching in Higher Education*, edited by Mang Li and Yong Zhao, 305–30. Berlin: Springer.

Fernández Collins, Elena. "The Deca Tapes—Lex Noteboom." *Radio Drama Revival*. April 21, 2021. Podcast. MP3 audio, 1:12:55. https://radiodramarevival.com/the-deca-tapes-lex-noteboom/.

Fisher, Dana R., and Larry Michael Wright. 2001. "On Utopias and Dystopias: Toward an Understanding of the Discourse Surrounding the Internet." *Journal of Computer-Mediated Communication* 6, no. 2.

Fisher, Danny. 2010. "Frozen Yoga and McMindfulness: Miles Neale on the Mainstreaming of Contemplative Religious Practices." Lion's Roar. December 15, 2010. https://www.lionsroar.com/frozen-yoga-and-mcmindfulness-miles-neale-on-the-mainstreaming-of-contemplative-religious-practices/.

Fischer, Mary Jane. 2007. "Settling into Campus Life: Differences by Race/Ethnicity in College Involvement and Outcomes." *Journal of Higher Education* 78, no. 1: 125–61.

Flores, Nelson, Tatyana Kleyn, and Kate Menken. 2015. "Looking Holistically in a Climate of Partiality: Identities of Students Labeled Long-Term English Language Learners." *Journal of Language, Identity & Education* 14, no. 2 (spring): 113–32.

Florini, Sarah. 2015. "The Podcast 'Chitlin' Circuit': Black Podcasters, Alternative Media, and Audio Enclaves." *Journal of Radio & Audio Media* 22, no. 2: 209–19.

———. 2019. *Beyond Hashtags: Racial Politics and Black Digital Networks*. New York: New York University Press.

———. 2020. "Podcasting Blackness." In *Race and Media: Critical Approaches*, edited by Lori Kido Lopez, 153–62. New York: New York University Press.

Forbes, David. 2019. *Mindfulness and Its Discontents: Education, Self, and Social Transformation*. Black Point: Fernwood Publishing.

Fournier, Lauren. 2021. *Autotheory as Feminist Practice in Art, Writing, and Criticism*. Cambridge: MIT Press.

Foussianes, Chloe. 2020. "10 Podcasts to Help You Fall Asleep." *Town & Country*, May 29, 2020. https://www.townandcountrymag.com/leisure/arts-and-culture/g32701236/best-podcasts-for-sleep/.

Fox, Kim, David O. Dowling, and Kyle Miller. 2020. "A Curriculum for Blackness: Podcasts as Discursive Cultural Guides, 2010–2020." *Journal of Radio & Audio Media* 27, no. 2: 298–318.

Fox, Kim, and Yasmeen Ebada. 2022. "Egyptian Female Podcasters: Shaping Feminist Identities." *Learning, Media and Technology* 47, no. 1: 53–64. https://doi.org/10.1080/17439884.2021.2020286.

Fox, Matthew P., Kareem Carr, Lucy D'Agostino McGowan, Eleanor J. Murray, Bertha Hidalgo, and Hailey R. Banack. 2021. "Will Podcasting and Social Media Replace Journals and Traditional Science Communication? No, but…" *American Journal of Epidemiology* 190, no. 8: 1625–31.

Fox, Neil, and Dario Llinares. 2018. "Cinematologists: Knowing Sounds." *Media Practice and Education* 19, no. 1: 48–51. https://doi.org/10.1080/14682753.2017.1362170.

Franklin, Bob, and Donica Mensing, eds. 2010. *Journalism Education, Training and Employment*. New York and London: Routledge.

Freire, Paulo. 2017. *Pedagogy of the Oppressed*. New York: Continuum.

———. 2002. *Education for Critical Consciousness*. New York: Continuum.

Frouws, Bram, Melissa Phillips, Ashraf Hassan, and Mirjam Twigt. 2016. "Getting to Europe the Watts App Way: The use of ICT in contemporary mixed migration flows to Europe." Danish Refugee Council and Regional Mixed Migration Secretariat. June 2016. https://mixedmigration.org/wp-content/uploads/2018/05/015_getting-to-europe.pdf.

Fryer, Wesley. 2005. "Podcasting as Disruptive Transmediation." In *E-Learn: World Conference on E-Learning in Corporate, Government, Healthcare, and Higher Education*. San Diego: Association for the Advancement of Computing in Education. https://www.learntechlib.org/primary/p/21140/.

Furlonge, Nicole Brittingham. 2018. *Race Sounds: The Art of Listening in African American Literature*. Chicago: University of Iowa Press.

Gallagher, Michael. 2016. "Sound as Affect: Difference, Power, Spatiality." *Emotion, Space and Society* 20: 42–48.

Garcia, Sonia, and Kate Barclay. 2020. *Adapting Research Methodologies in the COVID-19 Pandemic: Resources for Researchers*, 2nd edition. Sydney and Seattle: University of Technology Sydney and Nippon Foundation Ocean Nexus at EarthLab, University of Washington.

García-Marín, David. 2020. "Mapping the Factors that Determine Engagement in Podcasting: Design from the Users and Podcasters' Experience." *Communication and Society* 33, no. 2: 49–63. https://doi.org/10.15581/003.33.2.49-63.

Gaudet, Janice Cindy. 2019. "Keeoukaywin: The Visiting Way—Fostering an Indigenous Research Methodology." *Aboriginal Policy Studies* 7, no. 2: 47–64.

Gaudry, Adam J. P. 2011. "Insurgent Research." *Wicazo Sa Review* 26, no. 1: 113–36.

Geiger, R. Stuart, and Airi Lampinen. 2014. "Old Against New, or a Coming of Age? Broadcasting in an Era of Electronic Media." *Journal of Broadcasting & Electronic Media* 58, no. 3: 333–41.

Genette, Gérard. 1997. *Paratexts: Thresholds of Interpretation.* Translated by Jane E. Lewin. Cambridge: Cambridge University Press. https://doi.org/10.1017/CBO9780511549373.

Genova, Elena, and Elisabetta Zontini. 2020. "Liminal Lives: Navigating In-Betweenness in the Case of Bulgarian and Italian Migrants in Brexiting Britain." *Central and Eastern European Migration Review* 9, no. 1: 47–64.

Gerbner, George, and Larry Gross. 1976. "Living with Television: The Violence Profile." *Journal of Communication* 26, no. 2: 172–99. https://doi.org/10.1111/j.1460-2466.1976.tb01397.x.

Giles, Howard, Pamela Wilson, and Anthony Conway. 1981. "Accent and Lexical Diversity as Determinants of Impression Formation and Perceived Employment Suitability." *Language Sciences* 3, no. 1: 91–103.

Gillespie, Marie, Lawrence Peter Ampofo, Margie Cheesman, Becky Faith, Evgenia Illiou, Ali Issa, Souad Osserian, and Dimitris Skleparis. 2016. *Mapping Refugee Media Journeys: Smartphones and Social Media Networks.* Research report. The Open University and France Médias Monde. Accessed June 15, 2021.

Giuffre, Liz. 2013. "Top of the Tots: The Wiggles as Australia's Most Successful (Under-Acknowledged) Sound Media Export." *Media International Australia* 148, no. 1: 145–54. https://doi.org/10.1177/1329878x1314800116.

———. 2020. "Are We All 'BBC Dad' Now? What Covid-19 Restrictions Reveal about Comedy, Class, Paid Work, Parenting and Gender." *Journal of Working-Class Studies* 5, no. 1: 142–56. https://doi.org/10.13001/jwcs.v5i1.6265.

———. 2021a. "Bluey, Requestival, Play School and ME@Home: The ABC (Kids) of Communication Cultures during Lockdown." *Media International Australia* 176, no. 1: 63–76. https://doi.org/10.1177/1329878x20952520.

———. 2021b. "Handwashing Hits—Getting Cross-Generational Listeners to Rock during the Pandemic." *Rock Music Studies* 8, no. 1: 1–13. https://doi.org/10.1080/19401159.2020.1852771.

———. 2022. "Lessons on Popular Music Form, Creation and Reception through the *Song Exploder* podcast." *Radio Journal* 20, no. 1: 49–64.

Goffman, Erving. 1974. *Frame Analysis: An Essay on the Organization of Experience.* Cambridge: Harvard University Press.

Goldberg, Susan. 2018. "For Decades, Our Coverage Was Racist." *National Geographic,* March 13, 2018. Accessed January 7, 2022. https://www.nationalgeographic.co.uk/2018/03/decades-our-coverage-was-racist-rise-above-our-past-we-must-acknowledge-it.

Golding, Sarah, and Fiona Thraille. 2017a. "103—Audio Drama and Work/Life Balance." *Audio Drama Production Podcast.* January 25, 2017. Podcast. MP3 audio, 45:00. https://www.stitcher.com/show/audio-drama-production-podcast/episode/103-audio-drama-work-life-balance-49042563.

———. 2017b. "107—Business Models for Audio Drama." *Audio Drama Production Podcast.* March 28, 2017. Podcast. MP3 audio, 60:15. https://www.stitcher.com/show/audio-drama-production-podcast/episode/107-business-models-for-audio-drama-49576991.

Goldstein, Steve. 2018. "How Many of the 540,000 Podcasts Have 'Podfaded?'" Amplfi Media (blog). https://www.amplifimedia.com/blogstein-1/2018/8/22/how-many-of-the-550000-podcasts-are-actually-active.

Gordon, Avery F. 2008. *Ghostly Matters: Haunting and the Sociological Imagination.* Minneapolis: University of Minnesota Press.

Goriunova, Olga. 2011. *Art Platforms and Cultural Production on the Internet.* London: Taylor & Francis.

Grand View Research. 2021. "Podcasting Market Size, Share & Trends Analysis Report by
     Genre (News & Politics, Society & Culture, Comedy, Sports), by Format (Interviews,
     Panels, Solo, Conversational), by Region, and Segment Forecasts, 2021–2028." Grand
     View Research. https://www.grandviewresearch.com/industry-analysis/podcast-
     market.
"Graphic Design Trends." n.d. 99designs. Accessed December 12, 2021. https://99designs.
     ca/blog/trends/.
Gray, Colin. 2020. "Podcast Show Notes: The Potent Audience Growth Tool You're Under
     Using." The Podcast Host. November 3, 2020. https://www.thepodcasthost.com/
     websites-hosting/creating-great-podcast-shownotes/.
Gray, Jonathan. 2010. *Show Sold Separately: Promos, Spoilers, and Other Media Paratexts*.
     New York: New York University Press.
Greb, Fabian, Wolff Schlotz, and Jochen Steffens. 2018. "Personal and Situational
     Influences on the Functions of Music Listening." *Psychology of Music* 46, no. 6:
     763–94.
Green, Terrance. 2016. "From Positivism to Critical Theory: School-Community Relations
     Toward Community Equity Literacy." *International Journal of Qualitative Studies in
     Education* 30, no. 4: 370–87.
Greene, Seth. 2016. *Market Domination for Podcasting: Secrets from the World's Top
     Podcasters*. New York: Morgan James Publishing.
Gregg, Melissa. 2018. *Counterproductive: Time Management in the Knowledge Economy*.
     Durham: Duke University Press.
Gruber, John. 2022. The Talk Show. Podcast, Website. https://daringfireball.net/
     thetalkshow/.
The Guardian. 2022. "From *The Ranting Atheist* to *I Like Girls*: The Best African
     Podcasts." *The Guardian*. April 12, 2022. https://www.theguardian.com/global-
     development/2022/apr/12/the-best-african-podcasts.
Guay, Frédéric, Herbert W. Marsh, and Michel Boivin. 2003. "Academic Self-Concept and
     Academic Achievement: Developmental Perspectives on Their Causal Ordering."
     Journal of Educational Psychology 95, no. 1 (spring): 124–36.
Gumbs, Alexis Pauline. 2020. *Undrowned: Black Feminist Lessons from Marine Mammals*.
     Chico: AK Press.
Gunderson, J.L., and T.M. Cumming. 2022. "Podcasting in Higher Education as
     a Component of Universal Design for Learning: A Systematic Review of the
     Literature." *Innovations in Education and Teaching International* 60, no. 4: 591–601.
Gutsche, Robert. E., Jr., 2015. *Media Control: News as an Institution of Power and Social
     Control*. New York and London: Bloomsbury.
———. 2020. "Are Journalism Academics Worth a Listen? The New Podcast Says Yes."
     Poynter Institute. September 22, 2020. https://www.poynter.org/educators-
     students/2020/are-journalism-academics-worth-a-listen-this-new-podcast-says-yes.
———. 2021. "Critical Theory and Being Critical: Connections and Contradictions." *Media
     and Communication* 9, no. 2: 86–87.
Gutsche, Robert E., Jr., Xinhe Cong, Feihong Pan, Yiyi Sun, and LaTasha DeLoach. 2022.
     "#DiminishingDiscrimination: The Symbolic Annihilation of Race and Racism in
     News Hashtags of 'Calling 911 on Black People.'" *Journalism* 23, no. 1: 259–77.
Gutsche, Robert E., Jr., and Juliet Pinto. 2022. "Covering Synergistic Effects of Climate
     Change: Global Challenges for Journalism." *Journalism Practice* 16, no. 2–3: 237–43.
Hadwan, Leela. 2018. "Memorization Isn't Student Intelligence." *Energy Convertors*.
     Medium. Accessed March 11, 2022. https://medium.com/energy-convertors/this-
     is-a-message-to-all-teachers-stop-relying-on-memorization-to-determine-your-
     students-34cca2c2e328.
Haelewaters, Danny, Tina A. Hofmann, and Adrianna L. Romero-Olivares. 2021. "Ten
     Simple Rules for Global North Researchers to Stop Perpetuating Helicopter Research
     in the Global South." *PLoS Computational Biology* 17, no. 8, e1009277.
Hagood, Mack. 2021. "The Scholarly Podcast: Form and Function in Audio Academia."
     In *Saving New Sounds: Podcast Preservation and Historiography*, edited by Jeremy
     Wade Morris and Eric Hoyt, 181–94. Ann Arbor: University of Michigan Press.

Hamilton, Chel. 2022. "5 Minute Evening (or 'Letting Go') Meditation." *Meditation Minis*. February 14, 2022. Podcast, MP3 audio, 7:02. https://podcasts.apple.com/us/podcast/5-minute-evening-or-letting-go-meditation/id963597166?i=1000550989061.

Hamilton, Craig, and Simon Barber. 2022. "Rate and Review: Exploring Listener Motivations for Engagement with Music Podcasts." *Radio Journal* 20, no. 1: 17–32.

Han, Byung-Chul. 2015. *The Burnout Society*. Translated by Erik Butler. Stanford: Stanford University Press.

———. 2017a. *Pyschopolitics: Neoliberalism and New Technologies of Power*. Translated by Erik Butler. New York: Verso.

———. 2017b. *The Scent of Time*. Translated by Daniel Steuer. Cambridge: Polity.

———. 2021. *Capitalism and the Death Drive*. Translated by Daniel Steuer. Cambridge: Polity.

Hancock, Ange-Marie. 2016. *Intersectionality: An Intellectual History*. Oxford: Oxford University Press.

Hanlon Grohl, Virginia. 2017. *From Cradle to Stage: Stories from the Mothers Who Rocked and Raised Rock Stars*. UK: Coronet/Hatchette Books.

Hanna, Aoife. 2019. "These ASMR Podcasts and Videos Could Help Make Sleep Struggles a Thing of the Past." *Bustle*, March 16, 2019. https://www.bustle.com/p/the-best-asmr-for-sleep-because-these-podcasts-youtube-vids-are-super-satisfying-to-drift-off-to-16959189.

Hanna, Karen Buenavista. 2019. "Pedagogies in the Flesh: Building an Anti-Racist Decolonized Classroom." *Frontiers: A Journal of Women Studies* 40, no. 1: 229–44.

Hannerz, Ulf. 1992. *Cultural Complexity: Studies in the Social Organization of Meaning*. New York: Columbia University Press.

Hansal, Sophie, and Marianne Gunderson. 2020. "Toward a Fannish Methodology: Affect as an Asset." *Transformative Works and Cultures* 33. https://doi.org/10.3983/twc.2020.1747.

Hansen, Samuel. 2021. "The Feed is the Thing: How RSS Defined PodcastRE and Why Podcasts May Need to Move On." In *Saving New Sounds: Podcast Preservation and Historiography*, edited by Jeremy Wade Morris and Eric Hoyt, 195–207. Ann Arbor: University of Michigan Press.

Hanson, Aubrey Jean. 2020. *Literatures, Communities, and Learning: Conversations with Indigenous Writers*. Waterloo: Wilfrid Laurier University Press.

Haraway, D. 1998. "The Persistence of Vision." In *The Visual Culture Reader*, edited by Nicholas Mirzoeff, 677–84. London: Routledge.

Harp, Rick, Candis Callison, and Mary Lynn Young. 2020. "Value and Values in the Interstices of Journalism and Journalism Studies: An Interview with Candis Callison and Mary Lynn Young." *Sociologica* 14, no. 2: 235–47.

Harper, Hilary, and Michael Mackenzie. 2020. "Bedtime Stories for Adults." *Life Matters*. October 6, 2020. Podcast. MP3 audio, 15:20. https://www.abc.net.au/radionational/programs/lifematters/bedtime-stories-for-adults/12733554.

Harris, Jasmine. 2019. "Podcast Talk and Public Sociology: Teaching Critical Race Discourse Participation through Podcast Production." *About Campus: Enriching the Student Learning Experience* 24, no. 3 (summer): 16–20.

Harris, Jess, Kathleen Smithers, and Nerida Spina. 2020. "More than 70% of Academics at Some Universities Are Casuals. They're Losing Work and Are Cut Out of JobKeeper." The Conversation. May 15, 2020. https://theconversation.com/more-than-70-of-academics-at-some-universities-are-casuals-theyre-losing-work-and-are-cut-out-of-jobkeeper-137778.

Hartmann, Tilo. 2017. "Parasocial interaction, parasocial relationships, and well-being." *The Routledge Handbook of Media Use and Well-Being: International Perspectives on Theory and Research on Positive Media Effects* edited by L. Reinecke and M.B. Oliver, 131–44. Routledge/Taylor & Francis Group.

Hartsock, Nancy C. M. 1998. *The Feminist Standpoint Revisited and Other Essays*. Boulder: Westview Press.

Hatuqa, Dalia. 2021. "Recasting the Way Muslims Are Seen, One Actor at a Time." *The Washington Post*, May 7, 2021. https://www.washingtonpost.com/religion/2021/05/07/muslims-stereotypes-casting/.

Hausmann, Leslie R., Feifei Ye, Janet Ward Schofield, and Rochelle L. Woods. 2009. "Sense of Belonging and Persistence in White and African-American First-Year Students." *Research in Higher Education* 50, no. 1: 649–69.

Heeremans, Lieven. 2018. "Podcast Networks: Syndicating Production Culture." In *Podcasting: New Aural Cultures and Digital Media*, edited by Dario Llinares, Neil Fox, and Richard Berry, 57–79. London: Palgrave Macmillan.

Heider, Don. 2014. *White News: Why Local News Programs Don't Cover People of Color*. New York: Routledge.

Heilesen, Simon B. 2010. "What Is the Academic Efficacy Of Podcasting?" *Computers & Education* 55, no. 3: 1063–68.

Henderson, Stephen, and Karl Spracklen. 2017. "'If I Had My Way, I'd Have Been a Killer': Songwriting And Its Motivations For Leisure And Work." *Leisure/Loisir* 41, no. 2: 231–47.

Herbert, Daniel, Amanda D. Lotz, and Aswin Punathambekar. 2020. *Media Industry Studies*. Cambridge: Polity.

Hernandez, Patricia. 2018a. "The Twitch Streamers Who Spend Years Broadcasting to No One." *The Verge*. https://www.theverge.com/2018/7/16/17569520/twitch-streamers-zero-viewers-motivation-community.

———. 2018b. "YouTube is failing its creators." The Verge. https://www.theverge.com/2018/9/21/17879652/youtube-creator-youtuber-burnout-problem

Hesmondhalgh, David. 2002. *The Cultural Industries*. London: Sage.

Hess, Kristy, and Gutsche Jr, Robert. 2017. "Journalism and the "Social Sphere": Reclaiming a foundational concept for beyond politics and the public sphere." *Journalism Studies*, 19: 1–16. https://doi.org/10.1080/1461670X.2017.1389296.

Hetsroni, Amir. 2004. "The Millionaire Project: A Cross-Cultural Analysis of Quiz Shows from the United States, Russia, Poland, Norway, Finland, Israel, and Saudi Arabia." *Mass Communication and Society* 7, no. 2: 133–56. https://doi.org/10.1207/s15327825mcs0702_1.

———. 2005. "The Quiz Show as a Cultural Mirror: Who Wants to be a Millionaire in the English-Speaking World." *Atlantic Journal of Communication* 13, no. 2: 97–112. https://doi.org/10.1207/s15456889ajc1302_3.

Hill Collins, Patricia. 2009. *Another Kind of Public Education: Race, Schools, the Media, and Democratic Possibilities*. Boston: Beacon Press.

Hills, Matt. 2002. *Fan Cultures*. New York: Routledge.

Hilmes, Michele. 2022. "But Is It Radio? New Forms and Voices in the Audio Private Sphere." In *The Routledge Companion to Radio and Podcast Studies*, edited by Mia Lindgren and Jason Loviglio, 408–17. London and New York: Routledge.

Hilton, Nick. 2021. "Why Does Podcast Advertising Feel Different?" *Pod Culture* (blog). August 20, 2021. https://medium.com/pod-culture/why-does-podcast-advertising-feel-different-8fa340bf3959.

Hodapp, James. 2020. "Talking Books: The Paratextuality of African Literary Podcasts." *English Studies in Africa* 63, no. 2: 123–34. https://doi.org/10.1080/00138398.2020.1852707.

Hogan. Mél. 2008. "Dykes on Mykes: Podcasting and the Activist Archive." *TOPIA: Canadian Journal of Cultural Studies* 20: 199–215.

hooks, bell. 1989. *Talking Back: Thinking Feminist, Thinking Black*. New York: South End Press.

———. 2000. *Feminism Is for Everybody: Passionate Politics*. Cambridge: South End Press.

———. 2015. *Feminism Is for Everybody: Passionate Politics*, 2nd Edition. New York: Routledge.

Horváth, Ágnes. 2013. *Modernism and Charisma*. London: Palgrave Macmillan.

Horváth, Ágnes, Bjørn Thomassen, and Harald Wydra. 2009. "Introduction: Liminality and Cultures of Change." *International Political Anthropology* 2, no. 1: 3–4.

Howes, David, ed. 1996. *Cross-Cultural Consumption: Global Markets, Local Realities*. London and New York: Routledge.

"How to Write a Podcast Description That Gets You Listeners." 2021. *Captivate Unlimited Podcast Hosting & Analytics*. May 21, 2021. https://www.captivate.fm/blog/podcast-description/.

Hoydis, Julia. 2020. "Introduction: New Waves—Feminism, Gender, and Podcast Studies." *Gender Forum: An Internet Journal for Gender Studies* 77: 1–12.

Hoyt, Eric. 2021. "Saving Podcasting's Contexts." In *Saving New Sounds: Podcast Preservation and Historiography*, edited by Jeremy Wade Morris and Eric Hoyt, 237–56. Ann Arbor: University of Michigan Press.

Hoyt, Eric, and Jeremy Wade Morris. 2021. "Introduction." In *Saving New Sounds: Podcast Preservation and Historiography*, edited by Jeremy Wade Morris and Eric Hoyt, 181–94. Ann Arbor: University of Michigan Press.

Humphreys, Michael. 2005. "Getting Personal: Reflexivity and Autoethnographic Vignettes." *Qualitative Inquiry* 11, no. 6: 840–60. https://doi.org/10.1177/1077800404269425.

Hunter, Andrea. 2016. "Monetizing the Mommy: Mommy Blogs and the Audience Commodity." *Information, Communication, and Society* 19, no. 9: 1306–20. https://doi.org/10.1080/1369118X.2016.1187642.

Huntsberger, Michael, and Alan G. Stavitsky. 2007. "The New 'Podagogy': Incorporating Podcasting into Journalism Education." *Faculty Publications* 61, no. 4: 397–410.

Hutchby, Ian. 2006. *Media Talk: Conversation Analysis and the Study of Broadcasting*. Maidenhead: McGraw-Hill.

Hyland Wang, Jennifer. 2021. "The Perils of Ladycasting: Podcasting, Gender, and Alternative Production Cultures." In *Saving New Sounds: Podcast Preservation and Historiography*, edited by Jeremy Wade Morris and Eric Hoyt, 51–70. Ann Arbor: University of Michigan Press.

———. "The Sounds of Motherhood: Mediating 'Motherwhelm' in *ZigZag*." *Radio Journal* 21, no. 1: 7–27. https://doi.org/10.1386/rjao_00070_1.

Hyzen, Aaron, and Hilda Van den Bulck. 2021. "'The Most Paranoid Man in America': Alex Jones as Celebrity Populist." *Celebrity Studies* 12, no. 1: 162–66.

Illing, Sean. 2019. "Mindfulness Meditation in America has a Capitalism Problem." *Vox*, April 7, 2019. https://www.vox.com/science-and-health/2019/3/29/18264703/mindfulness-meditation-buddhism-david-forbes.

Ingham, Tim. 2021. "Spotify, Worth $67bn, Has Seen Its Share Price Triple in 10 Months. Should Daniel EK Pay Artists a 'Bonus' to Say Thank You?" *Music Business Worldwide*, January 11, 2021. https://www.musicbusinessworldwide.com/spotify-worth-67bn-has-seen-its-share-price-treble-in-10-months-should-daniel-ek-hand-cash-to-artists-as-a-thank-you/.

Inglis, Ian. 2001. "'Nothing You Can See That Isn't Shown': The Album Covers of the Beatles." *Popular Music* 20, no. 1: 83–97. https://doi.org/10.1017/S0261143001001325.

———. 2003. "'Some Kind of Wonderful': The Creative Legacy of the Brill Building." *American Music* 21, no. 2: 215.

Innes, Robert. 2013. *Elder Brother and the Law of the People: Contemporary Kinship and Cowessess First Nation*. Winnipeg: University of Manitoba Press.

Inoue, Asao B. 2015. *Antiracist Writing Assessment Ecologies: Teaching and Assessing Writing for a Socially Just Future*. Fort Collins: Parlor Press.

———. 2019. "Classroom Writing Assessment as an Antiracist Practice." *Pedagogy* 19, no. 3 (Fall): 373–404.

Irwin, Rita L., Ruth Beer, Stephanie Springgay, Kit Grauer, Gu Xiong, and Barbara Bickel. 2006. "The Rhizomatic Relations of A/r/tography." *Studies in Art Education* 48, no. 1: 70–88. https://doi.org/10.1080/00393541.2006.11650500.

Jackson, Alecia Y., and Lisa A. Mazzei. 2009. *Voice in Qualitative Inquiry: Challenging Conventional, Interpretive, and Critical Conceptions in Qualitative Research*. London: Routledge.

Jacobsen, Christine M., and Marry-Anne Karlsen. 2021. "Introduction: Unpacking the Temporalities of Irregular Migration." In *Waiting and the Temporalities of Irregular Migration*, edited by Christine M. Jacobsen, Marry-Anne Karlsen, and Shahram Khosravi, 1–19. New York: Routledge.

Jaffe, Sarah. 2021. *Work Won't Love You Back: How Devotion to Our Jobs Keeps Us Exploited, Exhausted and Alone*. London: Hurst and Company.

Jain, Andrea R. 2020. *Peace Love Yoga: The Politics of Global Spirituality*. New York: Oxford University Press.

Jarrett, Kylie. 2009. "Private Talk in the Public Sphere: Podcasting as Broadcast Talk." *Communication, Politics & Culture* 42, no. 2: 116–34.

Jenkins, Henry. 2000. "Reception Theory and Audience Research: The Mystery of the Vampire's Kiss." MIT. Accessed July 6, 2021. http://web.mit.edu/~21fms/People/henry3/vampkiss.html.

———. 2006. *Convergence Culture: Where Old and New Media Collide*. New York: New York University Press.

———. 2013. *Textual Poachers: Television Fans and Participatory Culture*. Updated 20th anniversary edition. New York: Routledge.

Jivan, Vedna, and Christine Forster. 2005. "What Would Gandhi Say? Reconciling Universalism, Cultural Relativism and Feminism through Women's Use of Cedaw." *Singapore Year Book of International Law* 9: 103–23.

Jobin, Shalene. 2016. "Indigenous Studies, Determining Itself." *Native Studies Review* 23, nos. 1 and 2: 91–122.

John, Nicholas A. 2011. "Representing the Israeli Internet: The Press, the Pioneers and the Practitioners." *International Journal of Communication* 5, no. 22. https://ijoc.org/index.php/ijoc/article/view/1091/627.

Join the Party Podcast. 2018. "The Podcaster's Guide to Transcribing Audio." *Medium*, March 19, 2018. https://bellocollective.com/the-podcasters-guide-to-transcribing-audio-2121f9e7992f.

Jones, Candace. 2002. "Signaling Expertise: How Signals Shape Careers in Creative Industries." In *Career Creativity: Explorations in the Remaking of Work*, edited by Maury Pieperl, Michael Arthur, and N. Anand, 209–28. Oxford: Oxford University Press.

Jones, Cheryl, Carla Reichard, and Kouider Mokhtari. 2003. "Are Students' Learning Styles Discipline Specific?" *Community College Journal of Research and Practice* 27, no. 5 (summer): 363–75.

Jordan-Zachery, Julia S. 2007. "Am I a Black Woman or a Woman Who Is Black? A Few Thoughts on the Meaning of Intersectionality." *Politics & Gender* 3, no. 2: 254–63.

Jorgensen, Britta. 2021. "The 'Cultural Entrepreneurship' of Independent Podcast Production in Australia." *Journal of Radio & Audio Media* 28, no. 1: 144–61.

Jorgensen, Britta, and Mia Lindgren. 2022. "Pause and Reflect: Practice-as-Research Methods in Radio and Podcast Studies." In *The Routledge Companion to Radio and Podcast Studies*, edited by Mia Lindgren and Jason Loviglio, 50–58. London: Routledge.

Justice, Daniel Heath. 2018. *Why Indigenous Literatures Matter*. Waterloo: Wilfrid Laurier University Press.

Kalin, Rudolf, and Donald Rayko. 2013. "The Social Significance of Speech in the Job Interview." In *The Social and Psychological Contexts of Language*, edited by Robert N. St. Clair and Howard Giles, 51–62. New York: Psychology Press.

Kalin, Rudolf, D.S Rayko, and N. Love. 1980. "The Perception and Evaluation of Job Candidates with Four Different Ethnic Accents." In *Language*, edited by Howard Giles, W. Peter Robinson, and Philip M. Smith, 197–202. Amsterdam: Elsevier.

Kane, Brian. 2014. *Sound Unseen: Acousmatic Sound in Theory and Practice*. New York: Oxford University Press.

Kasperkevic, Jana. 2015. "Poll: 30% of GOP Voters Support Bombing Agrabah, the City from *Aladdin*." *The Guardian*, December 18, 2015. https://www.theguardian.com/us-news/2015/dec/18/republican-voters-bomb-agrabah-disney-aladdin-donald-trump.

Katz-Kimchi, Merav. 2008. *Historicizing Utopian Popular Discourse on the Internet in America in the 1990s: Positions, Comparison, and Contextualization*. https://studylib.net/doc/7736683/.

Katz-Rosene, Joshua. 2020. "Protest Song and Countercultural Discourses of Resistance in 1960s Colombia." *Resonancias: Revista de Investigación Musical* 24, no. 47: 13–37.

Kellner, Douglas. 2011. "Cultural Studies, Multiculturalism, and Media Culture." In *Gender, Race, and Class in Media: A Critical Reader*, edited by G. Dines and J. M. Humez, 7–19. Thousand Oaks: Sage.

Kelty, Christopher. 2005. "Geeks, Social Imaginaries, and Recursive Publics." *Cultural Anthropology* 20, no. 2: 185–214. https://doi.org/10.1525/can.2005.20.2.185.

Kendrick, Robert L. 2014. "Iconography." In *The Routledge Companion to Music and Visual Culture*, edited by Tim Shephard and Anne Leonard, 43–49. London: Taylor & Francis.

Kennedy, Kristen. 1999. "Cynic Rhetoric: The Ethics and Tactics of Resistance." *Rhetoric Review* 18, no. 1: 26–45.

Kennedy, Rick, and Randy McNutt. 1999. *Little Labels—Big Sound: Small Record Companies and the Rise of American Music*. Bloomington: Indiana University Press.

Kermoal, Nathalie, and Isabel Altamirano-Jiménez. 2016. *Living on the Land: Indigenous Women's Understanding of Place*. Edmonton: University of Athabasca Press.

Kerrigan, Susan, Harry Criticos, Vicki Kerrigan, and Simon Ritchie. 2021. "Podcasting as a Creative Practice and the Spirit of Radio: Local Histories of Maitland." *Journal of Radio & Audio Media* 30, no. 2: 623–42. https://doi.org/10.1080/19376529.2021.1897986.

Kidd, Mary, Sarah Nguyen, and Erica Titkemeyer. 2020. "Subscribe, Rate and Preserve Wherever You Get Your Podcasts." *Journal of Archival Organization* 17, no. 1–2: 161–77.

King, Alison. 1993. "From Sage on the Stage to Guide on the Side." *College Teaching* 41, no. 1: 30–35.

Kinkaid, Eden, Kelsey Brain, and Nari Senanayake. 2020. "The Podcast-as-Method?: Critical Reflections on Using Podcasts to Produce Geographic Knowledge." *Geographical Review* 110, nos. 1 and 2: 78–91. https://doi.org/10.1111/gere.12354.

Kirk, Kate, Ellen Bal, and Sarah Renee Janssen. 2017. "Migrants in Liminal Time and Space: An Exploration of the Experiences of Highly Skilled Indian Bachelors in Amsterdam." *Journal of Ethnic and Migration Studies* 43, no. 16: 2771–87.

Kligler-Vilenchik, N., and O. Tenenboim. 2020. "Sustained Journalist–Audience Reciprocity in a Meso News-Space: The Case of a Journalistic WhatsApp Group." *New Media and Society* 22, no. 2: 264–82. https://doi.org/10.1177/1461444819856917.

Knoop-van Campen, C. A. N., E. Segers, and L. Verhoeven. 2020. "Effects of audio support on multimedia learning processes and outcomes in students with dyslexia." *Computers and Education*, 150, 103858. https://doi.org/10.1016/j.compedu.2020.103858.

Kosover, Maya. (producer and host of the podcast *Sipur Yisraeli*, FAO), in discussion with the authors. October 2022.

Krishnan, Madhu, and Kate Wallis. 2020. "Podcasting as Activism and/or Entrepreneurship: Cooperative Networks, Publics and African Literary Production." *Postcolonial Text* 15, nos. 3 and 4. https://www.postcolonial.org/index.php/pct/article/view/2483 Accessed 18 June 2021.

Kuehn, Kathleen, and Thomas F. Corrigan. 2013. "Hope Labor: The Role of Employment Prospects in Online Social Production." *The Political Economy of Communication* 1, no. 1: 9–25.

Kuhn, Virginia, and Vicki Callahan. 2012. "Nomadic Archives: Remix and the Drift to Praxis." In *Digital Humanities Pedagogy: Practices, Principles and Politics*, edited by Brett D. Hirsch, 291–308. Cambridge: Open Book Publishers.

Lacroix, Celeste. 2004. "Images of Animated Others: The Orientalization of Disney's Cartoon Heroines from *The Little Mermaid* to *The Hunchback of Notre Dame*." *Popular Communication* 2, no. 4: 213–29.

Låg, Torstein, and Rannveig Grøm Sæle. 2019. "Does the Flipped Classroom Improve Student Learning and Satisfaction? A Systematic Review and Meta-Analysis." *AERA Open* 5, no. 3: 1–17. https://doi.org/10.1177/2332858419870489.

Lane, Cara. 2006. "Podcasting at the UW: An Evaluation of Current Use." Office of Learning Technologies, University of Washington. https://itconnect.uw.edu/wp-content/uploads/2013/12/podcasting_report.pdf.

Larson, Sarah. 2020. "Field Recordings." *The New Yorker*, May 4, 2020. https://www.newyorker.com/goings-on-about-town/podcasts/field-recordings-05-04-20.

LA Times. 2020. "Editorial: An Examination of *The Times*' Failures on Race, Our Apology and a Path Forward." *LA Times*, September 27, 2020. Accessed January 7, 2022. https://www.latimes.com/opinion/story/2020-09-27/los-angeles-times-apology-racism.

Lauderdale, Diane S. 2006. "Birth Outcomes for Arabic-Named Women in California before and after September 11." *Demography* 43, no. 1: 185–201.

Lawless, Brandi, and Yea-Wen Chen. 2020. "Still a 'Sensitive' Subject? Unpacking Strengths and Struggles of Intercultural Communication Pedagogies." *Howard Journal of Communications* 31, no. 2: 171–86.

Leadbeater, Charles, and Kate Oakley. 1999. *The Independents: Britain's New Cultural Entrepreneurs*. London: Demos.

Lefebvre, Henri. 1991. *The Production of Space*. Oxford: Blackwell.

Leonard, Mark. 2017. "The Seven Most Common Podcast Formats: With Examples." Medium. https://mark-leonard.medium.com/the-seven-most-common-podcast-formats-87bbc3ecf40d.

Levin, Dan. 2020. "No Home, No Wi-Fi: Pandemic Adds to Strain on Poor College Students." *The New York Times*, October 12, 2020. https://www.nytimes.com/2020/10/12/us/covid-poor-college-students.html.

Levy, Adam. 2020. "Working Scientist Podcast: How the Academic Paper Is Evolving in the 21st Century." *Nature Careers Podcast*. May 5, 2020. Podcast. MP3 audio, 10:46. http://dx.doi.org/10.1038/d41586-020-00383-z.

Li, Ang, Alice Wang, Zahra Nazari, Praveen Chandar, and Benjamin Carterette. 2020. "Do Podcasts and Music Compete with One Another? Understanding Users' Audio Streaming Habits." In *Proceedings of the Web Conference 2020*: 1920–31.

Libeks, Janis, and Douglas Turnbull. 2011. "You Can Judge an Artist by an Album Cover: Using Images for Music Annotation." *IEEE MultiMedia* 18, no. 4: 30–37.

Library of Congress. n.d. "Israel: Supreme Court Authorizes Surrogacy Arrangements for Gay Men." Library of Congress. Accessed August 10, 2022. https://www.loc.gov/item/global-legal-monitor/2021-07-29/israel-supreme-court-authorizes-surrogacy-arrangements-for-gay-men/.

Lindberg, Sara. 2020. "The 21 Best Meditation Podcasts to Listen to Right Now." Verywell Mind. April 14, 2020. https://www.verywellmind.com/best-meditation-podcasts-4771686.

Lindgren, Mia. 2016. "Personal narrative journalism and podcasting." *The Radio Journal* 14, no. 1: 23–41.

Lindgren, Mia, and Michele Hilmes. 2016. "Editors' introduction to RJ 14:1 Podcast 2016." *Radio Journal* 14, no. 1: 3–5.

Lindgren, Mia, and Jason Loviglio. 2022. *The Routledge Companion to Radio and Podcast Studies*. London and New York: Routledge.

Lippi-Green, Rosina. 2012. *English with an Accent: Language, Ideology and Discrimination in the United States*, 2nd edition. London and New York: Routledge.

Liverpool, Layal. 2021. "Research from Global South Under-Represented in Development Research." *Nature*. September 17, 2021. https://www.nature.com/articles/d41586-021-02549-9.

Llinares, Dario. 2018. "Podcasting as Liminal Praxis: Aural Mediation, Sound Writing and Identity." In *Podcasting: New Aural Cultures and Digital Media*, edited by Dario Llinares, Neil Fox, and Richard Berry, 123–45. London: Palgrave Macmillan.

———. 2019. "Blindboy's Podcast Hug." Dario Llinares (blog). https://www.dariollinares.com/blog/tag/Blindboy.

———. 2020a. "A Cinema for the Ears: Imagining the Audio-Cinematic through Podcasting." *Film-Philosophy* 24, no. 3: 341–65.

———. 2020b. "In Conversation with Professor Lori Beckstead." *The Podcast Studies Podcast*. June 18, 2020. Podcast. MP3 audio. https://anchor.fm/newauralcultures/episodes/In-conversation-with-Professor-Lori-Beckstead-egtell.

———. 2020c. "In Conversation with Dr. Hannah McGregor." *The Podcast Studies Podcast*. October 1, 2020. Podcast. MP3 audio. https://anchor.fm/newauralcultures/episodes/In-conversation-with-Dr-Hannah-McGregor-ekdnd9.

———. 2020d. "Podcast Transcripts and the Slippage between Thought, Speech and Text." Dario Llinares (blog). October 21, 2020. http://www.dariollinares.com/blog/2020/10/18/some-notes-on-podcast-transcripts/.

———. 2022. "'Podcast Studies' and Its Techno-Social Discourses." In *The Routledge Companion to Radio and Podcast Studies*, edited by Mia Lindgren and Jason Loviglio, 408–17. London and New York: Routledge.

Llinares, Dario, and Neil Fox. 2015–Present. *The Cinematologists Podcast*. Podcast. MP3 audio. www.cinematologists.com.

———. 2022. "Intimate Conversations in Cinema's 'Elsewhere.'" MUBINotebook. 1: 95.

Llinares, Dario, Neil Fox, and Richard Berry. 2018a. *Podcasting: New Aural Cultures and Digital Media*. London: Palgrave Macmillan.

———. 2018b. "Introduction: Podcasting and Podcasts—Parameters of a New Aural Culture." In *Podcasting: New Aural Cultures and Digital Media*, edited by Dario Llinares, Neil Fox, and Richard Berry, 1–14. London: Palgrave Macmillan.

Logue, Anya. 2020. "How to Write Enticing Podcast Descriptions (w/ Template)." Podcast. co. May 11, 2020. https://www.podcast.co/create/podcast-descriptions.

Long, Paul, and Simon Barber. 2015. "Voicing Passion: The Emotional Economy of Songwriting." *European Journal of Cultural Studies* 18, no. 2: 142–57.

———. 2017. "Conceptualizing Creativity and Strategy in the Work of Professional Songwriters." *Popular Music and Society* 40, no. 5: 556–72.

Lopez, Lori Kido. 2009. "The Radical Act of 'Mommy Blogging': Redefining Motherhood through the Blogosphere." *New Media & Society* 11, no. 5: 729–47. https://doi.org/10.1177/1461444809105349.

Lorde, Audre. 1984. *Sister Outsider: Essays and Speeches*. Berkeley: Crossing Press.

Lowe, Robert J., Matthew W. Turner, and Matthew Y. Schaefer. 2021. "Dialogic Research Engagement through Podcasting as a Step Towards Action Research: A Collaborative Autoethnography of Teachers Exploring Their Knowledge and Practice." *Educational Action Research* 29, no. 3: 429–46. https://doi.org/10.1080/09650792.2021 .1908905.

Lule, J. 2001. *Daily News, Eternal Stories: The Mythological Role of Journalism*. New York: Guilford Press.

Lulle, Aija, and Elza Ungure. 2015. "Asylum Seekers Crisis in Europe 2015: Debating Spaces of Fear and Security in Latvia." *Journal on Baltic Security* 1, no. 2: 62–95. https://doi.org/10.1515/jobs-2016-0021.

Lund, Anna, and Andrea Voyer. 2020. "'They're immigrants who are kind of Swedish': Universalism, Primordialism, and Modes of Incorporation in the Swedish Civil Sphere." In *The Nordic Civil Sphere*, edited by Jeffrey C. Alexander, Anna Lund, and Andrea Voyer, 177–202. Cambridge: Polity Press.

Lundström, Markus, and Tomas Poletti Lundström. 2020. "Podcast ethnography." *International Journal of Social Research Methodology* 26, no. 5: 1–11.

Lundström, Tomas Poletti, and Markus Lundström. 2021. "Radical-Nationalist Podcasting under a Post-Fascist Condition: The Swedish Podcast *Motgift*." *Fascism* 10, no. 1: 186–201.

Lutz, Tom. 2021. *Aimlessness*. New York: Columbia University Press.

Lyall, Ben. 2021. "The Ambivalent Assemblages of Sleep Optimization." *Review of Communication* 21, no. 2: 144–60.

MacDonald, Jean. "Episode 53: Martin Feld, aka @martinfeld." Micro Monday. March 18, 2019. Podcast. MP3 audio, 17:41. https://monday.micro.blog/2019/03/18/episode-martin-feld.html.

MacDougall, R. C. 2011. "Podcasting and Political Life." *American Behavioral Scientist* 55, no. 6, 714–32. https://doi.org/10.1177/0002764211406083.

Magnat, Virginie. 2019. *The Performative Power of Vocality*. London and New York: Routledge.

Maharana, Adyasha, Morine Amutorine, Moinina David Sengeh, and Elaine O. Nsoesie. 2021. "COVID-19 and Beyond: Use of Digital Technology for Pandemic Response in Africa." *Scientific African* 14: e01041. https://www.sciencedirect.com/science/article/pii/S2468227621003422.

Malekebu, Marcel and Nora McInerny, "Terrible, Thanks for Asking," 2016-2021, in *Terrible, Thanks for Asking*, produced by American Public Media, podcast, MP3 audio, https://ttfa.org

Mama, A. 2017. "The power of feminist Pan-African intellect." *Feminist Africa* 1 no. 22: 1–5.

Markman, Kris M. 2012. "Doing Radio, Making Friends, and Having Fun: Exploring the Motivations of Independent Audio Podcasters." *New Media & Society* 14: 547–65.

———. 2015. "Considerations—Reflections and Future Research. Everything Old Is New Again: Podcasting as Radio's Revival." *Journal of Radio & Audio Media* 22, no. 2: 240–43.

Markman, Kris M., and Caroline E. Sawyer. 2014. "Why Pod? Further Explorations of the Motivations for Independent Podcasting." *Journal of Radio & Audio Media* 21, no. 1: 20–35.

Marks, L. U., 2020, "Let's Deal with the Carbon Footprint of Streaming Media." *Afterimage* 47, no. 2: 46–52. https://doi.org/10.1525/aft.2020.472009.

Mars, Roman. 2018. "The Shipping Forecast." *99% Invisible*. July 24, 2018. Podcast. MP3 audio, 30:00. https://99percentinvisible.org/episode/the-shipping-forecast/.

Marshall, P. David., Christopher Moore, and Kim Barbour. 2015. "Persona as Method: Exploring Celebrity and the Public Self through Persona Studies." *Celebrity Studies* 6, no. 3: 288–305.

Masinahikan iskwêwak. 2019. "Episode 10: Burlesque Storytelling with Brittany Johnson." *Masinahikan iskwêwak (Book Women Podcast)*. September 18, 2019. Podcast. MP3 audio, 1:06:19. https://anchor.fm/bookwomenpodcast/episodes/Episode-10-Burlesque-Storytelling-with-Brittany-Johnson-e5ecne/a-antm65.

———. 2021. "Episode 2: Split Tooth by Tanya Tagaq." *Masinahikan iskwêwak (Book Women Podcast)*. February 9, 2021. Podcast. MP3 audio, 1:03:53. https://anchor.fm/bookwomenpodcast/episodes/Season-3-Episode-2---Split-Tooth-by-Tanya-Tagaq-eq5042.

Massumi, Brian. 2002. *Parables for the Virtual: Movement, Affect, Sensation*. Durham: Duke University Press.

Massumi, Brian, Jacob Ferrington, Alina Hechler, and Jannell Parsons. 2019. "Affect and Immediation: An Interview with Brian Massumi." *disClosure: A Journal of Social Theory* 28: article 13. https://doi.org/10.13023/disclosure.28.09.

Mayer, Vicki. 2009. "Bringing the Social Back In: Studies of Production Cultures and Social Theory." In *Production Studies: Cultural Studies of Media Industries*, edited by Vicki Mayer, Miranda J. Banks, and John T. Caldwell, 15–24. London and New York: Routledge.

McClung, Steven, and Kristine Johnson. 2010. "Examining the Motives of Podcast Users." *Journal of Radio & Audio Media* 17, no. 1: 82–95.

McCombs, Maxwell E., and Donald L. Shaw. 1972. "The Agenda-Setting Function of Mass Media." *Public Opinion Quarterly* 36, no. 2: 176–87.

McDowall, E. (@Ellie_McDowall). 2020. "I've made a new podcast inspired by heartbreak and burnout. It's exactly what the name suggests it is." Twitter, March 16, 2020. https://twitter.com/Ellie_McDowall/status/1239496271049752577.

McGarr, Oliver. 2009. "A Review of Podcasting in Higher Education: Its Influence on the Traditional Lecture." *Australasian Journal of Educational Technology* 25, no. 3.

McGregor, Hannah. 2017–2022. *Secret Feminist Agenda*. Podcast. https://secretfeministagenda.com/.

———.2018–2019. "Peer Review of Secret Feminist Agenda." Wilfrid Laurier University Press (website). Accessed March 19, 2023. https://www.wlupress.wlu.ca/Scholarly-Podcasting-Open-Peer-Review/Secret-Feminist-Agenda.

———. 2019. "Yer a Reader, Harry: HP Reread Podcasts as Digital Reading Communities." *Participations: Journal of Audience & Reception Studies* 16, no. 1: 366–89.

———. 2020. "The Voice Is Intact: Finding Gwendolyn MacEwen in the Archive." *The SpokenWeb Podcast*. April 6, 2020. Podcast. MP3 audio. https://spokenweb.ca/podcast/episodes/the-voice-is-intact-finding-gwendolyn-macewen-in-the-archive/.

———. 2022. "Podcast Studies." *Oxford Research Encyclopedia of Literature*. https://doi.org/10.1093/acrefore/9780190201098.013.1338.

McHugh, Siobhán. 2012. "The Affective Power of Sound: Oral History on Radio." *The Oral History Review* 39, no. 2: 187–206.

———. 2014. "Audio Storytelling: Unlocking the Power of Audio to Inform, Empower and Connect." *Asia Pacific Media Educator* 24, no. 2: 141–56.

———. 2016. "How Podcasting Is Changing the Audio Storytelling Genre." *Radio Journal* 14, no. 1: 65–82.

———. 2022. *The Power of Podcasting: Telling Stories through Sound.* New York: Columbia University Press.

McHugh, Siobhán, Ian McLean, and Margo Neale. 2020. "Notes from a Cross-Cultural Frontier: Investigating Australian Aboriginal Art through Podcasts." *Liminalities: A Journal of Performance Studies* 16, no. 4.

McIntyre, Karen. 2019. "Solutions Journalism: The Effects of Including Solution Information in News Stories about Social Problems." *Journalism Practice* 13, no. 1: 16–34.

McIntyre, Phillip. 2008. "Creativity and Cultural Production: A Study of Contemporary Western Popular Music Songwriting." *Creativity Research Journal* 20, no. 1: 40–52.

McKinney, Dani, Jennifer L. Dyck, and Elise S. Luber. 2009. "iTunes University and the Classroom: Can Podcasts Replace Professors?" *Computers & Education* 52, no. 3: 617–23.

McLean, Matthew, and Robert Cudmore. 2014. "1—Why Start An Audio Drama?" *Audio Drama Production Podcast.* September 16, 2014. Podcast. MP3 audio, 14:24. https://www.stitcher.com/show/audio-drama-production-podcast/episode/001-why-start-an-audio-drama-64718566.

———. 2015. "48—Why Do You Make Audio Drama?" *Audio Drama Production Podcast.* June 3, 2015. Podcast. MP3 audio, 57:55. https://www.stitcher.com/show/audio-drama-production-podcast/episode/048-why-do-you-make-audio-drama-cast-gender-book-adaptations-49042618.

———. 2016. "78—Doing It All Yourself." *Audio Drama Production Podcast.* January 15, 2016. Podcast. MP3 audio, 24:35. https://www.stitcher.com/show/audio-drama-production-podcast/episode/078-doing-it-all-yourself-49042588.

McLeod, Katherine. Forthcoming. "Listening to the Listening: The Ghost Reading Series, 2018–2019." *SPOKENWEBLOG* (blog). https://spokenweb.ca/spokenweblog/.

McLuhan, Marshall. 1962. *The Gutenberg Galaxy: The Making of Typographic Man.* Toronto: University of Toronto Press.

McMurtry, Leslie. 2019. *Revolution in the Echo Chamber: Audio Drama's Past, Present, and Future.* Bristol: Intellect.

Medie, Peace A., and Alice J. Kang. 2018. "Power, Knowledge and the Politics of Gender in the Global South." *European Journal of Politics and Gender* 1, no. 1–2: 37–54.

Menduni, Enrico. 2007. "Four Steps in Innovative Radio Broadcasting: From QuickTime to Podcasting." *Radio Journal* 5, no. 1: 9–18.

Mertens, Jacob, Eric Hoyt, and Jeremy Wade Morris. 2021. "Drifting Voices: Studying Emotion and Pitch in Podcasting with Digital Tools." In *Saving New Sounds: Podcast Preservation and Historiography,* edited by Jeremy Wade Morris and Eric Hoyt, 154–78. Ann Arbor: University of Michigan Press.

Meyers, Peter J. 2019. "Podcasts in SERPs: Is Audio SEO the Next Frontier?" Moz (blog). May 22, 2019. https://moz.com/blog/podcasts-in-serps-is-audio-seo-the-next-frontier.

Millette, Mélanie. 2012. "Independent Podcasting as a Specific Online Participative Subculture: a Case Study of Montreal's Podcasters." *Selected Papers of Internet Research* 12.0.

Million, Dian. 2015. "Epistemology." In *Native Studies Keywords,* edited by Stephanie Nohelani Teves, Andrea Smith, and Michelle Raheja, 339–46. Tucson: University of Arizona Press.

Mills, Charles W. 2011. *The Racial Contract.* Ithaca: Cornell University Press.

Mindfulness Meditation Podcast. n.d. The Rubin Museum of Art. Podcast. MP3 audio. Accessed July 29, 2021. https://rubinmuseum.org/page/mindfulness-meditation-podcast.

Misener, Dan. 2018a. "Product Packaging for Podcasts." *Pacific Content Blog.* August 29, 2018. https://blog.pacific-content.com/product-packaging-for-podcasts-af173e05ed0f.

———. 2018b. "Product Packaging for Podcasts, Part 2: Episodic Elements." *Pacific Content Blog.* September 11, 2018. https://blog.pacific-content.com/if-your-latest-podcast-episode-was-a-book-how-thick-would-its-spine-be-f6cc9e9b1bb5.

Mitchell, Taylor. 2017. "Indigenous Podcasting: Resisting the Colonial Paradigm." https://www.thegrassrootsjournal.org/post/2017/11/06/indigenous-podcasting-resisting-the-colonial-paradigm.

Mohanty, Chandra Talpade. 1984. "Under Western Eyes: Feminist Scholarship and Colonial Discourses." *Boundary* 2 12, no. 3: 333–58.

Mollett, Amy, Cheryl Brumley, Chris Gilson, and Sierra Williams. 2017. *Communicating Your Research with Social Media: A Practical Guide to Using Blogs, Podcasts, Data Visualisations and Video.* Thousand Oaks: Sage.

Monteiro, Stephen. 2014. "Rethinking Media Space." *Continuum: Journal of Media and Cultural Studies* 28, no. 3: 281–85.

Mooallem, Jon. 2020. "A Minefield." *Walking.* November 24, 2020. Podcast. MP3 audio, 55:00. https://podcasts.apple.com/us/podcast/a-minefield/id1450757852?i=1000500102507.

Moore, Wendy Leo. 2008. *Reproducing Racism: White Space, Elite Law Schools, and Racial Inequality.* Lanham: Rowman & Littlefield Publishers.

Moreton-Robinson, Aileen. 2016. "Relationality: A Key Presupposition of an Indigenous Social Research Paradigm." In *Sources and Methods in Indigenous Studies,* edited by Chris Andersen and Jean M. O'Brien, 69–77. New York: Routledge.

Morris, Jeremy Wade. 2021a. "Infrastructures of Discovery: Examining Podcast Ratings and Rankings." *Cultural Studies* 35, no. 4–5: 728–49.

———. 2021b. "The Spotification of Podcasting." In *Saving New Sounds: Podcast Preservation and Historiography,* edited by Jeremy Wade Morris and Eric Hoyt, 219–34. Ann Arbor: University of Michigan Press.

Morris, Jeremy Wade, and Eleanor Patterson. 2015. "Podcasting and Its Apps: Software, Sound, and the Interfaces of Digital Audio." *Journal of Radio & Audio Media* 22, no. 2: 220–30.

Morrison, Aimée. 2011. "'Suffused by Feeling and Affect': The Intimate Public of Personal Mommy Blogging." *Biography* 34, no. 1: 37–55.

Moryl, Rebecca. 2013. "T-shirts, Moonshine, and Autopsies: Using Podcasts to Engage Undergraduate Microeconomics Students." *International Review of Economics Education* 13: 67–74.

Motlafi, Nompumelelo. 2018. "The Coloniality of the Gaze on Sexual Violence: A Stalled Attempt at a South Africa–Rwanda Dialogue?" *International Feminist Journal of Politics* 20, no. 1: 9–23.

Mountz, Alison, Anne Bonds, Becky Mansfield, Jenna Loyd, Jennifer Hyndman, Margaret Walton-Roberts, Ranu Basu, et al. 2015. "For Slow Scholarship: A Feminist Politics of Resistance through Collective Action in the Neoliberal University." *ACME: An International Journal for Critical Geographies* 14, no. 4: 1235–59.

Msuya, N. H. 2019. "Concept of culture relativism and women's rights in sub-Saharan Africa." *Journal of Asian and African Studies* 54, no. 8: 1145–58.

Mulki, Sapna, and Alison A. Ormsby. 2021. "Breaking Green Ceilings: Podcasting for Environmental and Social Change." *Journal of Environmental Studies and Sciences* 12, no.1: 18–27.

Mulvey, Laura. 1975. "Visual Pleasure and Narrative Cinema." *Screen* 16, no. 3: 6–18.

Mumford, Lewis. 1967. *Technics and Civilization.* London: Routledge and Kegan Paul Ltd.

Murray, Lars. 2019a. "What Is a Microcast, and Why Do You Need One? (Guest Column)." *Variety.* October 10, 2019. https://variety.com/2019/digital/news/what-is-microcast-1203364995/.

Murray, Sarah. 2019b. "Coming-of-Age in a Coming-of-Age: The Collective Individualism of Podcasting's Intimate Soundwork." *Popular Communication* 17, no. 4: 301–16. https://doi.org/10.1080/15405702.2019.1622117.

Mutsvairo, Bruce, Saba Bebawi, and Eddy Borges-Rey, eds. 2020. *Data Journalism in the Global South.* Cham: Springer Nature.

Narayan, Uma. 1997. *Dislocating Cultures: Identities, Traditions, and Third-World Feminism.* New York: Routledge.

Nayak, Bhabani Shankar. 2013. "Challenges of Cultural Relativism and the Future of Feminist Universalism." *Journal of Politics and Law* 6, no. 2: 83–89.

Nazari, Zahra, Christophe Charbuillet, Johan Pages, Martin Laurent, Denis Charrier, Briana Vecchione, and Ben Carterette. 2020. "Recommending Podcasts for Cold-Start Users Based on Music Listening and Taste." In *Proceedings of the 43rd International ACM SIGIR Conference on Research and Development in Information Retrieval*: 1041–50.

Neale, Jonathan. 2008. "Ranting and Silence: The Contradictions of Writing for Activists and Academics." In *Taking Sides: Ethics, Politics and Fieldwork in Anthropology*, edited by Heidi Armbruster and Anna Lærke, 217–55. New York and Oxford: Berghan.

———. 2015. "Why Radical Academics Often Find It Hard to Write, and What to Do about It." Social Informatics Blog. Accessed March 20, 2022. https://socialinfoblog. wordpress.com/2016/05/31/why-radical-academics-often-find-it-hard-to-write-and-what-to-do-about-it.

Nelson, Robin. 2013. *Practice as Research in the Arts: Principles, Protocols, Pedagogies, Resistances*. Basingstoke: Palgrave Macmillan UK.

Newman, Eryn J., and Norbert Schwarz. 2018. "Good Sound, Good Research: How Audio Quality Influences Perceptions of the Research and Researcher." *Science Communication* 40, no. 2: 246–57.

Newton, Philip M. 2015. "The Learning Styles Myth Is Thriving in Higher Education." *Frontiers in Psychology* 6, no. 1 (winter).

Nicholson, Tom. 2021. "How Sleep Podcasts Quietly Hack Your Brain." *Esquire*, February 23, 2021. https://www.esquire.com/uk/culture/a35562970/sleep-podcasts/.

Nicolai, Kathryn. 2022. "Auld Lang Syne." *Nothing Much Happens*. January 3, 2022. Podcast. MP3 audio, 36:00. https://podcasts.apple.com/us/podcast/auld-lang-syne/id1378040733?i=1000546750832.

Nnaemeka, Obioma. 2004. "Nego-Feminism: Theorizing, Practicing, and Pruning Africa's Way." *Development Cultures* 29, no. 2: 357–85.

Noh, Susan. 2021. "A Re-Emphasis on Context: Preserving and Analyzing Podcast Metadata." In *Saving New Sounds: Podcast Preservation and Historiography*, edited by Jeremy Wade Morris and Eric Hoyt, 135–53. Ann Arbor: University of Michigan Press.

North, Adrian C. 2010. "Individual Differences in Musical Taste." *The American Journal of Psychology* 123, no. 2: 199–208.

Nortje, Alicia. 2020. "20 Best Mindfulness Meditation Podcasts of 2020." PositivePsychology.com. November 18, 2020. https://positivepsychology.com/mindfulness-meditation-podcasts/.

NotePage, Inc. 2019. "What Is RSS?" RSS Specifications. http://www.rss-specifications.com/what-is-rss.htm.

Nyre, Lars. 2015. "Urban Headphone Listening and The Situational Fit of Music, Radio and Podcasting." *Journal of Radio & Audio Media* 22, no. 2: 279–98.

O'Bannon, Blanche W., Jennifer K. Lubke, Jeffrey L. Beard, and Virginia G. Britt. 2011. "Using Podcasts to Replace Lecture: Effects on Student Achievement." *Computers & Education* 57: 1885–92.

O'Brien, Dave, Kim Allen, Sam Friedman, and Saha Anamika. 2017. "Producing and Consuming Inequality: A Cultural Sociology of the Cultural Industries." *Cultural Sociology* 11, no. 3: 271–82.

Obrist, Hans Ulrich. 2015. *Ways of Curating*. London: Penguin.

O'Connor, Alan. 2008. *Punk Record Labels and The Struggle for Autonomy*. Lanham: Lexington Books.

O'Connor, Brian. 2018. *Idleness: A Philosophical Essay*. Princeton: Princeton University Press.

Odell, Jenny. 2019. *How to Do Nothing: Resisting the Attention Economy*. Brooklyn: Melville House Publishing.

Ofodu, Graceful O., and Senny O. Oso. 2015. "Technological Resources and English Language Teaching in Schools." *Journal of Literature, Language and Linguistics* 11, no. 4: 27–33.

Ogundipe, Leslie Molara. 1994. *Recreating Ourselves*. Trenton: Africa World Press.

O'Hagan, C. 2020. "Startling Digital Divides in Distance Learning Emerge." UNESCO.

Okeke, Philomina E. 1996. "Postmodern Feminism and Knowledge Production: The African Context." *Africa Today* 43, no. 3: 223–33.

Olagbaju, O.O., and A.G. Popoola. 2020. "Effects of Audio-Visual Social Media Resources-Supported Instruction on Learning Outcomes in Reading." *International Journal of Technology in Education* 3, no. 2: 92–104.

O'Meara, Jennifer. 2015. "'Like Movies for Radio': Media Convergence and the *Serial* Podcast Sensation." *Frames Cinema Journal* 8, no. 28.

O'Neill, Maggie, and Phil Hubbard. 2010. "Walking, Sensing, Belonging: Ethno-Mimesis as Performative Praxis." *Visual Studies* 25, no. 1: 46–58.

"Online Mini Music Licence." n.d. APRA AMCOS. Accessed March 1, 2023. https://www.apraamcos.com.au/music-licences/select-a-licence/online-mini-licence.

Onyango, Adelle. 2021. "Legally Clueless." Podcast. https://www.afripods.africa/podcast/25056b80-1f6e-4fc3-90fb-433f010441c7.

Orlin, Ben. 2013. "When Memorization Gets in the Way of Learning." *The Atlantic*. Accessed on March 11, 2022. https://www.theatlantic.com/education/archive/2013/09/when-memorization-gets-in-the-way-of-learning/279425/.

Oslawski-Lopez, Jamie, and Gregory Kordsmeier. 2021. "'Being Able to Listen Makes Me Feel More Engaged': Best Practices for Using Podcasts as Readings." *Teaching Sociology* 49, no. 4: 335–47.

Oyewunmi, Oyeronke. 2005. *African Gender Studies: A Reader*. London: Palgrave Macmillan.

Pabani, Aliya, Chandra Melting Tallow, Cheldon Paterson, Kaija Siirala, Jon Tjhia, and Phoebe Wang. 2019. "Resonant Bodies." Constellations. December 2, 2019. https://www.constellationsaudio.com/resonantbodies.

Parameswaran, Radhika. 1999. "Western Romance Fiction as English-Language Media in Postcolonial India." *Journal of Communication* 49, no. 3: 84–105.

Park, Chang Sup. 2017. "Citizen News Podcasts and Engaging Journalism: The Formation of a Counter-Public Sphere in South Korea." *Pacific Journalism Review* 23, no. 1: 245–62.

Pavelko, Rachelle L., and Jessica Gall Myrick. 2019. "Murderinos and Media Effects: How the *My Favorite Murder* Podcast and Its Social Media Community May Promote Well-Being in Audiences with Mental Illness." *Journal of Radio & Audio Media* 27, no. 1: 151–69.

Perks, Lisa Glebatis, Jacob S. Turner, and Andrew C. Tollison. 2019. "Podcast Uses and Gratifications Scale Development." *Journal of Broadcasting & Electronic Media* 63, no. 4: 617–34.

Perloff, Richard M. 2019. *The Dynamics of News: Journalism in the 21st-Century Media Milieu*. New York: Routledge.

Peterson, David A. 2020. "Dear Reviewer 2: Go F' Yourself." *Social Science Quarterly* 101, no. 4: 1648–52.

Pieterse, Jan Nederveen. 1995. "Globalization as Hybridization." *Global Modernities* 2: 45–68.

Pillow, Wanda. 2003. "Confession, Catharsis, or Cure? Rethinking the Uses of Reflexivity as Methodological Power in Qualitative Research." *International Journal of Qualitative Studies in Education* 16, no. 2: 175–96.

Pillsbury, Skye. 2021. "The Undervalued Work of the Audio Producer." *Hot Pod*. March 23, 2021. https://hotpodnews.com/the-undervalued-work-of-the-audio-producer/.

Pinheiro, Elton Bruno Barbosa. 2020. "*Podcast e Accessibilidade*." *Revista GEMInIS* 11, no. 2: 45–66.

Platt, Louise C. 2019. "Crafting Place: Women's Everyday Creativity in Placemaking Processes." *European Journal of Cultural Studies* 22, no. 3: 362–77.

"Podcast RSS Feed Requirements." 2021. Apple Podcasts for Creators. https://podcasters.apple.com/support/823-podcast-requirements.

Pollock, Griselda. 1999. *Differencing the Canon: Feminist Desire and the Writing of Art's History*. London: Psychology Press.

Price-Williams, Shelley R., Roger "Mitch" Nasser, and Pietro A. Sasso. 2020. "The Competition of an American Public Good: Performance-Based Funding and

Other Neoliberal Tertiary Effects in Higher Education." In *Leadership Strategies for Promoting Social Responsibility in Higher Education*, edited by Enakshi Sengupta, Patrick Blessinger, and Craig Mahoney: 175–89. Leeds: Emerald Publishing Limited.

Prior, Nick. 2010. "The rise of the new amateurs: Popular music, digital technology and the fate of cultural production." In *Culture: A Sociological Handbook*, edited by John R. Hall, Laura Grindstaff and Ming-Cheng Lo, 398–407. London: Routledge.

Pritchard, David, and Sarah Stonbely. 2007. "Racial Profiling in the Newsroom." *Journalism & Mass Communication Quarterly* 84, no. 2: 231–48.

Probst, Barbara. 2015. "The Eye Regards Itself: Benefits and Challenges of Reflexivity in Qualitative Social Work Research." *Social Work Research* 39, no. 1: 37–48.

Purser, Ronald E. 2019. *McMindfulness: How Mindfulness Became the New Capitalist Spirituality*. London: Repeater Books.

Quah, Nicholas. 2019. "The *Walking* Podcast is a Weird, Lovely Ode to Nature." *Vulture*, February 21, 2019. https://www.vulture.com/2019/02/jon-mooallem-walking-podcast-review.html.

Quah, Nicholas, and Caroline Crampton. 2020. "Coronavirus Is Changing Podcasting, Fast." *Vulture*, March 17, 2020. https://www.vulture.com/2020/03/coronavirus-changing-podcast-industry.html.

"Quick Facts about Arab Americans." 2018. Arab American Institute Foundation. https://www.aaiusa.org/demographics.

Quirk, Vanessa. 2016. *Guide to Podcasting*. New York: Tow Center for Digital Journalism.

Rachel, Daniel. 2013. *Isle of Noises: Conversations with Great British Songwriters*. London: Picador.

Radway, Janice A. 1984. *Reading the Romance: Women, Patriarchy, and Popular Literature*. Chapel Hill: University of North Carolina Press.

———. 2008. Foreword to *Ghostly Matters: Haunting and the Sociological Imagination*, by Avery Gordon, vii–xiv. Minneapolis: University of Minnesota Press.

Rae, Maria. 2023. "Podcasts and Political Listening: Sound, Voice and Intimacy in the *Joe Rogan Experience*." *Continuum: Journal of Media and Cultural Studies* 37, no. 2: 182–93.

Rae, Maria, Emma K Russell, and Amy Nethery. 2019. "Earwitnessing Detention: Carceral Secrecy, Affecting Voices, and Political Listening in *The Messenger* Podcast." *International Journal of Communication* 13: 1036–55.

Raetzsch, Christoph, Teke Ngomba, Cecilia A. Olivera, Unni From, and Henrik Bødker. 2021. "Towards Diversity in Global Journalism Studies. A Reply to Seth C. Lewis." *Digital Journalism* 10, no. 2: 360–7 1.

Ray, Victor. 2019. "A Theory of Racialized Organizations." *American Sociological Review* 84, no. 1 (winter): 26–53.

Reardon, Morgan. 2020. "Chill Out With 9 of the Best Podcasts for Mindfulness and Meditation." *Urban List*, March 27, 2020. https://theurbanlist.com/list/mindfulness-and-meditation-podcasts.

Reed, Mark, Anna Clair Evely, Georgina Cundill, Ioan Fazey, Jayne Glass, Adele Laing, Jens Newig, et al. 2010. "What Is Social Learning?" *Ecology and Society* 15, no. 4.

"Refugees on Air." 2023. Refugee Council of Australia, March 31, 2023. https://www.refugeecouncil.org.au/refugees-on-air/.

Reidpath, Daniel D., and Pascale Allotey. 2019. "The Problem of 'Trickle-Down Science' from the Global North to the Global South." *BMJ Global Health* 4, no. 4, e001719.

Reilly, Maura. 2018. *Curatorial Activism: Towards an Ethics of Curating*. London: Thames and Hudson.

Relay FM. 2022. *Connected*. Podcast, Website. https://www.relay.fm/connected.

———. 2022. *Upgrade*. Podcast, Website. https://www.relay.fm/upgrade.

Riener, C., and D. Willingham. 2010. "The Myth of Learning Styles." *Change: The Magazine of Higher Learning* 42, no. 5: 32–35.

Reinhard, CarrieLynn D., and Brenda Dervin. 2012. "Comparing Situated Sense-Making Processes in Virtual Worlds: Application of Dervin's Sense-Making Methodology to Media Reception Situations." *Convergence* 18, no. 1: 27–48.

Richardson, S., and H. Green. 2018. "Talking Women/Women Talking: The Feminist Potential of Podcasting for Modernist Studies." *Feminist Modernist Studies* 1, no. 3: 282–93.

Richardson, W. 2006. *Blogs, Wikis, Podcasts and Other Powerful Web Tools for the Classroom*. Thousand Oaks: Corvin Press.

Rime, Jemily, Chris Pike, and Tom Collins. 2022. "What Is a Podcast? Considering Innovations in Podcasting through the Six-Tensions Framework." *Convergence* 28, no. 5: 1260–82.

Ritzer, George. 2000. *The Mcdonaldization of Society*, New Century Edition. Thousand Oaks: Sage.

Robinson, Dylan. 2020. *Hungry Listening: Resonant Theory for Indigenous Sound Studies*. Minneapolis: University of Minnesota Press.

Rodgers, Tara. 2010. *Pink Noises: Women on Electronic Music and Sound*. Durham: Duke University Press.

Rodriguez, Nathian Shae, and Jennifer Huemmer. 2019. "Pedagogy of the Depressed: An Examination of Critical Pedagogy in Higher Ed's Diversity-Centered Classrooms Post-Trump." *Pedagogy, Culture & Society* 27, no. 1: 133–49.

Rogers, Dallas, Miles Herbert, Carolyn Whitzman, Eugene McCann, Paul J. Maginn, Beth Watts, Ashraful Alam, et al. 2020. "The City Under COVID-19: Podcasting as Digital Methodology." *Tijdschrift voor Economische en Sociale Geografie* 111, no. 3: 434–50.

Romero, Mary. 2017. *Introducing Intersectionality*. Cambridge: Polity Press.

Roush, Chris, ed. 2017. *Master Class: Teaching Advice for Journalism and Mass Communication Instructors*. Lanham: Rowman & Littlefield.

Royston, Reginold A. 2023. "Podcasts and New Orality in the African Mediascape." *New Media & Society* 25, no. 9: 2455–74.

"RSS Feed Guidelines for Google Podcasts" Podcasts Manager Help. 2021. https://support. google.com/podcast-publishers/answer/9889544?hl=en#podcast_tags.

Saarinen, Katariina, and Pertti Vakkari. 2013. "A Sign of a Good Book: Readers' Methods of Accessing Fiction in the Public Library." *Journal of Documentation* 69, no. 5: 736–54.

Saeed, Nauman, Yun Yang, and Suku Sinnappan. 2009. "Emerging Web Technologies in Higher Education: A Case of Incorporating Blogs, Podcasts, and Social Bookmarks in a Web Programming Course Based on Students' Learning Styles and Technology Preferences." *Educational Technology & Society* 12, no. 4: 98–109.

Salvati, Andrew J. 2015. "Podcasting the Past: Hardcore History, Fandom, and DIY Histories." *Journal of Radio & Audio Media* 22, no. 2: 231–39.

Sandlin, Jennifer A., Michael P. O'Malley, and Jake Burdick. 2011. "Mapping the Complexity of Public Pedagogy Scholarship: 1894–2010." *Review of Educational Research* 81, no. 3: 338–75.

Sandlin, Jennifer A., Robin R. Wright, and Carolyn Clark. 2013. "Reexamining Theories of Adult Learning and Adult Development through the Lenses of Public Pedagogy." *Adult Education Quarterly* 63, no. 1: 3–23.

Savage, Glenn C. 2010. "Problematizing 'Public Pedagogy' in Educational Research." In *Handbook of Public Pedagogy: Education and Learning Beyond Schooling*, edited by Jennifer A. Sandlin, Brian D. Schultz, and Jake Burdick, 103–15. London and New York: Routledge.

Savin-Baden, Maggi, and Lana van Niekerk. 2007. "Narrative Inquiry: Theory and Practice." *Journal of Geography in Higher Education* 31, no. 3: 459–72. https://doi. org/10.1080/03098260601071324.

Sayers, Jentery, ed. 2018. *The Routledge Companion to Media Studies and Digital Humanities*. New York: Routledge.

Schafer, R. Murray. 1973. *The Music of the Environment*. Vienna: Universal Edition.

———. 1993. *The Soundscape: Our Sonic Environment and the Tuning of the World*. Rochester: Vermont.

Schegloff, Emanuel A. 1999. "Discourse, Pragmatics, Conversation, Analysis." *Discourse Studies* 1, no. 4: 405–35.

Schindler, Johanna. 2020. "Negotiation, Translation, Synchronization? The Role of Boundary Objects in Artistic Research." In *Dialogues Between Artistic Research and*

Science and Technology Studies, edited by Henk Borgdorff, Peter Peters, and Trevor Pinch Abingdon, 103–16. New York: Routledge.

Schleiner, Anne-Marie. 2011. "Dissolving the Magic Circle of Play: Lessons from Situationist Gaming." In *From Diversion to Subversion: Games, Play, and Twentieth Century Art*, edited by David J. Getsy, 149–57. University Park: Pennsylvania State University Press.

Schlütz, Daniela, and Imke Hedder. 2022. "Aural Parasocial Relations: Host–Listener Relationships in Podcasts." *Journal of Radio & Audio Media* 29, no. 2: 457–74. https://doi.org/10.1080/19376529.2020.1870467.

Schrøder, Kim Christian. 2018. "Audience Reception Research in a Post-Broadcasting Digital Age." *Television & New Media* 20, no. 2: 155–69.

Scire, Sarah. 2021. "Vox Media Has Built a Visual Way to Experience Podcasts. It's Accessible to Deaf Audiences—and Gorgeous." *Nieman Lab* (blog). October 21, 2021. https://www.niemanlab.org/2021/10/vox-media-has-built-a-visual-way-to-experience-podcasts-its-accessible-to-deaf-audiences-and-gorgeous/.

Scolari, Carlos Alberto. 2012. "Media Ecology: Exploring the Metaphor to Expand the Theory." *Communication Theory* 22, no. 2: 204–25. https://doi.org/10.1111/j.1468-2885.2012.01404.x.

Scott, Karla D. 2018. "Check Yo' Stuff: A Black Feminist Rant to 'Allies' Seeking 'Dialogue' in Precarious Times." *International Review of Qualitative Research* 11. no. 2: 198–209.

Scott, Michael. 2012. "Cultural Entrepreneurs, Cultural Entrepreneurship: Music Producers Mobilising and Converting Bourdieu's Alternative Capitals." *Poetics* 40, no. 3: 237–55.

Seabrook, John. 2015. *The Song Machine: Inside the Hit Factory*. London: Jonathan Cape.

Sellas, T., and M. Bonet. 2023. "Independent Podcast Networks in Spain: A Grassroots Cultural Production Facing Cultural Industry Practices." *Convergence* 29, no. 4: 801–17.

"7 Reasons You Should Publish Your Podcast Show Notes." 2018. *Designrr* (blog). July 17, 2018. https://designrr.io/7-reasons-you-should-publish-your-podcast-show-notes/.

Shaheen, Jack G. 2001. *Reel Bad Arabs: How Hollywood Vilifies a People*. New York: Olive Branch Press.

Sharon, Tzlil. 2022. "Between Professionalism and Intimacy: An Analysis Model for Podcast Listening." Ph.D. dissertation, Hebrew University of Jerusalem.

———. 2023. "Peeling the Pod: Towards a Research Agenda for Podcast Studies." *Annals of the International Communication Association* 47, no. 3: 324–37, https://doi.org/10.108 0/23808985.2023.2201593.

Sharon, Tzlil, and Nicholas A. John. 2018. "Unpacking (the) Secret: Anonymous Social Media and the Impossibility of Networked Anonymity." *New Media & Society* 20, no. 11: 4177–94.

———. "Imagining an Ideal Podcast Listener." *Popular Communication* 17 no. 4: 333–47.

Shetty, Parinita. 2020a. "Episode 10 Reclaiming Stories: Representations of Dyspraxia and Autism in *Doctor Who*/Fandom." *Marginally Fannish*. June 9, 2020. Podcast. MP3 audio, 1:09:16. https://open.spotify.com/episode/7uwZKYzqapBFz8xCkDqDBv.

———. 2020b. "Episode 3 Just Let Me Hug a Tree in the Woods: Wicca, Paganism, and Religion in Fantasy Media." *Marginally Fannish*. February 28, 2020. Podcast, MP3 audio, 1:04:16. https://open.spotify.com/episode/76OpbNBJsW2v2NDwVoYott.

———. 2020c. "Episode 15 A Fascinating Tension: Multiple Interpretations of Religious Themes and Ideas in SFF," *Marginally Fannish*, September 2020, 2020. Podcast, MP3 audio, 1:16:13. https://open.spotify.com/episode/3qy1HnQ27oEfzZ8AosuBYz

———. 2020d. "Episode 1 More Inclusive: The Journey of Three Indian Fangirls." *Marginally Fannish*. January 31, 2020. Podcast. MP3 audio, 57:14. https://open.spotify.com/episode/349N9tlHDbC4p6zNULUREd.

———. 2020e. "Episode 7 There's Never Chicken Tikka Masala at Hogwarts: Different Cultures in Fantasy Media." *Marginally Fannish*. April 27, 2020. Podcast. MP3 audio, 1:01:40. https://open.spotify.com/episode/19FJM4lSKGWyqNAm6E8pvO.

———. 2022a. "Episode 18 We've Been Featured! Finally!: Questioning Cultural Norms in Mainstream Fantasy Books." *Marginally Fannish*. June 1, 2022. Podcast. MP3 audio, 1:26:21. https://open.spotify.com/episode/5s4W2ZnjslT67h8EAdaRKr.

———. 2022b. "Episode 20 Because We Couldn't See Ourselves: Cultural Representations and Cultural Imperialism in Western Media/Fandom." *Marginally Fannish*. June 26, 2022. Podcast. MP3 audio, 1:11:07. https://open.spotify.com/episode/06kpbaHboQNBOInj6vifKl.

Shields, Rob. 1999. *Lefebvre, Love and Struggle: Spatial Dialectics*. London and New York: Routledge.

Shoemaker, Pamela J., and Stephen D Reese. 1996. *Mediating the Message*. White Plains: Longman.

Sibanda, Makhosi Nkanyiso, and Mphathisi Ndlovu. 2023. "An Alternative Arena for 'Communities of Resistance'? Podcasting, Democratic Spaces, and Counterpublics in Zimbabwe." In *Converged Radio, Youth and Urbanity in Africa*, edited by S. Tsarwe and S. Chiumbu. 37–53. Cham: Palgrave Macmillan.

Sienkiewicz, Matt, and Deborah L. Jaramillo. 2019. "Podcasting, the Intimate Self, and the Public Sphere." *Popular Communication* 17, no. 4: 268–72. https://doi.org/10.1080/15405702.2019.1667997.

Skjerseth, Amy. 2022. "Ride-Along Listening: Inclusive Modes of Musical Analysis in *Switched on Pop*." *Radio Journal* 20, no. 1: 33–48.

Slow Radio. n.d. BBC Radio 3. Accessed February 16, 2022. https://www.bbc.co.uk/programmes/p05k5bq0.

Smith, Anna. 2018. "Episode 10: Us, Madeline's Madeline, Dirty Dancing, Eighth Grade and Bo Burnham interview." *Girls on Film*. 2018. Podcast, MP3 audio. https://podcasts.apple.com/gb/podcast/girls-on-film/id1439182513.

Smith, Barbara. 1989. "A Press of Our Own Kitchen Table: Women of Color Press." *Frontiers: A Journal of Women Studies* 10, no. 3: 11–13.

Smith, Terry. 2012. *Thinking Contemporary Curating*. New York: ICI.

spacejamorjelly. 2020. "*99% Invisible* is so calming I can no longer listen to it while driving. Roman Mars has the most sooooothing voice." Reddit. https://www.reddit.com/r/podcasts/comments/hhcasr/can_anybody_recommend_a_podcast_to_fall_asleep_to/.

Sparrow, Mark. 2021. "Podcast Radio Is a Radio Station For…Podcasts." *Forbes*, April 5, 2021. https://www.forbes.com/sites/marksparrow/2021/04/05/podcast-radio-is-a-radio-station-for-podcasts/.

"Special Eurobarometer 469: Integration of Immigrants in the European Union." 2018. Survey requested by the European Commission, Directorate-General for Migration and Home Affairs and co-ordinated by the Directorate-General for Communication. Accessed June 16, 2021. https://www.migrationsenquestions.fr/content/uploads/2019/09/EuroBarometer-IntegrationOfMigrantsintheEU_469_April2018_p12.pdf

Spinelli, Martin, and Lance Dann. 2019. *Podcasting: The Audio Media Revolution*. London: Bloomsbury.

Spinrad, Mark L., Stefani R. Relles, and Doris L. Watson. 2022. "Not in the Greater Good: Academic Capitalism and Faculty Labor in Higher Education." *Education Sciences* 12, no. 12: 912.

Spivak, Gayatri. 1988. "Can the Subaltern Speak?" In *Marxism and the Interpretation of Culture*, edited by Cary Nelson and Lawrence Grossberg, 271–313. Urbana: University of Illinois Press.

Spry, Tami. 2011. *Body, Paper, Stage: Writing and Performing Autoethnography*. London and New York: Routledge.

Stahlke Wall, Sarah. 2016. "Toward A Moderate Autoethnography." *International Journal of Qualitative Methods* 15, no. 1: 1–9.

Stanley, Christine A. 2007. "When Counter Narratives Meet Master Narratives in the Journal Editorial-Review Process." *Educational Researcher* 36, no. 1: 14–24.

Star, Susan Leigh. 2010. "This Is Not a Boundary Object: Reflections on the Origin of a Concept." *Science, Technology, & Human Values* 35, no. 5: 601–17. https://doi.org/10.1177/0162243910377624.

Star, Susan Leigh, and James R. Griesemer. 1989. "Institutional Ecology, 'Translations' and Boundary Objects: Amateurs and Professionals in Berkeley's Museum of Vertebrate Zoology, 1907–39." *Social Studies of Science* 19, no. 3: 387–420.

"Startling Digital Divides in Distance Learning Emerge | UNESCO." 2020. Accessed March 26, 2024. https://www.unesco.org/en/articles/startling-digital-divides-distance-learning-emerge.

Steinberg, Jacob J., Catherine Skae, and Barbara Sampson. 2018. "Gender Gap, Disparity, and Inequality in Peer Review." *The Lancet* 391, no. 10140: 2602–3.

Stelter, Brian, Irshad Manji, and Carl Bernstein. 2016. "Are Muslims Fairly Represented in News Coverage?" Transcripts. CNN. June 19, 2016. https://transcripts.cnn.com/show/rs/date/2016-06-19/segment/01.

Sterne, Jonathan, Jeremy Wade Morris, Michael Brendan Baker, and Ariana Moscote Freire. 2008. "The Politics of Podcasting." *The Fibreculture Journal* 13. https://thirteen.fibreculturejournal.org/fcj-087-the-politics-of-podcasting/.

Stoever, Jennifer Lynn. 2016. *The Sonic Color Line: Race and the Cultural Politics of Listening*. New York: NYU Press.

Strachan, Robert. 2007. "Micro-Independent Record Labels in the UK." *European Journal of Cultural Studies* 10, no. 2: 245–65.

Sullivan, Graeme. 2004. *Art Practice as Research: Inquiry in the Visual Arts*. Thousand Oaks, CA: Sage.

Sullivan, John L. 2018. "Podcast Movement: Aspirational Labour and the Formalisation of Podcasting as a Cultural Industry." In *Podcasting: New Aural Cultures and Digital Media*, edited by Dario Llinares, Neil Fox, and Richard Berry, 34–56. London: Palgrave Macmillan.

———. 2019. "The Platforms of Podcasting: Past and Present." *Social Media and Society* 5, no. 4. https://doi.org/10.1177/2056305119880002.

———. 2021a. "'Uber for Radio?': Professionalism and Production Cultures in Podcasting." In *The Gig Economy: Workers and Media in the Age of Convergence*, edited By Brian Dolber, Michelle Rodino-Colocino, Chenjerai Kumanyika, and Todd Wolfson, 92–106. New York: Routledge.

———. 2021b. Email to author. December 7, 2021.

Sutton, Rebecca, Darshan Vigneswaran, and Harry Wels. 2011. "Waiting in Liminal Space: Migrants' Queuing for Home Affairs in South Africa." *Anthropology Southern Africa* 34, no. 1–2: 30–37. https://doi.org/10.1080/23323256.2011.11500006.

Swartz, Ellen. 1992. "Emancipatory Narratives: Rewriting the Master Script in the School Curriculum." *The Journal of Negro Education* 61, no. 3: 341–55.

Swiatek, Lukasz. 2018. "The Podcast as an Intimate Bridging Medium." In *Podcasting: New Aural Cultures and Digital Media*, edited by Dario Llinares, Neil Fox, and Richard Berry, 173–88. London: Palgrave Macmillan.

Szakolczai, Arpad. 2015. "Liminality and Experience: Structuring Transitory Situations and Transformative Events." In *Breaking Boundaries: Varieties of Liminality*, edited by Agnes Horváth, Bjorn Thomassen, and Harald Wydra, 11–38. New York: Berghahn.

Taffel, Sy. 2019. *Digital Media Ecologies: Entanglements of Content, Code and Hardware*. New York: Bloomsbury Academic.

TallBear, Kim. 2017. "Standing with and Speaking as Faith." In *Sources and Methods in Indigenous Studies*, edited by Chris Andersen and Jean M. O'Brien, 78–85. New York: Routledge.

Tam, Cheung-On. 2012. "The Effectiveness of Educational Podcasts for Teaching Music and Visual Arts in Higher Education." *Research in Learning Technology* 20, no. 1.

Tamale, Sylvia. 2020. *Decolonization and Afro-Feminism*. Québec: Daraja Press.

Tang, Xin, Shengqi Zhang, Yucong Li, and Miqiang Zhao. 2013. "Study on Correlation of English Pronunciation Self-Concept to English Learning." *English Language Teaching* 6, no. 4 (spring): 74.

"10 Most Downloaded Podcasts of All Time!" 2021. Podchaser. June 13, 2021. https://www.podchaser.com/lists/10-most-downloaded-podcasts-of-all-time-107aDsn1Yu.

Terra, Evo. 2019. "Captioning Your Podcast with a Transcript for Those with Hearing Loss." Podcast Pontifications. August 20, 2019. https://podcastpontifications.com/episode/captioning-your-podcast-with-a-transcript-for-those-with-hearing-loss.

The Podcast Host. 2020. "Podcast Transcription: How to Get Your Show Transcribed." *The Podcast Host*, April 20, 2020. https://www.thepodcasthost.com/planning/podcast-transcription/.

Thomas, Bronwen. 2011. "What Is Fanfiction and Why Are People Saying Such Nice Things about It?" *Storyworlds: A Journal of Narrative Studies* 3: 1–24.

Thompson, Marie, and Ian Biddle. 2013. "Introduction: Somewhere Between the Signifying and the Sublime." In *Sound, Music, Affect: Theorizing Sonic Experience*, edited by Marie Thompson and Ian Biddle, 1–24. London: Bloomsbury.

"Three Updates on the Spotify Mobile Experience to Help Improve Accessibility." 2021. Spotify. May 18, 2021. https://newsroom.spotify.com/2021-05-18/3-updates-on-the-spotify-mobile-experience-to-help-improve-accessibility/.

Thumlert, Kurt. 2015. "Affordances of Equality: Ranciere, Emerging Media, and the New Amateur." *Studies in Art Education* 56, no. 2: 114–26. https://doi.org/10.1080/0039354 1.2015.11518955.

Tiffe, Raechel, and Melody Hoffmann. 2017. "Taking up Sonic Space: Feminized Vocality and Podcasting as Resistance." *Feminist Media Studies* 17, no. 1: 115–18.

Tischauser, Jeff, and Jesse Benn. 2019. "Whose Post-Truth Era? Confronting the Epistemological Challenges of Teaching Journalism." *Journalism & Mass Communication Educator* 74, no. 2: 130–42.

Tobin, Stephanie J., and Rosanna E. Guadagno. 2022. "Why People Listen: Motivations and Outcomes of Podcast Listening." *PLOS ONE* 17, no. 4. https://doi.org/10.1371/journal.pone.0265806.

Toffoletti, Kim, Holly Thorpe, Adele Pavlidis, Rebecca Olive, and Claire Moran. 2021. "Visibility and Vulnerability on Instagram: Negotiating Safety in Women's Online-Offline Fitness Spaces." *Leisure Sciences* 45, no. 8: 1–19.

Tolson, Andrew. 2005. *Media Talk: Spoken Discourse on TV and Radio*. Edinburgh: Edinburgh University Press.

Tomlinson, John. 2007. "Cultural Globalization". In *The Blackwell Companion to Globalization*, edited by George Ritzer, 352–66. New Jersey: John Wiley & Sons.

Towler, Luke. 2014. "Deeper Learning: Moving Students Beyond Memorization." Stanford Center for Opportunity Policy in Education. Accessed on March 11, 2022. https://edpolicy.stanford.edu/news/articles/1284.

Tuck, Eve. 2009. "Suspending Damage: A Letter to Communities." *Harvard Educational Review* 79, no. 3: 409–28.

Tuck, Eve, and K. Wayne Yang. 2014a. "R-Words: Refusing Research." In *Humanizing Research: Decolonizing Qualitative Inquiry with Youth and Communities*, edited by D. Paris and M.T. Winn, 223–48. Thousand Oaks: Sage.

———. 2014b. "Unbecoming Claims." *Qualitative Inquiry* 20, no. 6: 811–18.

Tuhiwai Smith, Linda. 1999. *Decolonizing Methodologies: Research and Indigenous Peoples*. London: Zed Books.

Turchi, Peter. 2004. *Maps and the Imagination: The Writer as Cartographer*. Texas: Trinity University Press.

Turner, Victor. 1969. *The Ritual Process: Structure and Anti-Structure*. Chicago: Aldine Pub.

———. 1974. *Liminal to Liminoid in Play, Flow, and Ritual: An Essay in Comparative Symbology*. Houston: Rice University Studies.

UNESCO. "Startling Digital Divides in Distance Learning Emerge." n.d. Accessed March 19, 2024. https://www.unesco.org/en/articles/startling-digital-divides-distance-learning-emerge.

UNHCR (United Nations High Commissioner for Refugees). 2016. *Global Trends: Forced Displacement in 2015*. Geneva: UNHCR. https://www.unhcr.org/576408cd7.pdf.

United Nations Office of the Special Adviser on Gender Issues and Advancement of Women and the Secretariat of the United Nations Permanent Forum on Indigenous Issues. 2010. "Gender and Indigenous peoples." https://www.un.org/esa/socdev/unpfii/documents/BriefingNote1_GREY.pdf.

Usher, Nikki. 2019. "#JStudiesSoWhite: A Reckoning for the Future." Keynote talk at Future of Journalism 2019, Cardiff University, September 5, 2019.

Van Cleaf, Kara. 2015. "'Of Woman Born' to Mommy Blogged: The Journey from the Personal as Political to the Personal as Commodity." *Women's Studies Quarterly* 43, no. 3–4: 247–64.

Vandenberg, Danielle. 2018. "Using Podcasts in Your Classroom." *Metaphor*, no. 2: 54–55.

Van den Bulck, Hilde, and Aaron Hyzen. 2020. "Of Lizards and Ideological Entrepreneurs: Alex Jones and Infowars in the Relationship between Populist Nationalism and the Post-Global Media Eecology." *International Communication Gazette* 82, no. 1: 42–59.

Varjú, Viktor, and Shayna Plaut. 2016. "Media Mirrors? Framing Hungarian Romani Migration to Canada in Hungarian and Canadian Press." *Ethnic and Racial Studies* 40, no. 7: 1096–113.

Venkatesan, Tara, Qian Janice Wang, and Charles Spence. 2020. "Does the Typeface on Album Cover Influence Expectations and Perception of Music?" *Psychology of Aesthetics, Creativity, and the Arts* 16, no. 3: 486–503.

Verma, Neil. 2021. "Sound and Pedagogy: Taking Podcasting into the Classroom." In *The Bloomsbury Handbook of Sonic Methodologies*, edited by Michael Bull and Marcel Cobussen, 141–53. New York: Bloomsbury Academic.

Vilceanu, Olguta, Kristine Johnson, and Alexis Burns. 2021. "Consumer Perceptions of Podcast Advertising: Theater of the Mind and Story Selling." *AMTP 2021 Conference Proceedings*. https://digitalcommons.georgiasouthern.edu/amtp-proceedings_2021/.

Villanueva, Silvia Toscano. 2013. "Teaching as a Healing Craft: Decolonizing the Classroom and Creating Spaces of Hopeful Resistance through Chicano-Indigenous Pedagogical Praxis." *The Urban Review* 45, no. 1 (spring): 23–40.

Voegelin, Salomé. 2010. *Listening to Noise and Silence: Towards a Philosophy of Sound Art.* New York: Continuum.

———. 2021. *Sonic Possible Worlds: Hearing the Continuum of Sound*, revised edition. New York: Bloomsbury.

Vox Media. 2021. "More Than This." Vox. https://voxmedia.github.io/vc-tracfone-more-than-this/.

Vrikki, Photini, and Sarita Malik. 2019. "Voicing Lived-Experience and Anti-Racism: Podcasting as a Space at the Margins for Subaltern Counterpublics." *Popular Communication* 17, no. 4: 273–87.

Wake, Alex, Kim Fox, and Catherine Strong. 2020. "Pandemic Podcasting: From Classroom to Bedroom." *Teaching Journalism and Mass Communication* 10, no. 1: 29–33.

Waldmann, Ella. 2020. "From Storytelling to Storylistening: How the Hit Podcast *S-Town* Reconfigured the Production and Reception of Narrative Nonfiction." *Ex-centric Narratives: Journal of Anglophone Literature, Culture and Media*, no. 4: 28–42.

Walker, Alice. 1983. *In Search of Our Mothers' Gardens: Womanist Prose*. San Diego, Harcourt Brace Jovanovich.

Wall Kimmerer, Robin. 2013. *Braiding Sweetgrass: Indigenous Wisdom, Scientific Knowledge, and the Teachings of Plants*. Minneapolis: Milkweed Editions.

Walls, Stephen M., John V. Kucsera, Joshua D. Walker, Taylor W. Acee, Nate K. Mcvaugh, and Daniel H. Robinson. 2010. "Podcasting in Education: Are Students as Ready and Eager as We Think They Are?" *Computers & Education* 54, no. 2: 371–78.

Warhol, Robyn, and Susan S. Lanser. 2015. *Narrative Theory Unbound: Queer and Feminist Interventions*. Columbus: Ohio State University Press. https://kb.osu.edu/handle/1811/68569.

Wayne, Teddy. 2015. "'NPR Voice' Has Taken Over the Airwaves." *The New York Times*, October 24, 2015. https://www.nytimes.com/2015/10/25/fashion/npr-voice-has-taken-over-the-airwaves.html.

Wenger, Etienne. 2010. "Communities of Practice and Social Learning Systems: The Career of a Concept." In *Social Learning Systems and Communities of Practice*, edited by Chris Blackmore, 179–98. London: Springer.

Werner, Jessie. L., Resa E. Lewiss, Gita Pensa, and Alyson J. McGregor. 2020. "Women in Podcasting: We Should Tune In." *Perm J* 24, no. 1: 1–3.

Weston, Deborah. 2013. "A Positive Constructivist: An Internal Debate on Opposing Educational Philosophies." *Teaching and Learning* 8, no. 1: 1–19.

"What Is Podfade? Tips for New and Seasoned Podcasters." 2020. BuzzSprout. https://www.buzzsprout.com/blog/podfade.

"What Is Programmatic Advertising?" 2017. *AcuityAds Inc.* (blog). December 15, 2017. https://www.acuityads.com/blog/2017/12/15/what-is-programmatic-advertising.

Wilding, Mark. 2020. "Rain on Rooftops, Crunching Gravel: The Strange Appeal of 'Slow Audio.'" *The Guardian*, May 23, 2020. https://www.theguardian.com/tv-and-radio/2020/may/23/rain-on-rooftops-and-crunching-gravel-the-strange-appeal-of-slow-audio-field-recordings.

Wilhelm, Claudia. 2021. "Gendered (In)Visibility in Digital Media Contexts." *Studies in Communication Sciences* 21, no. 1: 99–113.

Wilson, Robbie Z. 2018. "Welcome to the World of *Wandercast*: Podcast as Participatory Performance and Environmental Exploration." In *Podcasting: New Aural Cultures and Digital Media*, edited by Dario Llinares, Neil Fox, and Richard Berry, 273–98. London: Palgrave Macmillan.

Winn, Ross. 2019. "2019 Podcast Stats and Facts." Podcast Insights, April 11, 2019. https://www.podcastinsights.com/podcast-statistics/.

Wong, Rose. 2020. "Online Class, No WiFi: The Struggles of Students without Reliable Internet Access." *The Chronicle*, May 21, 2020. https://www.dukechronicle.com/article/2020/05/duke-university-online-class-no-wifi-struggles-students-without-reliable-internet-coronavirus-pandemic.

Woods, Charles, and Shane Wood. 2023. "Podcasts in Rhetoric and Composition: A Review of *The Big Rhetorical Podcast* and *Pedagogue*." *Computers and Computing* 67: 1–10.

World Health Organization. 2021. "Deafness and Hearing Loss." World Health Organization. April 1, 2021. https://www.who.int/news-room/fact-sheets/detail/deafness-and-hearing-loss.

Wrather, Kyle. 2016. "Making 'Maximum Fun' for Fans: Examining Podcast Listener Participation Online." *Radio Journal* 14, no. 1: 43–63.

Wright, Earl. 2009. "Beyond W. E. B. Du Bois: A Note on Some of the Little-Known Members of the Atlanta Sociological Laboratory." *Sociological Spectrum* 29, no. 6 (fall): 700–17.

———. 2016. *The First American School of Sociology: W. E. B. Du Bois and the Atlanta Sociological Laboratory*. London and New York: Routledge.

Wunker, Erin. 2016. *Notes from a Feminist Killjoy*. Toronto: Book*hug.

———. 2021. "Archiving Feeling: Feminist Friendship and Public Culture." In panel "The Feminist (Affective) Archive: Past and Present." Association of Canadian College and University Teachers of English, May 29–June 1, 2021.

Wyld, Jasper. 2020. "Collaborative Storytelling and Canon Fluidity in *The Adventure Zone* Podcast." *Convergence* 27, no. 2: 343–56.

Yee, Timothy. 2019. "Podcasting and Personal Brands: Mapping a Theoretical Path from Participatory Empowerment to Individual Persona Construction." *Persona Studies* 5, no. 1: 92–106.

Yosso, Tara J. 2005. "Whose Culture Has Capital? A Critical Race Theory Discussion of Community Cultural Wealth." *Race, Ethnicity, and Education* 8, no. 1: 69–91.

Younging, Gregory. 2010. "*Gnaritas Nullius* (No One's Knowledge): The Public Domain and Colonization of Traditional Knowledge." *Intergovernmental Committee on the Intellectual Property and Genetic Resources Traditional Knowledge and Folklore*. WIPO. December 6 to 10, 2010. https://www.wipo.int/edocs/mdocs/tk/en/wipo_grtkf_ic_17/wipo_grtkf_ic_17_inf_5_a.pdf.

———. 2018. *Elements of Indigenous Style: A Guide for Writing by and about Indigenous Peoples*. Edmonton: Brush Education.

Zehelein, Eva-Sabine. 2019. "Mummy, Me and Her Podcast: Family and Gender Discourses in Contemporary Podcast Culture: *Not by Accident* as Audio(Auto) Biography." *International Journal of Media & Cultural Politics* 15, no. 2: 143–61.

Zeleza, Paul T., and Garry Weare. 2002. *Rethinking Africa's Globalization, Volume 1: The Intellectual Challenges*. Trenton: Africa World Press.

Zelizer, Barbie. 2004. *Taking Journalism Seriously: News and the Academy*. Thousand Oaks: Sage.

Zollo, Paul. 2003. *Songwriters on Songwriting*. Cambridge: Da Capo Press.

Zuckerman, Ethan. 2014. "'Audio Never Goes Viral'...and Maybe That's a Good Thing." Ethan Zuckerman (blog). January 22, 2014. https://ethanzuckerman.com/2014/01/21/audio-never-goes-viral-and-maybe-thats-a-good-thing.

Contributor Biographies

Yemisi Akinbobola (Ph.D.) is a senior lecturer and research degrees coordinator at the Birmingham Centre for Media and Cultural Research (BCMCR) at Birmingham City University. She is an award-winning journalist and co-founder of African Women in Media (AWiM). AWiM's vision is that one day, African women will have equal access to representation in media. Yemisi holds a Ph.D. in media and cultural studies from Birmingham City University. Her research interest is in the intersection of women's rights, African feminism(s), journalism practice and media entrepreneurship. Yemisi hosts two podcast series: *HerMediaDiary*, a podcast by African Women in Media, and *She Stands for Peace*, a podcast by the United Nations Office to the African Union. She has been recognized as one of the "100 Most Influential African Women" and listed among the "Global Top 50 Women in Sustainability."

Tanya Ball is a Michif woman from Winnipeg, Manitoba, in Treaty One Territory. She is currently living in Amiskwaciwâskahikan (Edmonton, Alberta) where she is enrolled in the Ph.D. program with the Faculty of Native Studies at the University of Alberta. Here, she is working with her family from Saint Ambroise to research the connections between Michif storytelling and experience of religion. She is also a sessional instructor at the University of Alberta, Concordia University of Edmonton, and BCcampus. She is a co-host of the podcast *masinahikan iskwêwak: Book Women Podcast*, a podcast about Indigenous storytelling. Lastly (and most importantly), she is a mom of two weird ginger children and a giant coonhound who bays at the world from her window perch.

Simon Barber (Ph.D.) is a senior research fellow in the Birmingham Centre for Media and Cultural Research (BCMCR) at Birmingham City University. His work focuses on songwriting and the creative process, which he explores as co-lead of the BCMCR popular music cluster. He leads the Songwriting Studies

Research Network, edits the *Songwriting Studies Journal* and has published on songwriting in *Popular Music and Society* and the *European Journal of Cultural Studies*, among others. Simon is also the producer and co-presenter of the popular *Sodajerker* podcast, which features interviews with some of the most successful songwriters in the world.

Lori Beckstead is an associate professor in the RTA School of Media and director of the Allan Slaight Radio Institute at Toronto Metropolitan University, where she teaches courses in podcasting, radio, and sound studies. She is co-author, along with Ian M. Cook and Hannah McGregor, of *Podcast or Perish: Peer Review and Knowledge Creation for the 21st Century* (Bloomsbury, 2024), and the on-again, off-again co-producer and co-host of *The Podcast Studies Podcast* along with Dario Llinares.

Richard Berry is a senior lecturer in radio and podcasting at the University of Sunderland, UK. He is the program leader for their B.A. media production course and is the manager of the university-owned community radio station, Spark—winner of the Best Student Radio Station award at the 2022 UK Student Radio Awards. Starting in 2006, he has extensively published about the development of podcasting and the use of digital technologies by the radio and audio industries. Along with Kim Fox, he co-chairs PodAcademics, a global network of podcast studies researchers.

Kelli S. Boling (Ph.D.) is an assistant professor at the University of Nebraska–Lincoln. As a cultural studies scholar, her research focuses on the lived reality of media audiences (specifically women, women of colour, or victims of domestic violence), how those women are depicted, and how they interpret and make meaning from the media they consume. Her research has been published in *Mass Communication and Society*, *Feminist Media Studies*, *Journalism Studies*, and *Journalism History*. Her research on women in podcast audiences has also been cited by traditional media outlets such as *Time* magazine and *The Washington Post*.

Samuel M. Clevenger (Ph.D.) is an assistant professor of kinesiology at Towson University. His research centres on the history of physical culture and the moving body, particularly the historical role of sport in contexts of colonialism and environmental change. He also studies the intersections of physical culture and podcasting. His research has been published in such international journals as *Rethinking History*, *Leisure Studies* and *The International Journal of the History of Sport*.

Stacey Copeland (Ph.D.) is an assistant professor of cultural heritage and identity at the Research Centre for Media and Journalism Studies, University of Groningen, Netherlands. Copeland's work on sound, media, and culture has been published in top-ranking journals, including *Radio Journal: International Studies in Broadcast & Audio Media* and the *Canadian Journal of Communication*. She has published in various edited collections, co-published open-access guides on academic podcasting and soundscape assessment, and actively works to produce publicly accessible sonic scholarship that bridges research and creative practice. She is currently the co-director of Amplify Podcast Network.

Erin Cory (Ph.D.) is an assistant professor at Malmö University where she co-directs the M.A. program in media and communication studies. Before moving to Sweden she lived, taught, and researched in the US-Mexico border region, Lebanon, and Denmark. She is interested in and has published on decolonial media praxis, everyday art in the context of migration, and sound studies, and has produced media work in collaboration with cultural organizations committed to migrant rights in Scandinavia and Uganda.

Martin Feld works in digital communication and is undertaking a part-time Ph.D. at the University of Wollongong (UOW) in Australia on RSS-based technology podcasting. He holds an honours degree in communication and media studies from UOW and a graduate diploma in German from the University of New England (Australia). Martin's Ph.D. research podcast, *Really Specific Stories*, can be found at www.rsspod.net. He also records the solo podcast *Lounge Ruminator* and co-hosts the "tech-adjacent" podcast *Hemispheric Views*.

Kim Fox is a professor of practice at the American University in Cairo, Egypt. Her primary area of interest is radio, audio, and podcasting. With respect to podcasts, she is in the unique position of conducting academic research on them, producing them, and teaching about them. With a focus on feminist pedagogy, oral history methodology, and project-based learning, she has coached her students to win a long list of international audio awards and recognitions. Kim is the executive producer of the award-winning *Ehky Ya Masr (Tell Your Story Egypt)* podcast, a bilingual narrative non-fiction podcast about life in Egypt. She is also the executive producer of PodFest Cairo, Egypt's and Africa's first podcasting conference. Her scholarly research focuses on Black and African podcasters.

Neil Fox (D.Prof.) is professor of film practice and pedagogy at Falmouth University's School of Film & Television, where he is the research and strategy lead for the *Sound/Image Cinema Lab*. In this capacity has been associate producer on films such as *Enys Men* (Jenkin, 2022) and *A Year in A Field* (Morris, 2023). He also leads Falmouth's Research and Knowledge Exchange *Centre for Pedagogy Futures*. He has written for *The Quietus, Director's Notes, Little White Lies, Clash,* MUBI's *Notebook,* and *Beneficial Shock,* and is one half of *The Cinematologists* podcast, "consistently one of the finest film podcasts around" (*Sight and Sound*). His debut feature film as screenwriter, *Wilderness,* was released by Sparky Pictures in 2021 and his first monograph, *Music Films,* was published in 2024 (BFI/Bloomsbury).

Liz Giuffre (Ph.D.) is a senior lecturer in communications, music, and sound at the University of Technology Sydney. She specializes in popular music and culture, audience studies and (post) broadcast studies, and is a podcaster at *Music Mothers and Others.* Her most recent books are *Popular Music and Parenting* (with Shelley Brunt, Routledge, 2023); *Kylie Minogue's Kylie* (with Adrian Renzo, Bloomsbury, 2024), and *An Incomplete History of Community Radio: 2ser's 46 Boxes of Stuff* (with Demetrius Romeo, Halstead, 2022).

Robert E. Gutsche Jr. (Ph.D.) is an associate professor in the School of Communication and Multimedia Studies at Florida Atlantic University in the US, and visiting professor in the Faculty of Informatics at Vytautus Magnus University in Lithuania. He applies critical and cultural approaches to how digital content creators and journalists work as both power and change agents while adopting and reproducing hegemonic, authoritative explanations for local and world events. He is associate editor of *Journalism Practice* and produces and hosts its podcast, *The J Word: A Podcast by* Journalism Practice.

Jasmine L. Harris (Ph.D.) is professor and department chair of Africana Studies at Metropolitan State University of Denver. She completed her Ph.D. at the University of Minnesota in 2013. Her research examines Black life in predominantly white spaces, including Black students at Predominantly White Institutions (PWIs), Black Division 1 football and men's basketball players at universities in the Power Five conferences, and Black sociologists producing knowledge in a white-dominated discipline. Dr. Harris has been published in major newspapers across the country, including *Newsweek, The Washington Post,* the *Houston Chronicle,* and the *Chicago Tribune.* In 2021 she was featured in the *Vice News* documentary *College Sports, Inc.* Her latest book is *Black Women, Ivory Tower: Revealing the Lies of White Supremacy in American Education* (Broadleaf, 2024).

Nicholas John (Ph.D.) is an associate professor at the Department of Communication and Journalism at the Hebrew University of Jerusalem. He is the author of *The Age of Sharing* (Polity, 2016). In addition to podcasts and podcasting, his research interests include unfriending, sharing, and the limits of our knowledge about social media. He is the president of the Association of Internet Researchers.

Sheila Laroque is Métis and Scottish/Irish from Treaty Six Territory near Saskatoon, Saskatchewan. She currently resides in Saskatoon with her fiancé partner and their menagerie of animals. She works as an assistant librarian with Indigenous studies at the University of Saskatchewan, where she completed her undergraduate degree. After moving to Toronto, Ontario for her master's degree and Edmonton, Alberta, for work, coming home to Saskatoon has been a welcome change.

Kayla Lar-Son is Métis and Ukrainian from Treaty Six Territory, Tofield, Alberta. She currently resides on the unceded territories of the xʷməθkʷəẏəm (Musqueam), *Skwxwú7mesh* (Squamish), and *Selíĺwitulh* (Tsleil-Waututh) nations. She is one of the founding members of *masinahikan iskwêwak: Book Women Podcast*, and is the Indigenous programs and services librarian for the *Xwi7xwa* Library at the University of British Columbia.

Dario Llinares (Ph.D.) is an academic and podcaster whose research has focused on a range of cinema- and media-related themes. His Ph.D. thesis explored the cultural representation of the astronaut in literature, journalism, photography, and film, and he has published research on the status and practice of cinema-going in the digital age, the aesthetics of postmodern film, representations of masculinity in prison cinema, and podcasting as a media technology. He is the co-founder and co-host of the highly respected podcasts *The Cinematologists* and *The Podcast Studies Podcast*, and was co-editor of *Podcasting: New Aural Cultures and Digital Media* (Palgrave Macmillan, 2018).

Hannah McGregor (Ph.D.) is an academic, podcaster, and author living on the traditional and unceded territory of the Musqueam, Squamish, and Tsleil-Waututh First Nations. She is director and associate professor of publishing at Simon Fraser University, where her research and teaching focus on the intersection of publishing and social change. She is the co-director of the Amplify Podcast Network and the creator of its pilot podcast, *Secret Feminist* Agenda. She also co-hosts *Material Girls*, a pop culture podcast that uses critical theory to understand the zeitgeist, and co-created the *SpokenWeb Podcast*, part of a collaborative scholarly project exploring audio literary archives. She co-edited the collection *Refuse: CanLit in Ruins* (Book*hug, 2018). Her book *A Sentimental Education* was published by Wilfrid Laurier University Press in 2022. She is co-author of *Podcast or Perish: Peer Review and Knowledge Creation for the 21st Century* (Bloomsbury, 2024) and has a forthcoming book about dinosaurs.

Katherine McLeod (Ph.D.) is an affiliate assistant professor in the Department of English at Concordia University. She is writing a book that is a feminist listening to recordings of women poets on the radio, and she is the principal investigator for her Social Sciences and Humanities Research Council–funded project "Literary Radio: Developing New Methods of Audio Research." She has co-edited, with Jason Camlot, *CanLit Across Media: Unarchiving the Literary Event* (McGill-Queen's University Press, 2019) and she has published on poetry, performance, and archives in journals such as *Canadian Literature* and *Mosaic*. She produces *ShortCuts*—a monthly series about archival audio—for the *SpokenWeb Podcast*.

Leslie Grace McMurtry (Ph.D.) is a lecturer in radio studies at the University of Salford, UK. She has published on radio and podcast drama in journals such as *Gothic Studies, Palgrave Communications*, and the *Journal of Radio & Audio Media*. She makes podcasts for Lesser of 2 Weevils.

Tzlil Sharon (Ph.D.) is a postdoctoral researcher at the Amsterdam School for Cultural Analysis at the University of Amsterdam. Her Ph.D. dissertation focused on the cultural construction of the podcast listener, and her current research delves into the datafication of podcast listening. Her fields of interest include philosophy and theory of media and communication, history of media technologies, and sound studies. She has published in *New Media & Society, Popular Communication*, and *Communication Theory*, and produced the academic podcast *The SIP*.

Parinita Shetty (Ph.D.) is a researcher and children's book author who has worked with young people in India in various ways. She completed her M.Ed. in children's literature and literacies at the University of Glasgow in 2017. In 2022, at the University of Leeds, she completed her Ph.D. which examined intersectionality and public pedagogy in online fan podcasts of popular media. She launched her own fan podcast called *Marginally Fannish* as part of her research methodology. She is passionate about co-creating knowledge, including diverse voices in academic spaces, and finding creative ways to make academic research as accessible as possible to non-academic audiences. She is currently a public library assistant in North Lanarkshire, Scotland, and a post-doctoral researcher in education at Sheffield Hallam University, England.

Index